The Complete Films of
BUSTER KEATON

THE COMPLETE FILMS OF
Buster Keaton

by JIM KLINE

A CITADEL PRESS BOOK
Published by Carol Publishing Group

For the B man and the B woman in my life—
Buster and Beatriz—
both of whom I love dearly.

ACKNOWLEDGMENTS

I would like to thank the following individuals and organizations for assisting me with this book:

Eleanor Keaton, Marion Meade, William K. Everson, Kevin Brownlow, Joel Goss, Bob Borgen, Gere La Due, John Sebert, Ty Kistler of the Rohauer Collection, Bruce Lawton of the Killiam Collection, Charles Wolfe of the University of California/Santa Barbara, Mary Corliss of the Museum of Modern Art/Film Stills Library, Andrew Forberg of the National Archives of Canada, George Snyder of the Arvin Corporation, Ralph Hughes of John Deere and Company, Larry Austin of the Silent Movie Theatre/The Sound of Laughter, Murray Glass of the Em Gee Film Library, Jim Debold of CTN–New Jersey, the staff of the Academy of Motion Picture Arts and Sciences Library, the staff of the UCLA Film Archives and Theatre Arts Library, the gang at Eddie Brandt's Saturday Matinee, Turner Entertainment Company, Orion Pictures, the International Film Bureau, and the American Film Institute.

Special thanks to Joanna Rapf for the use of her filmography (cocompiled with Gary Green), Chuck Harter for his unflagging enthusiasm (and unlimited resources), and Alan Hoffman, whose unpublished book, *Buster*, was an invaluable and inspiring resource. Thanks also to my son, Dylan, for sitting through most of the films with me and for running the projector.

PHOTOGRAPH ACKNOWLEDGMENTS

The following individuals and organizations are gratefully acknowledged for contributing photographs:

Chuck Harter, Gere La Due, John Sebert, the Academy of Motion Picture Arts and Sciences, the Museum of Modern Art/Film Stills Library, Culver Pictures, George Eastman House, the British Film Institute/Stills, Posters and Designs, John Deere of Moline, Illinois, the Fantasy Cinemarchives of Forrest J. Ackerman, Hollywood, and the Historical Society of Long Beach, California. Also, for making most of these images possible, the film studios of Metro-Goldwyn-Mayer, Twentieth Century-Fox, Paramount, RKO, Columbia, and Educational are kindly thanked.

A Citadel Press Book
Published by Carol Publishing Group
Citadel Press is a registered trademark of Carol Communications, Inc.
Editorial Offices: 600 Madison Avenue, New York, N.Y. 10022
Sales and Distribution Offices: 120 Enterprise Avenue, Secaucus, N.J. 07094
In Canada: Canadian Manda Group, P.O. Box 920, Station U, Toronto, Ontario M8Z 5P9
Queries regarding rights and permissions should be addressed to Carol Publishing Group, 600 Madison Avenue, New York, N.Y. 10022

Carol Publishing Group books are available at special discounts for bulk purchases, for sales promotions, fund-raising, or educational purposes. Special editions can be created to specifications. For details, contact Special Sales Department, Carol Publishing Group, 120 Enterprise Avenue, Secaucus, N.J. 07094

Designed by A. Christopher Simon

Manufactured in the United States of America
10 9 8 7 6 5 4 3 2 1

Library of Congress Cataloging-in-Publication Data

Kline, Jim.
    The complete films of Buster Keaton / by Jim Kline.
        p.   cm.
    "A Citadel Press book."
    ISBN 0-8065-1303-9 (paper) :
    1. Keaton, Buster, 1895–1966—Criticism and interpretation.
I. Title.
PN2287.K4K65   1993
791.43′028′092—dc20   92-37553
                                                        CPI

CONTENTS

*All dates are release dates unless otherwise indicated

The Complete Films of
BUSTER KEATON

When it came to filmmaking, Buster was a one-man symphony of talents: actor, director, writer, stuntman, technician, all of these and more. This gag photo recreates a scene from his most visually dazzling short film, *The Playhouse*.

Joseph Frank Keaton, practicing his deadpan expression at age six months.

INTRODUCTION

His sad infinite eyes . . . are like the bottom of a glass, like a mad child's. Very ugly. Very beautiful. An ostrich's eyes. Human eyes in the exact balance of melancholy.

—*From* Buster Keaton Takes a Walk
by Federico García Lorca

There is a segment in Carl Reiner's charming, modestly successful 1989 film, *Bert Rigby, You're a Fool,* that accurately reflects the modern public's familiarity with the screen character of Buster Keaton. In it, British actor Robert Lindsay plays Bert Rigby, a coal miner from northern England who has a passionate love for the stars of the golden age of Hollywood and a talent for mimicking many of these screen personalities. One evening, while performing a tribute to the silent-era comedians in an amateur talent show, Bert is spotted by an American TV-commercial director, who offers him the chance to impersonate Buster Keaton for a series of athletic-footwear commercials. When the time comes for the first commercial to be made, Bert dons Buster's traditional costume—flat hat, tight vest, clip-on tie, baggy pants—as well as the featured footwear. Bert then assumes Buster's trademark stone-face expression and begins sprinting in front of a moving train as the cameras roll. When the commercial is later previewed in a screening room, the director congratu-lates Bert on a superb job. However, he says, the sponsor's demographics report has just come in, and it reveals that 94 percent of the public has never heard of Buster Keaton. Therefore, the commercial will never air and Bert is obligated to return home. A dejected Bert stares into the camera and remarks: "Buster Keaton and Bert Rigby. Two great careers shot down by demo-f***ing-graphics."

Fortunately—for movie fans in particular and mankind in general—Buster Keaton, a man with very little business sense, lived and worked during a time when public opinion polls and demo-f***ing-graphics weren't the all-powerful measure of a person's artistic worth. Otherwise, like poor Bert Rigby, Buster Keaton might have had a film career that was over before it ever began.

It was only by chance that Buster entered the world of filmmaking at all in 1917 at age twenty-one. Until then, he had been one of the most celebrated young stars of the vaudeville stage. Born Joseph Frank Keaton on October 4, 1895, in a boardinghouse in Piqua, Kansas, Buster began performing at the age of three with his mom and dad—billed as The Three Keatons—in some of the most prestigious theaters across the country, headlining with such performers as Harry Houdini, Louise Dresser, Bill "Bojangles" Robinson, Al Jolson, W. C. Fields, Eddie Cantor, and

The Three Keatons: Buster with his father, Joe, and his mother, Myra, circa 1900. The table was also an integral part of the act.

Buster at four years. He was already performing with his mom and dad as The Three Keatons on vaudeville stages across the country.

Buster as Little Lord Fauntleroy. He performed this part and others during times when his mother had to drop out of the family act in order to attend to the upbringing of Buster's two younger siblings—brother Harry (nicknamed Jingles) and sister Louise.

Buster and Joe with some of the props used in their roughhouse vaudeville act.

Will Rogers. It had been Houdini himself who, after witnessing the six-month-old boy fall down a flight of stairs without suffering any injuries or even crying, reportedly remarked to the child's parents, "That's sure some buster your baby took!" and thus earned the Keaton youngster his legendary nickname.

Throughout his years as a vaudeville headliner, Buster maintained a less than flattering opinion of the movies, one heavily influenced by his father's attitude toward the lowly "flickers." His father, Joe, a feisty, hard-drinking Irishman, believed movies to be merely a passing fad. In 1913, when The Three Keatons had been at the peak of their popularity, Joe had been approached by William Randolph Hearst to star the family act in a series of two-reel shorts based on the popular "Bringing Up Father" comic strip featured in his newspapers. Joe, insulted by the offer, turned Hearst down, saying he would be damned if Hearst or anyone else would dare film an act that had taken years to perfect and then charge ten cents to project it on a dirty bed sheet in some shabby back-room dive turned movie theater.

Joe was proud of the act he and Buster had developed, and deservedly so. Father and son had fashioned one of the most thrilling and dangerous acts in vaudeville, built around the idea of an Irish father demonstrating to the audience how to discipline a mischievous child. The two would dress up in exaggerated, look-alike Irish outfits, and then Joe would basically mop up the stage with little Buster, throwing him from one end of the floorboards to the other, hurling him into the painted backdrop, even tossing him into the orchestra pit or into the audience. Later, when Buster became too big to throw around, they developed a routine involving smacking each other with brooms in synchronized time to the music of "The Anvil Chorus." They also perfected a bit in which Buster would stand on a table center stage and swing around a basketball tied to a long rope. Joe would busy himself shaving with a straight-edge razor, oblivious to the swinging ball that whirled closer and closer, until it would finally hit him on the back of the head. Throughout the mayhem, Buster would remain poker-faced, never smiling, a trademark expression he had developed over the years after his father noticed that the act received a bigger laugh if the boy registered no emotional outrage while being flung around the stage. The routine appeared so brutal that many times Buster was asked to strip bare in front of law enforcement officials and child protection agencies to prove that he was in good physical condition and not being abused by his father. Over the years, Buster became an expert tumbler, able to stage the most harrowing stunts un-

scathed by subtly controlling his seemingly out-of-control body.

Buster reveled in the excitement, the endless variety of acts that paraded across the vaudeville stage every night—exotic dancers, hammy melodramas, Shakespearean soliloquists, ethnic comedians, high-wire artists, magicians, performing animals, opera singers, all-black revues. He and his father incorporated many aspects of these varying acts into their own routines, sometimes burlesquing the melodramas, kidding the excessive pomp of certain performers, and sometimes playing key parts in other productions. Buster even appeared as Little Lord Fauntleroy for an extended run during a time when his mother, Myra, herself an accomplished saxophonist-performer, had to drop out of the act for a while to take care of the growing family, which eventually included brother Harry (nicknamed Jingles) and sister Louise. At one time Joe had hopes of incorporating the entire family into the act, but after endless hassles with law enforcement agencies over the employment of children in stage performances, he gave up on the idea. This type of harassment, coupled with other running feuds he had with various promoters and theater owners, as well as the constant, stressful grind of the act, finally took its toll on Joe over the years. By the time Buster had reached the age of twenty-one, his father was a bitter, abusive alcoholic. It was Buster who finally made the decision to break up the family act. Joe's drinking had ruined his timing, and Buster was rightfully worried that their onstage roughhousing, which depended entirely on intricate timing for its success, would inevitably result in a crippling injury.

Looking forward to establishing himself as a solo performer, in March 1917, Buster began to develop routines for the show in which he had been signed to appear—the Shubert Brothers' *Passing Show of 1917,* an extravagant musical revue and popular rival to Ziegfeld's *Follies.* He had only a few weeks before the show was to open in New York and was feeling the pressure of coming up with new material for his solo debut. During a casual stroll through New York's East Side only days before starting rehearsals, he bumped into an old vaudeville friend, comedian Lou "Dutch" Anger, who was then working as a stage manager for a Manhattan movie studio. Anger asked Buster if he was familiar with the moviemaking process and when Buster replied that he knew nothing about filmmaking, Anger invited him to the studio for a look around. At first, Buster balked at the invitation, his old prejudices against the "flickers" influencing him. Buster was even more put off when Anger told him that one of the performers working at the studio was Roscoe "Fatty"

A joyous Buster romps with his early screen costars, Roscoe "Fatty" Arbuckle (bottom), Al St. John (middle), and Roscoe's multitalented dog, Luke. Buster's earliest film appearances were with the popular rotund comedian whom he called his cinematic mentor and best friend.

Arbuckle, the celebrated screen comedian known for his low-humor antics in the films he had made for Mack Sennett. Buster had a perceived grudge against Arbuckle; in one of his infrequent visits to the flickers, he had seen *The Waiter's Ball,* an Arbuckle two-reeler in which the rotund comic duplicated the broom-bashing "Anvil Chorus" routine that Buster and his father had originated in their stage act. Despite these personal prejudices against movies and movie actors, though, Buster also had an insatiable curiosity for anything new. Ultimately, he decided to accompany Anger to the studio, a decision that not only radically changed Buster's life, but also led to the creation of a body of work that ranks with greatest ever produced by any artist in any medium.

> His face went with silence. Its motionlessness and the film's soundlessness compounded each other. . . . Fundamentally bewildered yet completely matter-of-fact . . . it stared unblinking and unsurprised as mad mishaps and mad triumphs unfolded. . . . Never smiling, never moving a muscle or blinking an eye during all the horseplay; it gripped audiences strangely.
>
> —*From* Keaton *by Rudi Blesh*

Throughout his life, Buster Keaton unhesitatingly credited one man above all others as the major influence on his film career: Roscoe "Fatty" Arbuckle. This might, at first, seem hard to believe given the obvious radical differences between the two performers at the time they first met: Arbuckle, a bear of a man, weighing over 250 pounds, known for his chaotic farce comedies full of low-humor mayhem and exaggerated mugging; Buster, short, thin, and athletic, whose rough-house routines were built around intricate, meticulously planned stunts and executed with a restrained, deadpan offhandedness. However, during their initial meeting in March 1917, on Buster's very first visit to a movie studio, an instant rapport developed between the two men. Arbuckle, an extremely unselfish man with an open, carefree attitude, gave Buster a tour of the place—the Talmadge Studios, owned by independent producer Joseph Schenck and named after his wife, Norma, and her sister, Constance, both already well-known screen personalities. Even more famous than the Talmadge sisters was Arbuckle, whose only serious rival for the title of most popular screen comic was Charlie Chaplin, a friend and fellow alumnus of the Keystone Studios. Arbuckle had just recently been signed by Schenck to write, direct, and star in his own comedy shorts, and Buster's visit coincided with the shooting of the first Arbuckle two-reeler under his new contract.

Buster was instantly captivated by moviemaking. He asked a thousand questions, mostly about the workings of the camera, and was finally permitted to dismantle one so he could see just exactly how it worked. Later, Arbuckle showed him scenes that had been filmed the previous day, then invited him to participate in the shooting scheduled for that day. By then, Buster's objections to the "flickers" had dissolved, and his fascination with the making of films was at a fever pitch. Thus, on that very same day, Buster Keaton made his screen debut in *The Butcher Boy*. Afterward, he immediately instructed his agent to release him from his stage contract, one that would have paid $250 per week. Instead, Buster signed on with Arbuckle for $40 per week. It was the beginning of the screen career of a man who would ultimately be hailed by legions as the greatest film comedian of all time.

> You wouldn't believe a comedian could be so serious. He taught them all how to underact. He could tell his story by lifting an eyebrow. He could tell it by *not* lifting an eyebrow.
>
> —*Clyde Bruckman quoted in* Keaton *by Rudi Blesh*

From 1917 through 1920, Buster made fifteen two-reelers with Arbuckle. During that time, he learned everything there was to know about filmmaking, techniques that he would later master to perfection in his own movies. By the time the two men went their independent ways in 1920, it was Buster who was teaching Arbuckle about filmmaking. Before signing with Joe Schenck, Arbuckle had made over two hundred shorts, the majority of them for Sennett at Keystone. Nearly all of these shorts followed the same crude, freewheeling, slapstick style for which Sennett was famous. Despite their primitive comic histrionics, the Arbuckle shorts were extremely popular, due largely to his screen character, which was basically that of a mischievous, baby-faced fat man.

Arbuckle's first films under his new contract with Schenck followed the old Sennett format. However, Arbuckle, known for his magnanimous approach to filmmaking, heartily encouraged Buster to contribute gags and bits of routines picked up from vaudeville, until, according to Buster, he practically became Arbuckle's sole writing staff. The two soon were codirecting, and by the time of their final few films together, the Arbuckle shorts had taken on a much more elaborate and varied approach to film comedy that now included trick photography, black humor and satire, eccentric mechanical contraptions, and spectacular stunts. The later films also contained much more coherent story lines, as well as a more subtle approach to acting. In

other words, Buster had nearly single-handedly transformed Arbuckle's comedy style in three years and fifteen two-reelers, a style that had remained constant for over two hundred previous films.

When the Arbuckle troupe, known as the Comique Film Corporation, relocated from the Talmadge Studios in New York to the Los Angeles area in the autumn of 1917, Buster eagerly followed. Drafted into the army in 1918 and returning from post–World War I France ten months later, Buster immediately rejoined Arbuckle even though he was offered higher-paying contracts by both William Fox (later one of the founders of Twentieth Century-Fox) and Jack Warner of Warner Brothers.

In addition to their screen pranks, Keaton and Arbuckle earned a reputation around the new burgeoning Hollywood film community as offscreen pranksters. Buster had a long history of staging elaborate practical jokes. Back in his youth, living with his family in an off-season actors' community located near Lake Muskegon, Michigan, he had developed eccentric gags to entertain the local folks and astonish innocent bystanders (including a rigged outhouse that, when occupied, would collapse and set off a series of bells, gunshots, and music). In the most famous practical joke the two men concocted, Keaton pretended to be Arbuckle's butler and methodically sabotaged an elaborate dinner party given for Arbuckle's new boss, Adolph Zukor, the head of Paramount Studios. The two men, so different physically and intellectually, were bonded by their love of the gag and the freedom they enjoyed creating astonishing and innovative comic humor both on screen and off.

> The work of that rough and powerful mind, a clear but unspoken vision of the world, are what we see perfectly reflected in the face and eyes of Buster Keaton.
>
> —*From* The Look of Buster Keaton *by Robert Benayoun*

In 1920, Arbuckle was offered a million-dollar contract by Zukor and Paramount to star in feature films, an offer he accepted with little hesitation. Buster was then offered a new contract by Schenck, similar to the one Schenck had made with Arbuckle: Buster was given a studio of his own (Schenck bought him Chaplin's old Hollywood studio) and full creative control over his films. First, however, Schenck arranged for Buster to star in a feature film for the new Metro organization (eventually to become Metro-Goldwyn-Mayer). Metro, the distributor of Buster's movies under his new contract, hired him to star in *The Saphead,* a

Charlie Chaplin (in topcoat with bowler) welcomes Buster and the rest of Roscoe Arbuckle's New York-based production company to their new West Coast studio located in Long Beach, California. Also pictured are the studio's owner, H. M. Horkheimer (to the right of Chaplin), and Buster's studio manager, Lou Anger (far right).

filmed adaptation of the successful play *The New Henrietta.*

Buster's first official release under his new contract was *One Week*, a comedy about a newlywed couple's efforts to construct a prefabricated house. Full of whimsical inventiveness coupled with a unique approach to the construction of elaborate, intricate gags, and sporting a sophisticated technical mastery lacking in the average two-reeler, the film was immediately hailed as the comedy sensation of the year. A string of two-reelers followed, all infused with Buster's distinctive style.

During the shooting of his proposed ninth short, *The Electric House,* a film about a house designed by Buster and filled with wacky yet functional electrical gadgets, the star broke his ankle after catching his shoe on the escalator used in the movie. While he was convalescing, Buster's thoughts turned to a woman whom he had met during his first visit to Arbuckle's set in March 1917. Natalie Talmadge, the middle sister of

Buster and his first wife, Natalie Talmadge, on their wedding day, May 21, 1921. Also pictured are Natalie's two famous actress sisters, Norma (left), and Constance (right).

14

Norma and Constance, had worked for Arbuckle as an assistant and had followed the troupe when the Comique company moved to Los Angeles. She had even lived briefly with Buster and his family in their house near the Comique company's studio in Long Beach. During Buster's ten-month tour of duty in the army, Natalie had moved back to New York to live with her family. Now, Buster sent for her, asking her to marry him. He ended up traveling back to New York to finalize the engagement, and on May 31, 1921, he and Natalie were married at Norma and Joe Schenck's Long Island mansion.

Buster was very much a family-oriented man, having developed a special relationship with his parents and siblings while growing up on the road. Even though his relationship with his father became strained after the breakup of the vaudeville act, Buster later bought his family a house in Los Angeles and provided for them for his entire life, even featuring them in several of his films. This loyalty to family included Natalie, who,

Buster and Natalie enjoy a Christmas celebration with their two sons, James (left), and Robert.

A gag photo of Buster and Natalie that proved to be prophetic.

unfortunately, was unable to understand fully the type of relationship Buster wanted. Neither was she able to generate the enthusiasm for films that her husband and sisters enjoyed.

As soon as Buster was able to work again after *The Electric House* accident, he began filming *The Playhouse,* his most technically dazzling two-reeler, in which he played all the performers of a minstrel show as well as the orchestra members, stagehands, *and* the audience. During the filming of *The Playhouse* in September 1921, an event occurred that made headline news worldwide, an event that affected Buster deeply for the rest of his life. His best friend, Roscoe Arbuckle, was accused of raping Virginia Rappé, a Hollywood starlet, during a party hosted by Arbuckle at the St. Francis Hotel in San Francisco. Rappé died several days after the party, and Arbuckle was tried for manslaughter. Although he was eventually found innocent of all charges, the scandal caused by the event ultimately led to the Hollywood studio chiefs creating in 1922 a self-regulating censorship board, the Motion Picture Producers and Distributors of America (MP-PDA), headed by Will Hays, the U.S. Postmaster General in the Harding administration. One of the first official edicts of the MPPDA was to ban Arbuckle and his films from the screen. Keaton and Joe Schenck were able to help Arbuckle financially, arranging for him to receive a percentage of the profits from Keaton's films. Buster also hired him as a writer and codirector on some of his films. However, Arbuckle, devastated by the turn of events in his life, became a bitter alcoholic and difficult at times to work with. Later, he was able to find work as a director, using the first and middle names of his father, William Goodrich, as a pseudonym.

Meanwhile, Buster continued to turn out one superlative two-reeler after another. In his most famous short, *Cops,* made during the time of the Arbuckle manslaughter trial, Buster was mistaken for a bomb-throwing anarchist and was ultimately chased through the streets of New York by every cop in the city. The image of Keaton running frantically down the street while pursued by hundred of cops is one of the most indelible images of the cinema.

> Keaton's face ranked with Lincoln's as an early American archetype; it was haunting, handsome, almost beautiful, yet it was irreducibly funny. . . . No one could do as much with the deadpan. . . . Everything that he was and did bore out this rigid face and played laughs against it. When he moved his eyes, it was like seeing them move in a statue.
>
> —*From* Comedy's Greatest Era *by James Agee*

After completing his nineteenth short, *The Love Nest,* the story line of which was built around one of Buster's favorite props—an aimlessly drifting boat—Joe Schenck informed him that he was to begin work on feature films. Keaton's first independently produced feature was *The Three Ages,* a gag-laden, slapstick parody of D. W. Griffith's epic *Intolerance,* in which Keaton dramatized three distinct time periods to tell his irreverent story of love through the ages. Buster's next feature, *Our Hospitality,* was a radical departure in style, pacing, and content from everything he had previously done, reflecting a much more realistic approach to filmmaking. A period piece, set in rural Virginia in the early nineteenth century, it costarred his wife, Natalie, and featured his father, Joe, and Buster's one-year-old son, James. During the filming, Natalie became pregnant with their second son, Robert, who was born the following year.

In 1926, after releasing a string of wildly imaginative and innovative features, all of them solid box-office hits, Keaton began production on the film he considered his personal favorite, one that is now also considered among the greatest ever made. *The General,* a Civil War epic based on an actual historical episode from the war, featured Buster as a locomotive engineer trying to reclaim his beloved train after it is stolen by Union spies. The film, a long, elaborate screen chase, is filled with incredible action scenes and has one of the most spectacular disaster sequences of the silent era. However, when released, *The General* was a box-office disappointment and was responsible for Schenck's decision to assign a production assistant to Keaton's subsequent films to keep production costs down. Buster had never worried about them before—he was totally indifferent to financial matters both in his professional and personal endeavors.

His next two efforts, *College* and *Steamboat Bill, Jr.,* though filled with many terrific gags and spectacular stunt work, both were box-office failures. During the filming of *Steamboat Bill, Jr.* in spring 1928, Keaton was informed by Schenck that he was dissolving their contract. Schenck, one of the last of the maverick independent producers, had agreed to head financially unstable United Artists. Not wishing to take on any potentially risky endeavors by signing the box-office-beleaguered Buster to a contract with United Artists, Keaton was turned over by Schenck to his brother Nicholas, who was head of the more stable Metro-Goldwyn-Mayer. Buster always referred to this business deal as the worst decision of his life.

> Tears in Keaton's eyes . . . are redundant. Buster already always seems on the verge of tears. His stoicism and fixity bring tragedy. The beauty of Keaton's eyes comes from their recess, their depth; they are dryly, nakedly distant.
>
> —*From* The Look of Buster Keaton *by Robert Benayoun*

MGM, the premier movie studio of the era, was also the most rigidly structured. It was ruled by two pairs of iron fists belonging to studio head Louis B. Mayer and production chief Irving Thalberg. Full creative control for an artist was unheard of at MGM, and Buster found himself struggling to make the type of movies he wanted to. His first feature for the studio, *The Cameraman,* was 99 percent Keaton and one of his best films, although he had to fight hard to maintain creative control. Although he was able to work with most of his original crew on *The Cameraman,* it was for the last time. His next feature, *Spite Marriage,* introduced the screen character he was to play off and on for the rest of his career: Elmer, a humble, stumbling fool, a character possessing only the bumbling traits of his old screen persona and very little of the agile, eccentrically adept, and clever traits.

After making a successful sound film debut in the 1930 musical *Free and Easy,* one of the few MGM talkies he enjoyed making, Keaton attempted to per-

Buster playing baseball on the front lawn of his Beverly Hills mansion, "The Italian Villa." The villa was used as the setting for *Parlor, Bedroom and Bath*, one of the films he made as a featured star at MGM in the early 1930s.

suade Irving Thalberg to finance two original story ideas: one, a period film about a naive city slicker who accompanies his aunt across the country in a covered wagon; the second, a parody of the studio's hugely successful *Grand Hotel.* However, Thalberg, like everyone else at MGM, had a hard time understanding Buster's approach to comedy and ultimately turned down both of his ideas. Ironically, even though Keaton hated most of the films he was obligated to make at MGM, all were huge money-makers, grossing more than any of his own silent films. Creatively frustrated, unable to convince anyone at the studio that he was much more than merely an actor, Buster turned to alcohol for solace.

By the time he made *What! No Beer?* in 1932, Keaton had been reduced to costar status teaming with brash comedian Jimmy Durante. To protest his treatment, Buster began to purposely miss days of shooting, preferring instead to drink himself into oblivion. That same year, Natalie filed for divorce. Not long after the release of *What! No Beer?* Buster was fired by MGM.

The year 1933 was one of the worst of his life. In January, while in an alcoholic stupor, Buster married Mae Scribbens, a nurse with whom he had become acquainted while undergoing treatment for his drinking. Later, his best friend and mentor, Roscoe Arbuckle, died of a heart attack in New York at age forty-six.

Buster at his most sophisticated, taken during his MGM period.

Another prophetic gag photo. Shortly after being fired by MGM in 1933, Buster was incarcerated in various sanitariums specializing in alcohol rehabilitation. At times, Buster became so violent that he had to be restrained in a straight jacket.

Buster and his second wife, Mae Scribbens, married in January 1933. Mae had been hired as Buster's private nurse to take care of him as he struggled to conquer his alcoholism. Their marriage lasted less than three years.

Time has transformed the surface calm of Keaton's countenance into a subtle beauty.

—From The American Cinema *by Andrew Sarris*

The older Keaton got, the more one could see eternity in his look.

—From The Look of Buster Keaton
by Robert Benayoun

The rest of Buster's film career as a featured artist consisted of starring vehicles in cheap foreign movies such as *Le Roi des Champs-Élysées,* made in France in 1934; *The Invader,* made in England that same year;

Portrait of the artist as a bit player. Buster made two series of two-reel talkies as well as many supporting role appearances after losing his MGM contract in the early 1930s.

In 1944, Buster played a bus driver in *San Diego I Love You*, one of his best supporting role appearances.

Buster with his third wife, Eleanor Norris, on board friend Desi Arnaz's yacht. Buster and Eleanor were wed on May 29, 1940, and remained happily married for the rest of Buster's life.

Buster with fellow clown performers backstage at the Cirque Medrano in Paris. Buster performed with the celebrated French circus in the late 1940s and early 1950s.

Buster surrounded by some of his costars from a 1957 touring production of *Merton of the Movies*, in which he played the title role. He also appeared in several other plays in his later years.

19

In 1959, Buster received an Academy Award for his lifetime achievement in film. Wife Eleanor and Bob Hope help him celebrate the occasion.

Buster, the aging comic, still very active in film, television, and theater to the end of his life.

Buster and Eleanor relax in their San Fernando Valley ranch home. Buster bought the place with the money he was paid as technical adviser for *The Buster Keaton Story*, made in 1957 and starring Donald O'Connor in the title role.

and *El Moderno Barba Azul,* made in Mexico in 1946. All of these contain moments of inventiveness that bear Keaton's distinctive style, but because of budget constraints and the fact that he was denied full creative control, they pale in comparison to his own classic silent films. The same can pretty much be said about his two-reel shorts for Educational Pictures and Co-

Buster composing his thoughts in his study. On the wall are photos of his two sons and (just above his head) best friend, Roscoe Arbuckle.

lumbia during the years 1934 through 1941, although some compare quite favorably to the two-reelers he made in the 1920s.

In 1937, Buster was rehired by MGM as a gag writer and ended up contributing gags and routines for a large variety of films. He also began landing subordinate acting jobs at various other studios, most notably in such films as *Hollywood Cavalcade* in 1939, *The Villain Still Pursued Her* in 1940, *Forever and a Day* in 1943, *San Diego I Love You* in 1944, *Sunset Boulevard* in 1950, and *Limelight* in 1952 in which he appeared with Chaplin for the only time.

It wasn't until 1949, with the appearance of an excellent *Life* magazine article on silent comedy written by James Agee, that interest in Keaton's career experienced a revival of sorts. Buster began receiving offers to appear in many nonfilm projects, ultimately performing in several stage plays and vaudeville revivals, and staging some of his old film routines in Europe for France's prestigious Cirque Medrano. By that time, Buster had long been divorced from his second wife. In 1940, he had married his third, Eleanor Norris, a dancer under contract at MGM, to whom he remained happily wed for the rest of his life. He had also been able to conquer his drinking and, for the most part, remained sober for his remaining years.

Long having given up on the idea of reestablishing himself as a major filmmaker, Buster had come to accept the turn of events that had left him struggling to make a living after being one of the most celebrated stars of the silent-film era. He thought that no one really cared about the movies he had made during his heyday, and that his classic films would never be seen again, that, with the exception of *The General* and a couple of his silent shorts, his films had long been destroyed or lost. However, in 1952, actor James Mason, who at the time was owner of the mansion in which Keaton had resided in the twenties and early thirties with Natalie and their sons, informed Buster that he had discovered a secret storage closet in a private screening room. Inside were stacks of film canisters—Buster's classics.

Two years later, Buster and Eleanor attended a showing of *The General* at a revival house in Los Angeles owned by Raymond Rohauer, an avid film enthusiast and collector of classic movies. When Rohauer learned from Buster that he had stacks of his own movies still on nitrate film stock, which is highly unstable and extremely flammable, arrangements were made for them to be transferred to safety stock. Ultimately, Rohauer entered into a business agree-

With Elmer III. Buster loved animals and featured a variety of them in many of his films, most notably a cow in his 1925 film, *Go West*, and a monkey in *The Cameraman*, made in 1928.

ment with Buster and began to track down all existing prints of classic Keaton films, then secured the ownership rights and finally rereleased the movies to revival theaters and film festivals. A major European Keaton revival in 1962 marked the beginning of Buster's rediscovery by the world film community and his ultimately being hailed as a genius (an assessment that Buster himself never took seriously).

In the final years of his life, Buster was treated as a living legend. In 1957, he served as technical adviser on a film based very loosely on his life, *The Buster Keaton Story,* starring Donald O'Connor. Two years later he was presented with a special Academy Award for his lifelong contributions to screen comedy. He appeared in many cameo film roles, stage productions, guest shots on television, and commercials. He was also invited to such prestigious film gatherings as the Cinémathèque in Paris, and the Venice Film Festival where, in 1965, he received a tumultuous ovation. The final Keaton film appearances were in Richard Lester's version of *A Funny Thing Happened on the Way to the Forum,* made in Spain in 1965, and a Canadian educational film, *The Scribe,* made in October of the same year.

On February 1, 1966, after a night spent playing cards with Eleanor and some close friends, Buster Keaton died of lung cancer at the age of seventy in his San Fernando Valley ranch home.

The deadpan king cracks a smile.

The Great Stone Face, early in his film career, circa 1920. Although known for his eternally blank pan expression, Buster had one of the most beautifully expressive faces in film.

KEATON:
The Filmmaker and the Face

One of the most interesting and, ultimately, unanswerable questions plaguing someone fascinated with the life of a dynamic and innovative artist is, "Where the hell does he get his ideas?" In the case of Buster Keaton, I believe the key to understanding his genius, his distinct view of the world and how this view shaped his unique approach to comedy and filmmaking, lies in Buster's trademark, the one characteristic that distinguished him from all other performers: his unsmiling face.

Each of the four premier silent comedians—Chaplin, Keaton, Harold Lloyd, and Harry Langdon—had his own distinctive screen character. Chaplin, whom Buster called "the greatest comedian that ever lived," had his eternal Tramp character; Lloyd had his bespectacled, all-American go-getter persona; Langdon had his boy/man character accentuated by his baby face and slow, childlike mannerisms. However, all of these characterizations were created after each artist had experimented with other on-screen personas. Keaton's screen character was born the first moment he appeared on film in *The Butcher Boy* and remained constant throughout his entire career. Also, more than any of the other silent comedy giants whose characters were created for the screen, Keaton's sprang directly from his life and his reputation as a stone-faced stage performer.

Buster grew up surrounded by a mesmerizing, eclectic madness called vaudeville. He became part of this madness at the age of three and loved every minute of it, loved the onstage roughhouse that he and his father indulged in nightly before an audience. He delighted in the explosion of laughter that greeted him as he remained stoic and expressionless throughout the mayhem. The most important lesson he learned in vaudeville was: no matter what happens, don't smile.

Keaton makes an interesting comment in *My Wonderful World of Slapstick,* the book he wrote with Charles Samuels: "I guess people just never do expect any human mop, dishrag, beanbag, or football to be pleased by what is being done to him." Billed as "The Human Mop" in his vaudeville routine with his father, Buster was treated as an inanimate object, a thing, a prop to be used for the entertainment of others. Mayhem swirled around him onstage while he remained the calm eye of the storm. Yet he was acutely aware of and enthralled by the exuberant roar of the crowd, hearing the screams grow louder as he concentrated on maintaining his indifference.

On entering the world of filmmaking, he instinctively and naturally assumed the character he had grown up with onstage and applied it not only to his on-screen character but ultimately to his entire approach to the movies, visually expressing this subtle,

The Love Nest, 1923.

of them without the use of a double, earning the nickname Ace from other professional stuntmen. This insistence on never faking a stunt by using a double was an obsession; he felt that his stunts were a natural extension of his character, his "human mop" persona.

Clyde Bruckman also mentions in Blesh's biography the technical innovations Keaton introduced to filmmaking. Buster was the first to film his comedies at standard speed, unlike the other comics, who tended to undercrank the camera so that the action, when projected, would appear speeded up, more animated, more cartoonish, less real. Buster wanted a more natural, less artificially frenetic look to his films, another reflection of his vaudeville roots. Keaton the filmmaker always envisioned the reaction of an audience to his gags and therefore strove to present his action as if it were unfolding live and unrehearsed. He approached his screen gags the same way he had

understated "indifference in the midst of chaos" approach in all the films he wrote and directed with his unwavering staff of technicians and gagmen.

This deadpan approach enveloped his fellow actors as well. Although he smiled often in the films he did with Arbuckle—sometimes even laughing or crying hysterically—he returned to his unsmiling, understated vaudeville persona once he started making his own. As Clyde Bruckman, one of his most loyal and gifted gagmen and the codirector of *The General,* said in Rudi Blesh's biography, *Keaton,* "he taught them all how to underact." Buster was accused of treating his leading ladies not so much as love interests but as props to be thrown around and manipulated for gag purposes. Yet, this attitude toward women was a direct reflection of his stage and screen character. Buster, the former "human mop," was his own ultimate prop. He reserved the most harrowing, the most difficult, the most spectacular, stunts for himself. He performed all

The Navigator, 1924.

24

The General, 1927.

staged his vaudeville routines by making the gags appear spontaneous, understated, regardless of their incredible complexities or danger.

Always fascinated with the unique attributes of a particular piece of machinery, Buster took advantage of the motion picture camera's exclusive abilities, incorporating many cinematic tricks—double exposures, quick-cut editing, reverse action. However, reflecting the position he maintained regarding his own spectacular stunt work, he never faked a routine no matter how elaborate or even simple the stunt or gag might appear to be. For example, in his first independently produced feature, *The Three Ages,* there is a scene in which Buster as a caveman carrying a crude wooden club encounters an enemy carrying an armload of rocks. As his nemesis hurls one of his rocks, Buster swings his club like a baseball bat, hitting the rock and sending it smashing into his enemy's chest, knocking him out. This simple scene lasting only

"Buster Di Milo," circa 1927.

seconds and presented in one continuous take required more than sixty takes before the lumpy rock hit the irregularly shaped club in just the right way to send it hurtling back at the enemy. Keaton could have filmed the scene by showing the rock hitting the club, then cutting to his enemy to show the rock hitting him in the chest. But that would have robbed the scene of its purity, its spontaneity, its "live" look.

In keeping with his more realistic approach to screen comedy, Buster shot his movies with a strict and unflinching attention to detail. His films are some of the most beautifully photographed comedies of all time, with elaborate sets, gorgeous outdoor vistas, and an obsession for authenticity, especially in such period films as *Our Hospitality, The General,* and the Mississippi riverboat setting of *Steamboat Bill, Jr.* Keaton credited his cameraman, Elgin Lessley, for the look of his films. Yet, as with Orson Welles, who also credited the stylistically innovative look of *Citizen Kane* to his cameraman, Gregg Toland, there is a distinctive look to the films of these men that is consistent no matter which cameraman they used (Lessley wasn't the cameraman for Keaton's most visually beautiful film, *The General,* nor did he photograph *Steamboat Bill, Jr.*).

Buster has been called a surrealist, an existentialist, an absurdist, a fatalist, even a nihilist because of his use of death humor in many of his films. But he always insisted that he was first and foremost a comedian. His

Nothing But Pleasure, 1940.

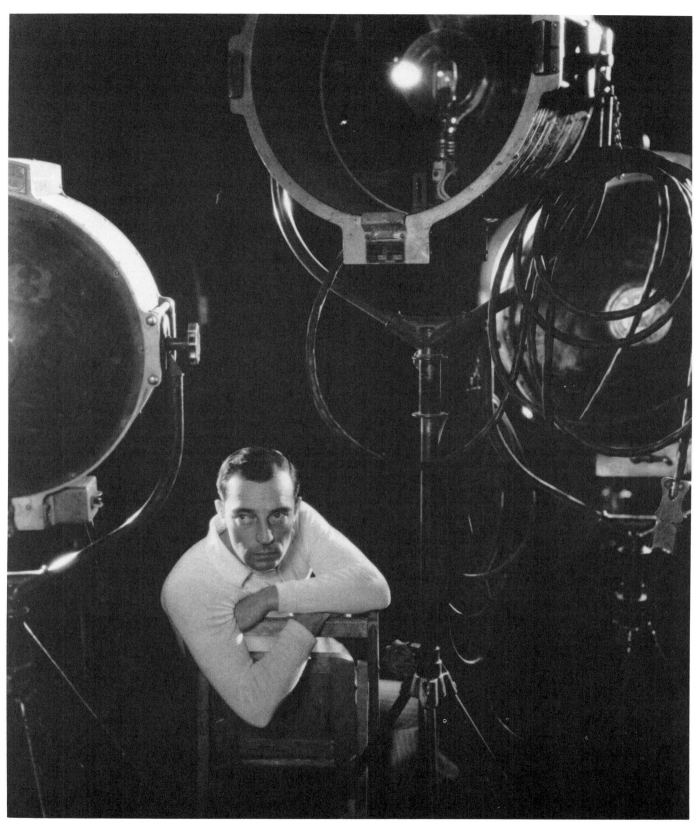

During his MGM period, circa 1930.

That's the Spirit, 1945.

You're My Everything, 1949.

Around the World in Eighty Days. 1956.

comedies do contain surreal, absurdist jokes acted out in an insane universe where humans are dominated by overwhelming mechanical complexities. But he used these absurdities and mechanistic monstrosities as gag material. In other words, while such people as Kafka, Sartre, and Nietzsche were making themselves nauseous trying to cope with modern, mechanistic society, Keaton was fashioning his horribly complicated and intimidating surroundings into gag props. In his best films, Buster is usually first introduced as a sedate character overwhelmed by the absurdity and chaos of modern society, but ultimately he triumphs, not by shunning the world but by calmly, matter-of-factly dismantling it and then redesigning it, making it just as functional but even more absurd than before to the point where confusion and despair are transformed into whimsy and laughter.

Buster transforms the world into his own image: stoic and unsmiling on the surface but filled with mirth and magic at its core. Because he had such a love for, and even an identification with, inanimate and mechanical objects, he was able to transform such massive props as trains, boats, houses, cars, and various other contraptions into objects of delight, reflections of his benign view of the world. He views the madness and the magnificence of life with the same deadpan expression, passing no judgment, accepting everything equally as part of the whole wonderfully insane phenomenon called life.

French film critic Robert Benayoun ends his beautiful book, *The Look of Buster Keaton,* with this moving passage:

The eyes of Buster Keaton see beyond mere story and script, encompass the cinema as a whole art, draw hope from frustration. . . . He gazes out upon America's landscape as a terrain for the poet to conquer, a place to be active and race down the hills and streets. His legs are pumping in a burst of speed. Headlong and unstoppable, imagination has run away with him and his look takes in the whole world.

Keaton's "look" is reflected in everything he ever appeared in. Sometimes the vision is jaundiced and blurred by too much booze; sometimes it is warped by the intrusive view of others; sometimes it is constricted and trivialized, as it was in his later years. But the look, the Great Stone Face, endures no matter what the situation, no matter what setting, no matter what death-defying stunt. From the first moment he appeared on screen in *The Butcher Boy* in 1917 to his last fade-out in *The Scribe* in 1965, Buster's beautiful, haunting face, reflecting every emotion and no emotion, remains constant, unflappable, eternal, a symbol of his all-encompassing, all-accepting view of the world.

A Funny Thing Happened on the Way to the Forum, 1965.

War Italian Style, 1965.

Buster (extreme right) makes his film debut in *The Butcher Boy*. Roscoe Arbuckle (second right) shrieks while Al St. John wields the pitchfork and leading lady Josephine Stevens (center) cowers.

THE
KEATON FILMS

The Butcher Boy: Roscoe, Al, and Josephine demonstrate the
less-than-subtle acting style that dominated the early two-reelers
Buster made with Arbuckle.

THE BUTCHER BOY

CREDITS:

Presented by the Comique Film Corporation: Distributed by Paramount Pictures. *Producer:* Joseph M. Schenck; *Director/ Scenario:* Roscoe Arbuckle; *Story:* Joe Roach; *Editor:* Herbert Warren; *Photography:* Frank D. Williams. *Release Date:* April 23, 1917. *Length:* two reels.

CAST:

Roscoe "Fatty" Arbuckle, Al St. John, Buster Keaton, Josephine Stevens, Arthur Earle, Agnes Neilson, Joe Bordeau, Luke the Dog.

While watching *The Butcher Boy* for the first time, I remembered certain comments made by Walter Kerr in his book *The Silent Clowns* concerning early screen comedy: "Silent film comedy began as though comedy never existed. . . . Here are genuine primitives at play, before laws were, before emotion was. The form is iconoclastic to the bone, its gestures are as gratuitous as they are extravagant, the conduct of all involved is utterly heartless." Kerr goes on to say that while researching his book, he viewed hundreds of these early comedy shorts and found them exciting to watch, filled with lots of action and lots of crazy stunts executed at an incredibly breakneck pace; but for the most part, the films were humorless, grotesque, and chaotic, lacking plot, character development, morality, and logic. This is precisely the reaction I had to *The Butcher Boy* and many of the early shorts Keaton did with Roscoe Arbuckle. Frenzied, brutal, lascivious, and amoral, they are spellbinding to watch, the most accurate visual representation of the uninhibited world of dreams that I have ever seen.

Arbuckle's approach to film comedy was basically the same as that of Mack Sennett, for whom he had made over two hundred shorts in a five-year span. The basic plot and structure of the shorts remain fairly consistent. First a basic setting is established (a general store, a hotel, a hospital, a garage, or an outdoor setting or event), then the characters are introduced, usually consisting of Roscoe, a girl, and a rival or two for the girl's affections. Then all hell breaks loose as Roscoe and the others battle for her attention. Sometimes after the first reel, the action switches to another setting and repeats itself.

This is essentially the structure of *The Butcher Boy,* which opens in a general store with customers and clerks engaging in extravagant horseplay. Lanky Al St. John, Arbuckle's real-life nephew and fellow Keystone alumnus (and one of the most frenetically unsubtle of all silent screen actors), helps a young woman customer with some items, nearly hanging himself on a pulley rope at one point. Then he assists a matronly woman with some pepper, which he grinds with the help of Roscoe's talented dog, Luke. Roscoe makes a humorous entrance as the butcher boy, exiting a huge walk-in freezer wearing a full-length fur coat. He then engages in some clever meat-cutting gags. He heaves slabs of meat against a wall lined with hooks, then tosses his cleaver in the air and has it twirl and land sticking point down on the chopping block.

Buster makes his film debut as a customer who wants to buy molasses. First glimpsed from behind, carrying a small pail, he enters the store dressed in overalls, slap shoes, clip-on tie, and flat porkpie hat. His deadpan expression, slow, methodical movements, and subtle curiosity about his surroundings are with him in that first moment on-screen and contrast profoundly with the flailing antics of the other cast members. After fiddling with a barrel full of brooms, he ambles over to Roscoe, pulls out a quarter, and drops it into his pail.

What follows is a classic comedy routine, one restaged by Keaton many times on television variety shows in his later years. After instructing Roscoe to fill up the pail with molasses, Buster tips his hat, sets it down on the counter next to the pail, and walks over to a group of old men playing checkers in a corner of the store. Roscoe fills the pail and beckons Buster over, demanding to be paid. When told that the quarter is at the bottom of the pail, Roscoe pours the molasses into Buster's hat on the counter and retrieves the quarter. Then he pours the molasses back into the pail. When Buster picks up his hat and pail and turns to leave, Arbuckle tips his trademark bowler hat. Buster tries to return the courtesy by tipping his hat, but can't because the sticky molasses has glued it tightly to his head. As a favor, Roscoe tries to wrench the hat from Buster's head, and Buster drops his pail and steps in the molasses. Roscoe finally loosens Buster's hat, then, to get him unstuck from the molasses on the floor, gives Buster a kick in the stomach, sending him flying across the store, out the door, and crashing into the proprietor, who is just entering.

Because both Buster and Arbuckle were so generous with their gags, freely crediting stories, routines, and technical assistance to others even when they actually contributed nothing at all, it is sometimes difficult to surmise just who originated what gag or routine in any of the films the comics made together. However, because this first filmed Keaton routine is so subtly executed with deliberate timing leading to a spectacularly effective conclusion, it is a very easy matter to credit him as the originator.

After tumbling out of the store, Buster returns to retrieve his hat. By this time, Roscoe and Al have begun to brawl over the store owner's pretty daughter, and Buster is hit in the face with a sack of flour that Roscoe has hurled at Al. Buster does a great, sprawling, feet-high-in-the-air fall on his rear, then gets up, smiles at the store owner, and proceeds to demolish the place along with Roscoe and Al. Buster spends the rest of the film as an accomplice to Al, who is trying to kidnap the daughter from a girl's boarding school, with both Roscoe and Al dressed up as coeds.

Buster's understated, deadpan screen persona is there from the first instant he appears. Even his traditional costume is already nearly intact. Only twenty-one at the time and yet nearly a twenty-year veteran of the stage, Buster instinctively knew how to improvise comic horseplay in his first screen appearance, which was also a first take, filmed during his first visit to a movie studio. An impressive movie debut indeed.

A RECKLESS ROMEO

CREDITS:

Presented by the Comique Film Corporation; Distributed by Paramount Pictures. *Producer:* Joseph M. Schenck; *Director/ Scenario:* Roscoe "Fatty" Arbuckle; *Story:* Joe Roach; *Editor:* Herbert Warren; *Photography:* Frank D. Williams. *Release Date:* May 21, 1917. *Length:* two reels.

CAST:

Roscoe "Fatty" Arbuckle, Al St. John, Buster Keaton, Alice Lake, Agnes Neilson, Corinne Parquet

A Reckless Romeo is one of the early Arbuckle-Keaton shorts considered lost. It has been confused with others made by Arbuckle when he was at Keystone, specifically the 1915 *Fatty's Tintype Tangle,* which has a similar plot description, and another Keystone two-reeler made in 1916 with the same title as this short. A contemporary review appearing in *Motion Picture News* noted that "the new all-star cast from *The Butcher Boy* is missing in this release," which makes one wonder whether this film could indeed be a rerelease of the earlier Keystone short. Since Roscoe liked to recycle his material, there is a chance the film is a remake of an earlier one.

In any event, the plot is clever. Roscoe plays a henpecked son-in-law. One day he storms out of his house and ends up at a park (Palisades Park in New Jersey), where he starts flirting with a girl played by Alice Lake, one of Arbuckle's favorite leading ladies. While he is flirting, a cameraman strolling through the park secretly films Roscoe and Alice. Later, after having been chased off by the girl's boyfriend, Roscoe returns home and generously offers to treat his wife and mother-in-law to a night at the movies. To his astonishment, his flirtatious encounter in the park that afternoon is the evening's featured attraction. Predictably, all hell breaks loose.

Although no contemporary review specifically mentions Buster's contribution to the film—if he did, in fact, appear—he more than likely played the cameraman in the park, while Al St. John, who usually received second billing in the early shorts, played the

A *Reckless Romeo*: Buster creates a human pinwheel with Roscoe, Alice Lake (left), and Viola Dana. Alice was Roscoe's most often-used leading lady in the films he made with Buster. Viola, a comic actress working at Metro, was one of Buster's girlfriends during his early days in Hollywood.

more substantial (and potentially volatile) part of the boyfriend. The *Motion Picture News* review mentions that Roscoe's filmed flirtation is projected in a way that "will have picture fans wondering how they photographed the picture brightly visible on-screen. Doubtless this is a trick of double exposure nicely executed." This special camera effect might be an early example of a trick Buster later used with spectacular success in his feature *Sherlock Jr.,* in which a scene also takes place in a movie theater where a film is being shown to an audience.

THE ROUGH HOUSE

CREDITS:

Presented by the Comique Film Corporation; Distributed by Paramount Pictures. *Producer:* Joseph M. Schenck; *Director/Scenario:* Roscoe Arbuckle; *Story:* Joe Roach; *Editor:* Herbert Warren; *Photography:* Frank D. Williams. *Release Date:* June 25, 1917. *Length:* two reels.

CAST:

Roscoe "Fatty" Arbuckle, Al St. John, Buster Keaton, Alice Lake, Agnes Neilsón, Glen Cavender.

According to Buster, by the time he made his third two-reeler with Arbuckle, he had practically become Arbuckle's sole writing staff. Since he was never cred-

The Rough House: A very supportive Roscoe gives Buster and Al St. John a lift.

ited as a writer on any of Arbuckle's shorts, the question of just how much he contributed depends on which gags a particular Keaton fan likes (the good ones are all Keaton's, the stupid ones are invariably somebody else's).

Many segments of *The Rough House* are easily recognizable as Keaton material. The plot of the film, of which the final footage is missing, centers around a seaside resort run by Roscoe, his wife, and mother-in-law. Buster plays three roles. He first appears as a thickly bearded gardener who helps put out a fire started by Roscoe, who has dropped off to sleep in bed with a lit cigarette. Then Buster turns up as a delivery boy who battles with the resort's cook, played by Al St. John, after Al catches him flirting with the maid, (Alice Lake). Finally, after both Buster and Al are arrested for nearly destroying the resort, Keaton returns as a cop to do battle with some crooks disguised as resort guests.

The first certifiably Keatonesque gag occurs during the fire sequence. With a deadpan matter-of-factness, Roscoe notices that his bed is on fire, gets out dressed in his nightshirt, strolls through the dining room to the kitchen, fills a teacup with water, then returns to the bedroom and flings the water at the flames. After he repeats this several times, once stopping to sample the food being served to the guests in the dining room, then another time drinking the water from his teacup, his wife and mother-in-law become aware of the fire and panic, resulting in a frenetic free-for-all. The entire segment, with its understated pacing in the midst of disaster, is pure Buster (although the teacup gag, which shows up in Buster's own short, *The Playhouse*, is from Arbuckle's 1915 two-reeler, *Fatty's Plucky Pup*.)

When Buster shows up as the delivery boy and gets into a brawl with Al, the two restage the broom-bashing routine from Buster's vaudeville act with Al spinning wildly around the kitchen while clutching a broom. Some of Al's actions are speeded up to emphasize his frenzied antics, the first use of camera trickery in the film. More cinematic tricks follow when Buster throws a knife at Al and he catches it in his teeth, a feat accomplished by reverse-action photography.

When Al and Buster are hauled off to the pokey, Roscoe becomes the new cook, and the gags that follow definitely have the Keaton touch. In the kitchen, Roscoe uses an electric fan to slice vegetables. When he sets the dining room table, he first wraps up the entire meal—including the dinnerware—in a tablecloth, then, once again with the aid of reverse-action photography, unwraps it onto the table with everything perfectly in place.

The most interesting camera trick occurs during the film's final segment when Buster and Al play Keystone-like cops. The two former foes, now officially part of the police force, magically appear with a colleague in front of the dispatch officer's desk, then just as magically vanish, a crude first example of a dazzling trick Buster would later perfect in *Sherlock Jr.*

The most famous gag of the film, however, must be credited to Arbuckle. Before assuming Al's duties as cook, Roscoe sits at the dining room table with his wife and mother-in-law and playfully sticks two forks into a pair of dinner rolls, then enacts an abbreviated version of the "Dance of the Rolls" routine that Chaplin later perfected in *The Gold Rush*. Although David Robinson, in his book on Buster's films, is eager to credit him as the originator, the routine is obviously by Arbuckle who blatantly imitates his old Keystone costar's mannerisms in the way he shuffles the rolls across the table, parodying the Tramp's distinctive walk.

Keaton wasn't stretching the truth when he claimed to be responsible for the majority of the gags by the third Arbuckle film. His fascination with the unique abilities of the motion picture camera is evident throughout the film, along with eccentric uses of machinery (the electric fan gag) and the use of material from his vaudeville days (the broom-bashing routine). However, the overall "roughhouse" brawling that dominates the short is still very much in the Arbuckle style.

HIS WEDDING NIGHT

CREDITS:

Presented by the Comique Film Corporation; Distributed by Paramount Pictures. *Producer:* Joseph M. Schenck; *Director/ Scenario:* Roscoe Arbuckle; *Story:* Joe Roach; *Editor:* Herbert Warren; *Photography:* George Peters. *Release Date:* August 20, 1917. *Length:* two reels.

CAST:

Roscoe "Fatty" Arbuckle, Al St. John, Buster Keaton, Alice Mann, Arthur Earle, Jimmy Bryant, Josephine Stevens.

In a variation of *The Butcher Boy* setting, *His Wedding Night* takes place in a drugstore (called Koff and Kramp Druggists) with Arbuckle as a combination soda jerk/general helper. Like most of his shorts, the film is filled with lots of wild horseplay centered around a battle for the affections of a pretty girl, this time played by Alice Mann. Al St. John plays Roscoe's rival for Alice, and at the start, they get into a watermelon-slinging melee before Roscoe (who has worked in some food-juggling bits and insulted various customers) finally flings Al out of the store. Later, Roscoe steps outside to attend to the gas pump, changing the price of gas according to the type of car—twenty-five cents per gallon for a jalopy and one dollar for a limousine (still later, Roscoe sips from the gas pump—it's actually a water hose).

As in *The Rough House,* Keaton appears as a delivery boy on a bike, this time bringing a wedding gown for Alice, who is Roscoe's fiancée. Buster helps her with her gown, volunteering to try it on while she puts some additional touches on it. In the film's most Keatonesque moment, Buster ducks behind a changing partition, then makes a spectacularly theatrical reappearance as it falls and a spotlight suddenly hits him while he strikes a feminine pose and begins modeling the gown. Prancing around in the wedding gown while maintaining his trademark frozen face, he milks the scene for all it's worth, and the effect is hilarious.

In the film's climax, the wedding-gowned Buster is mistaken for Alice and kidnapped by Al and his henchmen. Invading Alice's bedroom, located above the drugstore, they throw a pillowcase over Buster's head and haul him off to the local justice of the peace. On hearing about the kidnapping and thinking that Alice has been abducted, Roscoe rushes off to the rescue. When he catches up with the gang at the justice of the peace, all hell predictably breaks loose, ending with Buster—still wearing the pillowcase over his head—on the verge of becoming hitched to Roscoe. Alice suddenly shows up and Buster is unmasked at the altar, giving Roscoe a bashful smile and an all-knowing wink. (This refers back to when Buster entered the drugstore, nursing a sore eye, and repeatedly blinked at Roscoe, who misinterpreted the act as a secret request for some bootleg beer, which he supplies to his pleasantly surprised customer.)

The most wildly effective segment of *His Wedding Night* occurs earlier in the drugstore. To prevent customers from spritzing themselves with expensive perfume, Roscoe replaces the perfume with chloroform. A pretty young woman enters, picks up the perfume bottle, sprays herself, and promptly passes out into Roscoe's arms. Realizing he has a chance to have his way with the unconscious woman, Roscoe first hesitates, not because he feels any pangs of guilt but because his boss has been watching. Roscoe sneaks over to his boss, sprays him with the chloroform-laced perfume, then sneaks back to the woman, giving her a couple more spritzes to make sure she's sufficiently comatose, and begins kissing her. After satisfying his

desires, he passes some smelling salts under her nose until she perks up and saunters happily out of the store. This licentious gag, bold for its time and played with uninhibited abandon, is a prime example of Arbuckle's ability to get away with the most outrageously amoral antics and pass them off as harmless comedy. Erich Von Stroheim later used a similar routine in his masterpiece, *Greed,* but even Von Stroheim, a specialist in cinematic decadence, had his character show some guilt and remorse over his actions, while Arbuckle remains gleefully guiltless.

His Wedding Night, with its freewheeling amorality, is nearly pure Arbuckle with only a few recognizable gag contributions from Keaton. Gone are the playful camera experiments so prevalent in the previous short, *The Rough House,* all of them replaced by Arbuckle's special brand of low-humor horseplay. There is, however, a stronger story line in this short compared to previous ones, suggesting a minor contribution from Buster and resulting in a much more effective and fully integrated finale.

OH DOCTOR!

CREDITS:

Presented by the Comique Film Corporation; Distributed by Paramount Pictures. *Producer:* Joseph M. Schenck; *Director:* Roscoe Arbuckle; *Scenario:* Jean Havez; *Editor:* Herbert Warren; *Photography:* George Peters. *Release Date:* September 30, 1917. *Length:* two reels.

CAST:

Roscoe "Fatty" Arbuckle, Buster Keaton, Al St. John, Alice Mann.

Another one of the lost films that Buster made with Roscoe, *Oh Doctor!* sounds like a lively and anarchic Arbuckle-dominated romp, according to the plot summaries from reviews of the time. As a doctor with an overly congenial beside manner, Roscoe ends up smitten by a beautiful patient who turns out to be more interested in Mrs. Roscoe's jewelry than in Roscoe.

In addition to his professional duties, Roscoe dabbles in the horses. After winning a 500-to-1 bet on a race, he dashes out of his office to pick up his dough at the local bookie joint, leaving his son, played by Buster, in charge. (Al St. John apparently plays an intern and Alice Mann is a nurse. It seems to be the first time that Buster gets second billing to Roscoe, proof of

Buster tries to ring the bell but ends up making Roscoe see stars in a scene from *Coney Island*. Leading lady Alice Mann is awed at the sight of Roscoe's gravity-defying hat.

Arbuckle's keen awareness of Keaton's talents and his willingness to reward him for sharing these talents.) In his haste to leave the office, Roscoe throws on a patient's coat, a policeman's jacket. When he shows up at the bookie joint, the patrons think it's a raid and everyone scatters, except for Roscoe. Worried that he won't be able to collect his winnings, he gathers up the loot left by the fleeing patrons.

According to a contemporary review in *Variety*, "Buster Keaton plays the doctor's son with little to do, Arbuckle taking . . . center stage and holding it." One can only wonder what this "little to do" consisted of. *Oh Doctor!* is the first short in which scenario credit is given to Jean Havez, a rotund ex-vaudevillian who later helped Keaton with the stories for most of his features. The film has been confused by some critics with *Good*

Night, Nurse! which was made the following year. However, the plot to each is wildly different, so there is no chance the two are the same film under different titles.

FATTY AT CONEY ISLAND (aka Coney Island)

CREDITS:

Presented by the Comique Film Corporation; Distributed by Paramount Pictures. *Producer:* Joseph M. Schenck; *Director/ Scenario:* Roscoe Arbuckle; *Editor:* Herbert Warren; *Photography:* George Peters. *Release Date:* October 29, 1917. *Length:* two reels.

CAST:

Roscoe "Fatty" Arbuckle, Buster Keaton, Al St. John, Alice Mann, Agnes Neilson, Joe Bordeau, Jimmy Bryant.

At first glance (and even at second and third glance), *Fatty at Coney Island* is the most Mack Sennett/Keystone–influenced short Arbuckle did on his own. Sennett was fond of arranging his cameras at local events or familiar outdoor settings and then filming his stars as they ran wild, making up gags inspired by their surroundings. *Coney Island* fits this improvisational approach to filmmaking. It also has such Sennett-inspired touches as bathing beauties, Keystone Kops, and extreme overacting by everyone, including Buster, who smiles, laughs, and cries hysterically throughout the film, more than in any other one he ever made. However, in addition to the blatant Sennett touches, there are distinctive Keaton influences, namely the plot, which, although wild and convoluted, has an integrating thread around Buster's character tying all the action together and leading to a satisfying resolution. Also, several gags here are duplicated in later Keaton films.

The story revolves around Roscoe's trying to ditch his wife at the beach so he can cavort freely and enjoy the Coney Island attractions. He soon encounters pretty Alice Mann, who had originally arrived with Buster but had been wooed away from him by Al St. John. Now, Roscoe steals her away from Al, which compels both the scorned rivals to try to win her back. The wooing and competition take place throughout the amusement park, then later in a bathhouse where

Roscoe dons a matronly woman's bathing suit and is chased out of both the men's and women's dressing rooms. Buster spies on the bathing-suit-clad Roscoe and Alice while posing as a lifeguard, until Al and Mrs. Roscoe appear and uncover Roscoe's female disguise. A melee erupts between Roscoe and Al until they are hauled off to jail by the cops. Buster is reunited with Alice while Roscoe and Al continue to brawl in the hoosegow. The two rivals finally escape from their cell after a battalion of police tries to break up the battle and instead, all the cops end up unconscious. (One of the cops is played by a heavily mustached Buster.)

Coney Island's frenetic pacing, anarchic plot, and animated acting make it one of the wildest, crudest, most out-of-control two-reelers Keaton ever appeared in, thoroughly dominated by Arbuckle's low-humor comedy. Gags involving spitting, vomiting, fat butts, physical abnormalities, near-naked women, voyeurism, transvestism, and latent homosexuality abound. As usual, the crudities are all treated as just good fun and are presented at such a fast pace that they are, amazingly, almost completely inoffensive, thanks to Arbuckle.

Keaton's usual subdued acting technique is totally absent, replaced by the Al St. John–style of exaggerated mugging. Whenever one of Buster's rivals thwarts his efforts to win back Alice, he cries hysterically; whenever he successfully subdues his foes, he laughs excitedly. However, even though conforming to the acting style of his costars, Keaton still managed to inject some of his brand of humor. When Roscoe is changing in the bathhouse dressing room, he suddenly acknowledges the presence of the camera and, in the name of decency, asks the cameraman to raise the angle of the lens and film him from the waist up. This is an Arbuckle gag—he used it in the 1914 Keystone film *The Knockout.* However, it is the type of gag Buster loved, and he later reworked it for his short *One Week,* taking it to its extreme by actually covering the camera lens with his hand to protect his leading lady from exposing too much of herself. Also, there is a scene in *Coney Island* where Buster rescues Roscoe and Alice from drowning after they have been thrown from their seats while riding down a water chute (Buster doubled Alice for the stunt). Keaton restaged this comical scene for the dramatic finale of his 1928 feature *The Cameraman.*

After finishing *Fatty at Coney Island,* the Comique Film Corporation packed up and moved to southern California, where many other movie companies were relocating because of the moderate weather and varied outdoor locations, which were more suitable for year-round filmmaking. The fact that the Arbuckle players, with their maniacal carryings on, were dis-turbing the more subdued production efforts of their Talmadge Studio colleagues probably had something to do with producer Joseph Schenck's agreeing to the relocation.

A COUNTRY HERO

CREDITS:

Presented by the Comique Film Corporation; Distributed by Paramount Pictures. *Producer:* Joseph M. Schenck; *Director/Scenario:* Roscoe Arbuckle; *Editor:* Herbert Warren; *Photography:* George Peters. *Release Date:* December 10, 1917. *Length:* two reels.

CAST:

Roscoe "Fatty" Arbuckle, Buster Keaton, Al St. John, Alice Lake, Joe Keaton, Stanley Pembroke.

A Country Hero is the first Arbuckle two-reeler filmed in his new West Coat studio facilities. (Actually, the studio, located in Long Beach, was rented; its official name was the Horkheimer Brothers' Balboa Amusement Producing Company Studios.) The film unfortunately is one of the lost shorts. From the bits and

Al St. John, Roscoe, and Buster display their unique dancing styles in a scene from *A Country Hero.* Buster's father, Joe (smiling in background just to the right of Al), makes his screen debut in this two-reeler which, unfortunately, remains lost.

pieces known about it, *A Country Hero* undoubtedly contains many Keaton touches, the most obvious one being Joe Keaton, Buster's father, who makes his film debut here.

Joe Keaton, the confirmed movie hater, who, in 1913, had turned down a lucrative film contract offered by William Randolph Hearst, agreed to appear here only after much persuasion. He must have enjoyed the experience because he became one of Arbuckle's regulars and later appeared in many of Buster's films. Like Buster, Joe must have found many similarities between Roscoe's roughhouse comedy style and the freewheeling routines the Keatons had pioneered in vaudeville. Apparently, he took special pleasure in re-creating his head-bopping hitch kick in one scene, methodically kicking the principal cast members (Roscoe, Buster, Al St. John, and Alice Lake) into a horse trough.

Joe Keaton plays a key role in the film, which is set in a rural town called Jazzville with Roscoe as the owner of a blacksmith shop and Joe (known as Cy Klone) as a rival owner of a garage. The two men, already enemies, come to blows when they vie for the affections of a pretty schoolteacher, played by Alice Lake. However, with the arrival of city slicker Al St. John, Roscoe and Joe join forces to vanquish this new Romeo. The finale takes place during amateur night at the local village ball.

Apparently, the short contains an elaborate nightclub free-for-all in which Roscoe heaves a piano at a rival, and a spectacular two-car auto wreck with a passing locomotive. Like Keaton, Arbuckle was totally oblivious of financial matters and spent over $20,000 staging the wreck scene alone, an incredible amount of money to splurge on just one scene for a two-reel comedy, showing producer Joe Schenck's faith in Roscoe, who, at the time, was his most successful box-office performer. Buster later mirrored Roscoe's "Budget? What budget?" approach to filmmaking when he began making his own Schenck-produced movies, prompting Schenck to remark more than once: "If there is a costly way to make a movie, he'll find it."

Though hardly mentioned in the contemporary reviews of the film, Buster is one of the featured performers at the village ball. He originates a dance routine here that he revived in various incarnations in other Arbuckle shorts, as well as in the army when he was part of a troop entertainment act. He also performed the routine in the MGM feature *Hollywood Revue,* which contains its best filmed presentation.

The Cook: Charlie Chaplin (behind the camera) clowns with Buster (far right) at the Arbuckle troupe's film studio in Long Beach, California. Chaplin and Arbuckle were good friends, both having worked together at the Keystone Studios. Also pictured are studio manager Lou Anger (with hammer), and studio owner H. M. Horkheimer (about to be hammered).

40

OUT WEST

CREDITS:

Presented by the Comique Film Corporation; Distributed by Paramount Pictures. *Producer:* Joseph M. Schenck; *Director:* Roscoe Arbuckle; *Scenario:* Natalie Talmadge; *Editor:* Herbert Warren; *Photography:* George Peters. *Release Date:* January 20, 1918. *Length:* two reels.

CAST:

Roscoe "Fatty" Arbuckle, Buster Keaton, Al St. John, Alice Lake, Joe Keaton.

In *Out West*, Keaton and Arbuckle indulge in a brand of humor they both loved, gags built around killing and death. Extremely nightmarish, like a filmed dream, *Out West* is totally illogical, chaotic, and amoral. Its frenzied, violent action is, with the exception of Buster, executed by gleefully maniacal, slapstick demons.

The film opens on an old Western saloon setting. Dressed in a long, black coat and stovepipe hat, Buster plays a dude gambler who casually shoots a cheating cardsharp, then rolls the body through a trapdoor in the saloon floor. With the mood of the film now properly set, the scene shifts to Roscoe riding in the water car of a speeding train. His huge bottom adorned with his bowler hat bobs up and down in the water before his bawling face suddenly appears in the dark liquid. When he hauls himself out of the car and sits atop the train to dry, he is spotted by the conductors in the car below. In a beautifully timed scene, Roscoe jumps off and stands idly by the tracks, rolling a cigarette as the train speeds behind him. Then, as the caboose comes into view, he casually turns, grabs its railing, and swings back aboard.

After more high jinks on the train, Roscoe ends up stranded in the desert where he is chased by hostile Indians. ("And how!" grunts one Indian to his companions. "We catch, we can eat meat all winter!") Making a spectacular entrance into town, Roscoe barrels down the street and rolls into the saloon in time to interrupt a robbery by the ruthless Wild Bill Hiccup (played by a psychotic Al St. John). During the melee, the bartender is killed. After Buster disposes of the body, Roscoe becomes the new bartender.

A terrifying scene follows when rowdies begin taunting a black patron. When the man turns to Roscoe and Buster for help, they respond by shooting at him along with the rowdies as he runs frantically around the saloon. The man tries to take refuge in the death pit beneath the saloon's trapdoor, but after seeing the newly dead body of the ex-bartender staring at him, he jumps straight up out of the pit in horror and is finally rescued when a pretty Salvation Army representative (Alice Lake) enters and breaks up the melee.

Al suddenly reappears and saunters up to the bar for a couple of drinks, but gets fresh with Alice when she asks him for a donation. Buster tries to intervene, but Al's thirst and lust are insatiable and unstoppable. In the most frighteningly hilarious scene, Roscoe tries to subdue Al by smashing dozens of whiskey bottles over the latter's head, one after another, with no effect, the liquid from each splattering all over Al and Alice as he gleefully molests her. Roscoe then pulls out a gun and repeatedly shoots at Al, once more with no effect. Finally, finding a feather, Roscoe tickles Al into submission.

The seemingly invincible Al returns and lassos Alice, yanking her out of the saloon and riding off with her. While Roscoe jumps onto a horse and pursues them, Buster shoots the rest of Al's gang. Roscoe finally catches up with Al in a shack hideout where he spies the desperado trying to get Alice drunk. After she throws her drink in Al's face and flees, Roscoe shoves the shack off a cliff and watches it smash into splinters, the dazed Al staggering about in the rubble.

According to contemporary reviews, *Out West* is supposed to be a satire of westerns of the time. It is true that the action, although unsettlingly bizarre, is handled in an incongruously understated, satirical manner. For example, in the scene where the saloon is held up by Al and the bartender is gunned down, Buster instantly and matter-of-factly produces a sign, "Bartender Wanted," from underneath the bar. He reacts so casually, however, that his actions seem more heartless than funny. Then there's the running gag of rolling the dead bodies into a pit beneath the saloon floor, a routine much more disturbing than amusing because it is, again, played without the slightest hint of comedy.

Buster undoubtedly had a lot to do with the decision to satirize the well-established western. He and his father had similar burlesques in vaudeville, poking fun at the torrid melodramas of the time. Although *Out West* was Keaton's first attempt at cinematic satire, it was hardly his last and far from his best.

THE BELL BOY

CREDITS:

Presented by the Comique Film Corporation; Distributed by Paramount Pictures. *Producer:* Joseph M. Schenck; *Director/Scenario:* Roscoe Arbuckle; *Editor:* Herbert Warren; *Photog-*

raphy: George Peters. *Release Date:* March 18, 1918. *Length:* two reels.

CAST:

Roscoe "Fatty" Arbuckle, Buster Keaton, Al St. John, Alice Lake, Joe Keaton, Charles Dudley.

The Bell Boy, one of the best shorts Keaton made with Arbuckle, contains some of Buster's strongest and most easily recognizable touches. He obviously loved the gags he and Roscoe created since many show up in several other films of theirs. In fact, Buster practically remade *The Bell Boy* in 1937 as *Love Nest on Wheels,* his last talkie short for Educational Pictures.

The action takes place in the Elk's Head Hotel, a rural establishment operated by Roscoe and Buster, who appear as bellboys, and Al, as the desk clerk. The first Keaton gag is the oft-repeated one of cleaning a pane of nonexistent glass. Roscoe then mops the lobby by sitting on the floor and cleaning one small area before scooting on to another. He next shaves a heavily bearded guest, transforming the man into various historical personages as he removes layers of whiskers and hair. First the man appears as Ulysses S. Grant, then after some cutting, as Lincoln, and finally as Kaiser Wilhelm, a sight that compels the patriotic barber to smash the kaiser clone in the face with massive globs of shaving cream.

Buster then re-creates one of his vaudeville routines when his father, Joe Keaton, shows up as an elegantly dressed guest. While Buster mops the floor, Joe's top hat is knocked off by an overhead conveyor belt carrying hot towels from the kitchen to the barbershop. Suspecting Buster has insulted him, Joe kicks him in the rear, then upends his pail of water onto his head. When the conveyor belt again knocks off Joe's hat, he turns, spots Al walking by with a tray of food, and kicks him across the floor through several rooms. Joe then pulls out a close-fitting cap, slaps it on his head, and skulks out of the hotel.

Another Keaton gag follows, the most elaborate of the film. Buster tries to use the elevator to take several guests up to their rooms, but they get stuck between floors when it conks out. The elevator is powered by a horse, which is acting stubborn and refuses to budge. Al, who is trying to propel the horse, gets the bright idea of lighting a fire under it. As the horse moves out of the way of the flames, the rope attached to it that connects to the elevator catches fire. Meanwhile, Roscoe is trying to pry the elevator free by using a long plank. When he sets it down, one-half hanging over the empty elevator shaft, Alice Lake, as the hotel's new manicurist, wanders over and steps on the plank just as the burning rope snaps, causing the elevator to plummet and strike the board. Alice is propelled into the air and lands atop an elk's head nailed to the wall. The routine is pure Keaton and is a superb early example of his ability to create and stage incredibly elaborate mechanical gags.

Another intricate, Keaton-formulated scene follows. Roscoe instructs Buster and Al to stage a mock bank holdup so he can step in, thwart their robbery, and impress Alice with his heroics. (This blatantly contrived plot twist is an example of how some of Arbuckle's shorts begin with one premise and end with a completely new one.) When Buster and Al comply, real bank robbers show up and a melee erupts. Buster and Al perform some incredible stunt work as they vault from one room to the next trying to both escape

In *The Bell Boy,* Roscoe fraternizes with the hotel's new manicurist, Alice Lake, while Buster hangs around. The short is the first in which the two men are featured as a comedy team.

Revenuer Buster gets the drop on moonshiner Al St. John who, in turn, prepares to blast away at Roscoe in *Moonshine*. Alice Lake referees the shooting match.

from and subdue the robbers. (This scene is repeated at the climax of Buster's later two-reeler *The High Sign.*) When Roscoe shows up at the bank, he helps rout the robbers, who are finally arrested after a wild chase on a runaway trolley.

Except for the contrived robbery plot, *The Bell Boy,* rich in visual gags, most of them Keaton's, is a near-perfect comedy, virtually free of the usual crude, low-humor routines favored by Arbuckle. It is also the first strong example of Roscoe and Buster appearing as a comic team. Both are dressed throughout most of the film in matching bellboy uniforms, and they cavort together in some dazzling acrobatic stunts, playfully falling over one another while vying for the affections of Alice. Al, wearing a completely different costume, is presented as an obvious supporting player to the more dynamic and distinctive two-man team.

MOONSHINE

CREDITS:

Presented by the Comique Film Corporation; Distributed by Paramount Pictures. *Producer:* Joseph M. Schenck; *Director/ Scenario:* Roscoe Arbuckle; *Editor:* Herbert Warren; *Photography:* George Peters. *Release Date:* May 13, 1918. *Length:* two reels.

CAST:

Roscoe "Fatty" Arbuckle, Buster Keaton, Al St. John, Alice Lake, Charles Dudley, Joe Bordeau.

Moonshine is Keaton and Arbuckle's second attempt at cinematic satire following their sporadically effective black comedy *Out West.* Like that one, *Moonshine* is a burlesque of a particular type of entertainment. This time, Buster and Roscoe parody the florid style of stage melodrama with its invincible heroes, dastardly villains, implausible escapes from imminent death, and eventual triumph of good over evil. Dominated by Buster's distinctive approach to humor, *Moonshine* could easily be called his first independent two-reel short.

Like their previous film, *The Bell Boy,* the two are presented as a comedy team, this time both of them playing revenuers responsible for tracking down moonshiners in the backwoods of Virginia. Roscoe and his fellow agents make a hilariously effective entrance driving through the backwoods in a chauffeur-driven limousine. After Roscoe, sporting a floppy hat and monocle, hops out and surveys the scene, he beckons to Buster, his faithful lieutenant, to summon the rest of the revenuers from the car.

Buster and Roscoe romp in the backwoods of Virginia (actually California's San Gabriel Mountains) in *Moonshine*. Although technically an Arbuckle short, the film is dominated by Keaton's more satirical and visually dynamic style of humor.

What follows is an old clown gag in which a ridiculous number of people exit the car. However, because of the sophisticated way in which the segment is filmed, showing the entire car from a long shot and having a virtual army of men pile out and line up in row after row all in the same continuous shot, the effect is dazzling. This is an early example, later perfected by Buster, of double exposure achieved by masking one side of the camera lens, shooting the scene, then rewinding the film and masking the other side of the lens to produce the photographic effect. Keaton later used this effect in *The Playhouse* to achieve multiple images of himself.

Roscoe and Buster then begin to search for the moonshiners' secret hideaway. Their several wild adventures all emphasize the artificiality of melodrama. Many of the encounters blatantly call attention to the drama itself, either by poking fun at the illogical plot, acknowledging the presence of the camera, or using more cinematic tricks. In one of the more satirical scenes, revenuer Roscoe is captured by the moonshin-ers and thrown into the cellar of their hideout shack. Expecting squalid conditions, he is stunned to find himself in a luxurious parlor suitable for an English lord. When he sits in a large, comfy chair, Alice Lake, playing the head moonshiner's daughter, appears in an elegant evening dress and serves him dinner from a food tray sumptuously filled. Despite his less-than-barbaric surroundings, Roscoe still cries out in true melodramatic fashion, "How will I ever escape from these cutthroats?" The answer is conveniently and absurdly supplied when he picks up a nearby copy of *The Count of Monte Cristo* and reads how the hero of the book faked his death and ended up being tossed into the ocean by his captors. Roscoe, thanking Alexandre Dumas for the plan, promptly smears himself with catsup, picks up a gun given to him by the sympathetic Alice, and fires it into the air. Coming to investigate, the moonshiners dutifully carry him out of the cellar and throw him into the nearby river. Roscoe then floats away a free man.

After Buster has a hilarious encounter with mountain man Al St. John, in which the two mimic monkeys and chase each other up a tree, Buster again joins forces with Roscoe. The latter refers to the preplanned artificiality of the story by suggesting they cut to the climactic explosion scene. The moonshiners once again appear on cue, recapture Roscoe, and tie him up in their shack. Then they rig the place with dynamite and exit, waiting for the explosion that will blow Roscoe to bits. How will Roscoe, the symbol of goodness, the invincible hero of the melodrama, escape from this impossible predicament? Easy. When the explosion occurs, blowing Roscoe and the shack to smithereens, he (as director) merely reverses the film, and the cabin reassembles, allowing him to emerge triumphant and unscathed. This sequence, obviously a Keaton-inspired gag, could very well be the most purely cinematic one ever filmed. That the properties of filmmaking play a key role in the plot, actually rescuing the hero, illustrates the artificiality not only of melodrama but also of film itself. The joke is so sophisticated, so outrageously absurd, working on so many levels at once, that it takes a while for the viewer to grasp just exactly what has happened.

After the stunning explosion sequence, Buster disposes of the entire moonshine clan with rapid-fire gunshots, with all falling one by one in a neatly choreographed line of bodies. Thus, good has triumphed over the forces of evil, and Roscoe is free to marry Alice. However, at the last minute, Roscoe remembers that he is already married, so Buster claims Alice while the noble and heroic Roscoe walks off into the sunset.

Moonshine is so obviously dominated by Keaton's brand of comedy, even Arbuckle himself later admitted it was not in his typical style and objected to the more sophisticated approach, which he felt the average viewer wouldn't understand. The one major disagreement between the two during their career together was over the mentality of the average film audience. Roscoe maintained that its IQ was equal to that of a twelve-year-old, and he fashioned his comedies for that mentality. Buster adamantly argued that an intelligent film will always find an audience, citing D. W. Griffith's *Birth of a Nation* as an example of innovative and commercially successful moviemaking. Buster was soon to create more movies of this school of thought, *Moonshine* being his first fully realized example and one of his best.

GOOD NIGHT, NURSE!

CREDITS:

Presented by the Comique Film Corporation; Distributed by Paramount Pictures. *Producer:* Joseph M. Schenck; *Director/Scenario:* Roscoe Arbuckle; *Editor:* Herbert Warren; *Photography:* George Peters. *Release Date:* July 6, 1918. *Length:* two reels.

CAST:

Roscoe "Fatty" Arbuckle, Buster Keaton, Al St. John, Alice Lake, Joe Bordeau.

Doctor Buster flirts with nurse Roscoe as snubbed nurse Kate Price and crazy patient Alice Lake look on, in a scene from *Good Night, Nurse!*

Good Night, Nurse!: Buster demonstrates his surgical skills to his staff and prospective patients while Roscoe snuggles with Alice. Also pictured is Al St. John (far right) who plays Buster's assistant.

With a hefty assist from Keaton, *Good Night, Nurse!* emerges as, arguably, the best film Arbuckle ever made. It unquestionably contains one of his best opening sequences. Standing on a street corner in the pouring rain, a broad, benign grin on his face, an obviously drunk Roscoe tries to light a cigarette. Suddenly a woman (actually, Buster in drag) passes by carrying an umbrella. Moments later she literally blows back into the scene as a gust of wind catches her umbrella and propels her along the sidewalk. A scuffle results with Roscoe finally ripping off the woman's dress. She retaliates with a swift, two-feet-at-once kick in Roscoe's belly and departs. Soon afterward Roscoe is joined in the downpour by an elegantly dressed drunk, an organ-grinder and his monkey, a gypsy dancer, and finally a cop, before the eccentric troupe staggers off to Roscoe's house for a nightcap. This hilarious, wonderfully acted opening segment is filled with a loopy, freewheeling exuberance, a tone that dominates the entire film.

After Roscoe's companions are booted out of the house by Mrs. Roscoe, she insists that her chronically inebriated husband commit himself to the No Hope Sanitarium for the cure. An obliging Roscoe soon finds himself in the presence of the head doctor (played by Buster), who greets his new patient while dressed in a white doctor's smock covered with blood and a huge, bloody meat cleaver in one hand. A female patient in nothing but bloomers and a skimpy camisole sud-

denly appears and jumps into Roscoe's arms. The girl, played by Alice Lake, is taken away by Buster's assistant (Al St. John). While being examined by Buster and Al, Roscoe eats the thermometer placed in his mouth and is immediately rushed into the operating room for surgery.

When he awakes from his operation, Alice enters his room, still dressed in her underwear, and the two plan an escape. In a beautifully staged piece of mayhem, the escapees invade a communal ward and an incredible pillow fight erupts with feathers bursting forth and enveloping the entire screen while animated bodies career about. Roscoe emerges from the blizzard of feathers and bodies and races down the hall carrying Alice in a very large pillowcase. After she is recaptured, Roscoe dons a uniform stolen from a matronly nurse's locker. When Buster spots the disguised Roscoe, the two hilariously smirk, ogle, and blink at one another. However, when the matronly nurse returns and discovers her uniform missing, she spots Roscoe and rips off his outfit. In only his underwear, Roscoe races out of the hospital with Buster and Al in hot pursuit.

Sprinting down a dirt road, Roscoe somehow becomes part of a fat men's footrace. Soon he's leading the pack of rotund joggers while Buster and Al barrel along behind him. This entire scene is masterfully staged, filmed in a long shot showing the entire street littered with fainting fat men, each accosted and

Buster and Al prepare for a gun duel while Roscoe supplies the refreshments in *Out West*. The two-reeler contains the first examples of Buster's darkly humorous jokes about death.

methodically inspected by Buster and Al to make sure the perspiring victim isn't Roscoe. Ultimately, Roscoe wins the race and is surrounded by cheering spectators. Buster and Al burst on the scene, however, and wrestle Roscoe to the ground. Suddenly, the scene dissolves to a hospital room where Roscoe awakens from the operation performed earlier, the rest of his adventures having been a wild dream.

Good Night, Nurse! is fully entrenched in the freewheeling Arbuckle style. However, unlike the earlier comedies he and Buster made together, which contain far too many scenes of unmotivated mayhem, this time the mugging, roughhousing, and wild plot turns are all unified by a more purely frivolous tone. Keaton must be credited for this more understated approach as well as the more restrained acting by everyone. He also gets credit for the dream gimmick, one of his favorite plot contrivances.

In contrast to *Moonshine*, which was totally dominated by Keaton's brand of comedy, *Good Night, Nurse!* is an Arbuckle film in which Buster's contributions enhance Roscoe's style rather than clash with it. It is such a thoroughly entertaining film that its prophetic overtones—Keaton would later be incarcerated in several sanitariums during the worst period of his life, and he claimed to have escaped from one wearing only his nightshirt—are rendered meaningless by its indomitable joy.

THE COOK

CREDITS:

Presented by the Comique Film Corporation; Distributed by Paramount Pictures. *Producer:* Joseph M. Schenck; *Director/ Scenario:* Roscoe Arbuckle; *Editor:* Herbert Warren; *Photography:* George Peters. *Release Date:* September 15, 1918. *Length:* two reels.

CAST:

Roscoe "Fatty" Arbuckle, Buster Keaton, Al St. John, Alice Lake, Glen Cavender, Luke the Dog.

The Cook is one of the most obscure of all the alleged lost Arbuckle-Keaton films. It has been confused so many times with *The Rough House* that many believe the earlier film never existed and that it is

Buster takes a break from his culinary duties to dance with a Cleopatra admirer while Roscoe tries to remember a good recipe for baked sphinx in *The Cook*.

Al St. John tries to pay his restaurant bill with lead instead of silver, much to the surprise of Roscoe, Buster, and Alice Lake in *The Cook*. The film is one of the allegedly lost Keaton-Arbuckle two-reelers.

actually *The Cook.* This confusion was further aggravated by Keaton's later business partner, Raymond Rohauer, who mistakenly labeled *The Rough House* as *The Cook* when he tracked down a print of the earlier short somewhere in Eastern Europe. The obvious plot similarities of the films add to the mix-up.

In *The Rough House,* Roscoe is an owner of a seaside resort who ends up as the cook when the previous one, played by Al St. John, goes berserk after being spurned by Alice Lake as the maid. In *The Cook,* Roscoe is billed as the chef of a respectable ocean-front restaurant with Buster as his assistant and Alice as a waitress/cashier. A contemporary review of the latter film, appearing in *Moving Picture World,* mentions that complications result when the cooks, in the name of efficiency, destroy the tranquility of the restaurant. The key word here is *efficiency,* which conjures up images of Buster creating the most outlandish culinary inventions similar to the ones he devised for the opening breakfast-table segment of *The Scarecrow,* and the kitchen and dining room segments of *The Electric House.* One can only imagine what elaborate and eccentric mechanical contraptions he created for *The Cook.*

Apparently, in one more example of an Arbuckle two-reeler with a schizophrenic plot, the finale takes place at a seaside park where Roscoe once again battles Al St. John, who plays a restaurant holdup man. Arbuckle's dog, Luke, who was making over $200 per week when both were working for Sennett, joins in at the end, most likely chasing Al off into the horizon as he did in several Arbuckle-Keystone films.

One reviewer of the day, writing in *Motion Picture News,* suggests that *The Cook* is a remake of Arbuckle's Keystone film *The Waiter's Picnic* (aka *The Chef*).

In any event, the fact remains that several priceless film classics made by Arbuckle and Keaton remain lost. In Arbuckle's case, many were maliciously destroyed after the 1921 scandal that ruined his career.

The Cook was the last film Buster made before he was drafted into the army in June 1918. He spent ten months in the service, mostly in France at the tail end of World War I. When Keaton finished his tour of duty and returned to California in April 1919, his reputation as a screen comic was still intact; in fact, it was stronger than ever and he was offered lucrative contracts by both William Fox and Jack Warner. However, Keaton, who always valued loyalty more than financial security, returned to Arbuckle's company at his former salary.

BACK STAGE

CREDITS:

Presented by the Comique Film Corporation; Distributed by Paramount Pictures. *Producer:* Joseph M. Schenck; *Director:* Roscoe Arbuckle; *Scenario:* Jean Havez; *Photography:* Elgin Lessley. *Release Date:* September 7, 1919. *Length:* two reels.

CAST:

Roscoe "Fatty" Arbuckle, Buster Keaton, Al St. John, Molly Malone, John Coogan.

In what appears to be a welcome-home present for Buster following a ten-month military stint, *Back Stage* is a virtual showcase of the Keaton style of comedy. Set

Stagehands Buster and Roscoe are menaced by the burly strong man (in top hat) in *Back Stage,* one of the most thoroughly Keatonesque shorts Buster made with Arbuckle. Also pictured are leading lady Molly Malone (far left), and Jackie Coogan's father, John (background wearing straw hat).

in a vaudeville house, it features routines from his days as a stage performer as well as many new gags that he would rework in his later films.

The beginning segment is a prototype for a gag Buster would later use in *The Playhouse*. A scene complete with him asleep in a bed is suddenly and surprisingly dismantled in front of our eyes, the walls of the room turning out to be prop pieces from a small vaudeville theater. Roscoe is the stage manager and Buster is his assistant. Al St. John is also an assistant, but his part is minimal, this being the last short he made with Arbuckle before launching his own series of two-reelers.

As the stagehands prepare for the upcoming show, the performers begin arriving. When a conceited monologuist requests the star dressing room, Buster ushers the man through a door adorned with a star, then pulls on a rope, which swings the portable star up in front of another dressing room. The stagehands then gather around the new eccentric dancer (played by child star Jackie Coogan's dad, John) to watch him perform some fancy footwork, with Buster and Roscoe joining in with hilariously inept results. The hands, however, are appalled by the way the show's new Strong Man bullies his pretty assistant, played by Molly Malone, and they take turns trying to subdue the brute. After Buster hits the man over the head with an ax repeatedly to no avail, the crew attaches electrical wiring to the bully's bar weights and then watches as he picks them up and is finally jolted into submission. Unfortunately, after recovering from his shock, the bully organizes a strike with the other performers and they all end up walking out in protest. The panicked stagehands, encouraged by the bully's assistant, decide to go on with the show and begin working out routines that will feature their own talents.

On opening night, Roscoe, in leopard skins, and Buster, dressed as a deadpan Isadora Duncan, perform a wildly funny dance routine, both of them leaping and twirling about in synchronized rhythm. When the on-strike eccentric dancer appears in the audience and begins to heckle the performance, Roscoe ends up throwing Buster into the man's lap (a gag inspired by Keaton's dad having once thrown him into an audience to shut up a group of rowdy college kids).

Roscoe then appears as a serenading lover who woos Molly while she sits perched atop a two-story balcony. When the balcony facade collapses and falls on Roscoe, its window passes neatly over him. This elaborate Keaton gag is one he restaged later in *One Week*, and most dramatically in *Steamboat Bill, Jr.*

After the facade has been put back up, Roscoe cuddles with Molly onstage and kisses her. This sends the Strong Man, who is also in the audience, into a jealous rage. He bolts from his seat in the theater's balcony, pulls out a gun, and shoots Molly, who collapses at Roscoe's feet. Pandemonium erupts as patrons try to escape from the gun-wielding madman. Buster quickly rigs up a swing on the stage. In a spectacular stunt, he swings out over the audience into the balcony where he grabs the bully and swings with him back to the stage. Buster and others then pummel the brute, who is finally subdued when Roscoe drops a chest full of weights from the rafters onto the man's head. The film concludes in a hospital where Roscoe comforts the recuperating Molly in a playfully romantic fade-out.

Back Stage is nearly 100 percent Keaton. His influence is felt in virtually every scene and in every significant gag, as well as in the film's strong and unified story line. He and Arbuckle display adept comedy-team timing, especially in their dance scene, which is filled with understated yet exciting and hilarious action. What is shocking is the film's dramatic gunshot, played seriously and for sympathy, a radical departure in style and tone for both men. In their other teamings, gunplay is treated strictly for laughs. The scene is so unexpected that it seems out of place in this otherwise delightfully irreverent look at backstage life in a vaudeville theater, a setting with which Buster was intimately familiar and which he would use many times in his own films.

THE HAYSEED

CREDITS:

Presented by the Comique Film Corporation; Distributed by Paramount Pictures. *Producer:* Joseph M. Schenck; *Director:* Roscoe Arbuckle; *Scenario:* Jean Havez; *Photography:* Elgin Lessley. *Release Date:* October 26, 1919. *Length:* two reels.

CAST:

Roscoe "Fatty" Arbuckle, Buster Keaton, Molly Malone, John Coogan, Luke the Dog.

The Hayseed is one of the least inspired shorts Keaton made with Arbuckle. Filmed during a time when the two were earning a reputation around Hollywood as premier practical jokers, it appears that they put more effort into their offscreen gags than those they devised for this picture.

Most of the film's action unfolds in a rural general-store setting similar to the ones for *The Butcher Boy*,

After completing *The Hayseed* and *The Garage* with Arbuckle, Buster began his career as the star of his own series of two-reelers. Here, he introduces one of his favorite leading ladies, Sybil Seely, to an unappreciative Roscoe.

His Wedding Night, and *A Country Hero.* Roscoe and Buster run the place, which also serves as the local post office and community center. While Buster mans the store, Roscoe delivers the mail in a horse-drawn buggy with his faithful dog, Luke. As he passes each roadside mailbox, he tosses the letters and watches them slide smoothly into the slot of each box (reverse-action photography creates this amusing effect).

When he comes to sweetheart Molly Malone's house, Roscoe stops for an innocent game of hide-and-seek. While Roscoe hides in haystack (and of course, gets pitchforked by a farmer), Molly gets distracted by the unexpected arrival of the local constable, played by John Coogan, who is also Roscoe's sneaky rival for her. Later, back at the store, the constable appears in time to find Roscoe sorting more mail and noting to another clerk that a letter insured for $300 has arrived. When Roscoe leaves to fill another customer's order, the constable makes his way into the store, opens the letter, and steals the money.

Unknown to him, Buster has witnessed the theft and, as the crooked constable flirts with some women in front of the store, dumps pails of water on him from the roof. The entire melee is staged with little verve, surprising for an Arbuckle short, which normally contains the most feverishly demonic battles.

The liveliest scene of the film follows when the store is turned into a dance hall and Buster and Roscoe take turns literally throwing around an acrobatic female partner. Unfortunately, it is over quickly. The townspeople then gather as various audience members stage some entertainment. Buster performs some magic, making a rabbit disappear, but inadvertently exposes the trick when his assistant turns his back to the audience and reveals the rabbit pinned to his coat.

Roscoe sings a ballad and moves the audience to tears, which are brought on primarily by the effects of a plateful of onions he has just eaten. The constable, jealous of the emotional effect Roscoe has had on the audience, publicly accuses him of stealing the money from the insured letter. Buster then exposes the constable as the real thief and a fight erupts. Roscoe sics Luke on the constable, who tears out of the store and down the road with the dog in hot pursuit.

A limp effort, *The Hayseed* is almost totally devoid of the verve that dominates the other Arbuckle-Keaton shorts. Perhaps the two men suffered a creative block brought on by their surroundings. *The Hayseed* was filmed at the Thomas Ince Studios in Culver City, which at the time were being managed by Henry Lehrman. Also known as "Pathé" Lehrman because he once erroneously claimed to have studied moviemaking with the famous French film pioneers, he directed Arbuckle's first Keystone effort, *The Gangsters,* in 1913 and then promptly informed Sennett that Roscoe was a completely hopeless and untalented comic. On Lehrman's word, Sennett nearly fired Arbuckle but changed his mind when Mabel Normand, the famed comedienne (and Sennett's mistress), stepped in and spoke up for Roscoe.

Lehrman's own longtime mistress, ironically, was Virginia Rappé, the woman whom Arbuckle was accused of raping at the disastrous San Francisco party he hosted in 1921. During Arbuckle's three trials for manslaughter following Rappé's death, Lehrman was one of Arbuckle's most vehement denouncers, despite the fact that Virginia was in San Francisco at the time of the party to obtain an abortion for the child she and Lehrman had conceived. One of the reasons she attended Arbuckle's affair was to ask him for money to pay for the abortion after Lehrman had abandoned her and taken up with another woman.

With these apocalyptic vibrations distracting the filmmakers as they labored through the production of *The Hayseed,* it is little wonder that the film lacks the feverish, kinetic excitement that resonates so forcefully in all the other shorts Keaton made with Arbuckle.

Auto mechanics Buster and Roscoe demonstrate their professional skills in *The Garage*, the team's last two-reeler before Keaton began work on his own series of shorts and features.

THE GARAGE (aka Fire Chief)

CREDITS:

Presented by the Comique Film Corporation; Distributed by Paramount Pictures. *Producer:* Joseph M. Schenck; *Director:* Roscoe Arbuckle; *Scenario:* Jean Havez; *Photography:* Elgin Lessley. *Release Date:* January 11, 1920. *Length:* two reels.

CAST:

Roscoe "Fatty" Arbuckle, Buster Keaton, Molly Malone, Harry McCoy, Daniel Crimmins, Luke the Dog.

The Garage is the last and one of the best of the Arbuckle-Keaton two-reelers. After the creative block and distraction that affected their previous film, *The Hayseed,* their talents burst forth once again. Here they run a small-town combination garage and fire station. As Roscoe polishes up a recently repaired car, Buster inadvertently squirts grease all over it, and a fight breaks out between the two, which is ultimately joined by their assistant, an Al St. John clone. After some spirited roughhousing, all three end up in a tub of water. When the owner of the soiled car shows up, Roscoe hurriedly cleans it on a revolving platform. This clever, Keaton-tinged mechanical gag is taken to its absurd extreme when a suitor for the garage owner's daughter (Molly Malone) appears dressed in fancy duds. Predictably, the suitor and his duds don't remain fancy for too long, and Roscoe ends up gluing the poor guy to the revolving platform and matter-of-factly hosing him down as he spins by.

To avenge this mistreatment, the suitor borrows a friend's dog (the multitalented Luke) and, screaming "Mad dog!" has Roscoe and Buster chased all over town. Luke ends up ripping off Buster's pants, prompting Keaton to fashion a paper kilt from a billboard advertising a Scottish performer. He then breaks into a nifty Highland fling as a policeman and a woman pass by, but when he turns around and exposes his trouserless backside, he is chased down the street by the cop. In a deceptively simple yet expertly timed segment, the pursued Buster rounds a corner, spots Roscoe, jumps behind him, and walks along in lockstep with his pal, hidden behind the latter's huge bulk. When the policeman comes on the scene, he sees only Roscoe and passes him by. Then, before the cop can turn around, Buster swings around in front of Roscoe, both of them still in perfect synchronized step. When they march by a clothing store, Buster casually grabs a pair of pants from one of the racks set up outside, and as Roscoe lifts him up, he shoots his legs into the pants. Roscoe then sets Buster down and the two march off still in lockstep. This simple scene that takes only seconds of screen time is a brilliant example of perfectly timed, low-key Keaton humor. (He later repeated the gag in a segment on television's *Twilight Zone,* combining it with another pants gag from his short *Daydreams*).

The second half of *The Garage* emphasizes gags built around the place also being the town's firehouse. The city-slicker suitor returns and secretly sets off the fire alarm in order to get Buster and Roscoe out of the building so he can be alone with Molly Malone. However, when she scorns him, the suitor inadvertently sets fire to the garage, trapping them both in the burning building. The roving firemen spot the flames engulfing their own building, race back to the garage, and hurriedly hook up the water hose. When the hose springs a leak, Roscoe solves the problem by sitting on it. The impromptu repair job works until a trolley passes by and runs over the hose, cutting it to pieces.

With Molly and her suitor trapped in the building, Roscoe and Buster break out a net and yell for them to jump. As the suitor prepares to leap from the upstairs window, Molly appears at a separate one, and the firemen move the net over to her window 'ist as the suitor leaps, flying through the air and crashing to the ground. When Molly finally jumps, she bounces back into the air, getting entangled in some telephone wires. As the garage burns to the ground, firemen Roscoe and Buster climb up into the wires and rescue Molly.

Wildly inventive, fast and furious, *The Garage* is easily one of the best of the team's comedies. Like *Good Night, Nurse!* it is an excellent example of how the two men could create a film that enhances each other's nearly opposite comedic style. The gags of the film are nearly all Keaton's, but the pacing and crazy plot twists are Arbuckle's. Aside from a couple of gratuitous gags and some unsubtle mugging from the actor who plays Molly's suitor, it is hard to believe that the driving force behind *The Butcher Boy* is also the same man who fashioned *The Garage,* made only three years and fourteen two-reelers later. When *The Butcher Boy* is compared with *Moonshine* and *Back Stage,* films that contain much more overt examples of Keaton's brand of comedy, the change in style is so radical that no one watching them could possibly deny the presence of a new, distinctive creative force.

The completion of *The Garage* ended Buster's film apprenticeship, one that had provided him the opportunity to create an artistic base to which he would refer again and again throughout the rest of his career. All

the cinematic tricks he would later perfect, his subtle approach to staging elaborate gags, his fascination with machinery, and his eccentric use of common objects are all present throughout these early films.

Keaton never hesitated to credit Arbuckle as the prime influence on his screen career and always referred to this film apprenticeship as one of the happiest times of his life. Buster loved the jolly fat man, loved his exuberance, generosity, and total lack of ego when it came to encouraging colleagues to develop and expand their creative talents. Their friendship continued uninterrupted after their professional endeavors took them down separate creative paths, beyond Keaton's own two-reelers, beyond the features they fashioned individually, even far beyond the events that enveloped Roscoe and killed his creative spirit on that fateful day in September 1921, which Keaton referred to as "the day the laughter stopped." To the end, Buster kept a portrait of Roscoe hanging on the wall of his study, a tribute to the man who had dramatically changed his life from the moment they met on another fateful day—in March 1917, the day the laughter began.

THE SAPHEAD

CREDITS:

Produced and distributed by Metro Pictures. *Producer:* Winchell Smith; *Director:* Herbert Blache; *Script:* June Mathis, based on *The New Henrietta* by Winchell Smith and Victor Mapes, and *The Henrietta,* a play by Bronson Howard; *Photography:* Harold Wenstrom. Presented by John L. Golden and Winchell Smith in conjunction with Marcus Loew. *Release Date:* October 18, 1920. *Length:* seven reels.

CAST:

Buster Keaton (*Bertie "The Lamb" Van Alstyne*), William H. Crane (*Nicholas Van Alstyne*), Irving Cummings (*Mark Turner*), Carol Holloway (*Rose Turner*), Beulah Booker (*Agnes Gates*), Edward Alexander (*Watson Flint*), Jeffrey Williams (*Hutchins*), Edward Jobson (*Rev. Murray Hilton*), Jack Livingston (*Dr. George Wainright*), Helen Holte (*Henrietta Reynolds*), Odette Taylor (*Mrs. Cornelia Opdyke*), Edward Connelly (*Musgrave*), Katherine Albert (*Hattie*), Alfred Hollingsworth (*Hathaway*), Henry Clauss (*valet*).

The Saphead marks Keaton's first appearance in a feature, one he made as a favor for his new boss, Joseph Schenck, and for his new film distributor, Metro Pictures. It is based on one of the most popular plays of the period, *The Henrietta,* written in 1887 by Bronson Howard. The play had countless revivals, the most popular one on Broadway in 1913 and starring

A very dapper Buster makes his feature film debut playing Bertie "The Lamb" Van Alstyne in *The Saphead*. His creative input was limited to his acting abilities; however, the role he plays, that of a spoiled, innocent rich kid, was one he would re-create many times in his own independently-produced films.

Douglas Fairbanks in the title role. Fairbanks so enjoyed the part of Bertie "The Lamb" Van Alstyne that he played variations of the character in such films as *The Mollycoddle* and *The Lamb* before starring in a series that featured his most famous screen persona, the swashbuckling daredevil.

Watching Fairbanks in *The Lamb*, I found his performance as a bumbling Milquetoast painful, as if he were playing a very impatient Clark Kent dying to rip off his suit and tie and indulge in superhuman feats of daring. Fairbanks's mannerisms are terribly awkward, as if he is reminding himself to fumble around, to hesitate, to purposely drop his cane or hat or bump into a chair. In the final moments of the film he suddenly screws up his courage and single-handedly wipes out a horde of attacking heathens with a Gatling gun. Only in these moments does Fairbanks come alive.

Fairbanks recommended Keaton for the lead in *The Saphead* after other commitments got in the way of his playing the role. Unlike Fairbanks, Buster is totally convincing both as a sheltered Milquetoast and as a spirited dynamo. His vaudeville experience, where he was not only exposed to an endless variety of acting styles but also played several assorted parts himself, gave him the resources to adapt to the role. Seeing Keaton create a fully developed screen character, knowing that for the previous three years he had been indulging in roughhouse slapstick with Arbuckle, is a revelation, proving that Buster was a gifted actor as well as a superb comedian. Like Fairbanks, he was fond of the Bertie character and based many—argu-

The Saphead: Buster as Bertie has his wedding put on hold after a messenger arrives with some incriminating love letters. Also pictured are (from left) William H. Crane, Irving Cummings, Katherine Albert, Carol Holloway, Edward Jacobson, and Beulah Booker.

ably all—of his feature film portrayals on this type, one who appears weak and dim-witted at first but becomes the strongest, most resourceful and dynamic figure of all.

The Saphead is very much a filmed play, most of the action taking place in interior settings with the characters making grand, theatrical entrances and exits. Stage veteran William H. Crane plays Nicholas Van Alstyne, the wheeler-dealer "Wolf of Wall Street," a part he originated in the first production of the play in 1887. Nick is co-owner of the fabulously rich Henrietta silver mine, which has brought him immeasurable wealth and allowed him to establish a successful investment firm.

Buster plays Nick's son, Bertie, known as "The Lamb," or "The Saphead," because of his pampered upbringing and his inability to function in the real world. Nick is ashamed of his ineffectual son, who prefers to sit all day in his room munching on caviar and planning frivolous diversions rather than learning the family business. Bertie is hopelessly naive, even when it comes to having fun. He tries to develop a reputation as a rogue, hoping to impress his fiancée, Agnes Gates (Beulah Booker). But as in everything else he attempts, his naïveté and literal-mindedness thwart his efforts.

Nick also has a daughter, Rose (Carol Holloway), who is married to shifty investment broker Mark Turner (Irving Cummings), a scoundrel who relies on Nick to bail him out whenever his risky investments prove disastrous. Mark has also been involved for years with another women, Henrietta (Helen Holte), and is the father of her child.

When the crooked Mark tries to run Nick's investment business in Nick's absence, he nearly ruins the company by selling off shares of the Henrietta mine at ridiculously low prices. This occurs after Mark has messed up Bertie's wedding plans by getting the latter to confess that he, not Mark, has an illegitimate daughter by a woman named Henrietta.

In the film's exciting conclusion, Bertie, thinking he is saving his reputation as a gentleman rather than bailing out his father from financial disaster, races around the stock market floor, hurtling himself over other bidders to shout "I'll take it!" whenever he hears someone holler "Henrietta!" Buster performs some incredible acrobatic stunts, flying over the heads of the brokers, executing double flips, careening from one side of the stock market floor to the other as he buys up the mine shares, single-handedly saving his father's company and redeeming himself in both his father's and his sweetheart's eyes.

Although his contributions to *The Saphead* were strictly as an actor, the film contains nearly all the

"Henrietta!" shout the stockbrokers. "I'll take it!" answers Buster/Bertie, ultimately saving his father from financial ruin in the frantic climax to *The Saphead*.

essential elements of a typical Buster Keaton feature and must be viewed as having had a powerful influence on him. Unlike the frenetic, action-packed pacing and acting style of the films he had been making with Arbuckle, the pacing of *The Saphead* is slow to the point of rigor mortis. The acting, at least until the climax, is quite understated, and it is fascinating to watch Buster adapt to this sedate style by becoming even slower and more sedate than everyone else. This is in keeping with the slow-witted, duncelike character he portrays, and he embodies him with every look, nuance, and movement. His performance is astonishing, especially when he suddenly transforms at the end into a dynamo, still totally naive of the real implications of his actions but nevertheless becoming the vibrant, heroic son who saves his father from financial disaster, wins back his girl, and lives happily ever after.

THE HIGH SIGN

CREDITS:

Presented by the Comique Film Corporation; Distributed by Metro Pictures. *Producer:* Joseph M. Schenck; *Director/Script:* Buster Keaton and Eddie Cline; *Photography:* Elgin Lessley; *Technical Director:* Fred Gabourie. *Release Date:* April 12, 1921. *Length:* two reels.

Buster is surrounded by the dreaded Blinking Buzzards gang in *The High Sign*, his first independently-produced two-reeler. Dissatisfied with the results, he held up its release for a year.

Buster prepares to demonstrate his marksman's skills for leading lady Bartine Burkett Zane in *The High Sign*.

CAST:

Buster Keaton, Bartine Burkett Zane, Al St. John (cameo).

Keaton's first two-reel short as the featured artist of the Comique Film Corporation was his least favorite. After completing *The High Sign*, which he filmed simultaneously with *The Saphead*, Buster was so dissatisfied that he shelved the short for a year before finally releasing it in April 1921. Buster had wanted to make his debut effort something special, and he felt *The High Sign* was too much like the shorts he had been making with Arbuckle.

Although virtually all of Keaton's films contain bits from Arbuckle shorts, overall *The High Sign* is a solid Keaton effort, totally undeserving of Buster's harsh criticism. Buster plays a vagabond who is thrown off a train next to a seaside amusement park and finds work in a shooting gallery owned by the leader of a mob called the Blinking Buzzards. Assigned to bump off a wealthy businessman, Buster ends up protecting the man and his pretty daughter (played by Bartine Burkett Zane) by helping rig their house with assorted trap-doors, secret passageways, and illusionary and mechanical escape hatches.

The High Sign begins with Buster sitting on a bench to read the newspaper want ads. As he casually peruses the paper, he unfolds it, unfolds it some more, then unfolds it even more, until it dwarfs him, then envelopes him, and he ends up falling backward over the bench. Momentarily stunned, he looks back down at the paper and spots a job he feels suited for. While he is folding up the paper, the man from whom he sneakily stole it approaches him and, mistaking him for a paperboy, pays him for it. Buster gazes at the coin, than jauntily walks off to apply for the job.

The entire opening segment, so brief, so seemingly effortless, yet filled with intricate timing, is poetic, quintessential Keaton. The whole film continues in this vein, one gag logically setting up the next as each becomes more elaborate, more intricate, more absurd, and more dazzling, with the final moments erupting into a frenzied display of acrobatics and invention.

After his hiring as the shooting-gallery attendant, Buster demonstrates how easy it is for the shooter to win a prize. To ensure that he rings a bell with every shot, Buster has a hidden dog tied with a rope to a bell. A bone dangles from another rope in front of the dog, and when Buster steps on a foot pedal, it makes the bone dance. Lunging for the bone, the dog rings the bell. Taking his position, Buster shoots at the targets from various angles—over his shoulder, backward, looking through a mirror—stepping on the foot pedal after each shot and sounding the bell every time. All goes well until a cat happens by, causing the tied dog to lunge and lunge again, ringing the bell with maniacal frequency. This sends Buster into a shooting frenzy to keep up.

In the film's climax, Buster careens through the rich businessman's house, leaping through the various secret passageways to escape from and subdue assorted members of the Blinking Buzzards gang. The scene is filmed in a long shot, showing several rooms at once in stage-set cutaway as Buster hurls himself through walls, windows, trapdoors, even a picture hanging on a wall. Buster looks like a cog in an eccentric machine or clock, at one point hurtling up, down, and around the house from room to room in a repetitive pattern with various gang members following him. It is prototypical Keaton, amazing, awe inspiring, and uproariously funny.

An interesting observation in his autobiography helps explain why Buster ultimately hated *The High Sign* so much. A variation of the old slipping-on-the-banana-peel joke occurs late in the film after Buster has been inducted into the Blinking Buzzards. Instead of stepping on the banana peel, which is lying in the middle of a sidewalk, Buster looks at the camera out of the corner of his eye and gives the Buzzard's secret, kooky, nose-thumbing "high sign" as he jauntily walks on.

Later previewing the film in a theater, Buster felt that this audience-acknowledgment joke insulted the viewer, as if he were saying, "Ha, ha, fooled you that time, suckers!" His misgivings over the nose-thumbing scene are a perfect example of how he would condemn an entire film because of one gag about which he later had second thoughts.

Keaton gives credit to Eddie Cline, a colleague from vaudeville and a former Mack Sennett director, as cowriter and codirector of *The High Sign* and the majority of his other two-reel shorts. How much Cline actually contributed is anyone's guess. Like Arbuckle, Keaton generously acknowledged his coworkers as contributors to his films and refused to take sole writing-directing credit on all but one. Clyde Bruckman, who joined Buster later on as a gagman and codirector, confessed in Rudi Blesh's biography, *Keaton:* "You seldom saw his name in the story credits. But I could tell you . . . that those wonderful stories were ninety percent Buster's. . . . Most of the direction was his, as Eddie Cline will tell you. . . . Comedian, gagman, writer, director—then add technical innovator. . . . He had judgment, taste; he never overdid it and never offended. He knew what was right for him."

ONE WEEK

CREDITS:
Presented by the Comique Film Corporation; Distributed by Metro Pictures. *Producer:* Joseph M. Schenck; *Director/Script:* Buster Keaton and Eddie Cline; *Photography:* Elgin Lessley; *Technical Director:* Fred Gabourie. *Release Date:* September 1, 1920. *Length:* two reels.

CAST:
Buster Keaton, Sybil Seely, Joe Roberts.

> The very first film Keaton released as a star, once his association with Arbuckle had ended, was, breathtakingly, an explosion of style. To sit through dozens and dozens of short comedies of the period and then to come upon *One Week* is to see the one thing no man ever sees: a garden at the moment of blooming.
>
> —*From* The Silent Clowns *by Walter Kerr*

Buster released *One Week* one month before the premiere of his feature film debut in the long-delayed *The Saphead.* It created a sensation. In one review of the day, the critic wrote that it was "likely to produce the laugh heard round the world." Another called it "the comedy sensation of the year." Later, Buster admitted that *One Week* did more than any of his other films to establish his reputation as a master of screen comedy.

The premise for *One Week* came to Buster after he saw a promotional film detailing how a newly married couple could purchase an inexpensive, portable house and erect it on a vacant lot in one week's time. Buster's movie is divided into seven parts, introduced with the image of a calendar and the changing days of the week. On the first day, Monday the ninth, Buster and his leading lady, the wonderful Sybil Seely, are shown emerging from a wedding chapel, having just been married. Calmly accepting the cheers of his well-wishers as he walks down the chapel steps, Buster notices a pair of shoes on the ground amid the rice, ribbons, and other traditional wedding trappings. He pauses, picks up the shoes, inspects them, and takes them with him into the car waiting to carry him and his bride away. The little pause is a wonderful example of both Buster's offhanded acting style and his screen character's curious nature, a curiosity made even more humorous by his surroundings of the moment.

Newlyweds Buster and Sybil
Seely receive their wedding
gift, a portable house, with
mixed feelings in *One Week*.
His first film to be released
under his new contract with
independent producer Joseph
Schenck was praised as the
comedy sensation of the year.

The rest of the film details the mishaps that befall the couple as they attempt to assemble a portable house given to them as a wedding present. The task is challenging enough, but is made even more difficult when Handy Hank, Buster's rival for Sybil, spitefully swaps the numbers on the crates containing the various sections of the house.

By day three, after several hilarious disasters and lots of clever mechanical gags, the couple finally finishes construction. However, something looks wrong. In fact, everything looks wrong. The roof doesn't quite cover the top of the house, the windows are askew, the awning over the porch leans to one side, the kitchen sink is on the outside, the bathroom door leads to a ten-foot drop, and the easiest way to enter the place is through the downstairs window. Still, it's their home and they love it.

On day five, Friday the thirteenth, Buster and Sybil proudly hold a housewarming party. When Buster shows his guests around, it suddenly starts raining—inside. Going outside to check out the situation, Buster ends up in a violent wind and rain storm that sends the house twirling like a merry-go-round. Buster tries to jump into the house, hurling himself at the door whenever it passes by, an uproariously funny sight gag executed with great finesse. When he finally dives

58

through the door, he careens around inside along with the other guests until finally each is propelled out and into the mud.

Buster somehow manages to top this hysterically funny and amazingly intricate gag in the film's spectacular finale. Following the disastrous housewarming, the couple is informed by an inspector that they have built their house on the wrong lot and must move it to its proper location across the train tracks. The next day, they prop it up on barrels and roll it to its new location, using their car to inch it along. Naturally, when they get to the tracks, the house gets stuck. As they struggle to move it, they pick up the faint sound of a train whistle, then glance down at the tracks below

Buster admires the fruits of his labors in *One Week*.

them and jump. Frantically, they attempt to move the house before the onrushing train demolishes it. Finally, Buster pulls Sybil aside and they both cover their eyes, waiting for the crash. However, the train swishes by on a parallel track, just barely missing the house. The two, breathing a deep sigh of relief, begin figuring out another way to move the house when a train traveling in the opposite direction slams into it, sending them sprawling as bits of the house fly in every direction. No one watching this gag for the first time would anticipate this sudden turn of events, as the gag is staged so expertly and occurs so abruptly, maximizing the spectacular sight of the train turning the house to kindling.

Buster relished constructing routines around a central, eccentric object, piling them up until the film explodes in a flurry of wild, kinetic action and is then topped by one final, brilliant sight gag. Many of his strongest comedic trademarks are on display here: his love of inventive, offbeat mechanical objects, his superbly deadpan acting style, and his favorite theme of dealing with one's absurd surroundings by calmly accepting everything as just part of life. Ultimately this makes the surroundings appear simultaneously even more hilariously absurd and less intimidating. Sybil Seely, one of Keaton's favorite and most charming leading ladies, is a perfect match for his screen character. Endowed with an animated, girlish enthusiasm, she projects a pragmatic, accommodating attitude toward the disasters that befall her and, in this two-reeler, her new husband.

One Week, with its catastrophic depiction of the first days in the lives of newlyweds, is nevertheless Buster's most blissfully charming portrayal of marriage. In his later films, especially the ones he made after he was married in real life, the idea of living in a state of wedded bliss is presented in a radically different light.

CONVICT 13

CREDITS:

Presented by the Comique Film Corporation; Distributed by Metro Pictures. *Producer:* Joseph M. Schenck; *Director/ Script:* Buster Keaton and Eddie Cline; *Photography:* Elgin Lessley; *Technical Director:* Fred Gabourie. *Release Date:* October 27, 1920. *Length:* two reels.

CAST:

Buster Keaton, Sybil Seely, Joe Roberts, Eddie Cline, Joe Keaton.

Convict 13 introduces another, darker side of Keaton's humor. Many of his films are filled with references to death, suicide, murder, entrapment, mistaken identities, people accused of crimes they didn't commit. Although all the masters of silent comedy included jokes about death and falsely accused protagonists, Buster reveled in this type of humor, taking it to extremes, overloading his films with morbid, black comedy.

Convict 13 begins innocently enough on a golf course, with Buster and his socialite girlfriend (Sybil Seely) playing a comical round of golf. Sybil is obviously an adept golfer, and her friends, watching from the sidelines, applaud her efforts as she plays. Buster's skills, on the other hand, are sadly lacking; at one point, he smacks his ball into a tree and it careens off, hitting him in the head and knocking him out cold. At that moment, an escaped convict in inmate stripes runs across the golf course attempting to flee pursuing prison guards. Spotting the unconscious Buster, the convict quickly changes clothes with him and calmly walks off.

After regaining consciousness, Buster matter-of-factly resumes his golf game, unaware of his new prison garb. When he yells "Fore!" at the people ahead of him, they take one look at his prison stripes and flee. Briefly pondering their hasty retreat with mild interest, he then shrugs it off and prepares to hit his ball. When two guards show up and look him over, Buster tips his hat, then realizes that his usual outfit has somehow been transformed into prison stripes. Thinking this over, he returns to his golf game, hits the ball, then sneaks off while the guards admire his shot. Buster's wonderfully subtle expressions during this scene are used to uproarious advantage, accentuating the inexplicable developments.

Buster's attempts to elude the guards result in his finally taking refuge behind a huge locked gate. Of course, the gate is the entrance to the prison. To his surprise, he catches a glimpse of Sybil among the prisoners. She turns out to be the daughter of the warden, who scowls at Buster for eyeing his comely Sybil. Glancing at the number on Buster's outfit—thirteen—he informs the "prisoner" that he is scheduled to be hanged later that day.

The hangman, played by Keaton's cowriter-codirector Eddie Cline, measures the size of Buster's neck and adjusts the noose for a snug fit. Meanwhile, Sybil pleads in vain with her father to spare Buster, then steals the elastic arm-exercising bands from the pris-

Buster hopes for good news from hangman Eddie Cline (far right) in *Convict 13*, one of Buster's black comedy two-reelers. Cline received codirecting/writing credits on the majority of Buster's silent shorts and made frequent cameo appearances as well.

on's gym and switches them with the hangman's rope. While other prisoners cheer from the bleachers in front of the scaffold—a peanut vendor working the crowd— the trapdoor is tripped and convict Buster bounces up and down, up and down, dangling from the elastic rope in an outrageous sight gag.

Then assigned to pound some rocks with a sledgehammer, he ends up smacking a guard in the face with it and then changing into his clothes. Unfortunately, at that moment, a brute of an inmate, played by Buster's favorite heavy, the huge Joe Roberts, goes berserk and begins pummeling, hurling, and stomping on all the guards in sight. After the yard is littered with unconscious guards, Buster appears and scolds Joe for being too forward. Then, in his wonderfully deadpan manner, Buster notices the pile of bodies on the ground, realizes he is dressed as a guard, checks Joe's grimacing face, and stares blankly, helplessly at the camera as his heart begins to pound out of his chest.

The film's finale has Buster subduing the entire yardful of rebellious inmates by standing on a table and brandishing a ball and chain, braining the prisoners as they try to attack him. The segment faithfully re-creates a routine he did with his dad in vaudeville. After whacking the last one into unconsciousness,

Buster slips off the table and clunks himself on the head. As Sybil leans over him, the prison setting fades and Buster awakens on the golf course, having dreamed the rest of the story.

Many have attributed Buster's fascination with death humor to the fact that he had many close brushes during his vaudeville days, surviving various boardinghouse fires, train wrecks, cyclones, and other disasters. However, it might also have come from the fact that, beginning in his early days in vaudeville and continuing throughout his film career, Buster prided himself on his ability to stage the most spectacular, death-defying stunts, ones that would produce stunned amazement in his audiences followed by a surge of wild applause. Of course, the primary reason for Buster's use of death as a source for humor is probably far simpler and less symbolic: when it came to the business of creating gags for his films, there was no such thing as a taboo subject. Everything, every facet of life—including death—was a potential source for gags.

THE SCARECROW

CREDITS:

Presented by the Comique Film Corporation; Distributed by Metro Pictures. *Producer:* Joseph M. Schenck; *Director/ Script:* Buster Keaton and Eddie Cline; *Photography:* Elgin Lessley; *Technical Director:* Fred Gabourie. *Release Date:* November 17, 1920. *Length:* two reels.

CAST:

Buster Keaton, Sybil Seely, Joe Roberts, Joe Keaton, Eddie Cline, Luke the Dog.

The Scarecrow is a charmer, one of Keaton's most entertaining romps. It begins with a series of incredible mechanical gags staged inside a one-room cottage reminiscent of the eccentric house from *One Week*.

Buster and Joe Roberts are hired farmhands for Joe Keaton and live in their own cozy cottage, which they have transformed into a bachelor's dream. Everything there has a multiple function: the phonograph player doubles as a stove, the bookcase is also the icebox, the bed converts into an upright piano, and the kitchen table is also a wall plaque (its ironic motto: "What Is Home Without Mother"). While Buster cooks breakfast on the phonograph/stove, Joe readies the table/wall plaque by lowering a group of table items dangling

Buster auditions for the title role in *The Scarecrow*, one of his more Arbuckle-influenced shorts.

The Scarecrow: Buster bends down to tie his shoe and ends up engaged to Sybil Seely.

from strings from the ceiling. As they eat, the two reach up and grab items—salt and pepper shakers, catsup, sugar—swinging the containers back and forth to one another as they munch. The entire opening segment is filled with mechanical whimsy, a beautifully understated example of Buster's ability to transform mundane reality into a world endowed with magic and humor.

The rest of the film details the boys' exploits around the farm and their rivalry for the affections of Sybil Seely, their farmer boss's pretty daughter. By the midway point, the two Joes are both pursuing Buster around the farm while he is trying to elude them dressed as a scarecrow. When he first dons the scarecrow disguise, he assumes the figure's limp posture as he spots Farmer Joe Keaton approaching. Joe then secretly snatches a hidden bottle of booze out of the scarecrow's back pocket to sneak a drink before resuming his search for Buster. Moments later, Sybil and Big Joe Roberts pause in front of the scarecrow where Big Joe pleads with her to marry him. Scarecrow Buster overhears, turns around, and kicks Big Joe, then steals a kiss from Sybil. When the startled Sybil runs off, Farmer Joe appears and the two Joes huddle in front of the scarecrow. Buster then kicks each Joe in the rear, and the men, each thinking the other did it,

begin to fight. Finally Buster's scarecrow cover is blown and the chase resumes.

As Buster races across the farm, he loses a shoe and kneels to put it back on, striking a marriage-proposal stance just as Sybil appears, blushes, then "accepts." The gentle, graceful charm of this scene is capped by Buster's wide-eyed, perplexed expression. He blinks at his good fortune and accepts the sudden turn of events, and after stealing a motorcycle, he races off with Sybil to find a preacher. In a scene that illustrates Buster's unfazed acceptance of the inexplicable, the couple speeds around a corner and conveniently runs into a preacher crossing the street. The preacher ends up in Sybil's lap and Buster stares at him as if the man had somehow fallen out of the sky. Then the unfazed Buster asks the preacher to marry the couple as they continue to barrel down the road on the motorcycle. The preacher, also refusing to question the weird series of events, obliges, finishing the ceremony after the motorcycle careens out of control and plunges into a river.

The Scarecrow is very much in the Arbuckle style of comedy, full of fast, frenetic action, wild chase scenes, and spirited roughhousing. It even features Roscoe's dog, Luke, in a variation of the many scenes staged in the Arbuckle comedies where the maniacal mutt chases some poor victim off into the horizon. There is also a wonderful roll-in-the-hay scene reminiscent of one from *The Hayseed*, yet Buster's variation is far superior, introducing a confrontation with a hay-processing machine that supplies one of the film's most impressive sight gags.

The look of *The Scarecrow*, especially the outdoor scenes, is beautifully crisp and uncluttered, emphasizing the country freshness of the surroundings. Although the film lacks a strong, unified story line, it remains one of Buster's most effective shorts, filled with a simple yet inventive charm and propelled at a breakneck pace.

NEIGHBORS

CREDITS:

Presented by the Comique Film Corporation; Distributed by Metro Pictures. *Producer:* Joseph M. Schenck; *Director/Script:* Buster Keaton and Eddie Cline; *Photography:* Elgin Lessley; *Technical Director:* Fred Gabourie. *Release Date:* December 22, 1920. *Length:* two reels.

Neighbors: Buster and Virginia Fox make an unfavorable impression on Joe Roberts as they try to elope.

Buster receives a helping hand from big Joe Roberts in *Neighbors*. Roberts, an old vaudeville friend, played the heavy in the majority of Keaton's silent two-reelers.

CAST:

Buster Keaton, Virginia Fox, Joe Roberts, Joe Keaton, Eddie Cline, James Duffy, The Flying Escalantes.

Neighbors is a mischievous variation of the Romeo and Juliet story, this time played out in an unglamorous tenement setting. Buster and his girlfriend, Virginia Fox, his most frequent leading lady, live in adjoining buildings, their yards separated by a rickety wooden fence, their feuding families determined to keep the young lovers apart. However, Buster manages to rendezvous with his sweetheart in the most unorthodox ways, leading to a happily-ever-after ending.

Before the fade-out, Buster indulges in some spectacular stunts, providing many examples of his Human Mop persona. In an early scene, Buster sneaks into Virginia's third-story bedroom window, but is soon scared off by her dad (played by big Joe Roberts). In a superb display of acrobatics and intricate timing, Buster dives out of the tenement window, grabs the clothesline, and propels himself across the yard into the window of his own building, scooting down the stairway banister on his stomach, out the second-story window, and back across the yard via another clothesline, and into Virginia's window again, this time falling into the arms of big Joe. This brief yet amazing sight gag illustrates Buster's incredible ability to stage an elaborate stunt and execute it with breakneck precision, filming it in four quick-cutting segments to emphasize its sleek velocity.

The gag is then topped when big Joe hangs Buster outside the window and pins his feet to the clothesline, then pulls on the line as if he were hanging out a pair of pants to dry, cranking Buster across into his own yard. There Buster's dad (played by his real dad, Joe Keaton) is beating some rugs. In an astounding stunt that seemingly couldn't have been performed by a human—but nevertheless was by Buster—Joe, mistaking the dangling Buster for a rug, swats him on the back and propels him up and over the clothesline in a complete circle. Joe then attempts to rescue Buster from the clothesline, but ends up burying his head in the muddy yard. Twisting his son's body like a fence post, Joe finally dislodges Buster's head from the mud. All of these antics appear painfully impossible to perform, but not for Buster, the former Human Mop, who re-creates some of the brutal horseplay that he and his dad did back in vaudeville.

After more brawling encounters between the two families, both clans ends up in court where the judge orders them to permit Buster and Virginia to marry. The wedding ceremony is a disaster and ends with big Joe locking Virginia in her room before the preacher has had a chance to do the matrimonial honors. After Buster's parents send him to his room, too, the lovers end up staring at each other from their bedroom windows until Buster figures out a way to escape. With the help of friends living in the two rooms below his window, Buster stages the most elaborate acrobatic stunt of the film. He and his two buddies form a three-man pyramid with Buster on top. After the three balance their way across the yard, Buster enters Virginia's room through her third-story window, hoists her over his shoulder, then exits through a window, once again forming a three-man tier with his buddies. As the human pyramid hastens across the yard and down the street, the pile of acrobats becomes smaller as each member loses his lower partner until Buster is running along to the preacher's house with Virginia still slung over his shoulder.

The balancing feat, performed by Buster with the help of his vaudeville friends The Flying Escalantes, is literally the topper stunt to a film filled with amazing,

seemingly impossible acrobatic gags, so eye-popping that they overpower the simple story line. In other films he made, Buster admitted throwing out some of his best gags because they were too disruptive to the plot. In *Neighbors*, however, the gags run away with the film. Keaton was probably inspired by the presence of his acrobatic pals—with whom he worked again in one of his best sound shorts, *Allez Oop*, in 1934—and began constructing gags with them in mind. Fortunately, they are some of his best stunts and provide some breathtaking examples of his stunning athletic abilities.

THE HAUNTED HOUSE

CREDITS:

Presented by the Comique Film Corporation; Distributed by Metro Pictures. *Producer:* Joseph M. Schenck; *Director/Script:* Buster Keaton and Eddie Cline; *Photography:* Elgin Lessley; *Technical Director:* Fred Gabourie. *Release Date:* February 10, 1921. *Length:* two reels.

CAST:

Buster Keaton, Virginia Fox, Joe Roberts, Eddie Cline (extra).

The Haunted House, like *One Week*, centers around an eccentric house, this one a cold and intimidating chamber of horrors rather than a cockeyed yet lovable home. Although most of the film's antics occur in this spooky setting, the gags occurring outside it are the most effective.

The film opens with Buster arriving at a Wall Street bank where he is a clerk. After a comically sexy encounter with a pretty customer who charms him into opening the time-locked vault early, Buster accidentally spills a pot of glue all over his counter. Soon, clumps of bills are stuck to the floor, to hands, to feet, to just about everything. As the customers attempt to dislodge the bills from their bodies, they begin to shake their hands and stomp their feet in unison, creating a comical conga line. A fellow clerk tries to help but ends up with his rear stuck to the floor. Buster, re-creating the finale of *The Butcher Boy*'s molasses scene, pours hot water on the man's rear to dilute the glue, first knocking his colleague out so he's not bothered by the scalding water. Buster gives himself the same treatment—hitting himself over the head, then dousing himself with hot water to mask the pain of scraping off the sticky money. The topper gag comes

Buster and leading lady Virginia Fox are menaced
by animated bed sheets in *The Haunted House*.

when robbers invade the bank and order Buster to
"Stick 'em up!" He has difficulty complying because he
has jammed his sticky hands in his pockets and can't
get them out. Finally, he yanks his hands out of his
trousers, pulling with him the pockets, which look like
comical mittens. When the robbers try to stuff the
money into their bags, the bills again wad up and stick
to their hands. As they struggle to free themselves,
Buster grabs their guns and chases them off.

Buster is mistaken for a holdup man when the bank
president investigates the goings-on and spots him
holding the guns. Before the mix-up can be straightened out, Buster runs off and ends up hiding out in a
mansion owned by the bank holdup men, who have
rigged the place as a haunted house to keep the cops
away. The rest of the film is a series of haunted-house
jokes with Buster encountering robbers, theater actors, bank employees, and "ghosts" as he careens
through the house trying to escape from his spooky
surroundings. The bank president's pretty daughter,
played by Virginia Fox, joins in after she follows a
suspicious bank employee (Joe Roberts) to the house.

The film suffers somewhat from the hokey haunted-
house gimmick, which was obviously conceived so
Buster could indulge in spook-house gags, some of
which are quite clever. At one point, he encounters so
many ghosts walking around that he becomes a traffic
cop to keep them from bumping into one another. In
the most ingenious sight gag, two figures dressed as

skeletons are carrying various body parts. As Buster
watches, the skeletons methodically assemble the
parts, starting with the legs, then the trunk, then the
arms, and finally the head. As soon as the head is in
place, the figure comes alive and walks away. This
impressive trick photography stunt is thoroughly convincing and downright spooky.

The best gag is saved for last. After subduing the
thieves, Buster gets hit on the head and dreams he is a
white-robed angel climbing up the heavenly stairway.
However, upon his arrival at the pearly gates, he is
informed by St. Peter that he is not one of the chosen
few. St. Peter pulls a lever and Buster slides down the
stairway, plummeting past the other angels to earth,
where he continues on through the ground and down a
twisting chute, landing at the feet of the devil. There he
is welcomed with a smile and a pitchfork to the rear.

When compared to the film's wonderfully inventive
beginning and end, the haunted-house gags pale. In
fact, the setting seems so superfluous that it acts
merely as an elaborate preparation for the brilliant
finale, which uses two of the house's recurring mo-
tifs—a collapsing stairway and a costumed devil—as
the stimulus for Buster's fantastic dream. As in *Convict
13*, Keaton uses the dream gimmick to create amusing
images tinged with a devilish playfulness, a mixture of
antagonistic moods that he utilizes again and again in
later films.

HARD LUCK

CREDITS:

Presented by the Comique Film Corporation; Distributed by
Metro Pictures. *Producer:* Joseph M. Schenck; *Director/
Script:* Buster Keaton and Eddie Cline; *Photography:* Elgin
Lessley; *Technical Director:* Fred Gabourie. *Release Date:*
March 16, 1921. *Length:* two reels.

CAST:

Buster Keaton, Virginia Fox, Joe Roberts.

> The machine is friend or enemy, depending—no
> matter what you do—on luck.
>
> —*From* Keaton *by Rudi Blesh*

Hard Luck was Buster's personal favorite of all the
shorts he made. Long considered a lost film, a print
was reconstructed from various foreign ones found in
the mid-1980s by Raymond Rohauer and film historian

Kevin Brownlow. The ending to the film—one of Keaton's most outrageous conclusions—contains one of his most cherished sight gags. Unfortunately, the footage to this gag remains missing, although stills from the finale exist and were used to fill in the lost footage. Looking at the film in its reconstructed form, a casual observer would probably find it hard to understand why Buster called *Hard Luck* his favorite two-reeler.

As it begins, a down-on-his-luck Buster wanders into a town and is continually frustrated in his attempts to find a job. Finally, dejected and destitute, he decides on suicide, then indulges in a series of comically inept attempts on his life. He tries getting run over by a trolley and later by a car, crushed by a falling safe, and hung from a flimsy tree branch, all with no luck. Finally, he gulps down the entire contents of a bottle labeled "Poison" that he has stolen from a man's medicine cabinet. Instead of containing poison, however, the bottle is filled with bootleg booze, and Buster ends up snockered instead of dead.

Still feeling the effects of the hooch, Buster staggers onto the grounds of an exclusive sporting club and into a meeting of the board of directors. Buster listens attentively to the chairman's passionate speech about the need to hire an expert sportsman to promote the club's many activities and attract new members. Inspired by the speech, the still-inebriated Buster volunteers for the job and, incredibly, is hired on the spot.

The rest of the film is filled with gags centered around Buster's attempts to master the various sports. He tries fishing, hunting, and horseback riding and is about as successful with these as he was with his suicide attempts. The clever sporting gags show up in several other Keaton films, most notably a routine where he methodically catches larger and larger fish, and an equestrian gag that has him leaping from a bridge onto his horse and ending up riding a wild bull.

After his sporting adventures, Buster wanders into the clubhouse to enjoy an afternoon tea with the members. Moments later, the dastardly criminal Lizard Lip Luke, played by Joe Roberts, invades the club and holds everyone at gunpoint while the rest of his gang robs the patrons. When Joe attempts to ravish pretty Virginia Fox, Buster secretly tosses a box full of bullets into the club's stove. As the room explodes in a hail of bullets, Buster rescues Virginia while Joe and his gang are wiped out.

After escaping, Buster proposes to Virginia. She tells him she'd like to marry him, but her husband might object. Frustrated once again, Buster tries to make Virginia jealous by donning a bathing suit and showing off around the pool. He climbs to the top of an

Virginia Fox attempts to prevent Buster from taking his own life in *Hard Luck* (the actual scene in the film is different). This two-reeler, filled with gags involving death and suicide, was Keaton's personal favorite.

incredibly high diving platform and, with his female admirers waving encouragement, attempts a spectacular dive into the pool far below. However, when he leaps headfirst from the diving board, he completely misses the pool and plunges deep down into the surrounding deck. Virginia and the other women gather around the chasm and peer in, but Buster has hit so hard that he has disappeared from sight.

At the wonderfully surreal climax, the scene shifts: it is several years later and the club is long abandoned with weeds covering the empty swimming pool and surrounding area. Suddenly, out of the chasm made by his fateful dive, Buster emerges dressed as a Chinese coolie. Accompanying him are his Chinese bride and their two children.

This ironic sight gag was one of Buster's all-time favorites and by itself could easily explain why Keaton called the short his personal favorite. Just as he would condemn an entire film on the basis of one inappropriate gag—as he did in the case of *The High Sign*—he could also heap praise on a film because of one or two outstanding gags. However, I believe the real reason Buster loved *Hard Luck* more than his other shorts was because it presents his personal philosophy most concisely.

Hard Luck: Buster prepares to demonstrate his equestrian skills.

The core of the film's philosophy is in its title. It is also graphically illustrated in the series of suicide jokes that dominate the first half. Buster, trying to control his own fate, cannot do it. No matter what he attempts, whether taking his life or showing off around the swimming pool, the end result always differs from what he anticipated, being sometimes better, sometimes worse. It is only by fate or luck that he survives.

In *Keaton,* Rudi Blesh paraphrases Buster's comments on his philosophy, saying the comedian believed that the events of one person's life could result in the same fate as for another, even though the events making up the second person's life are totally different. As an example, Buster talks about the fate of his father, Joe, and his best friend, Roscoe Arbuckle, saying that Joe drank himself out of a successful career while Roscoe had his yanked away from him by others. "There may be a difference," Buster said. "If so, I don't see it."

For Buster, life was a series of random events. Try to control those events and your fate could be the same as if you did absolutely nothing. What Buster chose to do while waiting for fate to rear its capricious head was

In a variation to the ending of *Hard Luck*, Buster introduces his Chinese wife to a haughty Virginia. The film's final scene with him emerging from a deep hole in the ground with his Chinese family is still missing from the existing print.

Buster is mistaken for a murderer in *The Goat*, one of his best episodical two-reelers.

Buster and Virginia Fox attempt to elude sheriff Joe Roberts in the wild climax to *The Goat*.

to make people laugh. Fortunately, for him—and the rest of us—fate let him indulge in this most pleasurable and noble activity off and on for his entire life.

THE GOAT

CREDITS:

Presented by the Comique Film Corporation; Distributed by Metro Pictures. *Producer:* Joseph M. Schenck; *Director/ Script:* Buster Keaton and Mal St. Clair; *Photography:* Elgin Lessley; *Technical Director:* Fred Gabourie. *Release date:* July 14, 1921. *Length:* two reels.

CAST:

Buster Keaton, Virginia Fox, Joe Roberts, Mal St. Clair, Eddie Cline, Jean Havez.

Although *The Goat* is Buster's most purely episodic film, its random series of adventures make it quite similar to his previous—and personal favorite—film, *Hard Luck*. However, its inspired bits, all loosely connected, centering around some of Buster's favorite themes—mistaken identity, falsely accused victim, misleading first impressions—make it far superior and one of his most thoroughly enjoyable short masterpieces.

As an aimless, penniless vagabond, Buster is standing in a bread line, waiting for his handout, and ends up behind two store dummies set outside a clothing store. By the time he realizes this—after the clothing-store proprietor picks up the mannequins and carries them back inside—all the bread has been handed out for the day and Buster walks off hungry. The sight of Buster impatiently waiting behind the dummies is a marvelous bit of pantomime made hilariously effective by his subtly expressive body language.

Wandering off, Buster stops and watches through a barred window as a photographer prepares to take mug shots of Dead Shot Dan, the infamous desperado. In a beautifully staged gag that sets up the rest of the film's adventures, the nefarious Dan, played by Buster's gagman/collaborator Mal St. Clair, notices him looking through the window. While the photographer momentarily turns away, Dan ducks down and then trips the camera's shutter, taking a picture of Buster. When the photographer takes Dan's picture, Dan puts his hat over the lens, preventing him from being photographed. Then, while being transferred back to his prison cell, Dan escapes.

Much of the remainder of *The Goat* centers around

Buster's being mistaken for the notorious Dan. Buster strolls through town and joins a crowd gathered around a billboard. When the crowd suddenly flees in terror from him, he is confused until he discovers that the billboard contains a huge wanted poster for Dead Shot Dan with Buster's photo prominently featured. Attempting to flee from the incriminating photo, Buster tears off and slams into big Joe Roberts, as the local police chief. Buster then saunters away and finds himself again in front of the billboard. Picking up a piece of furry fabric left behind by a startled woman, Buster pins it under the nose of the photograph so it looks like a ridiculously bushy mustache. Thinking he is now safe, Buster casually stands in front of the billboard as Joe strolls by. However, when the "mustache" begins to sag, Joe gets suspicious and Buster takes off again.

In another equally wonderful segment (one used by Chaplin as the opening gag for *City Lights*), Buster runs into a park and hides under a huge sheet covering a statue soon to be revealed to the public. The proud artist, standing next to the statue with some park authorities, removes the sheet, revealing a horse and Buster posing majestically on its back. The statue begins to sag under Buster's weight, finally collapsing while the crowd gasps and Buster attempts to hold his proud pose. When Joe spots him trying to revive the horse, the chase is on again.

Having managed to bury Joe under a cartload of rocks, Buster bumps into a former acquaintance, pretty Virginia Fox, and she invites him home for dinner. After being introduced to her mother, Buster plays with Virginia's dog and is too preoccupied to notice the arrival of her father—big Joe. In an expertly timed segment, Joe sizes up Buster from across the dinner table, then locks the front door and begins to advance on the trembling guest. Suddenly Buster rises from his chair and leaps onto the table, steps on Joe's shoulder, and propels himself through the window above the door directly behind Joe.

By film's end, Buster has managed to trap Joe in an elevator and send it shooting out of the top of the building. Then, he and Virginia run off to the local preacher to be wed.

The Goat, basically one episodic gag after another, is impeccably staged, each scene barreling into the next, propelled by the brilliance of the gags and Buster's fever-pitch energy.

The Goat also contains one of the most haunting images in all of Buster's films. After Buster has boarded a train to elude some pursuing cops, the train is glimpsed from an extreme long shot, barely visible on the horizon. The stationary camera, set up on the tracks directly in the path of the train, records its progress as it rapidly chugs closer and closer, its black, steaming image gradually filling up the entire

One of the most haunting images from any of Buster's films is this one from *The Goat* in which he sits serenely on the front of a train.

screen. Just before it reaches the camera, the train suddenly slows down and the figure of a man sitting on the front of the engine looms dramatically before the lens. It is Buster, of course, looking straight into the camera, his passive stone face registering no emotion. This brief, dreamlike scene, so simple and yet so powerful, seems out of place with the rest of the film's frenetic action. It isn't really a gag nor does it set up any other funny business. Yet, more than any other, this simple image of Buster staring solemnly into the camera comes closest to summing up the essence of his screen character.

THE PLAYHOUSE

CREDITS:

Presented by the Comique Film Corporation; Distributed by First National. *Producer:* Joseph M. Schenck; *Director/Script:* Buster Keaton and Eddie Cline; *Photography:* Elgin Lessley; *Technical Director:* Fred Gabourie. *Release Date:* October 6, 1921. *Length:* two reels.

CAST:

Buster Keaton, Virginia Fox, Joe Roberts.

The Playhouse is a masterpiece of technical and acting brilliance. Based on Buster's experiences as a vaudeville performer, it is one of his most autobiographical films and easily the most visually dazzling short he made.

It opens with him buying a ticket to a minstrel show and entering the theater. The next series of images are first startling, then amazing, then hilarious. Buster, as an orchestra conductor, taps his baton and the various musicians begin playing. The musicians, shown three at a time, are all played by Buster. As they play, fumbling with their instruments, a stagehand, also played by Buster, raises the theater curtain on nine minstrel dancers, two in blackface and all played by Buster. As they perform, the camera cuts to various couples in the audience, again all played by Buster: a spoiled kid and his dour mother, an elderly couple, and an elegantly dressed woman and her husband. The husband gazes at the performers and then checks his program, which lists the name of the theater, Buster Keaton's Opera House, the name of the show, "Buster Keaton Presents Buster Keaton's Minstrels," and a list of the names of the technicians and performers, all of them credited as Buster Keaton. This prompts the man to comment to his wife, "This Keaton

fellow seems to be the whole show." The incredible visual effects conclude when two dancers appear—two Busters again—and perform together an expertly timed soft-shoe shuffle.

This dazzling display of technical wizardry and acting expertise is executed with Buster's usual low-key brilliance, thus increasing the already powerful effect of the scenes. He was able to achieve the multiple-exposure effects by placing the camera in a black box with removable slots in front of the lens and standing before an open slot to shoot his routine, then rewinding the film and repeating the process over and over again. Buster originally used this process to achieve a similar effect in *Moonshine.*

The inspiration for the opening of the film was provided by pioneer moviemaker Thomas Ince, who loved to give himself multiple credits in the films he made (produced by, directed by, written by, etc.). Buster, who was just the opposite—giving others credit for work he himself conceived—delighted in satirizing Ince's self-indulgent habits and, again, took the joke to an extreme.

The rest of *The Playhouse,* although not as technically stunning, is in its own way just as brilliant, with Buster gleefully indulging in two of his favorite themes—false first impressions and mistaken identities. When the minstrel show setting suddenly fades, Buster is shown asleep in a small bedroom, having dreamed the opening segment. Burly Joe Roberts appears and shakes Buster awake. Slowly, dejectedly rising from the bed, looking forlorn, as if he were being evicted from his room, Buster sadly shuffles out the door, and Joe gestures to some other men to begin removing the furniture. Suddenly the walls of the room collapse and Buster appears in the background pulling on a rope. He is hauling the room's walls up into the rafters of a theater stage. This scene, a recreation of the opening one from *Back Stage,* beautifully illustrates his fascination with illusion, obviously springing from his vaudeville years.

The Playhouse continues with various acts from the theater in which Buster is employed as a stagehand, all of them based on those with which he was familiar from vaudeville. Two of the segments are extremely autobiographical, one involving twin girls, which echoes the multiple images from the first half of the film. According to Tom Dardis in his book, *Keaton: The Man Who Wouldn't Lie Down,* Buster was very attracted to vaudeville acts featuring twin girls and enjoyed having amorous relationships with both girls. In the film, he attempts the same thing, but is first baffled by the amazing appearance and reappearance of the girls, believing only one girl is responsible for the multiple comings and goings. When he finally realizes that

In *The Playhouse*, Buster plays all the parts of a minstrel show, including the entire theater audience. Here, he is a snooty woman and her dozing husband.

Buster fills in for the performing monkey in *The Playhouse*, his most visually innovative short film.

In the balcony of the playhouse sits a youthful Buster and a crotchety Grandma Buster.

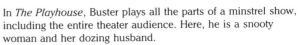

"This Keaton fellow seems to be the whole show!" says a gentlemanly Buster to his Busterette wife.

Buster picks up on the multiple image theme from the first half of *The Playhouse* and expands upon it in the film's second half as he confronts his own images in a mirror and later becomes involved with twin sisters.

71

there are identical twins, he tries to strike up a friendship with the one who is receptive, but keeps getting her mixed up with her sister, who is not so receptive.

The second overtly autobiographical segment of the film, brilliantly acted by Buster as a convincing monkey, is based on a routine that starred a performing chimpanzee called Peter the Great. According to Buster in his autobiography, Peter the Great was so humanlike in his abilities that he was once mistaken for another performer, a midget comedian named Marshall P. Wilder. Buster recalls a time when he was working in England and a soused Londoner stumbled into the theater, spotted Wilder onstage, and thinking the midget was the performing chimp, exclaimed, "My God! Now they have him *talking!*"

Another scene in the film is a summation of Keaton's unique approach to comedy. Big Joe, who is also in the stage show, is relaxing in his dressing room before his performance, enjoying a leisurely smoke. Suddenly, Joe's prop beard catches fire and he bursts out of his room yelling for help. Buster obliges by dashing over to a glass case labeled "For Fire Only." However, he pauses in front of the case, confused because it contains only a huge ax. Scratching his head, he finally gets an idea. Breaking the glass, Buster grabs the ax, rushes over to Joe, and smacks him in the face with the instrument, knocking him unconscious. Then Buster calmly cuts off Joe's smoldering beard with the ax and stomps out the fire. This is Buster the eccentric genius, adapting to the world's absurdities by becoming even more absurd. The joke, a capsule summation of his one-of-a-kind humor and view of life, is just one of the many highlights of this inventive film.

THE BOAT

CREDITS:

Presented by the Comique Film Corporation; Distributed by First National. *Producer:* Joseph M. Schenck; *Director/Script:* Buster Keaton and Eddie Cline; *Photography:* Elgin Lessley; *Technical Director:* Fred Gabourie. *Release Date:* November 1921. *Length:* two reels.

CAST:

Buster Keaton, Sybil Seely, Eddie Cline.

Buster's second-favorite two-reeler, *The Boat*, is a splendid companion piece to his second-favorite feature, *The Navigator*. Much more cartoonish than the feature, it is still delightful and contains some of his best gags as well as one of his most comically personal finales, a quick visual comment on his philosophy of life.

The film begins with Buster putting the finishing touches on a pet project of his, a full-size boat that he has constructed in the basement of his house. He then prepares to pull the boat, christened *The Damfino*, out of his basement and transport it down to the harbor where he plans to launch the craft on its maiden voyage. Realizing that the boat is too big to pass through the basement door, Buster widens the doorway. He then secures a rope to the boat and attaches the other end to his car and begins pulling. As *The Damfino* slowly rolls through the basement door, it rips open the side of the house. Buster, his kids, and his wife, played by Sybil Seely, gasp as they watch their entire house collapse. This incredible spectacle is another example of Keaton's ability to stage elaborate—and expensive—sight gags that first awe and then convulse the viewer with laughter.

Buster poses proudly next to his handmade pet project in *The Boat*. The film, one of his personal favorites, is one of several he made in which he frolics on board a doomed sailing vessel.

Buster, wife Sybil Seely, and their sons enjoy a little boating adventure on the high seas. Notice that the boys sport porkpie hats identical to their father's.

Disregarding the "minor" catastrophe with the house, the family proceeds to the harbor with the boat in tow. After accidentally running the car off the end of the dock and watching it sink to the bottom, Buster prepares to launch his precious vessel while standing proudly on the deck. What follows is one of his most memorable sight gags, one he asserted received the longest sustained laugh of any in his films. Buster rides the boat into the harbor, standing statuesque on the deck as the vessel slowly sinks down, down, until it completely disappears from sight, leaving its skipper floating alone in the drink. Buster claimed that, although the scene plays naturally and effortlessly—as do all of his gags, a Keaton trademark—the actual scuttling of the boat was quite complicated. To get the boat to sink completely and at just the right angle, the hull had to be loaded with tons of scrap metal.

After Buster, his family, and the resurrected boat finally set sail on its maiden voyage, several disasters follow, each showcasing Buster's love of the absurd and his mastery of elaborately staged mechanical gags. When the boat comes to a low bridge, Buster pulls a rope and the mast and smokestack slant back, permitting easy passage underneath, then pop back up. However, moments later, when Buster is busy installing a small flag at the back of the boat, he fails to notice another bridge, and the mast and smokestack collapse on top of him, knocking him overboard.

When evening arrives, the family gathers below deck. After the dinner sloshes off the galley table (caused by cartoonish hills and valleys in the middle of the ocean), a violent storm suddenly hits and threatens to capsize the craft. Buster frantically sends a distress signal, which is picked up by another boat, whose radio operator (Eddie Cline) sends back a message asking, "Who is it?" Buster replies with the name of his boat: *"Damfino."* Eddie, looking peeved answers, "Neither do I," and proceeds to ignore any further "frivolous" messages.

In another absurdly cartoonish gag, the boat begins to veer so radically that it turns a series of 360-degree circles. As he and the contents of the boat tumble around, Buster tries to remain upright by climbing the revolving walls. Finally admitting that his pride and joy is no longer seaworthy, Buster rounds up his family and loads them into a small bathtub-shaped lifeboat while he stubbornly goes down with his ship for a second time. The images of Buster sitting defiantly on the deck of the boat as it sinks, and then the pitiful sight of his porkpie hat floating alone in the ocean, are more distressful than funny.

The family is relieved when Buster finally bobs up again, conveniently under his hat, and climbs into the bathtub lifeboat. However, their disasters are not over yet; one of the kids, obviously possessing a curiosity rivaling his father's, playfully pulls the plug out of the bottom of the tub. As it sinks lower and lower into the water, Buster and the others close their eyes and huddle together, accepting their watery fate. However, when the tub suddenly stops sinking, Buster steps out and discovers the water is quite shallow. Relieved, saved from death at the last possible moment, the brave family clambers out of the tub and sloshes through the shallow water, finally beaching themselves on a foreign stretch of land. When Sybil turns to Buster and asks, "Where are we?" Buster faces the camera and mouths, "Damfino," and the family trudges off, swallowed up by the blackness.

It is easy to see why Buster loved *The Boat.* The film overflows with an amazing variety of wonderfully realized gags all centered around a central, comical prop. Buster is essentially playing a cartoon character, meeting one disaster after another with a steadfast, stubborn determination until all hope—well, almost all—is abandoned.

The ending to the film, downbeat yet hopeful, far from comical, is similar to the ending of *The Navigator,* yet here it carries an even stronger, more sober impact. The sight of the brave family marching out of the wet blackness, saved from death after having given up all hope, borders on the mythic. This touching, whimsical thumbnail summation of Keaton's philosophy of life was illustrated in his earlier and all-time favorite short, *Hard Luck.* Machines, as well as life itself, can be friendly or hostile, depending on one's luck. Better carry on as best as one can and leave such weighty matters as the fate of one's life to some cockeyed force of nature.

THE PALEFACE

CREDITS:

Presented by the Comique Film Corporation; Distributed by First National. *Producer:* Joseph M. Schenck; *Director/Script:* Buster Keaton and Eddie Cline; *Photography:* Elgin Lessley; *Technical Director:* Fred Gabourie. *Release Date:* January 1922. *Length:* two reels.

Buster holds a powwow with bigchief Joe Roberts and his tribe in the office of the land-hungry oil barons in *The Paleface.*

Buster enjoys a serene moment in his otherwise explosively fast-paced *The Paleface*.

CAST:

Buster Keaton, Joe Roberts.

The Paleface is a light romp through the woods highlighted by some terrific Keaton stunt work along with many humorous variations on old gags.

The film has a long expository introduction before getting down to some serious gagmaking. Big Joe Roberts plays the chief of a proud Indian tribe whose land is being stolen by a greedy oil baron. After one of the oilman's cronies swipes the land deed from a tribe member, the baron gives the natives twenty-four hours to vacate the land. The chief reacts by proclaiming to his tribe, "Kill first white man that comes in that gate."

Chief Joe has barely finished his proclamation when Buster jauntily passes through the gate of the reservation. Looking wide-eyed and innocent and carrying a butterfly net, Buster walks into the campground in pursuit of a butterfly flapping breezily in front of him, only to find the tribe gathering behind him. He acknowledges their presence with a polite tip of his flat hat, then suddenly tears off toward the front gate, the Indians chasing behind him. However, Buster is hardly trying to escape; he is merely in pursuit of his precious butterfly and slams his net down on it in triumph. This

marvelous beginning, one of Buster's best entrance scenes, sets up a series of wild confrontations between the innocent paleface and the very annoyed Native Americans.

In two of the most outrageous confrontations, Buster is tied to a stake for burning. He escapes the first time because the stake to which he is tied is loose; every time the Indians pile up wood around him for burning, he craftily scoots to another area with the stake. Later, after making his escape (tossed off a cliff, Buster uses a blanket as a parachute to float to safety), he takes refuge in an abandoned cabin where he has just enough time to fashion a pair of asbestos underwear (!) before being recaptured. When the Indians finally set him on fire, Buster calmly waits out the blaze, much to his captors' (and the audience's) astonishment.

After surviving this ordeal, Buster is made an honorary Indian complete with his own tepee, where he lounges in a smoking jacket while his valet, a member of the tribe, lays out his repaired clothes. When he learns from the chief of the oil baron's threat, Buster organizes a raid on the company's office. During the raid, he attacks one of the oilman's henchmen, threatening to scalp him. Very obligingly, the man removes the toupee he's wearing and hands it over. In another variation of an old gag, while being pursued by a rival Indian tribe, Buster escapes over a bridge missing most of its wooden planks by picking up the planks in back of him and setting them down in front of him. Once safe on the other side, he falls off the cliff anyway and plunges into a river.

In the film's final gag, after the Indians have returned victorious to their reservation, Buster eyes a pretty maiden and asks Chief Joe if it would be all right if he claimed her for his bride. With Joe's blessing, Buster races over to the maiden and embraces her. After the final title card appears—"Two years later"—Buster is glimpsed in the same embrace with his maiden and the film ends.

The Paleface is one of Buster's most frivolous two-reelers. The spectacular stunts he performs while racing through the beautiful outdoors, many of them impossible cartoon gags, are managed with the help of some very convincing special effects and some incredible acrobatic work on Buster's part. An enthusiastic outdoorsman, Buster enjoyed working in wild, wooded areas, where many of his films are set. Much of the special charm of his out-of-doors films derive from these stunningly photographed natural settings, *The Paleface* being one of his best, lighthearted wilderness romps.

The uneasy calm before the storm in *Cops*, Buster's most well-remembered two-reeler which many believe to be his best.

COPS

CREDITS:

Presented by the Comique Film Corporation; Distributed by First National. *Producer:* Joseph M. Schenck; *Director/Script:* Buster Keaton and Eddie Cline; *Photography:* Elgin Lessley; *Technical Director:* Fred Gabourie. *Release Date:* March 1922. *Length:* two reels.

CAST:

Buster Keaton, Joe Roberts, Virginia Fox, Eddie Cline.

If contemporary audiences remember who Buster Keaton was, they most often remember him as that short, sad-faced silent-movie guy in the porkpie hat who was chased through the streets of a city by hundreds and hundreds of cops. *Cops* is not only Buster's best-recalled short film, but also perhaps *the* best short he ever made. So well constructed, with so many themes and gags racing dizzyingly through its two reels, it is hard—make that impossible—to believe that, like the rest of Buster's films, much of it was conceived on the spot.

Buster's favorite mistaken-identity theme runs rampant throughout the film, most especially the first half. Everyone is mistaken for someone else in the beginning. First, the audience mistakes Buster for a criminal when he is first glimpsed behind what appear to be prison bars but are in fact the bars to the front gate of the mansion of his sweetheart (Virginia Fox), a snooty aristocrat who scorns him because he is a failure at business.

Setting out to prove her wrong, he ends up mistaken for a pickpocket when he finds a wallet full of money belonging to burly police chief Joe Roberts. Later, after eluding big Joe, Buster is conned into buying a pile of furniture from a man who he believes has just been evicted from his house. Buster then buys a horse and wagon from a hobo (played by Eddie Cline) whom he mistakes as the owner of the rig. Next, after the real owners of Buster's newly purchased furniture mistake him for a moving man and send him off to deliver their possessions to their new address, Buster ends up driving his rickety wagon into the middle of a parade of marching policemen.

As Buster mistakes the cheers of the crowd as praise for his smart business move, an anarchist appears atop a building and heaves a bomb at the parading cops. The fizzing bomb lands beside Buster, who, with an expression conveying "My, how convenient," picks it up to light his cigarette. Buster then realizes that his cigarette lighter does look somewhat odd and casually pitches it behind him into the squadron of marching policemen. Following the bomb explosion and the sight of blackened, dazed cops stumbling around in the street, the road apples hit the fan.

The rest of the film is visual poetry. Sight gags of Buster being pursued by every cop in the city erupt on the screen in a frenzy. The timing, staging, acrobatics, camera angles, and editing all come together in one of the great chase segments in film history. Hundreds and hundreds of cops fill the screen, all running madly after Buster, who, in one of the best-staged scenes, first runs down a street toward the camera followed by an army of policemen; then, after the street is empty of hurtling bodies for a heartbeat, Buster appears again, this time running away from the camera up the street, again followed by the horde of uniformed men.

In another impeccably timed and executed scene, Buster climbs a ladder, propped against a fence, trying to escape a dozen cops. Reaching the top of the fence, he sees another dozen cops on the opposite side waiting for him to jump down. As one group of cops grabs onto and pulls the ladder, Buster scrambles to

the other end of it. Soon both groups, separated from each other by the fence, struggle to pull the ladder down, with Buster riding it like a teeter-totter. When one group loses the tug-of-war, Buster is catapulted into the air, sailing over the heads of the men in blue and conveniently landing down the street on top of Joe Roberts.

Finally, Buster takes refuge in, of all places, the police station. An almost endless stream of cops all crowd through the precinct's front door, all eager to nab Buster. When the last cop finally enters, a lone uniformed figure emerges, closes the door, pulls out a ring of keys, locks the door, then drops the keys into a nearby trashbasket. If is, of course, Buster. Somehow, someway, he not only has managed to outrun and outmaneuver every cop in the city but is now on the

On your mark, get set, chase! The image of Buster running through the streets with every cop in the city after him is one of the most famous in all of film.

A romantic first encounter between Buster and his future bride, Kate Price, on the streets of a Polish community in *My Wife's Relations*.

Buster enjoys a quiet dinner at home with wife Kate's family in *My Wife's Relations*. Big Joe Roberts (center with carving knife) plays the meekest member of this aggressive family unit.

verge of making an easy getaway. However, after he drops the keys into the trash, he spots his sweetheart walking down the street and gestures to her. Seeing him, she gives him yet another look of contempt and walks away. Turning methodically, Buster digs the keys out of the trash, unlocks the door, opens it, and is yanked inside by the uniformed harpies, who tear him apart. On the film's last title card, the words *The End* appear chiseled on a small tombstone, on top of which rests Buster's porkpie hat.

Cops is beautifully understated, impeccably performed madness. If the film weren't so breathtakingly hilarious, it would be the perfect subject for a psychological thriller or a tortured existential novel. The initial idea for the film was more than likely inspired by one of the least humorous incidents of Keaton's personal life: at the time the film was made, Buster's best friend, Roscoe Arbuckle, was being tried for manslaughter after being falsely accused of rape and murder. The press had a field day with the case, printing speculative information gathered from unreliable sources, and doctoring up photos to show a nattily dressed Arbuckle behind bars awaiting trial (undoubtedly the inspiration for the opening scene of *Cops*). How Keaton managed to divorce himself from that traumatic experience and create comedy out of nightmare is probably the most extreme example of his amazing ability to find humor in every subject, every facet of his life.

MY WIFE'S RELATIONS

CREDITS:

Presented by the Comique Film Corporation; Distributed by First National. *Producer:* Joseph M. Schenck; *Director/Script:* Buster Keaton and Eddie Cline; *Photography:* Elgin Lessley; *Technical Director:* Fred Gabourie. *Release Date:* May 1922. *Length:* two reels.

CAST:

Buster Keaton, Kate Price, Joe Roberts, Monty Collins, Wheezer Dell, Tom Wilson.

My Wife's Relations is Buster's first full-fledged assault on the sacred institution of marriage, a subject he would return to again and again with even more savage—albeit less elaborate—satirical glee. At this time, Buster had been married to his first wife, Natalie Talmadge, for one year. The film is not exactly the most appropriate first-wedding-anniversary gift. However, given Buster's well-known reputation as a prankster, it might just be his unique way of saying, "Happy anniversary, Nat."

Like his previous film, *Cops,* the plot revolves around an elaborate series of mistaken identities. Buster, who works as baker in an ethnically diverse community, is falsely accused of breaking the window of a Polish judge and is hauled into court by his accuser, a large, matronly Irish woman played by Kate Price. Because the judge speaks no English, he thinks the couple has come to be married and promptly joins the two in holy matrimony. When the judge hands the couple their marriage certificate, Kate is overjoyed, and hauls her bewildered hubby, Buster, home to meet her family, made up of four Neanderthal-type brothers and one scrawny pop.

As Kate arrives with Buster in tow, the men gather around her new husband and inspect him from stem to stern, pulling his hair, pounding on his chest, checking his teeth, and finally picking him up to examine his feet. Buster plays a wonderfully limp mannequin, his vaudeville experience as a human mop coming in handy here. After one of the brothers, played by Joe Roberts, exclaims, "He won't last a week in this family," the brothers let go of Buster and he crashes to the floor.

Several comical domestic scenes follow. At the dinner table, Buster has no time to eat as he endlessly passes food back and forth to the others. When the main course is served—a huge pan of meat—the family pauses to say grace, then the instant "Amen" is uttered, the group stabs at the meat in unison, scoring the food while Buster stares wide-eyed at the empty pan. Later, after retiring for the evening, the newlyweds exchange some friendly love pats, which ends with Buster knocked unconscious by the brawling Kate.

In the morning, Joe goes through Buster's coat and finds a stray letter from an earlier encounter Buster had with a mailman. Joe opens the letter and gasps when he reads that the addressee is entitled to a $100,000 inheritance. Thinking Buster is the rightful claimant, the aggressive family suddenly turns into a bunch of pussycats, buttering up their new in-law and loaning him money to purchase a luxurious apartment. As bewildered as ever, Buster nevertheless goes along, and soon the uncouth lot is living it up in an elegantly furnished penthouse.

During a housewarming party, the clan and guests find out the truth about Buster's bogus inheritance, and soon the elegant surroundings are transformed into a battlefield. Finally, after the entire household nearly drowns in a vat of homemade beer, Buster flees and boards a train bound for Reno and relief from his state of marital bliss.

Many have interpreted *My Wife's Relations* as Keaton's way of dealing with the less than blissful aspects of his marriage, especially the way he was ridiculed by his in-laws for being a lowly slapstick comic. It is true that his first marriage was far from perfect. However, I believe that, in this instance, Buster was just as interested in poking fun at his own past, how he suddenly went from low-class vaudeville comic living in boarding rooms across the country to multimillionaire movie star living in a palatial Beverly Hills villa. This interpretation becomes more plausible after watching Buster's 1935 two-reel talkie, *Palooka from Paducah,* in which he restages the clever dinner table scene of *My Wife's Relations* with his own father, mother, and sister.

My Wife's Relations, although filled with many marvelous touches centered around domestic family life, is still somewhat flat. Buster's best digs at marriage would come later in quick, clever, creative bursts appearing at the end of several of his later films.

THE BLACKSMITH

CREDITS:

Presented by the Comique Film Corporation; Distributed by First National. *Producer:* Joseph M. Schenck; *Director/Script:* Buster Keaton and Mal St. Clair; *Photography:* Elgin Lessley; *Technical Director:* Fred Gabourie. *Release Date:* July 21, 1922. *Length:* two reels.

CAST:

Buster Keaton, Joe Roberts, Virginia Fox.

With its rural setting centered around a combination stable and auto repair shop, *The Blacksmith* is strongly reminiscent of the type of films Keaton made with his former partner and mentor, Roscoe Arbuckle. It is also his least inspired short film, one hampered by the overuse of cartoon gags and its now trite setting, one already well worked over for gags in such Arbuckle shorts as *A Country Hero, The Hayseed,* and *The Garage.*

Buster is an assistant to a small-town blacksmith played by the Arbuckle-sized Joe Roberts. With a clever opening, inspired by the classic Longfellow poem "The Village Blacksmith," Buster engages in some mildly amusing smithy gags, cooking his lunch over the blow furnace, burning his foot and rear on a smoldering horseshoe, and dousing his burnt body parts in a nearby water barrel.

Buster flexes his iron-band muscles for some youthful admirers in *The Blacksmith*. The two-reeler, Keaton's weakest effort, is highly reminiscent of the type of films he made with Arbuckle.

Buster and Joe Roberts try the soft and the hard sell approach on Virginia Fox in *The Blacksmith*.

When a huge horseshoe hanging over the shop's entrance suddenly develops magnetic powers and sucks up various objects out of Buster's hands, he and Joe accuse each other of sabotage. A fight breaks out between the two and Joe ends up in jail, leaving his assistant to wreak havoc on the shop.

In one segment, a pretty equestrienne (Virginia Fox) brings in her beautiful white stallion for a shoeing. Buster treats the horse as if it were a typical fashion-conscious customer shopping for the latest in footwear. He carefully measures the animal's hoof size, then fetches several different pairs of shoes for it to try on. After the horse rejects several of the styles—typical finicky customer that it is—Buster finally satisfies the beast by fitting it with a set of shoes that laces up the ankle. He finishes by brushing the horse's immaculate white coat, then smears one side of the animal with car grease until the poor horse looks like an abstract painting done by a crazed motor mechanic (not far from the truth).

Buster helps another equestrienne who limps in with a bruised backside, solving her problem by fixing her up with a springboard saddle, and she happily bounces out of the shop and down the road.

In the film's worst segment, a customer drives in a sparkling Rolls-Royce for minor repairs. While working on a car next to the Rolls, Buster smashes the elegant Rolls's windows with the backswings of a sledgehammer, smears it with axle grease, burns it with a blowtorch, dents it while using its hood as a surface for straightening nails, and then finally caves in its side when the other car's engine, hanging from the ceiling by a cable, suddenly begins swinging back and forth. All of this destructive horseplay is totally out of character for Buster, who acts like a mindless dunce, first oblivious of and then undisturbed by it.

The most interesting gag is staged during the film's fade-out, after Buster has been chased out of the blacksmith shop by the returning Joe and ends up running off with Virginia to get married. Following the title card—"Many a honeymoon express has ended thusly"—there is an iris-frame close-up of a toy train derailing from a small, circular track. The frame then expands to show Buster and Virginia married with a baby and living in a cramped, cluttered one-room apartment. Buster retrieves the toy train and sets it up again on the track, then with a bored expression punctuated by a wide yawn, he approaches the camera, reaches above it, and pulls down a black shade, the words *The End* appearing on the back of it.

This brief, bitter epilogue, its sardonic tone totally incongruous with the spirit of the rest of the film, is the first example of Buster's bleak view of married life. More unappetizing than humorous, it leaves a sour taste in the mouth coming after the rest of the film's limp yet harmless frivolity. It is almost as if the rest of the film were a dream and this brief spurt of nastiness were a jolt of reality, shocking the viewer back into the stark, depressing world that exists outside the movie theater.

THE FROZEN NORTH

CREDITS:

Presented by Buster Keaton Productions, Inc.; Distributed by First National. *Producer:* Joseph M. Schenck; *Director/Script:* Buster Keaton and Eddie Cline; *Photography:* Elgin Lessley; *Technical Director:* Fred Gabourie. *Release Date:* August 1922. *Length:* two reels.

CAST:

Buster Keaton, Joe Roberts, Sybil Seely, Bonnie Hill, Freeman Wood, Eddie Cline.

At this point in Keaton's career, the Comique Film Corporation became Buster Keaton Productions, and to celebrate the name change Buster fashioned the most bizarre film he ever made, *The Frozen North*. A parody of the florid melodramatic style employed by western star William S. Hart in his films, *The Frozen North* hurtles from one improbable, episodic adventure to the next, filling each scene with an endless stream of outlandish sight gags and hilariously heartless confrontations.

After the title card, "Last stop on the subway," Buster emerges from a subway kiosk in the middle of a snow-covered wilderness. His outfit, closely mirroring Hart's own, is a variation of a Canadian Mountie's uniform with Buster's flat hat replaced with the one he wore in his previous burlesque of melodramas, *Moonshine.*

Buster approaches a western saloon and eyes the heaps of money covering the many gambling tables. Then, spotting a poster featuring a gun-wielding cowpoke (who bears a strong likeness to Hart), he cuts out the figure and props it up in front of the saloon's window. Acting as this cardboard bandit's assistant, Buster strides commandingly into the saloon and gathers up the money. His goofy holdup plan works beautifully until a drunk staggers up to the two-dimensional desperado revealing it as a fake, and the patrons then grab Buster and heave him through another window.

Buster staggers off for home, entering one of the several cabins in the area, where he is startled by the sight of a tender scene between two lovers. Thinking

Buster emerges from a New York subway kiosk and finds himself in the Yukon wilderness in *The Frozen North*, a surreal and wickedly satirical parody of famed Western star William S. Hart's overly melodramatic films.

Buster prepares to stab rival Freeman Wood so he can have his way with Freeman's wife Bonnie Hill in the savage climax to *The Frozen North*.

he has caught his wife in the arms of another man, Buster nearly passes out with grief, tears streaming down his face. Then, feeling his grief turn to jealousy and revenge, he pulls out his gun and shoots the lovers. After taking a closer look at the couple lying dead on the floor, however, Buster exclaims, "I've made a mistake. This isn't my house or my wife," then politely tips his hat to the dead couple and leaves. This wonderful send-up of the standard jealous-husband-seeking-revenge ploy, typical of most melodramas, is played with Buster's unique blending of exaggeration and understatement, his face remaining stony throughout the embellished, absurd action.

Finally finding his own cabin, Buster is greeted with loving affection by his wife, played by Sybil Seely, but responds with a shove and a curt, "Shut up!" Then, catching sight of his pretty neighbor (Bonnie Hill), Buster dresses up in an all-white tuxedo and goes to her home, determined to have his way with her. When Bonnie's husband, played by Freeman Wood, tells Buster to go manhandle his own wife, the uncharacteristically villainous Buster, in typical melodramatic fashion, mouths a hilarious *"Grrr!"* in his rival's face.

Buster decides to follow the two, who board a

dogsled and take off across the snow-covered terrain. He hails a cab, operated by a cowering Joe Roberts, and the two head off in pursuit. The two men end up inside Joe's igloo where Buster borrows a couple of guitars to use as snowshoes. In a series of fishing jokes, Buster first falls through an ice hole, then snags another fisherman's line and pulls him in after.

Spotting Bonnie again, Buster makes another amorous attempt, striding triumphantly into her cabin and striking a lecherous pose. She stares at him in horror and, in an uproarious sight gag, imagines Buster to be Erich Von Stroheim, complete with white military outfit and black hip boots and sporting a monocle and a cigarette dangling from an elegant holder. When Bonnie's husband returns, the two men fight, and just as Buster subdues his rival and is about to stab him, his own wife, Sybil, saunters by the cabin, spots the two fighting, then pulls out a gun from underneath her shawl and shoots her husband in the back. Buster crumples to the floor mortally wounded, but then rises on one arm and pulls out a gun, leveling it at Bonnie and her husband. As he is about to pull the trigger, the scene dissolves to the interior of a movie theater. Buster, eyes closed, levels a candy wrapper at the screen in front of him while the theater's janitor (Eddie Cline) strolls by and shouts, "Wake up, the movie's over."

From the film's outlandish beginning to its startling, it's-only-a-dream conclusion, Buster manages to top each absurd moment with an even more bizarre scene of scandalously immoral behavior. The action is so unpredictable, with Buster's usual eccentric yet benevolent screen persona replaced by that of a bullying, lecherous cad, that the viewer is kept completely off balance, never knowing just what is going to happen next.

Buster had a ball satirizing William S. Hart, probably attracted to Hart's style of melodramatic heroics not only because it is the antithesis of his own understated style, but also because Hart's screen character shares Buster's trademark stoic, unsmiling demeanor. However, unlike Buster, who treated his screen character's expressionless puss with a kidding disrespect, Hart played his character's long-suffering stolidness with dead seriousness.

According to the Keaton autobiography, Hart was outraged by this blatant burlesque of his style, especially the way Buster portrayed Hart's "good-bad guy" character as a heartless, immoral lech. In author David Yallop's book, *The Day the Laughter Stopped,* he noted that Roscoe Arbuckle—not Buster and Eddie Cline— was the main creative contributor to *The Frozen North,* fashioning it out of revenge against Hart for refusing to support him during his manslaughter trials. Regardless of who contributed what, I don't believe *The Frozen North* was created out of revenge. Although unrelenting in its trashing of Hart's pretentious screen persona, the film is nevertheless in the same tradition as Keaton's other satirical ones and is as much a comment on his own stoic screen character as Hart's.

THE ELECTRIC HOUSE

CREDITS:

Presented by Buster Keaton Productions, Inc.; Distributed by Associated-First National. *Producer:* Joseph M. Schenck; *Director/Script:* Buster Keaton and Eddie Cline; *Photography:* Elgin Lessley; *Technical Director:* Fred Gabourie. *Release Date:* October 1922. *Length:* two reels.

CAST:

Buster Keaton, Joe Roberts, Virginia Fox, Joe, Myra, and Louis Keaton.

In *The Electric House,* Buster revels in one of his favorite hobbies: creating eccentric yet hilariously functional household gadgets. The film is powered by his love of, and identification with, inanimate objects as he turns a modern suburban dwelling into an electrical engineer's dream home.

In the film, Buster, dressed in the traditional cap and gown, is moments away from graduating from college.

Buster graduates with a botany degree but ends up an electrical engineer in *The Electric House.* This photo is from the first version of the film which was abandoned when he broke his ankle during shooting.

Buster and Virginia Fox comfort one another when his innovative and eccentric electrical gadgets go haywire in *The Electric House.* The electric stairway in the background is the one on which Keaton broke his ankle.

When the diplomas get mixed up, Buster, a botany major (!), ends up with a degree in electrical engineering. Before the graduation ceremony is over, Buster has been hired by the ceremony's director, played by Joe Roberts, to rewire his new home while he and his family, which includes daughter Virginia Fox, are away on vacation.

When Joe and family return, Buster is anxious to show off the features he has created for the house: an electric stairway, sliding doors, an automatic book retriever for the bookcase, mechanical ball rack for the pool table, a bed that folds into and out of the wall with a flick of the switch, and a dishwasher in the kitchen that not only washes and dries the dishes but puts them away as well. Outside, Buster demonstrates the automatic swimming pool drain, which empties and refills the pool in a matter of seconds.

Most impressive of all is the automatic food server, which consists of a miniature electric train that runs from the kitchen to the dining room and back again, a delightfully whimsical sight gag. A slight mishap occurs during dinner when the main course is served, again via train: Buster inadvertently disrupts the track laid out on the dining room table so that when the train arrives with the food, the plates end up chugging one by one into the wife's lap.

Despite the few electrical bugs, the family is pleased with Buster's efforts and invites friends over to show off the house. However, the real electrical engineer who lost his diploma to Buster seeks revenge against his fellow graduate and sneaks into the house to do a little creative wiring of his own. Soon the family and guests are racing through the house trying to escape from the appliances from hell. When Buster takes refuge in the kitchen, the electric dishwasher suddenly begins spitting out dishes in all directions. When he dashes into the game room, the automatic pool-ball rack flings balls at his head. When he tries to crawl out of the game room on his hands and knees, his head gets stuck in the automatic sliding doors.

Finally, Buster discovers the electrician sabotaging the wiring. Calmly walking to the kitchen, Buster fetches a variety of metal objects, then makes his way back to the closet where the saboteur is hiding and throws the objects into the room, electrically stunning the man, who staggers out of the closet. Buster entices him up the electric stairway, then switches its velocity to high and calmly watches as the man flies up the escalator and out the upstairs window into the swimming pool.

Finally fed up with Buster's innovations, Joe sends him packing. Even Virginia gives Buster a cold shoulder when he pleads for sympathy. Spurned and frustrated, he attempts suicide by tying a rope around his neck, then attaching it to a large rock and jumping into the pool. In the final scene, Buster floats out of a drainage pipe and ends up sitting next to the electrician, obviously another recent arrival from the swimming pool.

Although the gags in *The Electric House* are elaborately contrived delights, the story itself is a simple one, based on the well-worked idea of first demonstrating how a newfangled object works and then having the gadget go haywire. The story is also somewhat reminiscent of *The Haunted House*. However, *The Electric House* is far superior, with elaborate technical sight gags that are far more unusual and much more exciting to watch.

Keaton attempted to make *The Electric House* one year earlier, but shooting came to a sudden halt when one of his slap shoes jammed on the electric stairway and he broke his ankle. He took the injury as a personal insult, having always prided himself on his ability to stage—and survive—any and all types of stunts.

DAYDREAMS

CREDITS:

Presented by Buster Keaton Productions, Inc.; Distributed by First National. *Producer:* Joseph M. Schenck; *Director/Script:* Buster Keaton and Eddie Cline; *Photography:* Elgin Lessley; *Technical Director:* Fred Gabourie. *Release Date:* November 1922. *Length:* three reels.

CAST:

Buster Keaton, Renée Adorée, Joe Keaton, Joe Roberts, Eddie Cline.

One of Buster's most disjointed shorts, *Daydreams* consists, for the most part, of a series of self-contained gags and episodic vignettes.

Buster is visiting his sweetheart, played by Renée Adorée, and asking her father (Joe Keaton) for her hand in marriage. Joe is obviously hesitant to allow the marriage, prompting Buster to go off to the big city and prove his worth after telling Joe, "If I'm not successful, I'll come back and shoot myself." Joe calmly replies, "Very well, I'll lend you my revolver."

Buster, writing letters to his girl back home detailing his big-city exploits, includes impressive—though somewhat vague—descriptions of his many professional successes. Renée imagines Buster performing spectacularly with both finesse and expertise. Of course, the truth is somewhat less impressive, and much of the film's humor derives from the contrasts between Buster's hyperbolic descriptions, Renée's idealistic imaginings, and then the harsh and hilarious truth.

When Buster writes that he is the head of a big sanatorium where he looks after two hundred patients and performs operations "that you just couldn't imagine," Renée dreams that he is a brilliant surgeon (unfortunately, this daydream and two others are missing from the existing prints). Her fanciful daydream then fades to reveal the less-than-flattering truth. Buster is actually a veterinarian's assistant in a dog and cat hospital where his job is to feed and wash the various animals and keep the canines separated from the felines.

After some hilarious animal mishaps (the funniest one involving his mistaking a skunk for a runaway cat), Buster is fired, but he writes another letter to Renée describing his new position as a savvy financial entrepreneur. As Renée pictures him cleaning up on Wall Street, the scene fades to reveal Buster dressed in a

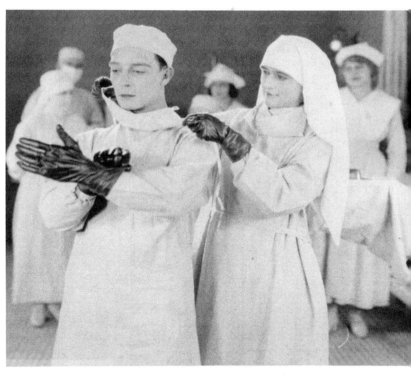

In one of the missing daydreams from the short, Buster's girl believes him to be an adept surgeon when in fact he is an assistant to a veterinarian.

Buster cleans up on Wall Street in one of the harsh reality segments from *Daydreams*. Joe Roberts points out a spot he missed.

85

Buster's sweetheart imagines him as the Bard's melancholy Dane in *Daydreams*, one of his most purely episodical two-reelers.

Buster does a variation of his "human mop" impersonation in the final moments of *Daydreams*. Here, he arrives back at girlfriend Renée Adoree's home as a special delivery package after his disastrous attempts to find fame and fortune in the big city.

In another classic moment from one of his films that is both haunting and hysterically funny, Buster rides a rotating paddle wheel in his efforts to elude pursuing policemen in *Daydreams*.

white custodian's uniform, dragging around a wheeled trash cart and cleaning up mounds of rubbish. During a ticker tape parade honoring politician Joe Roberts, Buster is inundated with huge mounds of confetti. To get rid of the unwieldy mess, he sets a match to it, resulting in a raging fire storm that overtakes Joe's campaign vehicle.

In his next letter to Renée, Buster writes, "I'm tired of cleaning up. I'm back at my artistic gift, and today I'm making my debut in Shakespeare's *Hamlet*." She imagines Buster in Renaissance garb, graciously accepting the bows of a wildly cheering audience seated in an elegant theater. The truth: Buster is actually a spear-carrier in the play, marching out of step with the others in the chorus, dropping his spear and sword, and finally getting kicked out of the production.

In Buster's final letter to his sweetheart, he writes, "Fantastic success! The crowds were so enthusiastic I just had to make a clean getaway." He is then shown barreling down the middle of the street, pursued by a horde of policemen. A series of chase jokes follow, most of them resembling outtakes from *Cops*. The chase ultimately leads to the harbor district where Buster leaps onto a ferry just pulling away from the dock, then races across the deck and jumps through a window, ending up sitting on the ferry's paddle wheel.

This sets up one of the most notable sight gags from any Keaton film. As Buster calmly sits on the paddle wheel, it slowly begins to rotate. He stands and begins to climb over the blades, then, as the wheel's rotations speed up, he crawls inside the wheel and walks along as if he were taking a casual stroll down the street. The wheel continues to turn faster, and Buster begins trotting inside it, then slipping, then tumbling, then rolling over and over again, finally grabbing onto one of the blades and rising up into the air, then plummeting down into the water, only to rise again as he makes a series of dizzying rotations around the outside of the paddle wheel. As this sequence illustrates, many of Buster's best sight gags, intentionally or not, have the power to transcend their context and tap into a realm of timeless, haunting beauty that at first is only mildly comical. Yet, ultimately, these moments are slowly sucked back into their comical surroundings and their more unsettling implications are purged, defeated by Buster's offhanded and irreverent attitude.

In the film's final segment, a mailman drives up to Renée's house, matter-of-factly picks up a tattered and bruised Buster from his truck, checks the mailing label wrapped around Buster's neck, and delivers him to her. Her dad nonchalantly signs for the shipment, then calmly retrieves his revolver from a desk drawer and hands it to Buster. When Buster fails to shoot himself, Joe boots him out of the house.

Although *Daydreams* contains several outstanding moments, the film still has the feeling of being merely a collection of stray comic events. The loosely constructed "letter writing" format is clever, presenting each segment from three different points of view, illustrating one of Buster's favorite themes, misleading

86

first impressions. Apparently, Harold Lloyd was so taken by *Daydreams*' letter-writing plot structure that he used it for his most famous film, *Safety Last,* made the following year. Lloyd also lifted a clever store-dummy gag from *Daydreams* and restaged it—twice—for his feature.

THE BALLOONATIC

CREDITS:

Presented by Buster Keaton Productions, Inc.; Distributed by Associated-First National. *Producer:* Joseph M. Schenck; *Director/Script:* Buster Keaton and Eddie Cline; *Photography:* Elgin Lessley; *Technical Adviser:* Fred Gabourie. *Release Date:* January 22, 1923. *Length:* two reels.

CAST:

Buster Keaton, Phyllis Haver.

The Balloonatic marked the first time Keaton attempted a more substantial and interactive relationship with his leading lady. In most of his other short films—and many of his features—the women, along with everyone else, were subordinate to the all-impor-

tant gags. Here, for once, Buster shared the spotlight, resulting in a more fleshed-out comedy.

In one of Buster's most unusual segments, the film opens on the full round top of Buster's porkpie hat appearing out of the darkness. Then it moves, revealing Buster's face in stark close-up, dramatically illuminated by matchlight, the flickering flame cradled in his hands. The mood is mysterious, foreboding, until the close-up cuts to a medium shot, revealing Buster's surroundings: an amusement-park fun house.

After being ejected from the house via a trapdoor hooked to a chute that deposits him roughly onto the boardwalk, Buster ends up sitting next to pretty Phyllis Haver on the tunnel-of-love ride. As their boat slowly slides out of the tunnel, Phyllis is sitting with a stern expression on her face while Buster is in shambles, his clothes ripped, his eyes blackened, his hat crumpled on top of his head. This old joke works well to set up the initial antagonism between the two, an antagonism that will later develop into a full-fledged battle of the sexes.

Buster wanders off again, soon captivated by another attraction, a huge hot-air balloon about to ascend. When he volunteers to attach a "Good Luck" banner to the top of the craft, the balloon suddenly lifts into the sky, leaving the intended passenger behind. After an initial jolt of fright, Buster quickly adjusts, setting up housekeeping in the balloon's basket. Later,

Buster searches for an uplifting experience in *The Balloonatic.*

Buster takes a refreshing nap after crashing his balloon in the wilderness in *The Balloonatic*, one of the few films he made featuring a strong and resourceful female costar, played by Phyllis Haver (no, that's not her in the bear costume).

he dangles several decoy ducks from the bottom of the basket, pulls out a rifle, and readies himself for a spot of duck hunting. Predictably, Buster ends up shooting a hole in the balloon, and after plummeting to the ground and pulling himself out of a tree in the middle of a wilderness, he salvages the remains of the balloon and sets up camp next to a river.

Buster uses a blatantly artificial plot contrivance by having Phyllis show up camped a few hundred feet downstream. Apparently, she is an avid sportswoman, and he two compete to prove who is the superior survivalist.

A resourceful adversary, Phyllis at one point escapes from a charging bull by grabbing the beast by its horns and flipping it on its side before Buster has a chance to rescue her. Determined to prove his superiority, Buster goes big-game hunting, stalking a tiny squirrel while being followed by a huge black bear. As Buster pauses to fix a bead on the frisky rodent, another bear suddenly rises out of a pit in front of the squirrel. Buster reacts by conking the bear on the head with his rifle butt, causing the weapon to fire and shoot the bear in back of him.

Phyllis, who has remained aloof throughout Buster's previous—and equally inept—outdoors adventures, now swoons with admiration after having witnessed his hunting exploits from afar. Seizing his advantage,

Buster invites her on a canoe outing, where he serenades her as the two are carried off down the rapidly flowing river and over a huge waterfall. Fortunately, Buster has rigged up the newly patched balloon to the canoe so when it reaches the falls, the tiny craft continues along into the air.

The Balloonatic benefits greatly from its emphasis on the playful boy-girl war. The two are equally matched, both displaying a fumbling helplessness as well as an ability to survive alone in the wilds. Unlike Chaplin and Lloyd, who usually present their leading ladies in a much more ethereal, romantic light, Keaton made sure his women are independent and resourceful, sort of female counterparts to his own character.

THE LOVE NEST

CREDITS:

Presented by Buster Keaton Productions, Inc.; Distributed by Associated-First National. *Producer:* Joseph M. Schenck; *Director/Script:* Buster Keaton; *Photography:* Elgin Lessley; *Technical Director:* Fred Gabourie. *Release Date:* March 1923. *Length:* two reels.

CAST:

Buster Keaton, Joe Roberts, Virginia Fox.

The Love Nest is Keaton's last silent two-reeler before embarking on his career in feature films for his producer, Joe Schenck. Dominated by a surreal, ironic playfulness, it is also his only film in which he took full directing and writing credit.

As the film opens, Buster is saying good-bye to his sweetheart, played by Virginia Fox, after a serious lovers' spat. He has decided to forsake all women and sail off alone across the ocean in search of peace. Buster writes Virginia a farewell letter and seals it with his tears, a funny touch that he plays with his usual ironically deadpan manner.

Clutching a picture of his beloved, Buster sets sail in his little canvas-covered love nest, which bears the name *Cupid*. The camera shows Buster in close-up, piloting, then fades out to indicate a passage of time. When the scene fades back, the camera angle is the same, yet now Buster sports a painted-on mustache and beard. As he checks his supplies—and the photo of his sweetheart, which he keeps next to his heart—he realizes that he is nearly out of food and water and collapses from hunger and remorse.

Later, Buster spots a sailing ship captained by a very

mean Joe Roberts. After being picked up by the ship, ironically named *The Love Nest*, Buster soon learns just how mean Joe is when a mate accidentally spills coffee on Joe's hand and is immediately tossed overboard with a wreath of flowers as a life preserver. The floral life preserver becomes a running joke as each subsequent infraction by other crew members is treated in exactly the same manner.

Agreeing to become a member of the crew, Buster is put to work swabbing the deck. Later, he picks up a rifle from Joe's gun collection and inadvertently points it at the large and looming captain, who reacts with a look of seething outrage. Buster, realizing the situation could be interpreted as mutiny, calmly takes the rifle and walks down a stairway leading to the ocean, marching right into the water until he is totally submerged. Several powerful underwater explosions follow with Buster finally reemerging and climbing back upstairs, the rifle in one hand and a load of fish in the other, as if this cockeyed act were his intent all the time.

An even more extreme example of Buster's love for the surreal occurs during the film's climax, after he has sunk Joe's ship and sailed off in a lifeboat, eventually running into a huge floating platform. Not realizing the platform is actually a navy target, Buster climbs aboard and calmly begins fishing. When a battleship begins shooting at the target, Buster pays the exploding shells no mind until a direct hit sends him flying into the air,

A "bearded" Buster displays his best table manners around Captain Joe Roberts in *The Love Nest*.

Buster tries to maintain his status as the last surviving mate on Captain Joe's ship in *The Love Nest*.

Buster ponders his fate aboard brutal captain Joe Robert's sailing ship in *The Love Nest*. Keaton's final silent two-reeler is the only film on which he took sole directing and writing credits.

his clothes tattered and his face blackened as he plummets to certain death.

Buster is saved when he wakens from a deep sleep, back on board his little *Cupid,* having dreamed the adventures with Joe and the encounter with the battleship. Now lost and without food or water, he drifts aimlessly, still clutching the picture of his beloved Virginia as he collapses from hunger. Suddenly, he notices Virginia swim by his craft, then glances out from his canopy-covered boat, seeing that he is still tied to the dock and has remained in the same spot all this time.

The Love Nest is, arguably, the best depiction of Buster's fatalistic philosophy of life. Filled with his special brand of cockeyed, surreal humor, most of it centered around the ordinarily depressing subjects of despair and death, the film is, amazingly, Keaton at his lighthearted best, the death jokes treated just like all the others with a loving, disrespectful offhandedness. The action circles back upon itself, the irony piles up, and Buster returns home—without ever having left— much sadder, no wiser, the only change being the stupid fake beard covering his face.

THE THREE AGES

CREDITS:

Presented by Buster Keaton Productions, Inc.; Distributed by Metro Pictures. *Producer:* Joseph M. Schenck; *Directors:* Buster Keaton and Eddie Cline; *Script:* Clyde Bruckman, Joseph Mitchell, and Jean Havez; *Photography:* William McGann and Elgin Lessley; *Technical Director:* Fred Gabourie. *Release Date:* September 24, 1923. *Length:* six reels.

CAST:

Buster Keaton (*The Boy*), Margaret Leahy (*The Girl*), Wallace Beery (*The Villain*), Joe Roberts (*The Girl's Father*), Lillian Lawrence (*The Girl's Mother*), Blanche Payson (*The Amazon*), Horace Morgan (*The Emperor*), Lionel Belmore.

Halfway through filming his nineteenth two-reeler, *The Love Nest,* Keaton was informed by his producer, Joe Schenck, that he would be making features from now on. Buster had wanted to start making independently produced features as early as 1920, but Schenck balked at the idea, preferring to star him in less costly two-reelers until he proved he was a competent—and profitable—filmmaker. Therefore, instead of being the first of the three comic geniuses to start making his own features, Buster was the last, with Chaplin having

made his first personal production, *The Kid,* in 1921 and Harold Lloyd launching into full-fledged features in 1922 with *Dr. Jack* after experimenting with four-reel comedies.

When he entered feature filmmaking, Keaton hired a staff of gag writers, some of them old friends from the Arbuckle days, the rest friends from vaudeville. In his autobiography, he comments on these gifted funnymen who helped create some of the most memorable comic moments on film: "Neither I, my director, nor my gagmen were writers in any literary sense. The writers most often on my staff were Clyde Bruckman, Joe Mitchell, and Jean Havez. They never wrote anything but gags, vaudeville sketches, and songs. I don't think any of them ever had his name on a book, a short story, or even an article for a fan magazine. . . . They were not word guys at all." They might not have been word guys, but along with Buster's technical people, they became an extremely close-knit creative staff, one that remained loyal for most of his silent features before going off to work for Harold Lloyd, Harry Langdon, and W. C. Fields, among others.

Keaton's first independently produced feature, *The Three Ages,* is very much in the kinetic, cartoonlike spirit of his two-reelers. As a creative base, he and his gagmen used the structure of D. W. Griffith's four-story epic, *Intolerance.* Instead of telling a tragic story of greed and corruption through the ages, though, Buster used the timeless subject of love and picked three wildly disparate epochs—the Stone Age, the Roman Age, and the Modern Age—on which to base his gag-strewn story.

Buster first appears dressed in black fur, sporting a ridiculous black wig and lying on what appears to be a slab of rock. When he slaps the slab underneath him, suddenly it begins to move as he stands up and peers off into the horizon. Then from a long shot, the audience sees what Buster is standing on: a gloriously fake, animated brontosaurus.

Soon Buster is engaged in a fight with rival caveman Wallace Beery, both brutes fighting for the affections of ex-beauty-queen Margaret Leahy, the rivals each pulling on one of her arms until her parents show up. Margaret's father (Joe Roberts, unrecognizable in a bushy black beard and full-length leopard skins) tests the two rivals' suitability by whacking them around with a club. Wally stands up to the whackings, but Buster crumples under the first blow to the head.

The story then switches to ancient Rome, introducing the same set of characters dressed in togas and riding horse-drawn chariots instead of dinosaurs. (The Roman set is impressively detailed and expansive, created by Buster's technical director, Fred Gabourie, from the remains of a lavish Hollywood exposition that

Caveman Buster, leading lady Margaret Leahy, and their primitive clan in one of the three historical periods dramatized in *The Three Ages*, his first independently-produced feature film.

Toga-adorned Buster poses with his Roman Age family in *The Three Ages*.

Buster tries to act casual after being thrown into the den of a ferociously fake lion in *The Three Ages*.

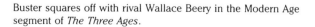

Buster squares off with rival Wallace Beery in the Modern Age segment of *The Three Ages*.

91

A triumphant Buster strolls with his Modern Age family in the satirical fade-out to *The Three Ages*.

had just closed.) The same scene from the Stone Age is played out with Buster and Wally both vying for Margaret's hand, and Margaret's parents showing up to choose who is more worthy. Joe looks at Wally and proclaims, "Thou rankest high in the Roman army." Then, turning to Buster, he says, "And thou art the rankest."

Next, the Modern Age of "speed, need, and greed" is introduced, and the two previous scenes are replayed in modern dress. Buster and Wally drive jalopies side by side down the street to Margaret's house, both snubbing each other until Buster hits a dip in the road and his car crumbles into a heap of scrap metal. This time when Margaret's parents show up, her mother (Lillian Lawrence) decides who is the most suitable by checking the men's bankbook balances. Wally again wins (he banks at First National while Buster uses the Last National).

The rest of the film follows this pattern of playing out a scene in one age, then replaying it in another. In the Stone Age, Buster attempts to make Margaret jealous by approaching another woman lying on a rock and playfully caressing her arm while Margaret watches from a distance. Then when Wally grabs Margaret by the hair and drags her away to his den, Buster does the same to his new girlfriend, who turns out to be a towering Amazon (Blanche Payson). She glares down at the diminutive Buster, then pulls out a club and

Buster poses with some of the collaborators who helped him create some of his finest silent features. Seated with him are Eddie Cline (saxophone), Clyde Bruckman (guitar), and Jean Havez (drum). Standing behind Buster is Joe Mitchell. The man with the microphone is friend Thomas Gray.

smacks him in the chest, sending him flying off a cliff and into a pool of water below. In the parallel scene from the Roman Age, Buster woos an attractive maiden, then ends up in a wrestling match in which he is finally pinned by the feisty young woman. Then in the Modern Age, Buster follows Wally and Margaret into a restaurant, only to be frustrated again when he tries to pick up another woman and her boyfriend suddenly returns and slugs him.

Rivals Buster and Wally then engage in contests of strength, dueling for Margaret in each of the eras. In the Stone Age, Buster beats Wally in a duel using clubs. In a wild chariot race from the Roman Age, Buster defeats Wally by converting his vehicle into a dogsled after a sudden snowstorm buries Rome. In the Modern Age, Buster and Wally are members of rival football teams, with the former scoring the winning touchdown.

In the exciting parallel finales, Buster wins a wild rock fight when he launches himself from a primitive catapult and flies into Wally's face, sending the villain over a cliff. Then, after escaping from a lion's den in the Roman Age (an adorably fake lion is used here), Buster does an effective Samson imitation and pulls down a column on top of his rival. Finally, in the Modern Age finale, Buster executes an astounding stunt—leaping from the top of one building to another, missing it, plummeting down, then grabbing onto a rainspout and swinging into the window of a fire station, careening across the floor, sliding down a pole, and ending up riding on the back of a fire engine. Filming this stunning segment, Buster suffered an injury when he missed the leap from the first building to the next (the rest of the scene had to be reworked to compensate for his misjudged leap; he later claimed the reworked gag received the biggest laugh of the picture). Buster ends up snatching Margaret from the wedding altar when he unmasks Wally as a bigamist.

In the parallel conclusions to each of the three ages, introduced by the title card, "And if anything more were needed to show that love has not changed. . . ," Buster takes a stroll with his Stone Age sweetheart accompanied by an endless line of leopard-skin-clad kids; then, he leads his toga-adorned family down the streets of Rome; and finally, in the last scene, Buster and Margaret stroll down the street leading a minuscule dog on a leash, a very funny, effective fade-out to a beautifully conceived and executed first independently produced feature.

OUR HOSPITALITY

CREDITS:

Presented by Buster Keaton Productions; Distributed by Metro Pictures. *Producer:* Joseph M. Schenck; *Directors:*

Buster's second feature film, *Our Hospitality*, a period piece set in early nineteenth century Kentucky, has a much more realistic and sedate approach to the story, a radical departure from his usual gag-infested comedies.

Buster rides his whimsical—yet historically accurate—bicycle in *Our Hospitality*.

Buster Keaton and Jack Blystone; *Script:* Clyde Bruckman, Joseph Mitchell, and Jean Havez; *Photography:* Elgin Lessley and Gordon Jennings; *Technical Director:* Fred Gabourie; *Electrician:* Denver Harmon; *Costumes:* Walter Israel. *Release Date:* November 19, 1923. *Length:* seven reels.

CAST:

Buster Keaton (*Willie McKay*), Natalie Talmadge (*Virginia Canfield*), Joseph Keaton (*Lem Doolittle*), Buster Keaton, Jr. (*Willie as a baby*), Kitty Bradbury (*Aunt Mary*), Joe Roberts (*Joseph Canfield*), Leonard Clapham [later Tom London] (*James Canfield*), Craig Ward (*Lee Canfield*), Ralph Bushman [later Francis X. Bushman, Jr.] (*Clayton Canfield*), Edward Coxen (*John McKay*), Jean Dumas (*Mrs. McKay*), Monty Collins (*Rev. Benjamin Dorsey*), James Duffy (*Sam Gardner*).

Keaton's second independently produced feature film, *Our Hospitality*, is his first attempt at telling a fully sustained, single story without relying on his usual brand of absurd, slapstick humor. Although he stated many times that the story line for all his films was always more important than the gags, this was not always the case. However, with *Our Hospitality*, the emphasis is profoundly on the story, to the point where there is no humor for several long—almost too long—stretches in the film. Also, Buster's approach to the humor and to the action are solidly grounded in a much more realistic world, one historically well-

founded. A period piece, shot in the Lake Tahoe and Truckee River areas of central California and Nevada, *Our Hospitality* is among his most beautifully photographed films, the only one in which he starred with his first wife, Natalie, and the only one in which three generations of Keatons appear together.

The film's story is based on the infamous real-life feud between the Hatfields and the McCoys. Buster changed the names of the families to the Canfields and the McKays and set the action in 1830s Kentucky, faithfully re-creating that period's frilly, fancy costumes, its primitive mechanical contraptions, and its sedate, rural surroundings. Buster plays Willie McKay, the last surviving male of the family dynasty. When he was an infant (baby Willie is played by Buster's son James in the film's prologue), his mother fled with him to New York in order to protect him from the feud that has wiped out the rest of his family.

When Willie, now a young man, learns of the family's Kentucky homestead via a letter from the estate's agent, he decides to travel back to stake his claim. Buster as Willie makes the trip from New York to Kentucky aboard one of the first trains ever used for

cross-country travel, the Stephenson Rocket. Buster created a replica of it from early historical records and later donated it to the Smithsonian. The train looks like a series of stagecoaches strung together and attached to a stove furnace on wheels. Naturally, Buster uses the train sequence (which, in truth, takes up far too much screen time) for a string of clever gags. At one point, when faced with a donkey blocking the tracks, the conductor (Joe Keaton), who has obviously encountered this type of problem before, jumps off the train and instead of moving the animal, yanks the tracks to its side. Later, the train ride becomes quite bumpy as the tracks were laid over boulders, tree stumps, and other large objects.

One of the passengers is a young woman whom Willie knows only by her first name, Virginia (Natalie Talmadge). Of course, Virginia turns out to be a Canfield, which leads to a comical confrontation after the train reaches its destination and Virginia invites Willie to her home for dinner.

Virginia's family includes her father, Joseph (Joe Roberts), and her two brothers, Lee (Craig Ward) and Clayton (Ralph Bushman). When they learn that a

Buster enjoys a musical interlude with Natalie before dodging bullets fired by her feud-obsessed family in *Our Hospitality*.

McKay has arrived in town and is looking for his family estate, they go out gunning for him. Imagine their surprise when he shows up later for dinner. Naturally, the brothers would like to gun down Willie before the first course is served, but Joseph reminds them that it would be rude and would violate proper Southern hospitality. Overhearing the two brothers talking about their plans to shoot him once he leaves the house, Willie decides to continue his stay as long as possible.

A wonderful, tension-filled dinner scene follows, in which the players eye one another around the table. The local reverend (Monty Collins) is also present, and he and Virginia sit innocently and enjoy the meal while the others fidget and jump with each minor disturbance.

Finally, Willie manages to sneak into a closet where he dons one of Virginia's Southern-belle gowns and saunters out the front door. His disguise is soon revealed, however, and the chase is on. Virginia, having learned the truth of the situation, is horrified over her family's plans to kill her new beau and follows her father and brothers as they search for Willie.

Willie's attempts to escape from the hotheaded Canfields lead to a river rescue climax with Willie tied by a long rope to a tree trunk that has lodged precariously next to a waterfall. When he spots Virginia

Buster boards one of the earliest cross-country trains ever built, another eccentric but historically accurate mechanical contraption featured in *Our Hospitality*. Also boarding the train is his leading lady, played by real wife Natalie Talmadge (center).

floating helplessly toward the falls, Willie struggles to rescue her. In the most spectacular stunt of his screen career, Buster as Willie—without the use of a double—swings like a trapeze artist out from the edge of the waterfall, grabs Virginia just as she is about to go over, then swings back to safety, a truly amazing scene guaranteed to produce gasps of wonder and awe from the first-time (and millionth-time) viewer.

With assistance from the reverend, Willie and Virginia make their way back to the Canfield mansion where they are married. When the Canfield men return home, the elderly Joseph, weary of the feud, finally lays down his gun and orders his sons to do the same. Realizing the feud is finally over, Willie pulls out his own weapons—an arsenal of pistols concealed all over his body—in a fade out touched with both humor and heartfelt drama.

Our Hospitality is a revelation in style, content, and emotional ups and downs, a total departure from Keaton's previous frenetic, slapstick approach to filmmaking. The characterizations are all fully realized and three-dimensional, especially Natalie's Virginia Canfield, captured in many loving close-ups. The film's pacing is unhurried, at times idyllic, reflecting the sleepy, small-town period setting. Even the chase sequences are shot in a much less frenzied style, a result of Buster's innovative habit of filming his comedies at standard speed rather than at an artificially increased one. Although Buster time and again credited Roscoe Arbuckle as the biggest influence on his film career, D. W. Griffith seems to be his second most influential cinematic mentor, with *Our Hospitality* very

much in Griffith's methodically detailed, reverential style (*The Three Ages* and *The General* are two other Keaton features that demonstrate the Griffith influence).

The extensive—and exhausting—river scenes nearly resulted in Buster's drowning on a couple occasions, first when a protective hold wire snapped and sent him tumbling into the fierce Truckee River rapids. Then, during the amazing waterfall stunt—which was actually filmed at the Keaton studios—he took in so much water hanging upside down underneath the falls that he had to have his stomach pumped. Also, tragically, Buster's longtime friend and costar, Joe Roberts, suffered a heart attack in midproduction. He was able to return and finish filming his segments; however, a month later, he experienced another attack and died soon afterward, a sad ending for the eternally exasperated villain of the majority of Keaton's short films.

SHERLOCK JR.

CREDITS:

Presented by Buster Keaton Productions, Inc.; Distributed by Metro Pictures. *Producer:* Joseph M. Schenck; *Director:* Buster Keaton; *Script:* Clyde Bruckman, Jean Havez, and Joseph Mitchell; *Photography:* Elgin Lessley and Byron Houck; *Costumes:* Clare West; *Technical Director:* Fred Gabourie. *Release Date:* April 21, 1924. *Length:* five reels.

Buster's dreams of becoming a famous detective are interrupted by his theater manager boss in *Sherlock Jr.*, one of the most visually exciting and innovative films ever made.

(*Opposite page*) Buster performs the most spectacular stunt of his film career in the breathtaking climax to *Our Hospitality*.

Buster returns to his unglamorous job as a movie projectionist, unaware that he soon will become the hero of the film he is about to project in *Sherlock Jr.*

CAST:

Buster Keaton (*The Boy/Sherlock Jr.*), Kathryn McGuire (*The Girl*), Ward Crane (*The Rival*), Joe Keaton (*The Girl's Father*), Erwin Connelly, Jane Connelly, Ford West, George Davis, John Patrick, Ruth Holley, Horace Morgan.

After the languidly paced *Our Hospitality,* in which Buster introduced a much more subtle and realistic approach to the humor, his next feature, *Sherlock Jr.,* seems like a return to his previous slapstick, gag-infested style of comedy. The main reason for making the film was to provide him the opportunity to stage some of his most outlandish, seemingly impossible gags, and the only way he felt he could get away with these stunts was to set the action in a dream, a format he'd used often previously. However, here for the first time Buster lets the audience know *beforehand* that the wild, absurd goings-on are happening in a dream.

Sherlock Jr. could be viewed as a companion piece to his most visually dazzling short, *The Playhouse,* whose innovative multiple images of Buster performing various stunts were also staged within a dream.

The "dream" Buster approaches the movie screen and prepares to enter its artificial reality in one of the most visually dynamic segments ever put on film. Also pictured is Buster's real-life father, Joe, who, along with Buster and the rest of the cast members, play dual roles.

Buster as the master "dream" detective, Sherlock Jr.!

The two films also share the theme of artificial realities being more vibrantly real and exciting than reality itself. With *The Playhouse*, Buster used the world of vaudeville to illustrate his fascination with illusion and how theater life is totally dependent on making its audiences believe in a world where the normal laws of the universe don't apply. With *Sherlock Jr.*, Buster uses the artificial reality of film to illustrate the same principle, that what we see and feel and relate to on-screen constitutes a false world that relies on illusion for its potency.

Sherlock Jr. begins as a simple boy/girl/rival tale. Buster plays a movie theater projectionist who longs to be a brilliant detective in the manner of Sherlock Holmes. In love with a pretty girl, played by Kathryn McGuire, whom he wants to marry, he has a rival in Ward Crane, who one day sneaks into Kathryn's house while she is entertaining Buster and steals her father's pocket watch. Later, when the theft is discovered, Buster pulls out his trusty book, *How to Be a Detective*, and attempts to solve the case of the missing watch to impress Kathryn and woo her away from Ward. However, Ward has arranged it so that Buster is accused of the theft and is banned from Kathryn's house by her father (Joe Keaton).

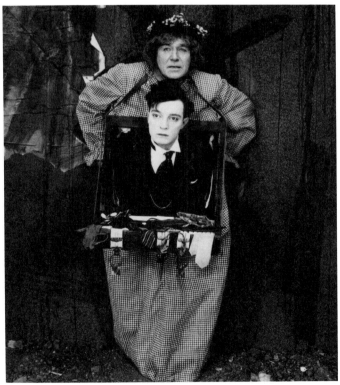

Sherlock Jr.: Buster pops out of his assistant's stomach in just one of several startling vaudeville magic tricks he stages without the use of camera trickery.

A crushed and dejected Buster returns to his projectionist job, and while the movie unreels, he falls asleep. Buster dreams a ghostly image of himself which rises out of his body and attempts to enter the movie on-screen. The plot to the film-within-a-film, *Hearts and Pearls, or the Lounge Lizard's Lost Love,* closely parallels Buster's own predicament with his girl: a sophisticated cad has stolen a pearl necklace from his girlfriend's father. As Buster's ghostly image watches the action, Kathryn, her father, her father's handyman, and the nefarious Ward all assume the roles of the characters in the film. At that point, the "dream" Buster marches down into the theater, past the audience and the musicians accompanying the film's action, and walks right into the screen.

What follows is one of the most amazing scenes of the cinema, a variation of one from Keaton's early Arbuckle short *Moonshine,* in which the film medium itself suddenly becomes an active participant in the action. Entering the screen, Buster finds himself locked outside the house where the movie action takes place. After pounding on the front door to no avail, he turns to leave, and the film abruptly cuts to a garden with Buster caught in midstep walking off a bench. As he attempts to rest on the bench, the film suddenly cuts again and he ends up sitting down in the middle of a busy street. Picking himself up and walking away, he nearly walks off a mountain cliff when the film jumps once more. As he peers over the cliff, the film cuts to a jungle scene with Buster looking into the face of a lion, and as the lion stands up, he tries to saunter nonchalantly away and ends up in a hole in the middle of a desert. Confused, Buster sits down on a small sand hill and suddenly finds himself on a rock in the ocean. He stands up and dives into the water, but the film cuts in midjump and he ends up stuck headfirst in a snowbank. Pulling himself out of the snow, he leans against a tree, and suddenly he's back in the garden falling over the bench again as the film cuts for the final time and fades out.

This stunning, magical sequence is flawlessly edited to give the impression of Buster being thrown from one random scene to the next, getting the full treatment from an outraged film world using its unique abilities to teach him a lesson. Precise measurements—achieved with the use of a surveyor's instru-

The master detective sails off triumphantly into the sunset with leading lady Kathryn McGuire in the final moments of the film-within-a-film segment from *Sherlock Jr.*

100

ments—of his body's position and his distance from the camera were worked out along with special lighting techniques to achieve the illusion of Buster's being at the mercy of the film medium.

After the fade-out on Buster lying confused and dazed in the garden, he returns after assuming the role of a cinematic character, brilliant detective Sherlock Jr. The rest of the film contains one amazing illusion after another coupled with astounding stunt work by Buster as he attempts to solve the mystery of the stolen pearls. In one stunt, Buster is riding on the handlebars of a runaway motorcycle, unaware that the vehicle is driverless. He swerves through traffic, breezes over the tops of two trucks passing through a narrow opening in a bridge, zooms through the middle of the exploding halves of a dynamited log, proceeds through the middle of a large mechanical contraption, and misses by inches a moving train before finally crashing into the secret hideout of the nefarious Ward and rescuing Kathryn from the clutches of one of Ward's cronies.

Buster also includes several eye-popping magician's tricks. In one, he escapes from Ward's hideout by leaping through a window rigged with a hoop containing women's clothing and then casually strolling down the street dressed as an old lady while Ward and his men pass him by. Moments later, he once again escapes from the bad guys by leaping through the stomach of his assistant and a wall behind the assistant, who then casually walks away as if nothing unusual has occurred.

In the end, Buster/Sherlock solves the mystery of the stolen pearls while the real Kathryn solves the mystery of the disappearing watch and confronts the real Buster in his projection booth to ask for his forgiveness. Taking cues from the couple on the screen, Buster woos her back with a hug and a kiss.

Much has been written about *Sherlock Jr.* and its amazing illusionary stunts, with many rightfully praising it as a brilliant exploration of the unique powers of the film medium. However, most fail to mention Buster's original intention, which was to use the cinematic dream format to show off illusionary tricks that he had learned in vaudeville. Buster goes to great lengths to present the stunts as if a magician were performing them onstage. Sometimes he uses theatrically inspired cutaway sets to ensure that all of the action will be viewed without relying on film's ability to cut from one scene to the next and thus fake a gag. Also, eternally proud of his athletic abilities, Buster always makes sure that his audience knows that that's him on-screen doing those amazing stunts: riding pell-mell on the handlebars of a runaway motorcycle, jumping off the tops of buildings, and running along the top of a moving train. (While performing the latter stunt, Buster fractured his neck.)

Although Buster has justifiably been called the most cinematic of the great silent comedians as well as one of the most accomplished film directors of his time, his moviemaking style and his view of the world are a direct reflection of his years as a vaudeville performer surrounded by magicians, tricksters, acrobats, comedians, all of them entrancing, amazing illusionists. That he was able to adapt this theatrically inspired view of the world to the cinematic universe is proof of his ability to master various forms of artistic expression in order to share his beguiling worldview with others.

In his book, *The Day the Laughter Stopped,* David Yallop credits Roscoe Arbuckle as both the scenarist and director of *Sherlock Jr.* Buster admitted in his autobiography that he hired Arbuckle to direct the film, but had to ease him out after he proved too belligerent, still suffering from the aftereffects of his blacklisting. Since the film is so thoroughly dominated by Keaton's distinctive style and filled with his favorite themes, it's safe to assume his was the main creative force.

THE NAVIGATOR

CREDITS:

Presented by Buster Keaton Productions, Inc.; Distributed by Metro Pictures. *Producer:* Joseph M. Schenck; *Directors:* Buster Keaton and Donald Crisp; *Script:* Clyde Bruckman, Joseph Mitchell, and Jean Havez; *Photography:* Elgin Lessley and Byron Houck; *Electrician:* Denver Harmon; *Technical Director:* Fred Gabourie. *Release Date:* October 13, 1924. *Length:* six reels.

CAST:

Buster Keaton (*Rollo Treadway*), Kathryn McGuire (*Betsy O'Brien*), The Steamship *Buford* (*The Steamship* Navigator), Fredrick Vroom (*John O'Brien*), Clarence Burton and H. M. Clugston (*Spies*), Noble Johnson (*Cannibal Chief*).

The Navigator, Buster's second-favorite feature and his second most financially successful, firmly established his reputation as a major filmmaking force. A companion piece to his short *The Boat,* the film takes place almost exclusively on a huge steamship, The *Buford* (here called the *Navigator*). Only after he had already paid $25,000 to lease the ship did Keaton and his loyal gagmen conceive of a story on which to base the action on board. Obviously inspired by the prop

Buster poses with one of his most famous costars, an aimlessly drifting steamship, in *The Navigator*. The film, one of his personal favorites, is considered among the funniest, most inventive comedies ever made.

Buster drops in on Kathryn McGuire after spending several hilariously frantic moments looking for one another on board *The Navigator*.

itself, Buster came up with some of his best gags for a feature film, ones that raised the art of screen comedy to new heights.

Buster plays Rollo Treadway, a spoiled, rich socialite modeled after his Bertie "The Lamb" Van Alstyne character from *The Saphead*. Glancing out his bedroom window one morning and noticing a pair of newlyweds driving past his mansion on their way to honeymoon bliss, he casually turns to his butler and announces, "I think I'll get married. Today." Rollo tells his butler to book him and his bride-to-be on a honeymoon cruise leaving in the morning for Honolulu. Then Rollo gets ready to propose to his sweetheart, Betsy O'Brien (Kathryn McGuire), whose father is a shipping magnate and the former owner of the steamship *Navigator*.

When Rollo meets with Betsy and blurts out that he wants to get married immediately, she chastises him for his seemingly frivolous attitude toward marriage and sends him on his way. A dejected Rollo ends up alone on his honeymoon cruise. He also ends up on the wrong ship, the *Navigator*. While it is still docked,

Betsy boards it in search of her father. Suddenly, a gang of foreign spies intent on destroying the ship appears and captures Betsy's dad. The spies then cut the ship from its mooring and watch as it drifts out to sea, the two hapless socialites still on board and unaware of each other's presence.

When the two awake the next morning, the real fun begins. In one of the most cleverly staged comedy moments on film, Rollo and Betsy, still not realizing the other is aboard, finally become aware of another human presence and begin to explore the ship, first calmly, then with more determination, finally racing around the decks, upstairs, downstairs, through passageways, running faster and faster, all the time just barely missing sight of one another. Eventually, Betsy tires of her frenzied search and stops to rest below deck on a wooden plank. Rollo, meanwhile, pauses next to a funnel-shaped air vent above deck, loses his top hat, then his footing, and falls inside the vent. The scene cuts back to Betsy, who notices the top hat fall out of the vent in the ceiling and land right next to her, followed shortly by Rollo. As they confront one an-

The two aren't so sure they are the only occupants of the supposedly deserted ship.

Buster is not exactly overjoyed at the idea of becoming a deep-sea diver in *The Navigator*.

other and recognition registers on their faces, Rollo calmly asks, "Will you marry me?"

The socialites struggle to adapt, first making a mess trying to cook breakfast in a galley better suited to feed hundreds than two sheltered twits. While Betsy uses ocean water to make coffee, Rollo attempts to open a small can of food with a hatchet. Later he boils—and breaks—a batch of eggs in a tub of water the size of Rhode Island.

Their gourmet breakfast is interrupted when they spot another ship approaching, and Rollo lowers a lifeboat over the side to row after it while towing the *Navigator,* one of the most extreme—and outrageously effective—examples of Buster's fondness for sight gags based on disproportionate sizes. Rollo's lifeboat sinks and Betsy attempts a rescue, followed by her falling overboard and Rollo rescuing her.

As they adjust to the rolling motion of the ship and the sights caused by their vivid imaginations, doors slam and objects fall. In Betsy's cabin, an evil-looking portrait of the former captain stares at her, finally prompting her to throw it overboard, where it ends up dangling outside Rollo's porthole and scaring him out of his wits. To investigate the creaky goings-on, the two inadvertently light Roman candles. And when they try sleeping in chairs on the top deck, Betsy nearly ends up overboard as her chair rocks toward the railing.

Eventually, the two adjust to their surroundings with the help of some wonderfully eccentric, Buster-designed contraptions, some of them resembling the culinary devices from *The Scarecrow* and the mechanical gadgets from *The Electric House.* Rollo and Betsy finally sight land, but it turns out to be an island inhabited by cannibals. Attempting to prevent the ship from drifting toward the island, they inadvertently cause it to run aground and spring a leak. Realizing their only chance for survival is to fix the leak in the ship's hull, Betsy persuades Rollo to venture overboard in a diving suit for a patch-up. The terrified Rollo dons a huge, cumbersome diving suit and goes into the water using a saw, a hammer, a lobster, and a swordfish as tools. (Of course, Buster insisted on doing all of his own underwater stunts, which were actually filmed with great difficulty in the crystal

103

The Navigator: Kathryn helps drain a thoroughly waterlogged Buster after his comically successful attempt to rescue her from island savages.

Buster helps *The Navigator*'s codirector Donald Crisp put the finishing touches on one of the film's cannibal extras. Keaton later claimed that he reshot the segments directed by Crisp.

clear—and icy cold—waters of Lake Tahoe over a grueling four-week period.)

As Rollo struggles below the water, the cannibals attack the ship and capture Betsy, cutting off Rollo's air hose in the process. He stumbles off toward land, finally emerging from the water just as the cannibals are preparing to molest poor Betsy. However, the frightening—and uproariously funny—sight of this strange sea god rising out of the water and doing a threatening shimmy dance as it slowly staggers toward land is too much for the savages and they run screaming into the jungle.

The two veteran seafarers make it back to the ship and thwart another attack with Roman candles and a pesky toy cannon. Unfortunately, another wave of attacking savages finally boards the ship, and Rollo and Betsy leap into the water, choosing death by drowning over death by barbecuing. As the two tenderly embrace and sink, they are saved by a surfacing submarine! After clambering on board the craft, Betsy gives Rollo a quick hug and kiss, which send him swooning against a stabilizing lever, causing the sub to roll over and over (a sight gag adapted from *The Boat*).

The Navigator is truly an inspired comedy, arguably Keaton's funniest film. The gags are all top-notch, seamlessly integrated into the lively action and breakneck pace. Unbelievably the gag that Buster deemed the film's best, an underwater stunt where he directs traffic when a school of fish interrupts his ship repair efforts, never made it to the screen. Because the joke came when Betsy is captured by the cannibals, Buster realized it interfered with the dramatic flow of the film and ended up cutting it.

Buster's acting in *The Navigator* is superb, easily one of his best performances, filled with subtly expressive facial and physical mannerisms. He and Kathryn McGuire make an excellent sparring couple, topping Buster's other encounter with a strong-willed female equal, Phyllis Haver from *The Balloonatic*. Obviously, the film deserves its designation as one of the best comedies ever made.

SEVEN CHANCES

CREDITS:

Presented by Buster Keaton Productions, Inc.; Distributed by Metro-Goldwyn. *Producer:* Joseph M. Schenck; *Director:* Buster Keaton; *Script:* Jean Havez, Clyde Bruckman, and Joseph Mitchell, based on the play by Roi Cooper Megrue; *Photography:* Elgin Lessley and Byron Houck; *Electrician:*

Denver Harmon; *Technical Director:* Fred Gabourie. *Release Date:* six reels.

CAST:

Buster Keaton (*Jimmie Shannon*), Ruth Dwyer (*Mary Brown*), T. Roy Barnes (*Billy Meekin*), Snitz Edwards (*The Attorney*), Frankie Raymond (*Mrs. Brown*), Jules Cowles (*Hired Hand*), Erwin Connelly (*The Minister*), Jean Arthur (*The Receptionist*), Loro Bara, Marion Harlan, Hazel Deane, Pauline Toler, Judy King, Eugenie Burkette, Edna Hammon, Barbara Pierce, Connie Evans, Rosalind Mooney.

Buster's least-favorite feature film, *Seven Chances,* is actually a delightfully funny and inventive work, totally undeserving of his disparaging opinion. He disliked it because his producer, Joe Schenck, bought the rights to the play on which the film is based without consulting him. Keaton and his writers were forced to adapt the play to fit his style of cinematic humor, a setup he thoroughly resented, but nevertheless, one that didn't prevent him from creating an excellent film.

Buster plays Jimmie Shannon, a financial broker on the verge of bankruptcy due to a disastrous deal with an investor who has proven to be a professional embarrassment. Unless he and his business partner, Billy Meekin (T. Roy Barnes), can raise money quickly, the firm will fold.

When an attorney (Snitz Edwards, one of Buster's favorite subordinate players) shows up in their office, Jimmie and Billy mistake him for a legal representative with an arrest summons. The partners sneak off to the local country club, but the attorney follows and finally presents his papers. The document is a will from Jimmie's grandfather leaving him $7 million. However, before the two have a chance to celebrate Jimmie's good fortune, the attorney informs Jimmie that, in order to inherit the money, he must be married before seven P.M. on the day of his twenty-seventh birthday. Naturally, his twenty-seventh birthday turns out to be that very day.

First, Jimmie runs off to propose marriage to his sweetheart, Mary (Ruth Dwyer), a proposal he has been trying to make for years. Mary has already been introduced in the film's clever prologue, in which she and Jimmie stand in front of her home as the various seasons of the year pass and title cards announce, with each passing season, Jimmie's desire to tell Mary that he loves her, which, unfortunately, he never does.

Once in Mary's presence, Jimmie bungles his proposal, blurting out that he must marry *some* girl by seven o'clock and it might as well be her. Infuriated by his seemingly heartless marriage proposal, Mary tells him to get lost. Returning to the country club, Jimmie

is persuaded by Billy and the attorney to get busy proposing to other prospective mates. A very reluctant Jimmie glances around the country club and makes a list of seven hopefuls. He then bungles every chance with increasingly disastrous—and hilarious—results.

After the seven chances have been exhausted, Jimmie's pal tells him they should meet at a local church before five P.M. and he will have a suitable fiancée. Billy then places an ad in the newspaper explaining Jimmie's predicament and offering a lucky woman the chance to become the bride of a millionaire. Meanwhile, Jimmie has taken to the streets in search of a prospective bride and ends up proposing to a fourteen-year-old girl, a woman he pulls up next to while driving, one who speaks no English, a barbershop dummy, and finally—in a gag that makes no sense to a modern audience—a famous female impersonator of the time named Julian Eltinge.

Giving up on his search, Jimmie arrives at the designated church, sits in the front pew, and falls asleep, exhausted from the day's activities. As he snoozes, the church slowly begins to fill up with an assortment of women dressed in thrown-together wedding gowns, all of them clutching Billy's newspaper ad. Soon the place is overflowing with hundreds of would-be brides. By the time Jimmie wakes from his nap, he is surrounded by a crush of anxious brides all giving him flirtatious winks. Their efforts, however are cut short when the minister appears, takes one look at the horde, and announces that they are all victims of a practical joke. When the women react with murderous glares, Jimmie dives out the window.

An army of would-be brides chases Jimmie through the streets of Los Angeles, some wanting to marry him, others wanting to tear him apart. (Buster puts on a display of his spectacular running abilities in these scenes.) The stampeding women upset pedestrians, stop traffic, mangle a parade of policemen, disrupt a football game, even chase Jimmie up a huge crane and spin him wildly around. Finally, after hearing from Mary's gardener—who has also been chasing him around town—that Mary has forgiven him and wants to get married, Jimmie escapes into open country on his way back to her, ultimately sliding, tumbling, and rolling down a steep embankment, loosening rocks and boulders, which begin cascading down behind him. Then—in one of Buster's most famous scenes—the cascading rocks slam into bigger ones, causing a massive rockslide that rumbles after him as he races down the hill. Just when he thinks he's safe from this new peril, the women, having taken an alternative route, appear at the foot of the hill and begin to advance on him. Deciding he has a better chance of survival with the rocks, Jimmie turns and begins to

Buster proposes to one of his many bride hopefuls in *Seven Chances*, which he called his least favorite silent feature, a disparaging opinion not shared by most who have seen it. Also pictured are T. Roy Barnes (tall man standing in background) as Buster's business partner, and Snitz Edwards (smiling short man) as an attorney.

Still searching for a bride, Buster asks a stagehand if the beautiful actress featured in the poster is single. The effectiveness of this gag is lost on the modern viewer who more than likely is unfamiliar with the person in the poster, Julian Eltinge, a famous female impersonator of the 1920s.

In the last serene moment before the stormy climax to *Seven Chances*, Buster confronts a church full of brides, all of them eager to become Mrs. Buster and share his seven-million-dollar inheritance.

dodge the boulders as they careen down the hill and ultimately chase off the retreating horde of women. After several more encounters with rocks, trains, and a pesky front gate, Jimmie arrives at Mary's and, with only minutes to spare, marries the girl of his dreams.

Seven Chances' stunning scenes of Buster being pursued by thousands of scorned and angry would-be brides—strongly reminiscent of the famous mass chase scenes from *Cops*—is another superb example of his ability to create strikingly powerful visual images that transcend their immediate context and tap into an archetypal netherworld, affecting the viewer on a more profound level, an intention Buster would flatly deny but is nevertheless true. The film's most famous scene—Buster's encounter with the rockslide—was created totally by accident after he previewed the movie and noticed that the audience let out a guffaw during the segment in which Jimmie/Buster scoots down the hill and knocks loose a couple of rocks. The scene originally faded out there, but because of the strong audience response to it, Buster and his crew reshot it after adding hundreds of artificial rocks to create a massive landslide. Looking at the film, it is hard to believe this scene was the result of a fluke.

Another visual highlight, one reminiscent of the quick-cutting movie-theater segment from *Sherlock Jr.*, is treated as a throwaway gag. When Jimmie runs off to propose to Mary, he jumps into his car, parked outside the country club, then sits unmoving while the club slowly dissolves in the background and, as if by magic, transforms into the front of Mary's house. The car has not moved an inch; however, somehow he has driven to Mary's and jumps out to propose to her. The effect—repeated later when Jimmie "drives" back to the country club—is treated so offhandedly that the casual viewer might miss it. However, this scene has the effect of watching a dreamy illusion performed by a master magician, which, quite frankly, is exactly the case.

GO WEST

CREDITS:

Presented by Buster Keaton Productions, Inc.; Distributed by Metro-Goldwyn. *Producer:* Joseph M. Schenck; *Director/Story:* Buster Keaton, assisted by Lex Neal; *Script:* Raymond Cannon; *Photography:* Elgin Lessley and Bert Haines; *Technical Director:* Fred Gabourie. *Release Date:* November 1, 1925. *Length:* seven reels.

In another visually dynamic scene that is both funny and unsettling, Buster is chased through the city streets by a mob of scorned brides in the film's stunning finale.

CAST:

Buster Keaton (*Friendless*), Howard Truesdale (*The Ranch Owner*), Kathleen Myers (*The Ranch Owner's Daughter*), Brown Eyes (*The Cow*), Ray Thompson (*Ranch Foreman*), Joe Keaton, Roscoe Arbuckle, Babe London (*cameos*).

In the summer of 1925, Charlie Chaplin's long-awaited second feature, *The Gold Rush,* was released to great acclaim. Keaton had recently released *Seven Chances* and was looking for a good subject for his next feature. His loyal staff of writers, Bruckman, Havez, and Mitchell, were all unavailable, having been romanced away with lucrative offers from Harold Lloyd and popular sophisticated comic Raymond Griffith. What Buster and his vaudeville friend Lex Neal finally came up with was a takeoff on Chaplin's Tramp character. Obviously inspired by the huge success of *The Gold Rush,* Buster created his own version of the immortal vagabond outcast. However, in his usual playfully ironic style, he made sure his character received mock sympathy and pathos instead of the overly sentimental kind that Chaplin loved to immerse his character in. In addition, Buster made sure his leading lady was one upon whom he could lavish affection and love and, at the same time, send up Chaplin's reverential, cow-eyed approach to his love interests. The result was *Go West,* one of his most slyly satirical films.

Buster plays Friendless, an aimless, eternally displaced drifter who never seems to fit in. He specializes in train travel and, after literally rolling out of his boxcar fortress in a barrel, ends up in the middle of the Arizona desert and trudges off in search of civilization, finding it in the form of a cattle ranch. There he quickly dons some discarded duds and applies for work as a seasoned cowpoke. The ranch owner (Howard Truesdale) takes one look at this diminutive hand with his greenhorn cowboy gait (Buster is uproariously funny as he tries to master the appropriate cowboy walk) and assigns him the task of cow milking rather than cowpunching. Of course, Friendless knows absolutely nothing about milking cows, and when he finally locates the beast, he calmly places his pail underneath the animal's udder. Then he uses his milking stool to sit down in front of the cow and patiently wait for it to do its thing. The entire milking scene is an effective bit of pantomime accentuated by Buster's slow, patient, and eternally blank pan delivery (which, strangely enough, matches the cow's own disaffected look).

After his milking debacle, Friendless encounters another cow among the herd. This is Brown Eyes, the film's heroine, who falls head over udder in love with Friendless after he compassionately removes a pesky pebble from her hoof. When she reciprocates by saving him from being gored by a charging bull, the two lonely critters walk off to the bunkhouse together, friends for life.

Friendless is so smitten with his new love that he can hardly concentrate on his ranch chores. In between bungling his assigned tasks, he rescues Brown Eyes from the branding iron by personally lathering up her backside and shaving the brand into her hide with a razor. Later, when his beloved is attacked by a pair of bulls, Friendless attaches deer antlers to her crown to help her fend off any would-be mashers.

Ranch owner Truesdale, meanwhile, is facing financial ruin if he doesn't immediately ship his cattle to the stockyards. When he decides to move his herd by rail, a hostile neighboring rancher tries to prevent the shipment by sending his hands to hold up the train. A gun battle erupts, resulting in Friendless riding off with the herd as the train's only human passenger. When he arrives at the end of the line, he decides to lead the cattle single-handedly to the stockyards. Friendless and his herd end up wandering through downtown Los Angeles, disrupting traffic, panicking the populace, and overrunning local establishments.

In one of the funniest stampede moments, several head of cattle invade a barbershop. At the sight of the threatening beasts, one barber shaves a wide bald streak in the head of a customer, while another customer (Buster's dad, Joe, in a cameo), oblivious to the intruders, relaxes as two bulls lick the shaving cream off his face. The shop's shoeshine man, attempting to escape from the invading herd, jumps over a partition and ends up on the back of a steer that tears out of the place, giving the man just time enough to grab his hat off the hat rack.

Finally, Friendless looks for something red to attract his wandering herd's attention and finds what he's looking for in a costume shop: a red devil's outfit. Putting it on, he wanders into the street and models it for the herd (Buster's expression here is a wonder to behold; he comes extremely close to losing his concentration and laughing hysterically in front of the camera). Buster sprints off and runs into a group of policemen, one of them grabbing onto his devil's tail as he races by, others latching onto the coattails of their fellow officers until a long line of cops is being pulled down the street by Friendless. Eventually, he catches sight of Brown Eyes and leaps on her back, both of them then galloping down the street in front of the stampeding beasts and ultimately leading them to the stockyards and a triumphantly satisfying fade-out.

Gun-totin' cowpoke Buster helps ranch owner Howard Truesdale and his pretty daughter, Kathleen Myers, round up their herd of cattle in *Go West*.

Keaton, who loved animals and featured many in his films, personally trained the cow he used in *Go West*. In his autobiography, he states, "I never had a more affectionate pet or a more obedient one. After a while, I was able to walk her through doors, in and out of sets, even past bright lights. The only difficulty we had was when I sat down and she tried to climb into my lap." However, while on location in Kingman, Arizona, where most of the film was shot, Brown Eyes went into

Buster and Brown Eyes, his most affectionate leading lady, in *Go West*. The film is a parody of Charlie Chaplin's overly sentimental approach to comedy.

In *Go West*, Buster plays Friendless, a Tramp-like figure who travels through the country by stowing away on freight trains, eternally searching for a place to call home.

"When you say that, SMILE!" commands ranch foreman Ray Thompson when Buster accuses him of cheating at cards in one of the funniest scenes from *Go West*. Here, Keaton takes time out from poking fun at Chaplin's Tramp character to ridicule his own poker-faced screen persona.

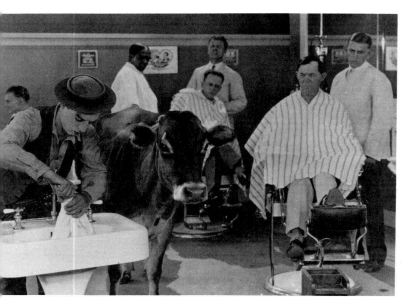

Buster rounds up Brown Eyes from a barbershop during the hysterical cattle stampede climax from *Go West*. Seated in the barber chair (to the far right) is Buster's father, Joe, making a cameo appearance. Buster's blacklisted best friend, Roscoe Arbuckle, also appears briefly in the film.

heat and refused to obey any of Buster's commands, holding up two weeks' worth of shooting until her condition passed.

Although Buster playfully kids Chaplin's Tramp character throughout *Go West,* one of the film's best moments has him lambasting his own screen persona when Friendless and some other ranch hands engage in a game of poker. When Friendless notices the dealer feeding himself cards from the bottom of the deck and accuses him of cheating, the steely-eyed dealer pulls a gun and says, "When you say that, *smile!*" Buster as Friendless pauses to give the audience just enough time to let the ironic implications of this request sink in, then gives his adversary one of his best blank-pan expressions before finally pushing up the corners of his mouth with two fingers. The scene is a prime example of Buster's "nothing is sacred, least of all me" attitude toward comedy.

Go West is Buster's last silent feature in which he appears in his trademark costume of slap shoes, baggy pants, vest, and flat hat, although his porkpie does make brief cameo appearances in the other silent features he made. And look for the blacklisted Roscoe Arbuckle to make a brief if illegal appearance dressed as a woman in a department store during the stampede scene.

BATTLING BUTLER

CREDITS:

Presented by Buster Keaton Productions, Inc.; Distributed by Metro-Goldwyn-Mayer. *Producer:* Joseph M. Schenck; *Director:* Buster Keaton; *Script:* Ballard MacDonald, Paul Gerard Smith, Albert Boasberg, Lex Neal, and Charles Smith, based on the musical comedy by Stanley Brightman, Austin Melford, Philip Brabham, Walter L. Rosemont, and Douglas Furber; *Photography:* Dev Jennings and Bert Haines; *Electrician:* Ed Levy; *Technical Director:* Fred Gabourie. *Release Date:* September 19, 1926. *Length:* seven reels.

CAST:

Buster Keaton (*Alfred Butler*), Sally O'Neil (*The Mountain Girl*), Snitz Edwards (*Martin, the Valet*), Francis McDonald (*Alfred "Battling" Butler*), Mary O'Brien (*His Wife*), Tom Wilson (*His Trainer*), Eddie Borden (*His Manager*), Walter James (*The Mountain Girl's Father*), Buddy Fine (*The Mountain Girl's Brother*).

Battling Butler earned the most money of any of Keaton's silent features. Ironically, it is now the most obscure feature he made, hardly ever revived at festival showings featuring Buster's films. Although it contains several of his favorite themes and boasts one of his most adept and subtle performances, *Battling Butler* still seems very un-Keatonesque and remains one of his least inspired efforts.

Like *Seven Chances,* the film is based on a stage play, a very successful musical comedy, which was obviously a factor contributing to its phenomenal commercial success. Buster's character, Alfred Butler, could very well be the long-lost older brother of Bertie "The Lamb" Van Alstyne from *The Saphead;* the two characters are very much alike, both effete, sheltered, helpless twits. Alfred is first glimpsed sitting in the elegant living room of the family mansion sipping tea while his mother and his valet, Martin (Snitz Edwards), dote over him. His father finally gets fed up with the sight of his helpless son hanging around the house all day and convinces him to go on a hunting trip in the mountains, thinking the experience might help make a man out of him.

It turns out that Alfred's idea of roughing it isn't much different from his everyday living. His camping equipment is practically the entire contents of his father's house. He lounges in a spacious tent, sleeps in a king-size bed, has a suit for every occasion in his massive portable closet, and has the eternally faithful Martin fix his gourmet meals and carry his sporting equipment when the two venture into the countryside.

Buster as Alfred has never looked so sedate, so passive, so . . . twitty. Here, the Stone Face placidity takes over his entire body.

During a hunting jaunt, Alfred and Martin walk by every type of animal in the forest before finally shooting at a chicken and nearly hitting a passing mountain girl (Sally O'Neil). The girl is a feisty sprite and tells off the two, resulting in Alfred's falling madly in love with her on the spot. Later, Alfred meets the girl while duck hunting in a rowboat and, after sinking his tiny craft, politely tips his hat to her while floating neck deep in the water as she paddles by in her own boat. Determined to woo the girl, Alfred has Martin arrange a formal proposal and sends the diminutive valet off to meet with the girl and her family. When Martin confronts the girl and her beefy father (Walter James) and brother (Buddy Fine), the two lugs scoff at the idea of her marrying a weakling like Alfred. Martin, remembering an item in the morning paper, blurts out that his boss is none other than the famous Alfred "Battling" Butler (Francis McDonald), the celebrated boxer scheduled for a championship fight later in the week. In truth, the two Alfred Butlers have only their names in common. However, the girl's father and brother end up believing her beau to be the prospective champ and enthusiastically embrace their future in-law.

Assuring his boss that the real Battling Butler will be defeated in his bid for the championship, Martin boards a train with Alfred headed for the boxing arena, where they watch the dynamic Battling soundly beat his opponent, prompting Alfred to turn to his valet and matter-of-factly proclaim, "I'm champion." Alfred decides to return to the mountains and confess his masquerade to the girl, knowing that he will lose her. But arriving by train, he is given a hero's reception with banners, marching bands, and adoring fans. Before Alfred has time to say one word (actually he does say two words: "I do"), he is married.

After the wedding reception, Alfred, to keep up his masquerade, leaves with Martin for Battling's training camp where they plan to hide out until after the next fight. Before departing, Alfred orders his new bride to stay behind, telling her he never wants her to see him as the fighting brute that he really is. She disobeys, however, and follows. When she shows up, Alfred has already gotten into deeper hot water with the real Battling Butler, who, after several mix-ups, believes Alfred is having an affair with his wife (Mary O'Brien). Soon Battling tells his trainer (Tom Wilson) he's tired of men flirting with his wife and that if this other guy wants to impersonate him so badly, let him train for the fight. And so begins Alfred's boxing impersonation in earnest.

Finally, after three weeks of disastrous training—a segment filled with only mildly amusing boxing gags, the best involving his struggling to follow his trainer's commands while being unmercifully pummeled by his sparring partner—Alfred arrives at the arena to face his opponent, the Alabama Murderer. As Alfred cowers in his dressing room, the arena crowd soon begins chanting, "Butler! Butler!" and he looks outside to see the real Battling Butler standing triumphantly over the comatose Alabama Murderer in the center of the ring. The trainer then reveals the truth to Alfred, telling him that they never had any intention of his fighting and ruining Battling's career.

The most uncomical finale to any of Buster's features follows as Battling corners Alfred in his dressing room and proceeds to slug him into submission. Alfred tries to escape by running for the door, but when he opens it, his wife stands in the doorway, stunned at the sight of her terrified husband. Then, after the camera holds briefly on a touching close-up of her, Alfred explodes in a frenzy of violence, landing blow after blow on the bewildered Battling, who staggers back to regain his composure.

Battling's trainers finally show up and carry the near-comatose champ away, and Alfred tells his wife the truth. Thinking that their marriage is now over, he is stunned by her response: "I'm glad," resulting in a touching fade-out.

In many ways, *Battling Butler* would seem to be a perfect Keaton vehicle with its well-developed mistaken identity theme and elaborately amusing mix-ups cleverly handled. Also, Buster is playing one of his favorite character types and is thoroughly convincing as the elegant, upper-class twerp who ultimately goes through a dynamic transformation in the film's finale. Most of the gags are too sedate, though, lacking the Keaton sparkle and outrageousness. One of the best low-key scenes has a subtle, cinematic touch when Buster as Alfred drives off for Battling's training camp after saying good-bye to his wife, whose face remains framed in the back window of the car as it pulls away, creating a beautiful cameo effect.

What is totally surprising is the film's brutal—and very realistically staged—climax, played for all of its dramatic punch, a total departure from the original play, which lacked the final violent encounter between Alfred and Battling. Buster rightfully felt that the play's ending was an anticlimax and robbed the audience of a dramatic conclusion that the rest seemed to be leading up to.

Buster was once quoted as saying that *Battling Butler* was his favorite film. The source of this unbelievable assertion is someone who would seem to

Battling Butler: Buster congratulates the brutal Battling Butler (Francis McDonald), hoping to appease the fighter's wrath, in the film that was the most financially successful Keaton silent feature.

Battling Butler (Francis McDonald) wants to discuss a little personal matter with Buster, something that has to do with Mrs. Butler's (Mary O'Brien) black eye. Also pictured is Sally O'Neil, who plays Buster's wife.

know better: Keaton's business partner, Raymond Rohauer. Since Buster was also once quoted as saying that the "falling house" stunt from *Steamboat Bill, Jr.*—one of his most dangerous and spectacular stunts—was faked by filming the scene in reverse, I believe that Rohauer's leg was being firmly yanked at the time.

Buster swears off fighting and regains the admiration of his wife in the touching final moments of *Battling Butler*, as Martin, his manservant, shares in his glory.

Battling Butler gives Buster a few boxing tips, like how to enter the ring without tripping over the ropes.

In the startling conclusion, the vengeful Battling Butler pummels Buster unmercifully until Buster catches sight of his wife. Then, in the most purely dramatic finale to any of his films, Buster transforms into an even more brutal fighter than Battling and beats the fighter senseless. Snitz Edwards plays Buster's faithful manservant, Martin.

THE GENERAL

CREDITS:

Presented by Buster Keaton Productions, Inc.; Distributed by United Artists. *Producer:* Joseph M. Schenck; *Director/Script:* Buster Keaton and Clyde Bruckman, based on the book *The Great Locomotive Chase* by William Pittinger; *Adaptation:* Al Boasberg and Charles Smith; *Photography:* Dev Jennings and Bert Haines; *Technical Director:* Fred Gabourie; *Electrician:* Denver Harmon; *Editors:* J. Sherman Kell and Buster Keaton; *Assistant Editor:* Harry Barnes; *Wardrobe and Makeup:* Bennie Hubbel, J. K. Pitcairn, and Fred C. Ryle. *Release Date:* February 5, 1927. *Length:* eight reels.

CAST:

Buster Keaton (*Johnnie Gray*), Marion Mack (*Annabelle Lee*), Glen Cavender (*Captain Anderson*), Jim Farley (*General Thatcher*), Frederick Vroom (*A Southern General*), Charles Smith (*Mr. Lee*), Frank Barnes (*His Son*), Joe Keaton, Mike Donlin, Tom Nawn (*Union Generals*), Ray Thomas, Bud Fine, Jimmy Bryant, Red Rial, Ross McCutcheon, Red Thompson, Ray Hanford, Charles Phillips, Al Hanson, Tom

Moran, Anthony Harvey (*Raiders*), Edward Hearn (*Union Officer*), Frank Hagney (*Recruiter*).

> Buster Keaton shows signs of vaulting ambition in *The General;* he appears to be attempting to enter the "epic" class. That he fails to get across is due to the scantiness of his material as compared with the length of his films; he has also displayed woefully bad judgments in deciding just where and when to stop.
>
> —*From* Life *magazine review, February 24, 1927, by Robert E. Sherwood*

> A comedian's qualities are not at all what an epic wants. An epic wants an event of great scale and significance, one rooted in a historical moment, a moment so representative that it takes on mythological status. And it wants a hero at its center who certainly need not be perfect but whose high aspirations are matched by his capabilities. It is an elevated form, the epic as such, and it is a deeply serious one.
>
> —*From* The Silent Clowns *by Walter Kerr*

> Comedy is a serious business.
>
> —*Buster Keaton*

If someone wanted to know just who the real Buster Keaton was, what kind of personality he had, what he was really like as a flesh-and-blood human being, one need only watch *The General.* Although hardly autobiographical, being based on an actual incident from the Civil War, it is Keaton's most personal film, embodying his personality, his essence, his spirit, more than any other one he ever made, more than any interview he ever gave, more than any book ever written about his work or his life.

The essence of Buster Keaton is understatement, vividly exemplified by his stolidly handsome, deadpan puss. The fact that he doesn't smile in his films, that his face remains gravely serious throughout every imaginable—and unimaginable—situation, is not merely a gimmick created for the screen. It is his artistic philosophy. *The General* is an eight-reel close-up of Buster's face. Every inch of the film is fabulously rich, emotionally understated brilliance. Because Buster was so successful at downplaying the film's subtly dazzling attributes, it proved a box-office flop and, ironically, contributed to his losing his artistic independence.

Filmed in Cottage Grove, Oregon, in the summer of 1926, *The General* was Buster's favorite film and is now considered one of the greatest, most expertly directed and beautifully photographed cinema works. Buster plays Johnnie Gray, a competent and well-liked railroad engineer from 1860s Georgia. He has two loves in his life: his train, called The General, and his girlfriend, pretty Southern belle Annabelle Lee (Marion Mack). When war breaks out between the states, Johnnie tries to enlist but is turned down because the recruiter believes him to be more valuable as a civilian train engineer than a Confederate foot soldier. However, because the recruiter doesn't tell Johnnie why he was turned down, his sweetheart brands him a coward and tells him she wants nothing more to do with him until he is in uniform. A year later, Union spies steal Johnnie's train—with Annabelle aboard—intending to disrupt Southern communication and supply lines as they proceed north. Johnnie pursues the raiders on another train and recaptures The General and rescues his sweetheart. He returns to Confederate lines, warns the troops of an impending attack by the Union army, and after the Southern troops repel the advancing Northerners, Johnnie is hailed a hero.

This simple story, dramatized in painstakingly accurate historical detail, seems tailor-made for Buster, who enjoyed playing characters first perceived as failures but who ultimately triumph. Like other films of his, the story and gags are built around a major prop, this time a train. It is also a chase film, another Keatonesque ingredient. Here, though, there is a unique emphasis to the film. All of his others focus squarely on comedy, on creating humor. Here the emphasis is profoundly on Buster's character.

Buster as Johnnie is never presented as a bumbling incompetent. He acts somewhat bewildered at times, misinterprets the causes for various incidents, and has a habit of becoming intensely involved with minor details that distract him from more dramatic developments. (The most extreme example: Johnnie's energetic wood-chopping on his speeding train, causing his failure to notice both a Confederate and a Union battalion parade behind him, a brilliantly directed scene.) From the beginning of the film to its conclusion, however, Buster's character is always strongly in command, fiercely efficient, galvanized into action by the desire to recapture his stolen train. His Johnnie Gray is the central theme of the film. Everything else about it—the story, the setting, the gags, the train, the way it is directed, photographed, edited—is a reflection of this character.

Buster shows off his beloved train to some young admirers in *The General*, the film he called his personal favorite and one that is now considered among the screen's greatest.

Buster as Johnnie is nearly always filmed on the move, running, jumping, stoking the fire, leaping off his train either to clear the track or, later, to sabotage it. Although some of his actions are eccentric—using one railroad tie to catapult another off the track while riding on the front of the moving train—he is dynamically efficient. His beloved train is never presented as merely a gag toy/prop. It is, instead, an extension of his dynamic character.

His efficient, "always in control" approach to his character is vividly illustrated by the way he treats his leading lady—strictly as a prop, a focal point for his gags, ridiculing her inefficient, bungling actions, at one point stuffing her in a potato sack, throwing her inside a supply car, stepping on her as he digs her out of her hiding place, then carrying her around like a rag doll and later drenching her with water pouring from a huge spout. This is where the misconception that Buster treated all of his leading ladies as props originates. However, only in *The General* does he actually treat his love interest thusly. Here, as never before, Buster is the master of his swiftly moving universe, and his girl better conform to the laws of this universe or face ridicule.

Probably the most impressive aspect about the film is how Buster uses the medium to faithfully capture the time period. It wasn't until after seeing the film several times that I realized how many tracking shots there are. For easily 70 percent of the time, the camera is moving, recording the action from the point of view of a speeding train, either on board riding with Buster or on a parallel track. Somehow, Keaton incorporated the remarkably sophisticated tracking shots—all of them beautifully composed, maximizing efficiency and presenting the action from the most dramatic points of view—so well into the film's overall atmosphere and action that the anachronistic presence of a twentieth-century moving picture camera on an elaborately recreated nineteenth-century setting is completely unobtrusive.

Keaton's understated cinematic approach to his epic story is best illustrated by the climactic train wreck scene in which a Union train, The Texas, crashes into a river from a burning bridge. This single scene cost $42,000 to stage, one of the most expensive single shots of the silent film era. However, Buster crashed the train not to impress his audience with epic grandeur, but to record the reaction of the Union commander's face as he stares in stunned disbelief at the result of his gross misjudgment in ordering the train across the bridge. Keaton built a bridge across a river, then sent an actual full-size locomotive to a spectacular death just so he could get a gag reaction shot from a bit player. No wonder the film was a financial disaster.

Buster and friends are off to visit Buster's second love, Annabelle, played by Marion Mack. Filmed in Cottage Grove, Oregon, *The General* recreates the Civil War period in painstakingly accurate detail.

Buster attempts to remove various obstacles from the tracks in his efforts to recapture his beloved train from Union spies.

Buster dutifully chops up firewood for his train, totally oblivious to the Union troops marching behind him, in one of the many visual highlights of *The General*.

Buster overhears Union battle plans while he hides in a house occupied by the enemy in yet another stunning scene from *The General*. Also pictured are Buster's father, Joe (far left), and Glen Cavender (second from right), both playing Union officers.

In the most expensive single shot of the silent film era, the "Texas" chugs across a bridge set afire by Buster, then crashes into the river below. Buster wrecked the train in order to get a funny reaction shot from the Union officer who had pronounced the bridge safe enough to cross.

Buster clowns around in the wreckage of the "Texas." The wrecked train remained a tourist attraction for years until it was finally carted off and used for scrap metal during World War II.

When I think about how *The General* was initially received and how that first impression changed over the years, I am reminded of a two-panel cartoon I saw many years ago in a humor magazine. In the first panel, a rugged-looking mountain-man type lies on the ground playing with a bunch of flat, domino-shaped pebbles, piling them on top of one another. In the second, a group of tiny humans in modern dress stares up in awe at this massive construction of rocks. The rocks are in fact Stonehenge; the man in the first panel is actually an ancient giant who, years ago, had stopped briefly to play, leaving an offhanded masterpiece behind before passing into oblivion.

It took the world nearly forty years to stumble upon the magnificence of *The General*. Yet, like Buster himself, its deadpan brilliance and subtle beauty had always been there, created by a cinematic giant who had paused briefly to play one summer long ago before passing into a dark period of personal and professional oblivion.

COLLEGE

CREDITS:

Presented by Buster Keaton Productions, Inc.; Distributed by United Artists. *Producer:* Joseph M. Schenck; *Director:* James W. Horne; *Script:* Carl Harbaugh and Bryan Foy; *Photogra-*

Buster is given a friendly reception by college dean Snitz Edwards and a not-so-friendly one by his fellow rommates in *College*. Also pictured is Harold Goodwin (far right) who became a frequent Keaton costar and one of his closest friends.

phy: Bert Haines and Dev Jennings; *Editor:* J. Sherman Kell; *Technical Director:* Fred Gabourie; *Lighting:* Jack Lewis; *Production Supervisor:* Harry Brand. *Release Date:* September 10, 1927. *Length:* six reels.

CAST:

Buster Keaton (*Ronald*), Ann Cornwall (*Mary Haines*), Florence Turner (*Ronald's Mother*), Harold Goodwin (*Jeff, a Rival*), Buddy Mason, Grant Withers (*Jeff's Friends*), Snitz Edwards (*The Dean*), Carl Harbaugh (*Rowing Coach*), Sam Crawford (*Baseball Coach*), Flora Bramley (*Mary's Friend*).

After the box-office disaster of Buster's expensive pet project, *The General,* producer Joe Schenck insisted that his next film be a less ambitious (i.e., cheap) endeavor. To ensure that the budget was kept in line, Schenck hired a supervisor, Harry Brand, to watch over the production, a decision that infuriated Buster. Schenck also appointed a director and a scriptwriter—James Horne and Carl Harbaugh respectively—for both of whom Buster had no respect. Although Buster could hardly know it at the time, Schenck's more active influence on the production was the beginning of the end of Buster's creative control over his films. As a result of all these financial pressures, Buster's *College* is one of his lesser efforts, strongly derivative of one of the biggest box-office successes of the silent film era, Harold Lloyd's *The Freshman,* released in 1925.

Buster plays Ronald, a bookish, bumbling high school senior. During graduation ceremonies, Ronald, the valedictorian, gives a speech praising books and ridiculing sports, not the best topic for a class full of college-bound athletes. During Ronald's address, his cheap suit, drenched from a sudden downpour, begins to shrink, a sight gag made funnier by Buster's expressions of calm, in-control panic.

After the speech, which empties the auditorium, he meets with his high school sweetheart, Mary (Ann Cornwall), who berates him for being so antagonistic toward sports. Realizing he might be losing her to his athletic rival, Jeff (Harold Goodwin), Ronald decides he had better become less of a bookworm and more of a physical specimen. He also decides to follow Mary's and Jeff's example by enrolling at the local college, vowing to support himself by working odd jobs.

After arriving at college and locating his dormitory room (which he shares with Jeff and Jeff's friends), Ronald unpacks his two suitcases, which are stuffed with every type of sports equipment imaginable along with instruction books on baseball, football, and track. Of course, Ronald fails at every sport he attempts. When he tries out for the baseball team and gets up to bat, he stands at the plate rigid, wide-eyed, and clueless as to how to proceed. Then, after being hit in the rear by a fastball, Ronald runs delicately around the bases, passing his fellow base runners, and doing a head-over-heels slide into home, where he is informed that not only is he out but so are the rest of the runners he passed.

Trying to emulate the other athletes in various track and field events, Ronald hurls the discus into the bleachers, trips over each hurdle while sprinting, throws the javelin nearly straight up into the air (it lands only a few feet in front of him), has an altercation with an uncooperative crossbar while attempting to high jump (and then does a headfirst dive over the bar, landing with his head buried in the sawdust), and finally stalls out in midair while pole-vaulting. During all these endeavors, Buster has never looked more childlike; he walks, runs, and holds his body with a stumbling, infantile charm.

While failing miserably at every athletic event, Ronald also messes up two part-time jobs. As a drugstore soda jerk, he tries to maintain a cool, professional demeanor while spilling ice cream and milk, breaking glasses, and drenching customers and himself. Later, after being fired, he slaps on a coat of blackface and lands a position as a waiter at an "All Colored Help" restaurant. There he gets knocked head over heels by

The bookish Buster tries to impress his girl by trying to become a star athlete. Here, he bungles at baseball, forcing his team into a triple play.

rudder, dragging his rear in the water and steering his team to victory.

After the race, Ronald looks for Mary, who had promised that she would attend. Unknown to him, Jeff, who has just flunked out, is holding her hostage in her dormitory. When she manages to distract Jeff long enough to call the locker room, Ronald answers the phone. Racing to the rescue, Buster as Ronald performs all the athletic feats he had failed at before. His babylike run transforms into a jackrabbit sprint as he bounds down the street, hurtling massive hedges, leaping over ponds. He then grabs a clothesline post and vaults into Mary's second-story window. When he confronts the dastardly Jeff, he hurls plates at him like a champion discus thrower, tosses cups like an ace pitcher, bats back objects like a pro slugger. Then when Jeff jumps out the window to escape, Ronald throws a javelinlike stand after him, clipping the masher on the heels and sending him sprawling.

Buster is a failure at everything he tries in *College*, even attemping to disguise himself as a black waiter in an "All Colored Help" restaurant. His use of racial stereotypes in several of his films serves to date his material. In this scene, however, he ridicules himself for behaving like a stereotypical black.

the swinging kitchen door while carrying a cup of coffee and executes a complete backward somersault without spilling a drop. However, some of his black-face makeup comes off on his shirt, and he's chased out of the restaurant by the outraged employees.

Finally, in the film's ineffective climax, Ronald succeeds at something. After being appointed coxswain on the rowing team, he not only barks out rowing commands at his team but also doubles as the boat's

Buster puts on a dazzling display of athletic abilities to save his sweetheart, played by Ann Cornwall, from his dastardly rival in the climax to *College*.

In a sardonic coda to *College*, Buster and Ann are an old, bitter, married couple. The film's final image is of their graveyard headstones. These harsh scenes were most probably prompted by Buster's mounting personal and professional problems.

The final moments of *College* have Ronald and Mary dashing off to the preacher to get married and live happily ever after. No, wait a minute. Buster, obviously somewhat perturbed by the loss of control over his film, tacked on one of his sardonic fade-outs, first showing the couple in a cramped apartment with two small kids frolicking, then cutting to Ronald and Mary as aged, bitter marrieds exchanging recriminations, and finally focusing on two simple headstones in a graveyard. With this sour finale, Keaton seems to have been working out some pent-up frustrations, as if saying, "There, take that, Natalie! Take that, Schenck! Up yours, Harold Lloyd!"

Although *College* was obviously inspired by Lloyd's *The Freshman* and was lorded over by a production supervisor, it is still very much a Buster Keaton film. His distinctive style is fully integrated into the story and the action. It is Buster who makes the soda-jerk scene effective by the way he keeps his face stolidly concrete during his behind-the-counter disasters. It is Buster with his babylike stumblings that empower his athletic atrocities with the playfully inept vigor needed to make them all uproariously funny. And it is Buster's real superb athletic abilities that finally make his transformation from stumbling wimp to physical dynamo a revelation to watch.

In one scene, however, Buster's style doesn't dominate: the pole-vaulting stunt at the film's climax was performed by Olympic athlete Lee Barnes. This is the only documented instance in which Keaton admitted to using a stunt double. He tried to perform the stunt himself but finally gave up and called in a professional, a decision that was said to have depressed him for days.

Despite—or because of—Schenck's tighter production control over *College,* the film ended up making less money than *The General.* Ironically, Buster, who never worried about money matters either on or off screen, was ultimately done in by the almighty dollar.

STEAMBOAT BILL, JR.

CREDITS:

Presented by Buster Keaton Productions, Inc.; Distributed by United Artists. *Producer:* Joseph M. Schenck; *Director:* Charles F. Riesner; *Script:* Carl Harbaugh; *Photography:* Dev Jennings and Bert Haines; *Editor:* J. Sherman Kell; *Assistant Director:* Sandy Roth; *Technical Director:* Fred Gabourie; *Production Supervisor:* Harry Brand. *Release date:* May 1928. *Length:* seven reels.

CAST:

Buster Keaton (*Willie Canfield*), Ernest Torrence ("*Steam-*

Steamboat Bill, Jr.: Buster plays the effete, sheltered son of burly Steamboat Bill (Ernest Torrence, left) in his last independently-produced film. Tom Lewis, as Bill's faithful first mate, looks on.

boat Bill" Canfield), Tom Lewis (*Tom Carter*), Tom McGuire (*John James King*), Marion Byron (*Mary King*), Louise Keaton (*cameo/stunt double*).

Steamboat Bill, Jr. was Keaton's last independently produced feature before his producer, Joe Schenck, dissolved their contract and pushed Buster onto Joe's brother, Nicholas, the president of MGM. Although Buster's name doesn't appear in the film's scripting and directing credits, *Steamboat Bill, Jr.* is his most autobiographical feature, the title character loosely based on his feisty, aggressive father, Joe. It also contains many gags based on his vaudeville experiences as well as a finale inspired by an apocryphal tale from his childhood. Beautifully filmed along northern California's Sacramento River, the film's look and style are strongly reminiscent of his two gorgeously detailed period movies, *Our Hospitality* and *The General*.

As with *College*, Schenck insisted that Buster keep filming costs down and once again assigned Harry Brand to supervise. Ironically, it was Brand who was responsible for *Steamboat Bill, Jr.*'s becoming the most expensive Keaton film ever, exceeding its originally planned $300,000 budget by nearly one-third. The additional expenses were the result of a last-minute change in the climax. Buster and his writers had planned to take advantage of the film's setting, a small riverboat town situated along the Mississippi,

Buster tries to copy his dad's mannerisms and style of dress in *Steamboat Bill, Jr.*, having more luck with the latter than the former.

121

Buster brings a freshly baked loaf of bread packed with special ingredients for his poor, incarcerated father.

dandy collegiate duds, a French beret on his head, a pencil-thin mustache under his nose, and a ukulele under one arm. Bill finally spots Willie at an unfortunate moment while his son is entertaining a baby—the baby hidden from Bill's sight—prancing and dancing around and strumming on his ukulele. This entire segment is a riot to watch, Buster ridiculing male virility with his masterful portrayal of a mincing little twerp.

After a less than tearful reunion between father and son, Bill begins an aggressive but ineffective campaign to turn his sissy offspring into a junior image of himself. In the local hat shop, Bill attempts to find a more manly hat for his son than the floppy beret. Buster as Willie poses in front of a mirror while Bill plops hat after hat on his head and discards each one in rapid succession. The scene's topper gag occurs when Bill fits Willie with a familiar-looking porkpie model and Willie stares at it wide-eyed before flinging it away himself.

Bill's disappointment in his son shifts into high when Willie falls for a pretty former college chum, Mary (Marion Byron), who just happens to be the daughter of Bill's rich adversary, John King (Tom McGuire). King owns most of the town's businesses

After subduing the sheriff with a surprise punch to the stomach, Buster almost succeeds in springing his dad from jail.

and create a finale with a flood. However, when Brand saw documentary footage taken earlier in the year of the real Mississippi flooding its banks and causing many fatalities and much damage, he notified Schenck, who then ordered Buster to rework the climax into something less potentially offensive. Furious at first, Buster finally gave in and came up with an ending that is now recognized as the most inventive and spectacular finale to any of his films.

Buster plays young Willie Canfield, the sheltered, effete son of burly, brawling Mississippi riverboat captain "Steamboat Bill" Canfield (Ernest Torrence). When the film opens, father and son are about to be reunited after many years of separation, Willie having grown up with his mother in the East. Newly graduated from college, Willie sends a telegram to his dad telling him that he will be arriving by train.

While Bill and his first mate, Tom (Tom Lewis), wait at the train station, they speculate on young Willie's appearance, imagining him a muscular giant like his dad. When Willie finally appears, he's dressed in

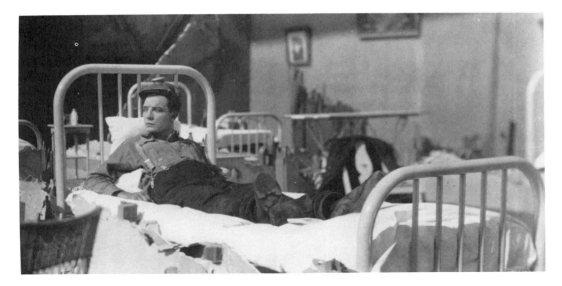

Recovering from his less-than-successful jailbreak attempt, Buster rests in his hospital bed while studying the destructive effects of a cyclone in the amazing climax to *Steamboat Bill, Jr.*

This gag photo shows the near-complete destruction of the riverboat setting by the cyclone. Buster had originally wanted the finale to involve a flood; however, once he hit upon the idea of a cyclone, his creative juices began to flow, resulting in the most spectacular climax to any of his films.

In the most dangerous stunt of his career, Buster stands in the middle of the street while the front of a building crashes down on top of him. The stunt was so potentially hazardous that even director Charles Riesner couldn't bear to watch it being filmed.

Buster ends up saving his girl (Marion Byron), his dad and hers from the effects of the destructive cyclone. However, Buster couldn't save the picture from being a financial flop. Its failure, coupled with the disastrous box-office performances of his two previous films, led to the dissolution of his contract with producer Joseph Schenck.

including the new luxurious steamboat, which he confidently believes will put Bill's old eyesore boat, the *Stonewall Jackson,* to shame and eventually out of business. When Bill catches Willie trying to rendez-vous with Mary after being forbidden to associate with her, he sends his son packing, ordering him to catch the next train back east. However, before Willie boards the train, he sees his father arrested for assaulting King in public and decides to spring Bill from jail.

Willie attempts to deliver to his dad a loaf of bread laden with hammers, saws, and other tools that he believes will help Bill escape. When Bill refuses to accept the loaf, Willie pantomimes that there's more than just dough in the bread. Bill dismisses his son's peculiar actions until finally Willie, out of desperation, rips off the top of the loaf, exposing the tools, then hastily replaces the top before the sheriff notices.

Willie's efforts to spring his dad from jail nearly succeed, but after the sheriff ends up nearly comatose from a sneaky blow to the stomach by Willie, Bill remains behind bars and Willie is carted off to the hospital, suffering a whack to the head by the vengeful lawman.

The rest of the film is literally based on stories and legends from Buster's past. When Buster was growing up in vaudeville, his father, Joe, loved to concoct tales about his famous son as promotional gimmicks to advertise their act. In Joe's favorite story, Buster, as a toddler, gets sucked out of a boardinghouse window by a tornado.

After Buster had been ordered by producer Schenck to change the film's finale, the tornado incident became his creative springboard, with gags created about the near total destruction of the riverboat town by a powerful cyclone. Using cables to tear buildings apart, cranes to lift sets into the air, and airplane engines to produce the cyclone-caliber winds, Buster romped through his disaster-prone set, riding through the studio streets on a runaway hospital bed, then leaning into the wind while dodging wind-propelled machinery, flying houses, and splintering buildings. At one point, Buster as Willie takes refuge from the cyclone by running into a wrecked theater where he ends up wrestling with an eerie, animated ventriloquist's dummy. Then he tries to escape by attempting to leap through the stage's painted backdrop, and he finally disappears—momentarily—behind a magician's magic curtain. All of these theater gags are from his vaudeville past, as if Buster/Willie's life were passing before his eyes as he is sucked into the eye of a hurricane. Finally, Willie becomes airborne, clinging to the trunk of an uprooted tree as the winds carry him and it high into the air before dumping him into the river.

Willie goes on to rescue the three other principal characters, first saving Mary from drowning (Buster's sister, Louise, doubled for actress Marion Byron in the rescue scene), then commanding Bill's steamboat to save his father, and finally performing a spectacular dive into the river to save Mary's dad as he clings to the wreckage of his luxury craft. In these breathtaking rescue scenes, Buster has never been more assertive as he leaps, dives, and springs into action like a human dynamo.

Before Willie proves himself a hero in the eyes of his father and his girl, Buster performs the most dangerous stunt of his career, one so potentially hazardous that even director Charles Riesner couldn't bear to watch it being filmed. After Willie has scooted through the streets on his hospital bed, he ends up in front of a house about to rip apart from the force of the wind. As he stands up in the gale, the front portion of the house breaks away and falls with a powerful crash on top of him. He survives the catastrophe when his body passes through the building's second-story window, clearing the opening by inches. This stunt required painstakingly precise calculations to guarantee its success and Keaton's safety. If he had been out of position by a couple of inches, his body would have

been crushed by the force of the falling house, which had to be loaded down with weight to prevent it from buckling in the wind.

Steamboat Bill, Jr. ended up as Buster's least profitable feature, a fact that, ironically, had more to do with the film's financially unstable distributor, United Artists, than its escalating budget. (United Artists had also distributed Buster's two previous box-office duds.) Despite its initially disastrous draw, *Steamboat Bill, Jr.* is easily one of Buster's best and most spectacularly inventive films. It also contains some of his most ingeniously subtle yet intricately timed pantomime segments. In addition to the ones already mentioned, Buster and Marion Byron act out a series of near-miss encounters in the middle of town with the two actors conveying an amazing range of emotions with simple facial glances and expressive body language. Beautifully filmed, wonderfully acted by all, and containing the most exciting climax of any of his films, *Steamboat Bill, Jr.* comes close to matching the all-around perfection Buster achieved with his masterpiece, *The General.*

THE CAMERAMAN

CREDITS:

A Metro-Goldwyn-Mayer Production; Distributed by MGM. *Producer:* Lawrence Weingarten (uncredited); *Director:* Edward M. Sedgwick; *Script:* Richard Schayer; *Story:* Clyde Bruckman and Lew Lipton; *Titles:* Joseph Farnham; *Photography:* Elgin Lessley and Reggie Lanning; *Editors:* Hugh Wynn and Basil Wrangell; *Technical Director:* Fred Gabourie; *Costumes:* David Cox. *Release Date:* September 22, 1928. *Length:* eight reels.

CAST:

Buster Keaton (*Luke Shannon*), Marceline Day (*Sally Richards*), Harold Goodwin (*Harold Stagg*), Harry Gribbon (*Officer Henessey*), Sidney Bracey (*The Editor, Edward J. Blake*), William Irving (*A Photographer*), Edward Brophy (*Man in Dressing Room*), Vernon Dent (*Man in Tight Bathing Suit*), Dick Alexander (*The Big Sea Lion*), Ray Cooke (*Office Worker*), Josephine (*The Monkey*).

Buster's first feature for MGM, *The Cameraman*, ranks with the best of his independently produced films. Unfortunately, it proved to be the last in which his distinct cinematic style fully dominated a feature. It was also the last time he worked with some of his old staff members on a feature—writer Clyde Bruckman,

In his first MGM-produced film, *The Cameraman*, Buster plays a newsreel photographer out to impress his girl with his photographic feats. His rival for the girl and the news is played by his old friend, Harold Goodwin.

Buster's girlfriend is played by the beautiful Marceline Day. Here, she boosts up his flagging confidence by tentatively accepting his date proposal.

technical director Fred Gabourie, and cameraman Elgin Lessley.

Buster plays Luke Shannon, a tintype photographer struggling to make a living on the streets of New York by convincing passersby to pose for portraits. In one of his most expressive cinematic moments, Buster as Luke is thrown next to Sally (Marceline Day), an attractive newsreel assistant assigned to help cover a street parade, resulting in a swooning, slow-blink close-up as he buries his face in her hair and rests his head on her shoulder. Later, the entranced Luke follows Sally back to her office and, attempting to impress her with his photographic expertise, trades in his tintype camera for a primitive—very primitive—newsreel apparatus, determined to woo her away from hotshot cameraman Stagg (Harold Goodwin, Buster's nemesis from *College*).

This thoroughly Keatonesque premise allows Buster to indulge in some wonderfully staged newsreel-reporter gags. Hearing of a warehouse fire, Luke dashes out of the newsroom along with the other cameramen; then, spotting a fire truck careening down the street, he manages to jump on its running board and cling to its side as it races off . . . back to the fire station. Later, when he shows up at Yankee Stadium hoping to capture some exciting baseball action only to find the place deserted, Buster as Luke performs one of his most purely theatrical pantomime bits as he plays a baseball game all by himself, first playing the pitcher, then the batter, throwing and hitting an invisible ball,

tagging invisible runners, slamming an inside-the-park home run, and sliding headfirst into home. The scene is one of Buster's personal favorites, no doubt because he was able to indulge simultaneously in two of his favorite passions—moviemaking and baseball.

Thinking he has captured several hot news items, Luke turns in his film to the boss at the office only to find out that the footage is a mishmash of double exposures, speeded-up sequences, and backward-motion scenes, leaving a less than positive impression on his editor. Later, Sally comforts Luke and even tentatively agrees to a date with him, telling him she'll phone the following day.

Luke impatiently waits for Sally's call and nearly destroys his apartment as he attempts to break open his piggy bank. Then, when Sally does call, Luke races down several flights of stairs to answer the phone, the entire scene expertly filmed in one long take with the use of a cutaway set and the camera perched on a slowly descending elevator crane. Hearing Sally tell him that she's free for the day, Luke races out of the building, dashes through traffic, and arrives at her apartment just as she hangs up the phone (a scene that captures Buster's dynamically expressive running style.)

For their first date, the two decide to visit the local swimming pool. Luke tries to change into his swimsuit in a cramped dressing room shared with a belligerent fellow bather (Buster's unit manager, Ed Brophy). Both men become entangled in each other's clothing, flinging shirts and pants at one another as they struggle to undress. Finally emerging wearing a suit several sizes too large, Luke tries to impress Sally with his swimming and diving expertise. He executes a painful belly flop off the high-diving board, losing his swimsuit as well.

In the film's funniest sequence, Luke, returning to the newsroom the following day, gets a tip from Sally about a Chinatown parade, which quickly turns into a Tong war. Accompanied by an organ grinder's monkey he's picked up along the way—another of Buster's excellent animal costars, this one named Josephine—he calmly records the two rival Chinese gangs battling each other with machine guns, swords, and knives. Luke even stages confrontations between the rival gangs so he can get better action shots, throwing light bulbs into the crowd to simulate gunfire to keep the war going, then placing a knife in the hand of one gang member as he battles an aggressive attacker. The entire scene is literally a riot to watch.

Back at the newsreel office with his exclusive footage, Luke is crushed when he finds out that his camera

Buster emerges from the bathhouse dressing room wearing a swimsuit a few sizes too large for his lean frame. Marceline, however, looks just fine.

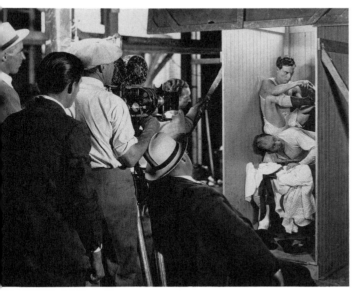

This scene from *The Cameraman*, in which Buster struggles to undress in a cramped bathhouse dressing room with character actor Ed Brophy, was filmed in one take after being conceived on the set by himself, writers Clyde Bruckman and Lew Lipton, and director Edward Sedgwick (seated in foreground).

was apparently loaded with an empty film canister. Feeling totally defeated, he vows never to bother Sally or the other cameramen again.

In the film's thrilling climax, Luke and his monkey assistant cover a yacht club regatta. Also in attendance are Sally and Stagg, who zoom around the bay in a speedboat, then find themselves in the water when Stagg loses control of the craft. Abandoning his camera, Luke jumps into a rowboat and rescues the stunned Sally, then races off to find smelling salts. Returning, he watches dumbfounded as Sally, mistaking Stagg for her rescuer, walks off with the deceitful rival. As Luke stares at the couple, the camera pulls back to reveal the loyal Josephine cranking away at Luke's newsreel camera, having filmed the entire rescue.

The heartbroken Luke ends up handing over the film

In one of the film's two exciting action scenes, Buster calmly cranks away at his news camera while the streets of Chinatown erupt into a full-scale gang war.

Buster with his furry costar, Josephine, along with his favorite MGM director, Edward "Junior" Sedgwick. The two men would later become gagmen for MGM after their respective falls from grace with that studio.

cartridge with the boat race footage to his boss without bothering to see what it contains. When the newsreel staff gathers to watch the footage "for a laugh," they are stunned to find that it contains both the Chinatown war footage and the spectacular boat rescue sequence. Sally then races out of the office and tracks down Luke. When she tells him about the footage and that everyone wants to give him a hero's welcome, throngs of cheering spectators and streams of ticker tape suddenly envelop them. Not knowing the reception is actually for Charles Lindbergh, Luke graciously tips his hat and acknowledges the wild cheers from his new, enthusiastic fans.

The Cameraman was a huge box-office success, attributable not only to the superb comedy sequences but also to the film's emphasis on the love relationship between Keaton and his lovely costar, Marceline Day. The result is his most genuinely poignant feature, filled with an emotional depth rivaling the films of Chaplin. Because of this stronger emphasis on the relationship between the two principals, Buster's crushing setbacks and his ultimate triumph pack a more powerful emotional wallop.

MGM was so impressed with the film that for years it was required viewing for all new studio comics. *The Cameraman* was screened so many times that it became damaged and lost two key sequences, one of Buster filming a hotel doorman whom he mistakes for a navy admiral, the other of his covering a ship launching ceremony and ending up sliding into the ocean along with the vessel. MGM apparently never realized that Buster was responsible for the film's success, that he was not only a superb screen comic but a brilliant moviemaker as well. His battles with the studio heads all had to do with their refusal to treat him as more than just a contract studio player.

SPITE MARRIAGE

CREDITS:

A Metro-Goldwyn-Mayer Production; Distributed by MGM. *Producer/Director:* Edward Sedgwick; *Production Supervisor:* Lawrence Weingarten; *Script:* Lew Lipton and Ernest S. Pagano; *Continuity:* Richard Schayer: *Titles:* Robert Hopkins; *Photography:* Reggie Lanning; *Editor:* Frank Sullivan; *Art Director:* Cedric Gibbons; *Costumes:* David Cox. *Release Date:* April 6, 1929. *Length:* nine reels (silent and synchronized-sound versions).

CAST:

Buster Keaton (*Elmer Edgemont*), Dorothy Sebastian (*Trilby Drew*), Edward Earle (*Lionel Denmore*), Leila Hyams (*Ethyle Norcrosse*), William Bechtel (*Frederick Nussbaum*), John Byron (*Giovanni Scarzi*), Hank Mann (*Stage Manager*), Pat Harmon (*Ship Captain*).

> Buster had no one to look after him at MGM, a thing he really needed in a place like that. He was really all on his own, right from the start. And it never changed. Never.
>
> —*Buster Collier, quoted from* Keaton: The Man Who Wouldn't Lie Down *by Tom Dardis*

With *Spite Marriage,* Keaton's second feature for MGM, his loss of creative control over his films becomes apparent for the first time. Although the film contains some of his best segments, ones he fought hard to keep in despite fierce objections from his production supervisor, Lawrence Weingarten, it is apparent in the unfocused, rambling plot that Buster had too many "creative advisers," all insisting they knew what was best for their new contract actor.

Ironically, all of Keaton's MGM films, beginning with *Spite Marriage,* were shot from detailed scripts; yet they play more like the chaotically plotted shorts he made with Roscoe Arbuckle. This is especially true of *Spite Marriage,* which starts out as a story of a simple pants presser who hangs around a theater trying to impress the current production's leading lady. It then turns into a gangster film taking place on board an abandoned yacht.

Buster with vivacious Dorothy Sebastian in the uproarious play-sabotaging scene from *Spite Marriage*, not only his last silent film but the last he made for a major studio in which his unique approach to comedy is prominently on display.

Buster tries to impress Dorothy with his unorthodox equestrian skills in a gag photo staged for *Spite Marriage*.

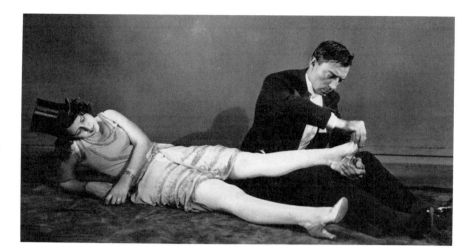

In one of Buster's most famous—and often copied—routines, one he had to fight hard to keep in the film, he struggles to put a thoroughly sloshed Dorothy to bed after celebrating their spiteful marriage. Buster restaged this routine in several of his other films as well as on stage with his third wife, Eleanor.

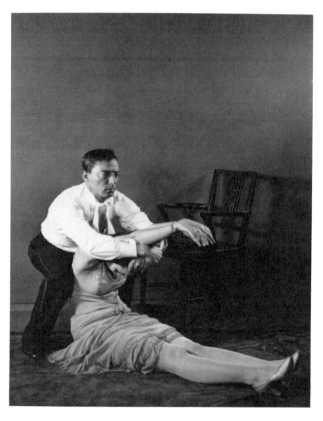

Buster plays Elmer, a type of character he would reprise in every subsequent film he made at the studio. He runs a dry cleaning shop catering to wealthy aristocrats. Borrowing the clothes of his rich customers, Elmer appears at ritzy locales frequented by the beautiful girl of his dreams, stage actress Trilby Drew (vivacious Dorothy Sebastian, Buster's favorite leading lady). Each evening, he attends the play in which she appears as a Civil War belle fending off the lecherous advances of a Union officer and his troop of soldiers.

Elmer gets a chance to play a key role in the stage production, replacing the actor who gets to kiss Trilby at the end of act one. Elmer proceeds to turn the floridly melodramatic production into a slapstick farce. First he prepares for his part with a visit to the makeup room, methodically gluing on a full beard, ending up covering his face with random clots of hair. Then during the play, Elmer misses all of his cues, destroys the set, and stumbles into his fellow actors. When it finally comes time to hold his beloved Trilby in his arms and kiss her, he hesitates just long enough for the entire backdrop to fall on top of him. Buster performs his unintended sabotage with a look of offhanded bewilderment, a superb example of his ability to act a scene that requires precise timing and make it look totally unrehearsed.

Escaping the wrath of the theater manager (Hank Mann) and quickly changing back into his borrowed tux and tails, Elmer meets backstage with Trilby, who, after being spurned by the production's caddish lead actor, turns to Elmer and gives him the eye. Before he has a chance to realize that Trilby is using him to make her lecherous costar Lionel Denmore (Edward Earle) jealous, she has asked him to get married.

After a whirlwind courtship and quickie marriage, Elmer and Trilby check into their honeymoon suite and later visit a nightclub to celebrate. When Trilby spots her playboy costar, Lionel, at another table with a blond socialite, she gets plastered and staggers out of the club with the help of her bewildered new husband. This sets up one of the most famous and most often repeated scenes of Keaton's career, one he used in later films and onstage with his third wife, Eleanor: the "putting the drunk woman to bed" routine. As Elmer drags Trilby into their hotel room, she passes out on the floor. He tries to pick her up, but she slips limply through his hands. When he at last gets her into a chair, she slinks out of it to the floor again. Finally, he lays her out on the bed and turns her over to remove her clothes, rolling her off the bed and onto the floor once more. When he picks her up again, he trips over a nightstand and the two tumble to the ground in a heap. And so it goes for several masterfully staged minutes of pantomime, ending with Buster/Elmer ultimately getting Trilby into bed only to have it collapse to the floor.

In the morning, Elmer learns from Lionel that Trilby has left him and bops the playboy in the face. Then Elmer runs out of the hotel, down the street, and into a completely new plot development, jumping into a car occupied by gangster Giovanni Scarzi (John Byron). After driving off the end of a pier, Elmer is fished out of the water by Scarzi, who then forces him to become one of his rum-running cronies. Elmer escapes from Scarzi's thugs when he falls overboard from a boat and is rescued by a yacht carrying a group of socialites, two of whom are Lionel and Trilby. Elmer is put to work on the yacht, but it catches fire and everyone abandons ship except for, that's right, Elmer and Trilby. He ends up proving himself in Trilby's eyes when Scarzi and his gang attempt to hijack the yacht and Elmer subdues them all.

Despite the film's chaotic plot, *Spite Marriage* is an exciting comedy. Because Buster remains subdued while surrounded by the inexplicable, the story contrivances seem less forced, and the film's breakneck pacing also helps propel it along. Buster's character, although suffering from a bad case of idol worship, still remains true enough to the spirit of his former screen persona to make his Elmer a figure with great

Buster (seated right) poses with some of the cast and crew of *Spite Marriage*.

future potential (a potential that, unfortunately, remained unrealized in Keaton's subsequent MGM features). Here, Buster plays a much more realistic and mature character, a suitable match for his more sophisticated and aggressively independent leading lady. He and Dorothy Sebastian make an excellent screen couple, working their routines together with a flair that rivals the work of such later screwball screen couples as Katharine Hepburn and Cary Grant in *Bringing Up Baby,* and Barbara Stanwyck and Henry Fonda in *The Lady Eve.*

After *Spite Marriage,* Buster's days as a total master of the film medium were over. His talents as a superb comic actor continued to the end of his life. But never again was he given the artistic freedom he enjoyed throughout his early years when he was able to fashion a body of work that ranks with the greatest ever created by any artist in any medium.

HOLLYWOOD REVUE OF 1929

CREDITS:

A Metro-Goldwyn-Mayer Production; Distributed by MGM. *Producer:* Harry Rapf; *Director:* Charles Riesner; *Dialogue:* Al Boasberg and Robert E. Hopkins; *Photography:* John Arnold, Irving G. Reis, Maximillian Fabian, and John M. Nickolaus; *Editors:* William S. Gray and Cameron K. Wood; *Art Directors:* Cedric Gibbons and Richard Day; *Recording Engineer:* Douglas Shearer. *Dances and Ensembles:* Sammy Lee, assisted by George Cunningham; *Music:* Gus Edwards; *Lyrics:* Joe Goodwin; *Costumes:* David Cox. *Release Date:* November 23, 1929. *Running Time:* 130 minutes.

CAST:

Buster Keaton, Joan Crawford, Norma Shearer, John Gilbert, Jack Benny, Cliff Edwards, Conrad Nagel, Laurel and Hardy, Bessie Love, Lionel Barrymore, Marion Davies, Marie Dressler, and a cast of hundreds.

Hollywood Revue of 1929 is basically an MGM promotional feature made shortly after the conversion to sound. Once the studio made the expensive transition from silent films, it did so with as much fanfare as possible, creating many lavish, all-star, all-singing, all-dancing, all-talking (emphasis on the talking) extravaganzas. Unfortunately, as with most of the films made during the early days of the talkies, none of the stars appearing in *Hollywood Revue* has much to say.

Buster was not intimidated at all by the conversion to sound; in fact, he was excited by its possibilities and developed a cinematic philosophy that reflected his overall, understated approach to filmmaking. Buster felt sound should be used not as a gimmick—not

Buster does his exotic Egyptian dance number in *Hollywood Revue of 1929.* He originated the dance in vaudeville and repeated it in various films he made with Roscoe Arbuckle.

Buster dances but he doesn't sing or talk in *Hollywood Revue of 1929.* The film was basically a promotional piece featuring MGM's major stars.

merely as sound for sound's sake—but for a purpose, to punctuate the action, to enliven gags, to move the story along. Like most of the ideas Buster pitched to the heads of MGM, though, this common-sense idea seemed too radical and fell on . . . well, it wasn't fully understood.

Everyone in *Hollywood Revue of 1929* makes noise and lots of it. Everyone except Buster, whose segment is by far the highlight. He performs the routine he originated in the Arbuckle shorts *A Country Hero* and *Back Stage*, and used as part of the act he staged for the troops while in the army shortly after World War I. His number is introduced by a provocative dance routine by a scantily clad woman who is supposedly Venus, goddess of love and beauty. After finishing her gyrating, she enters a huge shell, which then sinks into the depths of the sea. When the shell reopens in front of King Neptune and his mermaid companions, a new figure emerges covered in a black robe, the face hidden by a thin, black veil. Suddenly the maiden loses her footing and slides on her rear down a long staircase, hitting the bottom with a thud and knocking off her veil, revealing a familiar deadpan puss. Then, to Egyptian belly-dance music, the lovely "maiden" begins to gyrate, striking Nefertiti-like poses as she sways to the exotic sounds. Buster's wonderfully staged exotic cavortings end in a frenzied, twirling dance, complete with expertly executed no-hands cartwheels and an incredible neck-twisting flip.

To see Keaton surrounded by some of the most .talented performers at MGM during its early prime is to realize how painfully underappreciated he was by the studio heads and how radically different his style of comedy was from everyone else's. The sad fact is that the studio was more interested in reflecting the trends of the day rather than encouraging artists to create strikingly innovative cinemagic.

FREE AND EASY
(aka Easy Go)

CREDITS:

A Metro-Goldwyn-Mayer Production; Distributed by MGM. *Producer/Director:* Edward Sedgwick; *Scenario:* Richard Schayer; *Dialogue:* Al Boasberg; *Adaptation:* Paul Dickey; *Photography:* Leonard Smith; *Editors:* William LeVanway and George Todd; *Art Director:* Cedric Gibbons; *Recording Engineer:* Douglas Shearer. *Songs:* Roy Turk and Fred E. Ahlert. Release Date: March 22, 1930. *Running Time:* 92 minutes. (French Version: *Le Metteur en Scene;* Spanish Version: *Estrellados*.)

CAST:

Buster Keaton (*Elmer Butts*), Anita Page (*Elvira Plunkett*), Trixie Friganza (*Ma Plunkett*), Robert Montgomery (*Larry Mitchell*), Fred Niblo (*The Director*), Edward Brophy (*The Stage Manager*), Edgar Dearing (*An Officer*), David Burton (*A Director*), Gwen Lee, John Miljan, Lionel Barrymore, William Collier, Sr., William Haines, Dorothy Sebastian, Karl Dane, Jackie Coogan, Cecil B. DeMille (*cameos*).

Buster talks! Buster sings! Buster dances! Buster looks depressed!

Actually, *Free and Easy*, the first film in which Keaton actually speaks, is one of the few talkies he enjoyed making at MGM, despite the fact that his creative input was pretty much reduced to featured actor/singer/dancer. It gave him the opportunity to show off some of his more purely theatrical/ vaudevillian talents as opposed to his more stunt-oriented, acrobatic ones, which dominated his independently produced films.

Free and Easy is a lavish, enjoyable MGM musical comedy, a typical early talkie. Buster plays Elmer Butts, a variation of the character he originated in *Spite Marriage*. Elmer, an auto shop mechanic, is in love with his small-town sweetheart, Elvira Plunkett (Anita Page), who has recently been crowned "Miss Gopher City, Kansas," entitling her to a trip to Hollywood and a chance at movie stardom. Elmer has proclaimed himself Elvira's manager to help establish her movie career in Tinseltown. Along for the ride to glory is Elvira's domineering mother (Trixie Friganza), who believes Elmer's former position as owner of Butts' Auto Garage has not adequately prepared him to manage "The Flower of Kansas and America's Future Greatest Movie Star."

During their train trip to Hollywood, Elvira bumps into Larry Mitchell (Robert Montgomery), the popular movie star. Larry is immediately struck by Elvira and invites her and Ma Plunkett to the MGM studio lot to see him shoot his next feature. Later, as the women watch Larry warble "It Must Be You" in front of the movie cameras to his leading lady (Lottice Howell), the abandoned Elmer attempts to sneak onto the studio lot. Trying to elude the studio guard (Edgar Dearing), Elmer confronts a bevy of MGM stars and creates chaos as he dashes through various sound stages. Cecil B. DeMille, Dorothy Sebastian, Karl Dane, Gwen Lee, John Miljan, and Lionel Barrymore all make effective cameo appearances.

When Elmer appears on the set where Larry's musical is being filmed, Larry finds out that Elmer is Elvira's "agent" and arranges a screen test for him so that he

In *Free and Easy*, one of the few MGM films he enjoyed making, Buster sings, dances and talks . . .

. . . and auditions for the part of a comical king.

(Larry) can woo her while Elmer is busy auditioning. Both Ma Plunkett and Elmer attempt to prevent Larry from corrupting poor Elvira, but instead, both end up with featured roles in Larry's musical. Ironically, they become the film stars while Elvira remains just another pretty hopeful.

The production numbers with Buster and Trixie Friganza are the main attributes of *Free and Easy,* all marvelously exaggerated hokum full of playful stunts, songs and acrobatics. During one musical number, the two of them, playing a comical king and queen, fight and rip off each other's clothing until both stand shivering in their underwear. At that point, they stage a mock ballet full of energetic stunt work, particularly on Buster's part, ending in a spectacular dive by him into a shallow pool of water that suddenly becomes bottomless. This illusion gag was undoubtedly an original idea of his.

Later, Buster sings the film's title song while dancing with a line of exotic harem girls, performing all of this with great ease and expertise; his deep, baritone voice is delightfully distinctive and comically complementary to his small physical size. He does, however, have trouble with some of the hokey, pun-filled dialogue, as do most of the cast members.

In the film's final scene, Buster as the heartbroken Elmer is dressed as Pagliacci, and staring sadly at

Buster as the king and Trixie Friganza as his queen in one of the comedy highlights of *Free and Easy*.

Elvira. She is swooning, though, over Larry, who again warbles "It Must Be You" before the cameras while gazing in her direction, a fade-out more suitable for a Chaplin film than a Keaton one. It is still quite touching, the one purely dramatic moment to a stodgy but overall entertaining sound film debut for MGM's new comic.

DOUGHBOYS

CREDITS:

A Metro-Goldwyn-Mayer Production; Distributed by MGM. *Producer:* Buster Keaton; *Director:* Edward Sedgwick; *Scenario:* Richard Schayer; *Dialogue:* Al Boasberg and Richard Schayer; *Story:* Al Boasberg and Sidney Lazarus; *Photography:* Leonard Smith; *Editor:* William LeVanway; *Art Director:* Cedric Gibbons; *Recording Engineer:* Douglas Shearer. *Dances:* Sammy Lee. *Songs:* Edward Sedgwick, Joseph Meyer, Howard Johnson. *Release Date:* August 30, 1930. *Running Time:* 81 minutes. (Spanish Version: *De Frente Marchen;* British Title: *Forward March!*)

CAST:

Buster Keaton (*Elmer Stuyvesant*), Sally Eilers (*Mary Rogers*), Cliff Edwards (*Cliff Nescopeck*), Edward Brophy (*Sergeant Brophy*), Victor Potel (*Svendenburg*), Arnold Korff (*Gustave*), Frank Mayo (*Captain Scott*), Pitzy Katz (*Abie Cohn*), Williamm Steele (*Lieutenant Randolph*), Ann Sothern (*Wac*), Edward Sedgwick (*Guggleheimer, Camp Cook*), John Carroll (*Soldier-Singer*).

Doughboys is loosely based on some of Buster's World War I experience, which he sorely disliked. Keaton was extremely antiwar, being influenced by his close and totally benign association with vaudeville performers from all over the world.

Although he had some creative input on *Doughboys*, it was still not enough to prevent it from being a fairly routine military comedy, with Buster playing Elmer Stuyvesant, a character similar to his aristocratic types of *The Saphead, The Navigator,* and *Battling Butler*. He is smitten with a pretty clerk, Mary (Sally Eilers), and waits for her every afternoon outside the store where she works, standing beside his Rolls, dressed in tux and top hat, carrying a bouquet of flowers. However, every afternoon Mary snubs him, indicating she wants nothing to do with him. Elmer nods his head in agreement, then replies, "How about a little dinner and a show?"

In top hat and morning coat, Buster, playing a snooty, rich aristocrat, lines up with the rest of the new recruits in *Doughboys*, loosely based on several of his own World War I experiences. Also pictured are Pitzy Katz (in straw hat), Victor Potel (in derby), and Cliff "Ukelele Ike" Edwards (with loud sweater and ukelele).

In one of the funniest scenes from *Doughboys*, Buster is subjected to a surprise physical examination.

Buster performs a brilliant Apache dance number in *Doughboys*. The scene is the film's highlight and shows off Keaton's adept comic dancing abilities.

Next to the store is a military recruiting station, and on this particular day, Elmer's chauffeur, stirred by a recruiter's speech about fighting the Huns in the Great War, decides to enlist and abandons Elmer and his butler, Gustave (Arnold Korff). Elmer decides to hire another chauffeur and enters what he thinks is an employment agency but what is actually the recruiting station. There he is asked a lot of questions that he thinks are unnecessary for hiring a chauffeur, but he snootily obliges anyway. Then, told to go into an adjoining room, he is outraged when two men order him to take off his clothes. When Elmer attempts to flee, the men jump him and rip off his clothes, prompting him to yell, "I changed my mind, I don't want a chauffeur!" as he is dragged behind a partition, given a physical exam, and inducted into the army.

The next scene finds him sporting a black eye, his tux and top hat rumpled, as he lines up with other recruits, all of them being ordered around by a shrill, belligerent sergeant (Ed Brophy). Of the weak military gags that follow, one of the better ones has Elmer and his motley squad of recruits watching their sergeant demonstrate the proper use of the bayonet. Ripping the guts out of a sawdust-engorged dummy, the sergeant rants in explicit detail about the damage he is inflicting, causing the entire squad to keel over one by one.

The best segments are nonmilitary scenes, the first

taking place on a ship en route to France where Elmer and his buddies are destined to fight the nasty Huns. As he relaxes, Elmer and Nescopeck (Cliff "Ukulele Ike" Edwards), a fellow recruit, enjoy a musical interlude, the two men scat singing, Buster booming in his baritone voice while Cliff meows in a falsetto, and both strumming Cliff's trademark ukulele. This intimate scene is seemingly off the cuff.

Another musical number occurs just before the big battle finale. Mary, who has also enlisted, joins Elmer's battalion as part of the entertainment division and, still holding a grudge against him, refuses his advances once they have settled into their French military barracks. Then Nescopeck helps arrange a meeting between the two by sneaking Elmer into Mary's show, where he becomes part of the male chorus. All of the men in the chorus don women's clothing and perform a lead-footed dance number for the enthusiastic crowd with Cliff providing music and Mary dancing friskily around the makeshift stage. Elmer, stumbling around in the background, ends up as the female partner to an aggressive male Apache dancer. Buster is a joy to watch as he is thrown roughly around the stage, executing flips, twists, stumbles, and mock wrestling moves, all of which appear unrehearsed but are in fact brilliantly choreographed movements.

In the film's fairly predictable climax, Elmer sneaks into the German's trenches and encounters his old butler, Gustave, who, along with his fellow soldiers, is starving, prompting Elmer to volunteer to supply food for them from the Allies. Before he can accomplish this, the war ends. Back in the States, Elmer and Mary get hitched, and he and his army buddies end up business partners manufacturing gold-plated ukuleles.

Only in fleeting moments of *Doughboys* does Buster's unique approach to humor emerge, adding a special flair to the otherwise standard military comedy. Buster's Elmer character is also much more charming than his usual dense, bungling persona. His aristocratic stuffiness contrasts effectively with his otherwise lowbrow surroundings. He is also much more aggressive around his leading lady, another appealing change, one that should have been emphasized more in his later MGM features but unfortunately only shows up again in one of his best sound films, *Speak Easily.*

Both Keaton and Cliff Edwards shared a love for eccentric vaudeville tunes, and a lifelong friendship developed between them. Buster himself was an accomplished ukuleleist, and the two men enjoyed strumming together on the set between takes on the three features they made with one another at MGM.

PARLOR, BEDROOM AND BATH

CREDITS:

A Metro-Goldwyn-Mayer Production; Distributed by MGM. *Producer:* Buster Keaton; *Director:* Edward Sedgwick; *Adap-*

Mistaken for a notorious ladies man, Buster is pampered by some entranced females in *Parlor, Bedroom and Bath.* Also pictured are Natalie Moorhead (center) and Dorothy Christy who plays a woman attracted to "unpredictable" men.

137

For *Parlor, Bedroom and Bath*, Buster (here with Joan Peers) repeats a gag from *One Week*, this time having a train run over a car instead of a house.

Buster asks bellboy Cliff Edwards's advice on proper seduction attire before launching his series of attacks on a stream of female subjects.

tation: Richard Schayer and Robert E. Hopkins, from the play by Charles W. Bell and Mark Swan; *Photography:* Leonard Smith; *Editor:* William LeVanway; *Recording Engineer:* Karl Zint. *Release Date:* February 28, 1931. *Running Time:* 73 minutes. (French Version: *Buster Se Marie;* German Version: *Casanova Wider Willen;* British Title: *Romeo in Pyjamas.*)

CAST:

Buster Keaton (*Reginald Irving*), Charlotte Greenwood (*Polly Hathaway*), Reginald Denny (*Jeffery Haywood*), Dorothy Christy (*Angelica Embry*), Joan Peers (*Nita Leslie*), Sally Eilers (*Virginia Embry*), Cliff Edwards (*Bellhop*), Natalie Moorhead (*Leila Crofton*), Edward Brophy (*Detective*), Walter Merrill (*Frederick Leslie*), Sidney Bracy (*Butler*).

At first glance, *Parlor, Bedroom and Bath* seems all wrong for Buster. Based on a popular play (and already filmed once before at MGM in 1920), it is a farce about a meek, sheltered nobody being mistaken for an irresistible Romeo and becoming involved with several women at the same time. Buster objected to farce comedy, saying that most of the plots were horribly contrived and based on a simple misunderstanding that could be cleared up if one character merely explained the truth of the situation to the other princi-

138

pals. He also said the pacing of farce was not right for him, with the action becoming more shrill, unrealistic, and out of control as the story progressed. In this case, I believe Buster was really objecting to the fact that he had no control over the basic plots to his MGM films. In reality, *Parlor, Bedroom and Bath* turns out to be well suited to his comedy approach and is one of his best sound films, containing many Keatonesque touches and providing him with the opportunity to play a satisfying variation on his old dynamic silent film persona.

The main drawback to *Parlor, Bedroom and Bath* is its "filmed play" theatrical style, most obvious in the first half. It opens poolside at Buster's Beverly Hills mansion, affording an excellent view of the villa's beautiful grounds, the sight of many of his famous barbecue and swim parties.

The film's basic premise is quickly established in the first scene. English aristocrat Jeff Haywood (Reginald Denny) wants to wed Virginia Embry (Sally Eilers), but she refuses to do so until her rich, flitty older sister, Angelica (Dorothy Christy), is married first. The problem with Angelica is that she's only attracted to gigolo types. "Oh, if I could only have a husband that could make me jealous," she says while lounging around the pool. "I'd send him out nights just to get a thrill when he came home."

Enter Buster playing his bumbling Elmer character, although this time his name is Reginald Irving. Reggie, a lowly sign tacker, pauses at one of the trees surrounding the villa to tack up one of his posters, lingering to catch a glimpse of Angelica as she dives into the pool. In a love-struck reverie, Reggie turns and is hit by a car driven by Jeff.

Reggie ends up in Angelica's bed recuperating from his injuries, and Jeff persuades him to pose as a notorious playboy to woo Angelica. Later, Jeff hires several women to pretend to be some of Reggie's former conquests. This causes a panicked Reggie to jump out of bed, climb out the window, and run across the grounds to escape from the weird goings-on. This segment offers a quick tour of Buster's estate as he dashes across the lawn and down the staircase leading to the pool. There he makes a spectacular leap into the water, swims to the other side, and continues racing until finally being captured and wrestled back into bed.

Several weeks later, the smitten Angelica learns the truth about Reggie and sends him packing. Jeff immediately plans to get Reggie caught with another woman in Angelica's presence. Setting up Reggie in a hotel room, Jeff then calls his friend, society columnist Polly Hathaway (Charlotte Greenwood), and convinces her to pose as Reggie's lover.

Parlor, Bedroom and Bath: Buster checks his "seduction" notes before pouncing upon Charlotte Greenwood in one of the most outrageously scandalous lovemaking scenes of the pre-Production Code era.

En route to the hotel, Buster as Reggie restages the classic train gag from *One Week*. He also picks up another woman, Nita (Joan Peers), a friend of Angelica's whom he mistakes as his date for the evening, leading to a frenetic scene at the hotel when everyone piles into Reggie's room, including Nita's maniacally jealous husband (Walter Merrill), who shows up with a gun. Before the bullets fly, however, Buster engages in one of the most scandalously licentious scenes of the pre–Production Code period after Polly arrives and tries to give him a crash course in lovemaking, easily the highlight of the film. At one point, lanky comedienne Charlotte Greenwood, reprising her stage role as Polly, passionately embraces Buster/Reggie, planting on him a long, intense kiss as his short, wiry body shakes and squirms, his legs finally sticking straight up in the air while he is wrapped around her neck. Then, after the panting couple finally breaks apart and she orders Reggie to try the same technique on her, Polly's towering frame shakes and swings around his diminutive form as he returns a long, lingering smooch. After his lesson, Reggie suddenly turns into a kissing, woman-pawing dynamo, ferociously attacking every female who shows up in an incredibly effective variation on his old, acrobatically dynamic silent screen persona. Each time Reggie pounces, the hotel bellboy, played by Cliff Edwards, appears and is amazed at the sight of Reggie attacking yet another woman, at one point exclaiming, "Oh, no, he's a Mormon!" before running out of the room. In the end, Reggie tries his technique on Angelica when she shows up, and the two have a happy reconciliation.

Parlor, Bedroom and Bath is a vivid example of Buster's more dynamic approach to filmmaking at war with the movie's stodgy, theatrical roots. While its origins slow down the pacing in the first half, the second half, dominated by Buster's own gag-laden material, not only picks up the pace but also gives the proceedings a much more cinematic feel even though the action remains confined for the most part to the cramped hotel suite. Unfortunately, Buster wasn't as lucky in his subsequent studio battles as to the proper vehicles in which to feature his unique talents.

SIDEWALKS OF NEW YORK

CREDITS:

A Metro-Goldwyn-Mayer Production; Distributed by MGM. *Producer:* Lawrence Weingarten (uncredited); *Directors:* Jules White and Zion Myers; *Story/Scenario:* George Landy and Paul Gerard Smith; *Dialogue:* Robert E. Hopkins and Eric Hatch; *Photography:* Leonard Smith; *Editor:* Charles Hochberg. *Release Date:* September 26, 1931. *Running Time:* 75 minutes. (French Version: *Buster Millionaire.*)

CAST:

Buster Keaton (*Homer Van Dine Harmon*), Anita Page (*Margie*), Cliff Edwards (*Poggle*), Norman Phillips, Jr. (*Clipper*), Frank Rowan (*Butch*), Frank La Rue (*A Policeman*), Oscar Apfel (*The Judge*), Syd Saylor (*Mulvaney*), Clark Marshall (*Lefty*).

> I knew before the camera was put up for the first scene that it was practically impossible to get a good motion picture. . . . Absolutely impossible.
>
> —Buster Keaton, from a 1958 taped interview

Although Keaton was generally dissatisfied with all the sound films he made at MGM, he was most outspoken about *Sidewalks of New York*. He was right in believing that the material was unsuitable for his approach to comedy. The film itself, however, is not the total disaster that Buster insisted it was.

Sidewalks of New York is Buster's only MGM film that wasn't directed by Edward Sedgwick, with whom he had developed a close working relationship. In-

stead, producer Lawrence Weingarten appointed two new directors, Jules White and Zion Myers, whose previous assignments consisted primarily of a series of one-reelers featuring dogs (called "all barkie" comedies by the movie trade papers). Buster was not at all happy about their approach: "They alternated telling me how to walk, how to talk, how to stand, and how to fall—where and when, how fast or slow, how loud or soft. I was Trilby with two Svengalis."

Possibly, the two men mistook Keaton for one of their canine actors, one of which was also named Buster. It was insulting enough to have to star in a film that he felt was totally unsuited to his talents; then to be treated like a circus animal had to be the ultimate indignity.

The story is typical of the type of film that was then popular, involving a clash between upper and lower classes with a gangster subplot thrown in for good measure. Playing yet another variation of his sheltered, rich Bertie "The Lamb" Van Alstyne character from *The Saphead*, Buster is Homer Van Dine Harmon (called simply Harmon throughout), owner of several tenement buildings in New York's lower East Side. One of the most Keatonesque touches occurs in Buster's first appearance: he is glimpsed lying in bed with a Saint Bernard. The dog is his own, whom he named Elmer, after his MGM-created screen persona. My feeling is that Buster's opening scene was one of his subtle jokes, a comment on the way he was perceived by his two director-graduates from the Rin Tin Tin School of Filmmaking.

When Harmon's assistant, Poggle (Cliff Edwards), returns from rent-collecting covered with shoe print marks on his face from some of the young residents in the tenements, Harmon decides to visit and teach the young hoodlums a lesson. But Harmon and Poggle end up in a full-scale riot when they attempt to break up a game of street baseball. When Harmon confronts the juvenile-gang leader, Clipper (Norman Phillips, Jr.), the boy's pretty older sister, Margie (Anita Page), joins the melee, warning Harmon to pick on someone his own size. Harmon immediately becomes smitten with Margie and attempts to woo her by building a gym for the neighborhood so Clipper and his gang can have a decent place to play.

The ungrateful Clipper, however, is more interested in pleasing local mobster Butch (Frank Rowan), who encourages the youngster to sabotage Harmon's philanthropic efforts. Harmon is determined to win over Margie by attempting to rehabilitate Clipper and continues his efforts to transform the rough neighborhood into a more hospitable environment by putting on sports and entertainment benefits for the kids. These shows provide some of the film's few highlights with

Buster and Cliff Edwards show off some new gym equipment to leading lady Anita Page and a gang of street kids in *Sidewalks of New York*. The film was Keaton's least favorite MGM feature.

In one of the film's few highlights, Buster and Cliff perform in a stage play to benefit the new gym. The scene is a weak re-creation of a routine Keaton originally performed with Arbuckle in *Back Stage*.

Buster and Cliff Edwards in wrestling and boxing matches and later restaging the amateur-show scene from the Arbuckle-Keaton short *Back Stage*. Buster, dressed as a peasant woman, saves this restaged

scene from becoming a total disaster by dancing and twirling spiritedly around the stage. The film's climax is a frenetic confrontation between Butch's gang and Clipper's as the youth finally sees the light and rescues Harmon from the gangsters.

Sidewalks of New York is saved from total mediocrity by its lively pacing and effectively rambunctious young cast. The film plays like a prototype for Warners' later popular Dead End Kids movies, full of colorfully aggressive "toughs" who, along with Anita Page, banter in thick Brooklyn accents. Of course, the film is a waste of Buster's time; any B-movie comic could have played his part. It seems, however, that the studio heads couldn't forget that Buster's most financially successful silent films featured him as a bumbling aristocrat and, therefore, believed that the story line to his films was irrelevant so long as he appeared dressed in tux and tails and spoke in a prissy, upper-class tone.

Despite the film's predictable action, its bland comedy, and the fact that Buster's part is beneath his talents, *Sidewalks of New York* ended up a box-office success. Obviously, its strong popular acceptance astonished Buster, who was hoping it would flop and thus prove he was right in labeling it totally unsuitable for him.

Another factor contributing to Keaton's disillusionment with his MGM career was that he was required to make foreign-language versions of the films, sometimes remaking one movie two or three times, in German, French, and Spanish. Buster acted with different cast members for each foreign version, speaking his lines from cue cards written out phonetically. This was like sadistic torture, forcing him to make over and over again films he already detested.

THE PASSIONATE PLUMBER

CREDITS:

A Metro-Goldwyn-Mayer Production; Distributed by MGM. *Producer:* Harry Rapf (uncredited); *Director:* Edward Sedgwick; *Adaptation:* Laurence E. Johnson, from the play *Her Cardboard Lover* by Jacques Deval; *Dialogue:* Ralph Spence; *Photography:* Norbert Brodine; *Editor:* William S. Gray. *Release Date:* February 6, 1932. *Running Time:* 73 minutes. (French Version: *Le Plombier Amoureux*.)

CAST:

Buster Keaton (*Elmer Tuttle*), Jimmy Durante (*McKracken*), Irene Purcell (*Patricia Alden*), Polly Moran (*Albine*), Gilbert

Buster accepts Gilbert Roland's challenge to a duel by slapping Roland in the face with his towel in one of the best scenes from *The Passionate Plumber*, as a shocked Irene Purcell looks on.

Buster (far left) prepares to do battle with Gilbert Roland (far right) with some inept assistance from Jimmy Durante (pointing sword) in the famous dueling scene from *The Passionate Plumber*. Keaton restaged the scene many times in subsequent films and on stage in his later years.

Roland (*Tony Lagorce*), Mona Maris (*Nina Estrada*), Maude Eburne (*Aunt Charlotte*), Henry Armetta (*Bouncer*), Paul Porcasi (*Paul Le Maire*), Jean Del Val (*Chauffeur*), August Tollaire (*General Bouschay*), Edward Brophy (*Pedestrian*).

Then, of course, when you give me a Jimmy Durante . . . well, Durante just can't keep quiet. He's going to talk no matter what happens. You can't direct him any other way.

—Buster Keaton, from a 1958 interview

The Passionate Plumber, the first of a trilogy of films in which Buster was teamed with loudmouthed comic Jimmy Durante, is my candidate for Keaton's worst at MGM. Considering the talent involved and the fact that it was made at the most prestigious studio of that time, it could also be the worst film he ever made, period. Based on Jacques Deval's stage farce, *Her Cardboard Lover*, and filmed once before in 1928 with Marion Davies, it was obviously thought to be the perfect starring vehicle for Buster after the success of his previous attempt at farce comedy, *Parlor, Bedroom and Bath*. Keaton's objections to farce comedy, that it is based on easily resolved misperceptions that are never explained until the climax and involves hysterical characters becoming even more hysterical as the action progresses, accurately sum up everything wrong with this film.

Buster plays Elmer again, this time working as an American plumber in Paris. Summoned to the house of rich socialite Patricia Alden (Irene Purcell) to fix a leak in her bathroom, he ends up being mistaken for one of her lovers by her boyfriend, caddish playboy Tony Lagorce (Gilbert Roland). Finding Elmer in a compromising position—holed up in Patricia's bathroom dressed only in a towel—the outraged Tony pulls out a pair of gloves and slaps Elmer in the face, challenging him to a duel at sunrise. Elmer accepts the challenge by removing his towel and using it to slap Tony in the face, much to Patricia's surprise.

The following morning, Tony and his entourage arrive by limousine at the outskirts of a secluded forest, ready to duel. Elmer arrives moments later in a dilapidated jalopy accompanied by his second, Patricia's butler/chauffeur, McKracken (Jimmy Durante). What follows is the classic pistol-dueling scene, one of

142

Buster's favorite routines and one he repeated in subsequent film and stage appearances. However, in my opinion, the scene is ruined by incessant, mindless chatter and director Sedgwick's staging. The extreme long shot, cluttered with too many black-caped figures, makes it hard to determine who is battling whom. The best moment occurs after a hunter walks into the scene (supposedly oblivious to the half dozen figures only a couple feet away from him) and starts shooting at ducks, causing the two duelists to panic and sprint through the forest until Elmer knocks himself out by running into a low tree branch. Buster's head-clunking stunt is a real gasp-producer, the only surprise in the film.

In a casino, Elmer is reunited with Patricia and Tony and then causes a near riot when he destroys several gambling tables. Elmer agrees to help Patricia fend off the philandering Tony's advances by becoming her bodyguard. This sets up the overly shrill and chaotic finale in which Patricia and Nina (Mona Maris), another of Tony's lovers, take turns yelling at Tony and smashing things over his head while chasing him around Patricia's mansion. In the end, Patricia declares her love for Elmer while Spanish spitfire Nina forgives Tony for his boorish behavior. In the hamfisted fade-out, McKracken mugs for the camera with the comical housemaid, Albine (Polly Moran).

Because the film's dominant mood is one of vein-popping hysteria, and because the actions of the principals are all contrived and passionless, there is nothing remotely appealing about any of the characters or the story. To illustrate just how unsubtle the film is, it's Durante who gives the most sedate performance; his muggings and asides spring from his true comic persona, while everyone else struggles to embody the film's artificial, cardboard spirit.

Although Keaton hated working with Durante, they eventually became good friends offscreen. He also became close chums with Gilbert Roland. In fact, some of Buster's strongest friendships developed out of his MGM studio days, the one positive aspect to his otherwise disastrous association with the studio.

SPEAK EASILY

CREDITS:

A Metro-Goldwyn-Mayer Production; Distributed by MGM. *Producer:* Lawrence Weingarten (uncredited); *Director:* Edward Sedgwick; *Adaptation:* Ralph Spence and Lawrence E. Johnson, from "Footlights," a story by Clarence Budington Kelland; *Photography:* Harold Wenstrom; *Editor:* William Le-

In *Speak Easily,* Ed Brophy (right) informs Jimmy Durante and Buster that the show won't go on due to lack of funds. Buster, playing a sheltered university professor, gives one of his best sound film performances.

A modest Buster confers with an aggressive Thelma Todd after spending the night together in a scene that should have been one of the film's highlights but isn't.

Buster and Jimmy save the show by wrecking it in the effective climax to *Speak Easily*. Although Keaton disliked working with loudmouth Durante, they later became offscreen friends.

Vanway; *Costumes:* Arthur Appell. *Release Date:* August 13, 1932. *Running time:* 82 minutes.

CAST:

Buster Keaton (*Prof. Timolean Zanders Post*), Jimmy Durante (*James*), Ruth Selwyn (*Pansy Peets*), Thelma Todd (*Eleanor Espere*), Hedda Hopper (*Mrs. Peets*), William Pawley (*Griffo*), Sidney Toler (*Stage Manager*), Lawrence Grant (*Dr. Bolton*), Henry Armetta (*Tony*), Edward Brophy (*Reno*).

Speak Easily, Buster's favorite MGM sound feature, is a hodgepodge of comedy bits and plot variations from most of his previous films for the studio. The reliance on recycled routines unfortunately weakens the film's effectiveness, since the basic story is well suited for Buster, resulting in one of his better performances, an amazing feat because he was on the verge of a total physical and mental collapse during production. Because of severe personal problems complicated by his heavy drinking—wife Natalie filed for divorce shortly after the film was completed—Buster missed a number of days of shooting, which increased the budget, ultimately making this his second most expensive movie.

Buster plays a prim and sheltered university professor, Timolean Zanders Post, whose specialty is classical Greek literature. The professor, dressed formally, carrying an umbrella and sporting pince-nez, dreams of journeying out into the world to find adventure. What keeps him at the university is a fear of the outside world and a lack of funds.

In an effort to motivate his boss into action, the professor's valet delivers a bogus letter informing him that he has inherited $750,000. After staring at the letter and staggering around his office, the professor does several double takes and finally falls on the floor. He then gets up and immediately begins packing for an extended excursion into a world he has never fully experienced.

The scene shifts to a railroad station where a financially strapped stage troupe is preparing to leave for its next scheduled performance When its stage manager, Reno (Ed Brophy), tells the featured comic, Jimmy (Jimmy Durante), that what the show might need to increase its popularity is a better comedian, Jimmy decides to demonstrate his talents on a stranger to prove his jokes still have punch. Spotting the professor, who is about to board the train, Jimmy proceeds to try out some of his lame jokes on the literal-minded intellectual. However, the professor ends up more entranced by the troupe's lead dancer, Pansy (Ruth Selwyn), than the aggressively unfunny comic.

After a long, shrill train-boarding sequence with misplaced luggage and a perpetually screaming baby, the professor goes to see the troupe at their next stop and watches enraptured from the front row as the performers put on a horribly amateurish musical revue. Afterward, Jimmy invites the professor backstage to meet everyone. When a law enforcement official shows up and threatens to confiscate the troupe's belongings unless it can pay off some former debts, the professor ends up not only paying the outstanding bill but also agreeing to manage the outfit, vowing to star them on Broadway.

With Jimmy energetically singing "I Know Darn Well I Can Do Without Broadway but Can Broadway Do Without Me," the scene shifts to the newly established New York office of T. Z. Post—Theatrical Enterprises. The professor meets with a stage director (Sidney Toler) who has just watched the troupe's act and declares it the worst he has ever seen. However, he agrees to direct the show, but only if it is totally revamped. At that moment, a vamp shows up— Eleanor Espere (Thelma Todd)—who is interested in becoming the show's lead dancer. She begins making advances toward the professor, ultimately stripping off her dress to give him a better sampling of her talents.

Later, the professor accepts Eleanor's offer to come up to her room and share a cup of tea. Instead of tea, Eleanor fixes a "Thomas Collins" for him and the two become quite drunk, passing out together—in separate beds. This scene could have been playfully risqué; however, it ends up as a weak re-creation of the "putting the drunk woman to bed" routine from *Spite Marriage* with Buster's uninspired fumblings and Thelma's inane squeals spoiling the segment's pacing.

The following day, the professor learns from Jimmy that creditors are threatening to close down the show, having discovered that the professor's inheritance is a fake. Jimmy advises him to flee to New Jersey so he can't be served with papers until after opening night. He first obeys Jimmy's request, but then changes his mind and turns up backstage just before showtime.

What follows is a variation of the performance-sabotaging scenes from both *Spite Marriage* and *Free and Easy*. The variation, however, is exciting enough to give the film an effective finale. In the best scene, Buster as the professor performs some exciting stunt work, dangling headfirst from a rope and swinging across the stage, bumping into the actors and the scenery while simultaneously apologizing to the audience for the interruption. The show, naturally, becomes a huge success. The professor is able to pay off his creditors, and after telling Eleanor, "Nuts to you," he and Pansy embrace in the film's fade-out.

Because of Keaton's superb portrayal of an effete innocent lost in a world of wisecracking sharpies, *Speak Easily* emerges as one of his best sound features. The clash between his professorial snootiness and Durante's slangy loudness works due mainly to Buster's ability to remain in character throughout the

mostly predictable action. Only once, during the apartment scene with Thelma Todd, does he slip out of character and rely on standard stumbling-drunk behavior to cover up the scene's triteness. Otherwise, he is a joy to watch and works especially well with Durante, who essentially plays himself and is, not unexpectedly, quite good at it.

WHAT! NO BEER?

CREDITS:

A Metro-Goldwyn-Mayer Production; Distributed by MGM. *Producer*: Lawrence Weingarten (uncredited); *Director*: Edward Sedgwick; *Script*: Carey Wilson; *Story*: Robert E. Hopkins; *Additional Dialogue*: Jack Cluett; *Photography*: Harold Wenstrom; *Editor*: Frank Sullivan. *Release Date*: February 10, 1933. *Running Time*: 66 minutes.

CAST:

Buster Keaton (*Elmer Butts*), Jimmy Durante (*Jimmy Potts*), Roscoe Ates (*Schultz*), Phyllis Barry (*Hortense*), John Miljan (*Butch Lorado*), Henry Armetta (*Tony*), Edward Brophy (*Spike Moran*), Charles Dunbar (*Mulligan*), Charles Giblyn (*Chief*).

Before filming was completed on *What! No Beer?* in January 1933, studio chief Louis B. Mayer had already drafted Keaton's termination notice. Buster had again missed several days' shooting, preferring to camp out in the woods in his land yacht far away from the studio and drink away his sorrows. Natalie had been granted an interlocutory divorce decree in August of the previous year and had taken possession of nearly everything they owned, with full custody of their two boys, ultimately changing their names from Keaton to Talmadge.

Buster's ghastly physical condition is apparent in his final MGM starring vehicle. His face is chalk white, heavily made up to compensate for his bloated features; he speaks in a congested, cracked voice; and his movements are, at times, sluggish and clumsy. Although Buster's frailty sometimes makes the film painful to watch, *What! No Beer?* still manages to be quite enjoyable with its best moments supplied not by the equally billed Jimmy Durante but by Buster himself.

The plot was inspired by the headlines of the time about the repeal of Prohibition. Buster is Elmer again, this time a taxidermist in love with a rumrunner's moll, Hortense (Phyllis Barry). In the opening scene, Elmer attends a political rally given for a "dry" politician enthusiastically supported by rumrunner Butch Lorado (John Miljan) and his cronies, who figure his stance will be good for their business. As the politician rambles on about the need for abstinence, Elmer stares dreamily at Hortense and is eventually ejected from the rally when it becomes obvious that he is more interested in pining than abstaining.

Elmer's barber friend, Jimmy (Durante), however, is aggressively in favor of repealing Prohibition. After the election vote results in favor of repeal, Jimmy convinces Elmer to invest in the refurbishing of an abandoned brewery. Soon Elmer and Jimmy retrieve the former's life savings from the wild assortment of stuffed animals in the taxidermy shop. An extremely shrill scene follows when Elmer and Jimmy, with the help of three comical bums, attempt to make a batch of

beer in the decrepit old brewery, with Jimmy screaming commands at his bumbling cohorts.

Once their first batch of suds is delivered to a local speakeasy, the two beer entrepreneurs run into trouble with the law, then later with Butch and his gang. Jimmy tries to remedy the situation by passing off the brew as nonalcoholic near beer, satisfying the authorities for a while but not so Butch and another rival gang headed by Spike Moran (Edward Brophy). Putting pressure on Elmer, Spike ends up convinced that the would-be beer baron is a super-salesman and becomes an enthusiastic supporter.

On hearing about Spike's conversion, Butch sends Hortense over to entice information out of Elmer. She, too, is eventually won over by his naive sincerity, which sends Butch into a frenzy. First, Butch knocks

Buster smells something fishy in Jimmy's proposal to buy a beer brewery during the final days of Prohibition in *What! No Beer?* The film proved to be Keaton's last starring role for a major studio.

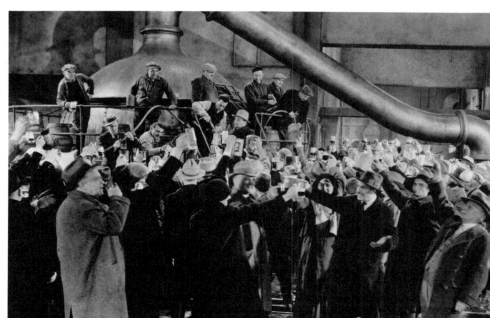

Eager for a sip of legalized suds, Jimmy and Buster do a little ballot box stuffing to make sure Prohibition is repealed.

Buster (in shirt sleeves at the top of the stairs) saves the brewery from a police raid by inviting the townspeople to drink up the evidence, in the effective climax to *What! No Beer?*

In Buster's final scene as a featured MGM star, he and Jimmy celebrate the opening of their new beer garden. While Jimmy samples the brew, Buster smooches with leading lady Phyllis Barry.

off Spike, then attempts to prevent the brewers from delivering any more of the boys' suds to local vendors, resulting in two excellent confrontations between Elmer and the rumrunners. First there is a re-creation of the rock avalanche scene from *Seven Chances,* this time with Buster as Elmer dodging barrels of beer rolling down a hill and smashing into roadsters filled with pursuing gangsters. The second is the film's highlight, occurring after Butch had taken over the brewery, demanding that Elmer and Jimmy hand over the majority of the profits. Elmer escapes by rolling out of the building in an empty barrel, then riding through the streets inviting the townspeople to the brewery to sample as much beer as they want. A thirsty mob shows up, subduing the gangsters and ultimately "drinking up the evidence" before the police arrive to break up the riot.

In the end, Prohibition is officially repealed and Elmer and Jimmy become local heroes. In the happily-ever-after fade-out, the two partners open a beer garden and end up millionaires, Elmer smooching with Hortense as Jimmy delivers one last "Hot-ch-ch-cha" straight into the camera.

On this ironically uplifting note, Buster's career as one of the highest-paid stars at the country's most prestigious movie studio ended. Plans had already been made to team Keaton again with Durante in a film

tentatively titled *Buddies*. But L. B. Mayer had finally made the decision to fire Buster, and shortly after filming was completed on *What! No Beer?* at the end of January, he delivered Buster's termination notice. *What! No Beer?* was a box-office smash, setting attendance records at New York's Capitol Theater, MGM's Broadway showcase, where it was held over for an additional week, a rare honor for any film premiering in the depths of the Depression. However, Mayer couldn't overlook Buster's out-of-control behavior. Nearly two weeks' shooting time had been lost because of his failure to show up for work.

During one of his absences, Buster, in an alcoholic stupor, had flown to Mexico and returned several days later married to his nurse, Mae Scribbens, who had been hired to keep him from drinking. After his termination from MGM, Buster ended up in a sanatorium suffering from the DTs, caused by his nonstop drinking.

What! No Beer? was made under these difficult conditions. Keaton's final appearance as a star studio actor is proof of his ability to project a sense of stolid, beguiling charm while surrounded by incessant chatter and engulfed in a vortex of self-destructive delirium. Unfortunately, the film's story line about the legalization of booze makes his appearance an ironic example of the horrors of overindulgence.

THE GOLD GHOST

CREDITS:

An Educational Pictures Production Presented by E. W. Hammons; Distributed by Fox Films. *Producer:* E. H. Allen; *Director:* Charles Lamont; *Story:* Ewart Adamson and Nick Barrows; *Adaptation/Continuity:* Ernest Pagano and Charles Lamont; *Photography:* Dwight Warren. *Release Date:* March 16, 1934. *Length:* two reels.

CAST:

Buster Keaton, Dorothy Dix, William Worthington, Lloyd Ingraham, Warren Hymer, Leo Willis, Joe Young, Al Thompson, Billy Engle.

After his humiliating departure from MGM in early February 1933, Keaton was deemed unemployable by all the major studios; his reputation as an unreliable alcoholic had made him too much of a risk. Throughout the rest of the year, easily the most disaster-prone of his life, Buster struggled to find work. Finally, a former MGM colleague, Ernest Pagano—who had

Buster poses with some of the cast and crew of *The Gold Ghost*, his first two-reeler for Educational Pictures. Also pictured are director Charles Lamont (seated to the left of the camera), scriptwriter Ernest Pagano (seated to right of camera), and studio president Earl W. Hammons (seated, wearing suit and hat).

Buster interacts with ghostly dames and desperadoes in one of the most effective scenes from *The Gold Ghost*. His first talkie two-reeler for Hollywood's cheapest film studio contains excellent examples of his innovative "sound" approach to film comedy.

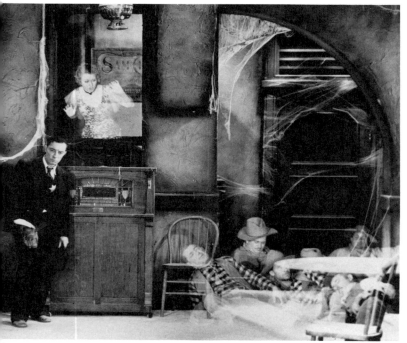

worked on the script for *Spite Marriage*—persuaded him to accept an offer from Educational Pictures to star in a series of two-reel sound comedies. Pagano was employed at Educational at the time as a scriptwriter and felt that Buster could make a lucrative deal with Educational's president, Earl W. Hammons, who was always on the lookout for new—and not so new—talent.

Educational Pictures specialized in cheaply made two-reelers and used this slogan: "The best of the old comedy favorites, the brightest of the new stars." It is true that many newcomers got their start at Educational. Danny Kaye, Bob Hope, and Imogene Coca, among others, made their screen debuts there before graduating to more illustrious endeavors. However, Educational also had a reputation for hiring stars whose sheen was somewhat tarnished. Roscoe Arbuckle, Harry Langdon, and Mack Sennett all ended up at Educational after experiencing declines in their careers. And so in late 1933, after a series of crippling personal and professional disasters, Buster signed on at the cheapest studio in town.

Buster's director for most of his sixteen Educational shorts was an old vaudeville friend, former child acrobat Charles Lamont. Lamont also received writing credit on many of the shorts, although he later admitted that Keaton contributed a great deal of material, making him (Lamont) look like "a smart director." Buster hired many of his old friends to star with him in the Educationals; he even persuaded his mother, father, and siblings to appear with him in two of the shorts.

Although the look of the films is definitely cheap, the content of many is quite good, some having the creative flair of Buster's silent shorts. The first, and one of the best of the series, is *The Gold Ghost*, which contains many strong Keaton touches. Buster plays a character called Wally, a spoiled, rich bumbler in the tradition of his Elmer and Bertie the Lamb characters.

This time, after overhearing a conversation in which his girlfriend, played by Dorothy Dix, calls him a jerk, Buster stumbles out of his father's Boston mansion, borrows the family car, and drives to the Nevada ghost town of Vulture City. There his car finally breaks down. As he investigates the long-abandoned town, Buster in a long, wordless segment, enters the local saloon and imagines himself the sheriff. As he dons a holster and gun and pins a badge to the lapel of his city slicker duds, he conjures up an encounter with a beautiful dancing girl—actually Dorothy dressed in saloon-gal getup—and some rough desperados. Throughout the scene, the dominant sound is tinkly, old-time piano music, which adds a ghostly aura to the pantomime. This is an example of Buster's unique approach to sound comedy, which emphasizes natural, atmospheric sounds rather than unnecessary talk and intrusive sound for sound's sake.

The ghost town doesn't remain deserted for long. First, a gangster on the lam (Leo Willis) shows up, then a couple of prospectors who have rediscovered gold in the area. Soon the place is once again bustling. Buster appears washing his clothes in a horse trough, his apparently naked body strategically blocked by the trough (the visible portions of his body—his upper torso, arms, and legs—appear shockingly white and frail, quite a contrast to his wiry, athletic physique from his early films). As he hangs the clothes to dry on the limbs of a nearby tree, a fleet of cars drives up behind him until the background is alive with street traffic and pedestrians hurriedly rushing about. This marvelous segment recalls the famous scene from *The General* where Buster is totally immersed in the task of chopping up firewood for his train while troops of soldiers pass behind him unnoticed.

Later, Buster, who has been mistaken for the town's sheriff, must battle claim jumpers out to steal a gold mine owned by the father of his old girlfriend, who, along with Buster's father, all show up in town. In the middle of a traditional saloon brawl, Buster inadvertently trips the handle of an old slot machine, then calmly stares at it as it begins spitting coins into his hat lying on the floor. He finally replaces his hat snugly on his head before rejoining the battle. Then, spotting a gun-toting varmint sneaking up on him from a corner of the room, Buster quickly leaps on one end of a shattered table, causing the other end to snap up, knocking the desperado's gun from his hand and into the air. Buster catches the weapon and subdues his attacker. The entire sequence, filmed in a single take without cutting away from the action, has the precise, "unfaked" feel of his earlier silent shorts.

In the end, Buster triumphs over the bad guys with his sudden display of newfound bravado, winning back his girl and the respect of the rest of the townspeople in a climax that conjures up the Keaton character of yore. Buster himself looks weary throughout the film's action; his movements are sluggish, his expression more deadpan than ever. Yet, his performance remains strong and the film itself is a superb example of his new approach to sound comedy, resulting in an excellent two-reeler and a dynamic debut as Educational Pictures' new "best of the old comedy favorites."

ALLEZ OOP

CREDITS:

An Educational Pictures Production Presented by E. W. Hammons; Distributed by Fox Films. *Producer:* E. H. Allen; *Director:* Charles Lamont; *Story:* Ernest Pagano and Ewart Adamson; *Photography:* Dwight Warren. *Release Date:* May 31, 1934. *Length:* two reels.

CAST:

Buster Keaton, Dorothy Sebastian, Harry Myers, George Lewis, The Flying Escalantes.

Buster is reunited with Dorothy Sebastian in the circus-flavored short, *Allez Oop*, which also features his acrobatic friends, the Flying Escalantes.

Allez Oop reunites Buster with Dorothy Sebastian, his leading lady from *Spite Marriage*. Like him, Dorothy had had a falling out with MGM and was finding it hard to land a job elsewhere. As the new star of the Educational lot—a dubious honor at most—Buster had little trouble persuading the studio's executives to team him with his favorite leading lady for his second talkie two-reeler. In casting old friends, he didn't stop with Dorothy. His vaudeville buddies the acrobatic Flying Escalantes, who had appeared in his silent short *Neighbors*, are also in *Allez Oop*. In fact, they are its central focus, proof that Buster also had control over the story content of his Educational shorts even though he received writing credit on only one of them.

Buster again plays Elmer, this time the owner of a watch repair shop. When an attractive female customer—Dorothy Sebastian—shows up with a broken wristwatch, Buster gives her a little more personal attention than usual and promises to personally deliver the repaired watch.

Soon afterward, he arrives at her place, the watch wrapped in a gift box. With a great flourish he opens the box and then digs through wads of cotton, finally finding the watch after having torn the box apart and thrown cotton all over the floor.

Buster wants to take Dorothy to the local circus but can't find the courage to ask her. Instead, before leaving her apartment, he secretly stops her grandfather clock and then tells her that if she needs him for anything else, just call. Then, after accidentally dropping his circus tickets on the floor, he races back to his shop and sits by the phone waiting for her to call. A series of just-missed encounters follows, the two finally ending up at the circus together where Dorothy becomes smitten by one of the handsome trapeze artists. Determined to win Dorothy away from the high-flying masher, Buster decides to become a trapeze artist himself.

Buster rigs up a crude trapeze set in his backyard, attaching ropes to a tree and a clothesline, then climbing up on a ladder and attempting to swing from one rope to the next. After placing a mattress underneath the ropes as a safety precaution, he manages to miss it as he plummets to the ground, prompting him to move it to another location. Restaging his acrobatic stunts, he becomes tangled in the ropes and gets bounced up and down by the sagging tree limbs and then deposited on the ground, once more missing the mattress. Keaton's stunt work here is brutal yet very funny, but the intrusive, cartoonish music and speeded-up action segments intrude on Buster's more subtle approach to screen comedy.

Meanwhile, Dorothy has invited her new beau to dinner, and he immediately makes bold advances. She is outraged and slaps him, finally telling him to leave when he forces himself on her again. In the ensuing struggle, Dorothy is knocked unconscious and the cad inadvertently sets her apartment on fire before escaping out the window, leaving Dorothy to fend for herself. Just then, Buster shows up and springs into action, climbing up a fire escape and using the telephone wires to swing over to her window, then pulling her out of the burning apartment and dropping her to safety in a fireman's net below. (The Flying Escalantes doubled for Buster and Dorothy in this scene, which probably depressed Keaton for days afterward.)

Although *Allez Oop* has several elaborate action sequences, the film overall betrays its skimpy budget by looking slapdash and hurried. However, dominated by Buster's distinct touches—the story itself is obviously Keaton-inspired—many segments play effectively, especially his backyard trapeze act.

LE ROI DES CHAMPS-ÉLYSÉES

CREDITS:

A Nero Films Production; Distributed in France by Paramount (no U.S. release). *Producer:* Seymour Nebenzal; *Director:* Max Nosseck; *Production Supervisor:* Robert Siodmak; *Script:* Arnold Lipp; *Dialogue:* Yves Mirande; *Photography:* Robert LeFebvre; *Art Directors:* Hugues Laurent and Jacques-Laurent Atthalin; *Music:* Joe Hajos. *Release Date:* December 1934. *Running Time:* 70 minutes. (British Title: *The Champ of the Champs-Élysées.*)

CAST:

Buster Keaton (*Buster Garnier/Jim Le Balafre*), Paulette Dubost (*Germaine*), Colette Darfeuil (*Simone*), Madeline Guitty (*Madame Garnier*), Jacques Dumesnil, Pierre Pierade, Gaston Dupray, Paul Clerget, Frank Maurice, Pitouto, Lucien Callamand.

After completing two shorts for Educational Pictures, Buster received an offer to star in a French film produced by Seymour Nebenzal, the president of the Paris-based Nero Films. Nebenzal was hoping to profit from Buster's international popularity, which remained strong despite his personal and professional problems of the past several years. Unfortunately, the film received limited distribution—it was never re-

Buster and his second wife, Mae, set sail for France where he starred in his first foreign-produced feature, *Le Roi Des Champs-Élysées*.

A promotional ad for *Le Roi Des Champs-Élysées*. Although the film received limited distribution, it is a better showcase of Buster's talents than most of his MGM sound features.

leased in the United States—and did nothing to benefit Buster's career or increase Nero Films' profits.

Although Buster receives no script credit, the film is a virtual showcase of gags and plot lines from several of his silents and from his MGM features. Buster is first glimpsed riding down the Champs-Élysées in the back of an elegant limousine convertible. Dressed in tuxedo and top hat, he stands up and tosses advertising fliers in the shape of French paper currency to the people strolling along the boulevard. The sight of Buster in these surroundings is a shock; it is almost as if he were involved in a documentary and these clownish antics filmed on the streets of Paris are for the benefit of his French fans.

After distributing his batch of money-shaped fliers, Buster returns to his employer's headquarters to pick up more handbills. However, this time he inadvertently carts off a pile of real French currency. Ambling down the street handing out his bills, he creates a riot in his wake as people begin pouncing on one another to scoop up more of the notes when they realize they are real. Buster's wanderings lead him to an apartment complex where he ends up smitten at the sight of a young resident, Germaine (Paulette Dubost). However, when he again returns to his employer's office, he is immediately fired for handing out the pile of real money.

Buster wanders off to visit his mother (Madeline Guitty), who works as a script prompter at a local theater. In a variation of the show-sabotaging scene from *Speak Easily,* Buster dons a medieval suit of armor, then struggles with the stuck helmet while sitting on a mock throne. When the throne is hoisted above the stage, he falls off the platform and lands on a lever that starts the stage revolving, throwing him into the midst of a group of dancers, who struggle to remain standing as the stage spins.

Echoing the inept-suicide gags from *Hard Luck,* Buster returns to his apartment and prepares to asphyxiate himself with the kitchen gas stove, first bidding adieu to his pet parrot and goldfish, then lying in front of the oven and setting a potted plant on his stomach before turning on the gas. These preparations are rudely interrupted when the gas man shows up and turns off the stove. Undaunted, Buster purchases a bottle of sleeping pills, visits a restaurant, and drops them into his glass of wine, adding sugar to kill the poison's bitter taste. However, one of the waitresses turns out to be Germaine. Calling off his suicide attempts, Buster makes a date with her and runs back to his apartment.

Encouraged by his mother, Buster auditions for a part in her stage troupe's new play, *Le Roi des Champs-Élysées,* and lands the lead part of a gangster escaping from prison. During a break in rehearsals, Buster, dressed in his prison uniform, relaxes in a park, unaware that a real convict is nearby staging an escape. In a cleverly contrived mixture of plot lines from *Convict 13* and *The Goat,* Buster ends up mistaken for the real convict, who is the mirror image of Buster. (Buster also plays the convict, Jim Le Balafre.)

When cops begin chasing him through the park, he is rescued by the real convict's cronies, who, mistaking him for their cohort, hoist the bewildered Buster onto their shoulders and carry him into their hideout. There he is greeted by the rest of the gang members, who suddenly break into a lively song-and-dance number in honor of their returning leader.

The film's heretofore sluggish pacing now gains momentum as Buster pretends to be the leader. One member gives him a tour of the hideout, pointing out new secret compartments, revolving walls, and trapdoors, all of which are amusing variations of the booby-trapped house in *The High Sign.* Later, the gang hands him a strongbox and tells him he is the only one who knows how to open it. Buster innocently fiddles with the dials on the box, causing it to erupt in a hail of machine gun fire that sends everyone diving for cover. Then, as the gang eyes him suspiciously, a woman claiming to be his girlfriend turns up and smothers him with kisses, ultimately dragging him off to her suite and trying to seduce him. In a scene that is reminiscent of his romantically inept encounter with Thelma Todd in *Speak Easily,* Buster struggles to disentangle himself from his "girlfriend," who is puzzled by his cool reception. She is even more perplexed when he wanders off, then returns as a sexual dynamo—not realizing that this time it is her real lover, who has finally managed to make it back to the hideout.

The two Busters ultimately encounter one another and the chase is on throughout the hideout, with one Buster eluding the other as well as the gang members via the various secret escape mechanisms. At last escaping from the hideout with the crooks hot on his trail, Buster hijacks a car and speeds through the streets hurling objects at strolling policemen in an effort to get them to follow him. His plan works, and soon he is pursued by both cops and crooks.

Buster drives to the theater and ends up onstage just in time for his part. The audience, lulled to sleep by the play's slow pace, suddenly perks up as Buster is joined onstage by the horde of battling policemen and mobsters. Buster eventually subdues the look-alike convict, saving the stage play and winning the heart of Germaine, resulting in a startling smile from the Great Stone Face when Germaine plants a kiss on his puss.

The effectiveness of Buster's first foreign-produced effort is dulled by his badly dubbed voice, some awkward staging in the action scenes, and the film's low production values, most glaringly evident in the final car chase, which is actually from another Nebenzal-produced film, Fritz Lang's *The Testament of Dr. Mabuse.* Despite these shortcomings, *Le Roi des Champs-Élysées* remains a solid Keaton feature, recapturing the feel of his independently produced films. Buster manages the innovative dual-character role with great expertise. Buster as a vicious gangster illustrates well how easily his usual deadpan demeanor can reflect menacing evil rather than benign innocence.

Buster's startling smile during the fade-out, although totally unexpected, is nevertheless anticlimactic, as if he were playing a blind character who miraculously regains his sight in the film's final moments. Buster probably agreed to a smiling fade-out for *Le Roi des Champs-Élysées* believing that it would be a fitting coda to his career as a featured star. Fortunately, it was far from his last fade-out and hardly the last time the Great Stone Face blessed the screen with a smile.

The effectiveness of Buster's second foreign-produced feature, *The Invader* (also known as *An Old Spanish Custom*) was sabotaged by severe budget limitations. Keaton felt the film had enough good material to remake it as a two-reel short, *Pest From the West*, in 1939.

THE INVADER (aka An Old Spanish Custom)

CREDITS:

A British and Continental Production (MGM); Released in the United States by M. H. Hoffberg. *Producers:* Sam Spiegel and Harold Richman; *Director:* Adrian Brunel; *Script:* Walter Greenwood; *Photography:* Eugene Schufftan; *Editor:* Dan Birt; *Music:* John Greenwood and George Rubens; *Recording Engineer:* Scanlan. *Release Date:* January 2, 1936 (filming completed November 1934). *Running Time:* 61 minutes.

CAST:

Buster Keaton (*Leander Proudfoot*), Lupita Tovar (*Lupita Malez*), Esme Percy (*José*), Lyn Harding (*Gonzalo Gonzalez*), Andrea Maladrinos (*Carlos*), Hilda Moreno (*Carmita*), Clifford Heatherly (*David Cheesman*), Webster Booth (*Serenader*).

While in Paris filming *Le Roi des Champs-Élysées*, Buster received an offer from producer Sam Spiegel (in the days before he emigrated to Hollywood) to star in an English production with the promise of creative control over the story. Although he received no writing credit, Buster supplied the film's story outline as well as a flurry of gag material. The result was *The Invader,* an abysmal failure despite many fine Keatonesque touches, doomed from the start by an extremely low budget. Its production values are so blatantly cheap that it makes Keaton's Educational shorts look like big-budget extravaganzas.

Buster plays Leander Proudfoot, a rich American yachtsman who drops anchor off the coast of a small Spanish town and ventures forth to revel in the charming ambience. The town actually has about as much authentic Spanish appeal as a mountain of painted cardboard, which is basically what the tiny, claustrophic set is made of. Soon, Buster is attacked by a swarm of maniacal street vendors and ends up purchasing a wild assortment of trinkets. Taking refuge in a local cantina, he becomes a key player in a scheme hatched by the establishment's pretty hostess to take over ownership of the place by making the current bar owner jealous to the point of murdering her patsy lover. Guess who gets chosen as the woman's bogus Romeo.

Buster remains enchanted with the cantina cutie, Lupita (Lupita Tovar), even after watching her in one of the most unintentionally inept musical numbers ever staged. According to director Adrian Brunel, the finished print ran too short for a feature, so a bevy of hand-flapping dervishes was hired for a gratuitous dance number to increase the running time.

After the free-for-all chorus number, Lupita asks Buster to dance, hoping the owner, Gonzalo (Lyn Harding), will spot them and fly into a jealous rage. When he fails to take notice, however, Lupita storms out of the cantina. Buster then imagines himself a romantic balladeer, strumming a love song on a guitar while Lupita gazes enraptured from her balcony window. The dream Buster then tosses aside his guitar and boldly scales the wall to Lupita's balcony and embraces her. His wall-scaling feat is accomplished with the use of invisible wires attached to the back of his coat, resulting in a blatantly faked—and hysterically funny—sight gag. Buster tops the segment when he finally does serenade Lupita, plucking the strings of a ukulele and singing "In a Little Spanish Town," while an annoyed neighbor from an adjoining balcony drops various objects on Buster's head in perfect time to the song.

After being chased back to his yacht by the annoyed neighbor, Buster is shocked to find Lupita waiting for him in his cabin. The two have an intimate dinner, which is interrupted by the jealous Gonzalo and Lupita's other lover, José (Esme Percy), resulting in a duel at sunset. A weak variation of the pistol-dueling scene from *The Passionate Plumber*, it concludes in a win for Buster as his two adversaries end up in a fistfight while he and Lupita hightail it back to the yacht and sail off together.

The Invader could have been a fine starring vehicle for Buster if only someone would have spent enough money on it. He was obviously fond enough of the material, for he reworked it as a two-reeler for Columbia in 1939 called *Pest From the West*. Although the two-reeler is far superior technically, it lacks the elaborate pantomime routines and subtle throwaway gags that inundate the feature. Buster seemed to be attempting to put his theoretical approach to sound comedy into practice, staging several long routines without the use of dialogue. In fact, he speaks only a few more lines of dialogue in this feature than he did in *Le Roi des Champs-Élysées* where his lines were purposely reduced due to his unfamiliarity with French.

PALOOKA FROM PADUCAH

CREDITS:

An Educational Pictures Production Presented by E. W. Hammons; Distributed by Fox Films. *Producer:* E. H. Allen; *Director:* Charles Lamont; *Story:* Glen Lambert; *Photography:* Dwight Warren. *Release Date:* January 11, 1935. *Length:* two reels.

CAST:

Buster Keaton, Joe Keaton, Myra Keaton, Louise Keaton, Dewey Robinson, Bull Montana.

The Three Keatons—Plus One—make their film debut in Buster's third Educational two-reeler, *Palooka From Paducah*. This portrait, taken in the mid-1920s, shows Buster with his entire family: sister Louise, mother Myra, brother Harry, Buster, and father Joe. All but Harry appear in the film.

After appearing in two low-budget features overseas and returning home to a coldly indifferent Hollywood, Buster picked up where he had left off—turning out cheaply made two-reelers for Educational Pictures. His third effort for Educational is one of his most memorable because the Three Keatons—Plus One—appear together for the first time on-screen. Buster had attempted to feature his family in previous films—*Convict 13* and the first version of *The Electric House* supposedly contained glimpses of Joe, Myra, Louise, and Harry Keaton. However, with the exception of Joe making a brief high-kicking cameo in *Convict 13,* the rest of the Keaton clan is absent in both. Since nearly one reel of footage from *Convict 13* is still considered lost, there is a chance that the official film debut of the Three Keatons will be marked as 1920 rather than 1935.

In *Palooka From Paducah* the Keatons play a back-woods family of moonshiners whose business has fallen off a bit since the repeal of Prohibition. It opens on a touching family interlude between mother and daughter: Sis sits in a rocking chair playing the Jew's harp while Ma puffs on her pipe and grinds tobacco in her own rocker. Myra and Louise—in fact the entire family—look like refugees from Al Capp's Dogpatch, especially Myra, who is a near dead ringer for Li'l Abner's dear, sweet Mammy Yokum.

Outside in the woods, Buster—who is called Jim—dressed as a country hick and sporting fake whiskers, tosses horseshoes with his burly, bearded brother, Elmer (of all the names to choose), played by big Dewey Robinson. In between tossings, they check on their homemade brew cooking in the woods behind them. When big Elmer samples two different stills and asks brother Jim why one costs more than the other when the batches taste the same, Buster matter-of-factly explains that the more expensive batch is the one the cat *didn't* fall into.

With their more lucrative brewing days behind them, Pa comes up with an alternative money-making venture: professional wrestling. He and Buster set up a ring in the barn and begin to train big Elmer for the tournament to be held in nearby Paducah. Several predictable wrestling gags follow, with Buster getting his head stuck in a huge bale of hay and wandering about in search of Elmer.

Training is interrupted by the dinner bell. An amusing variation of the supper scene from *My Wife's Relations* follows, with Buster continually passing dishes around the table until finally, having run out of items to pass, he removes his boot and passes that around.

In the Paducah wrestling match, Buster referees while Elmer, in long johns and checkered boxer shorts, battles mountainous Bullfrog Kraus, played by professional wrestler Bull Montana. Buster tries to keep his "little brother" from getting hurt, but fails miserably as the brutal Bullfrog slaps Elmer around. Finally, the sight of Elmer being pummeled by the merciless brute is too much for Ma, and she jumps out of her ringside seat and attacks Bullfrog, quickly joined by Pa and Sis. When Bullfrog turns around and decks Buster, Elmer erupts into a wrestling maniac. He flings Bullfrog around the ring, throwing him on the ground and then leaping on his back, sending him right through the floorboards. Buster awakens from his blow and pronounces Elmer the winner. An elated Ma flings herself into the arms of her victorious son, then nearly decks him when he almost drops her. The film ends with a shot of the triumphant family strolling down the streets of Paducah dressed in their newly acquired city slicker outfits, still looking hopelessly hick.

Palooka From Paducah is a real charmer, quite lively, and full of irreverent slapstick and delightfully caricaturish performances by the Keatons, a film dominated by a feeling of frolicsome family horseplay. It almost seems as if Buster were trying to crack up his family—especially Joe—with his exaggerated pratfalls. However, in true Keaton fashion, the family remains just as poker-faced as the king of deadpan himself.

ONE-RUN ELMER

CREDITS:

An Educational Pictures Production Presented by E. W. Hammons; Distributed by Fox Films. *Producer:* E. H. Allen; *Director:* Charles Lamont; *Story:* Glen Lambert; *Photography:* Dwight Warren. *Release Date:* February 22, 1935. *Length:* two reels.

CAST:

Buster Keaton, Lona Andre, Harold Goodwin, Dewey Robinson, Jim Thorpe (uncredited).

One-Run Elmer was filmed in the California desert after a sudden rainstorm had held up two days of shooting. Buster reportedly spent those two days drinking; however, his performance remains solid throughout, showing little evidence of his illness.

The film opens on a long shot of a small, one-shack

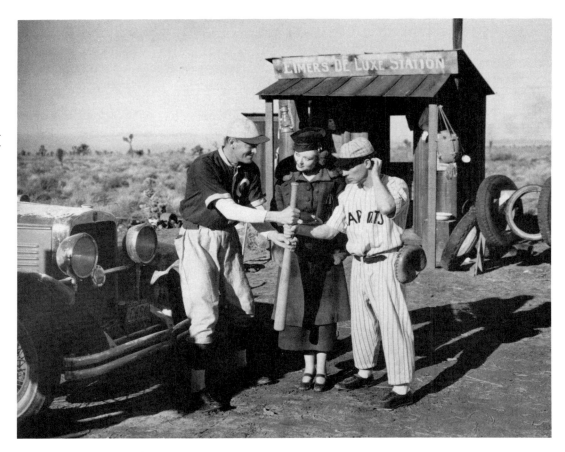

Buster uses bats and balls to woo Lona Andre away from rival Harold Goodwin in *One-Run Elmer*, another superb Educational two-reeler filled with his effective use of sound in a nearly non-dialogue short film.

desert gas station in the middle of nowhere. Buster emerges from the shack and settles into a rocking chair. Somehow, the sight of the Great Stone Face surrounded by the majestic quiet of the desert is more hauntingly poignant than mirthful, with the stillness of the landscape perfectly complementing the stolidly silent figure hunched in his rocker.

A good five minutes of nearly silent action passes with Buster attempting to sell his gas to people who only want directions. At one point, he pulls out a rifle and stalks game until a customer pulls up, spots Buster with the rifle, and swerves off the road into the dusky desert in a gag that is more surrealistically beautiful than funny.

The silence is temporarily broken when a truck laden with equipment pulls up and starts unloading. At first, Buster is excited over the idea of construction going on right next door. However, he is soon sulking in his rocking chair at the sight of another station being built right across the dirt road from his. The station is run by Harold Goodwin—Keaton's old friend and costar from *College* and *The Cameraman*, as well as five Educationals. Soon the two are engaged in a silent but escalating gas war.

After a couple botched attempts at selling gas,

Buster scores a coup when he waits on pretty Lona Andre. Quickly, he and Harold find out that she will be staying in town, and Harold begins rattling off the town's entertainment possibilities. Lona perks up at the mention of a local baseball-team rivalry scheduled to resume the following day.

After she pulls away, both men dive into their respective offices and emerge dressed in rival baseball uniforms, then engage in some throwing and batting practice. Buster's shack gets hit with several stray balls, and one even knocks a brick from the foundation, causing the entire structure to wobble whenever Buster enters it to retrieve a missed ball. Then he hits a ball through a motorist's car window and the man bats him around in the wildly swaying shack.

The following day, the rivals and their teammates gather in a baseball field in the middle of the desert (another comically surreal image), with Lona offering to date the man whose team wins. The game erupts into series of baseball gags, most of which were originally conceived by baseball fanatic Buster for charity games he staged for Los Angeles' Mount Sinai Hospital throughout the 1930s (and would continue into the 1940s). The gags are all visual with only the umpire's calls occasionally intruding on the nonverbal

156

antics. Once, an apple is mistaken for the ball, then hit and frantically put back together by Buster and his teammates in time to tag out the runner as he slides into home. The topper gag has Buster sneaking a bullet into the tip of his bat, which explodes when he hits the ball, knocking down the opposing players and sending the ball deep into the outfield (legendary athlete Jim Thorpe fields it in an uncredited cameo appearance). Then, as Buster rounds the bases and digs in for home (here his running is once again spectacular), he slams into the catcher feet first, sending the player flying backward. Buster scores the winning run, showing off some of his old, dynamic physical powers for a few exciting moments.

One-Run Elmer is dominated by the Keaton touch from beginning to end and benefits greatly from its natural outdoor location, giving the short a big-budget feel. Even the pacing of the film seems more assured and unrushed, surprising since the shooting was shortened by the two-day thunderstorm and Keaton's one-day hangover. Buster was trying to create a silent film surrounded by sound rather than dominated by it, and he accomplishes this better than he ever did with any of his MGM sound features. Although the story is slight, the film's overall effect is solidly satisfying.

HAYSEED ROMANCE

CREDITS:

An Educational Pictures Production Presented by E. W. Hammons; Distributed by Fox Films. *Producer:* E. H. Allen; *Director/Story:* Charles Lamont; *Dialogue/Continuity:* Glen Lambert; *Photography:* Gus Peterson. *Release Date:* March 15, 1935. *Length:* two reels.

CAST:

Buster Keaton, Jane Jones, Dorothea Kent.

Hayseed Romance is one of the more average two-reelers Buster made for Educational. Buster (billed as Elmer again) answers a "Handyman Wanted" ad placed by a matronly woman, played by Jane Jones, who he thinks eventually wants to marry him. However, he falls in love with the woman's cute, squeaky-voiced niece (Dorothea Kent). Buster begins helping out around the house by first tackling a mountain of dirty dishes in the kitchen and breaking most of them. Afterward, he relaxes in the living room with Dorothea and Auntie, but the silence is shattered when Auntie sits down at the piano and launches into a booming

ballad that knocks Buster and Dorothea out of their chairs and sends them racing around the house rescuing objects in danger of rattling off their perches.

After Auntie's serenade, Buster climbs up to his attic bedroom to turn in for the evening. Disaster strikes when it begins raining, causing the roof to collapse and propelling Buster through the floor, into bed with Dorothea and Auntie. The gag is repeated—with an elaborate variation—when Buster returns to the attic and again plummets down the hole in the floor into the bed below, then out the window into the mud, across the yard, and into the barn.

In the morning, Buster has a heart-to-heart talk with himself about his growing feelings for Dorothea. A ghostly double suddenly pops out of Buster's body and scolds him for having fallen in love with Dorothea when he is expected to marry Auntie. In a melodramatic flourish, Buster wrings his hands and turns his head away from his ghostly conscience, then decides to run away to forget about Dorothea. However, Auntie catches him and hauls him off at gunpoint to the preacher with Dorothea following close behind. Unexpectedly, Auntie barks at the parson to hitch up Buster and Dorothea as quickly as he can. While the couple embraces, Buster's ghostly conscience appears and taps him on the shoulder. Turning and giving his double a scowl, Buster grabs Auntie's rifle and aims it at the meddling ghost. In the fade-out, the ghost races out of the chapel and down the dirt road, but suddenly

Hayseed Romance: Although many consider Buster's Educational two-reelers trashy, several are filled with excellent examples of his unique approach to humor. Buster himself had a low opinion of all but one of the films.

flies into the air and flops dead on the ground after Buster fires and hits his mark.

Hayseed Romance contains enough distinctive Keatonesque qualities to make it a pleasant minor addition to his unique body of work. The double-image effect supplies its best moments and is a superb example of Buster's ability to rework an old effect (from *Sherlock Jr.*) into a clever variation, one that can easily stand on its own.

TARS AND STRIPES

CREDITS:

An Educational Pictures Production Presented by E. W. Hammons; Distributed by Fox Films. *Producer:* E. H. Allen; *Director/Story:* Charles Lamont; *Adaptation:* Ewart Adamson; *Photography:* Dwight Warren. *Release Date:* May 3, 1935. *Length:* two reels.

CAST:

Buster Keaton, Vernon Dent, Dorothea Kent, Jack Shutta.

Tars and Stripes is a mediocre Educational two-reeler with nothing outstanding to recommend it, unless the sight of Buster in a navy uniform happens to strike a person's fancy. The short was filmed at the U.S. Naval Training Station in San Diego and contains lots of elaborately staged—and pretty much pointless—footage of troop formations marching, posing, and scurrying about the deck of a huge battleship. If these scenes were spliced together, they would make for a nice navy promotional ad, superior to the tepid comedy within the rest of the footage.

Buster (playing another Elmer) first appears perched atop a flagpole in an uninspired re-creation of the mast-varnishing scene from *Spite Marriage.* After he dumps paint on his commanding officer, played by the eternally exasperated Vernon Dent, Buster is ordered to march in place until he learns how to behave like a proper sailor. The rest of the film is a series of encounters between Buster and his increasingly frustrated CO. Dent is dunked in the harbor twice, gets a faceful of gunk from an artillery gun, and is finally humiliated when Buster ends up a hero after rescuing a lieutenant from drowning. Buster hangs around Dent's pretty girlfriend, played by Dorothea Kent and, on one of her visits, ends up rolling around in the grass with her as he attempts to fix her shoe. Later, he tries to carry her to safety after she twists her ankle. Both times Dent sees him and gives chase. Finally, when the

Buster shows his alcoholic battle scars in this portrait taken from *Tars and Stripes*, one of his less-than-sterling Educational two-reelers. Shortly after completing this film, he stopped drinking and remained sober for the rest of the decade.

commander has good news for Buster—a letter of commendation for his rescue efforts—the latter takes off and locks himself in the brig just to be on the safe side. His hunch pays off after Dent presents him with the letter, then spots Dorothea's broken shoe in Buster's hand. The chase resumes and Buster ends up back in the brig with the commander personally locking him in. In the weak final gag, after Buster has been thrown into the brig, he suddenly slumps to the ground at the sight of Dorothea, who has arranged to be locked up with him.

Buster does next to nothing with the nearly nonexistent story line, which is based on a subplot from *Doughboys* where army private Buster competes with his sergeant (Ed Brophy) for the affections of leading lady Sally Eilers. Buster also looks far too old to be playing a navy recruit, the effects of his battle with alcohol painfully apparent on his deeply lined face.

THE E-FLAT MAN

CREDITS:

An Educational Pictures Production Presented by E. W. Hammons; Distributed by Fox Films. *Producer:* E. H. Allen;

Director: Charles Lamont; *Story:* Charles Lamont and Glen Lambert; *Photography:* Dwight Warren; *Sound:* Karl Zint. *Release Date:* August 9, 1935. *Length:* two reels.

CAST:

Buster Keaton, Dorothea Kent, Broderick O'Farrell, Charles McAvoy, Si Jenks, Fern Emmett, Jack Shutta, Matthew Betz (uncredited gang leader).

The E-Flat Man attempts to re-create the episodic style of such previous Keaton shorts as *The Goat* and *The Scarecrow*. Eloping with his sweetheart (Dorothea Kent), Buster ends up fleeing from her parents in a car belonging to gangsters. When the couple is then pursued by the police, Buster believes it is because Dorothea's father has reported their elopement. Then, when they hear a report over the police radio alerting patrolmen to "be on the lookout for a little shrimp wearing a flat hat and his blond moll in a plain evening dress," Buster realizes he is not driving his own car, and the two jump out and run off into the night.

After taking refuge in a huge haystack—populated by a beefy cow and three bums—Buster and Dorothea arise the next morning in search of food. They find it on the windowsill of a nearby farmhouse: a freshly baked stack of doughnuts. Trying to spear the doughnuts with a rake handle, Buster succeeds only in knocking them off the sill, and they land neatly around the neck of a goose, which promptly runs off.

Discovered by the farmer, they are put to work doing chores in exchange for food. However, after the farmer's kitchen radio croaks out another report about the shrimp and the moll, the couple takes off and begins hitchhiking. When no cars stop to pick them up, Buster remembers a surefire way to get a driver to pull over and encourages Dorothea to raise her skirt to show some leg (stealing the scene from *It Happened One Night* which premiered the previous year). The trick works, but their prospective chauffeurs turn out to be two patrolmen, and the couple heads off into a cornfield to escape capture. Buster then creates a variation of his scarecrow impersonation from *The Scarecrow*, and he and Dorothea elude the cops, ending up in a train yard and hopping inside a refrigerated freight car. Miles later when the car is opened, a train employee finds Buster and Dorothea around a small fire in the middle.

Realizing it is hopeless to keep trying to run from the law, the two stagger into a local police station and give themselves up. Unknown to Buster and Dorothea, the cops have already straightened out the mix-up in cars and tracked down the real crooks.

If the episodic adventures had been spiced up with a few more playful variations of old gags, *The E-Flat Man* could have been a lot more fun. As it is, it is too predictable and hardly one of the best examples of Buster's work at Educational.

THE TIMID YOUNG MAN

CREDITS:

An Educational Pictures Production Presented by E. W. Hammons; Distributed by Twentieth Century-Fox. *Producer/ Director:* Mack Sennett; *Script:* uncredited; *Photography:* Dwight Warren; *Sound:* Karl Zint. *Release Date:* October 25, 1935. *Length:* two reels.

CAST:

Buster Keaton, Lona Andre, Stanley J. Sandford, Kitty McHugh, Harry Bowen.

Many have assumed that Keaton, like Arbuckle, Chaplin, Lloyd, and Langdon, worked with Sennett at the Keystone Studios early in his career. Even Sennett himself, in his autobiography, had Keaton working with him at Keystone. However, they first worked together professionally at Educational on *The Timid Young Man*. With two such mighty creative forces involved, it is a shame that the film is so mediocre.

Buster (called Milton here, but he could easily have been Elmer) is a confirmed woman-hater who picks up pretty Lona Andre along the road and is relieved to find out she's a confirmed man-hater. On a narrow mountain lane, they ram head-on into a belligerent motorist, played by burly Stanley Sandford, who then tries to force them backward down the mountain but ends up driving off into a gully.

In a setup faintly reminiscent of the *The Balloonatic*, the woman-hater and the man-hater decide to camp out together and pitch a tent beside a lake. Buster goes fishing and uses Mexican jumping beans as bait, catching the fish in his net when they pop up out of the water.

While he continues to net the bouncing fish, Stanley shows up and makes a move on Lona. Buster ends up preparing a salad for the brute using a special ingredient—gasoline—for the dressing. He then saunters sheepishly away, watching from the safety of a nearby tree while Stanley digs into his meal and remains totally unaffected by the lethal dressing. After eating, Stanley gets frisky and begins to chase Lona around the camp, ultimately cornering the unsuspecting Buster in a tent and planting a kiss on him. Staggering out and rushing over to the salad bowl, Buster gargles with the potent salad dressing in the film's best sight gag.

To keep their aggressive unwelcome guest occupied long enough for them to make a getaway, Lona suggests they all go swimming. Their plan works when Buster's old flame (Kitty McHugh) hitchhikes into the midst of their party and starts a fight with Stanley, giving Buster and the bathing-suit-clad Lona enough time to escape down the road after dodging a fleet of randy motorists lusting after her.

Except for a few brief Keaton bits, the film's humor seems totally uninspired. Perhaps the two great silent screen legends were each depending on the other to act as the film's principal creative force. Perhaps they were only anxious to finish shooting and collect their paychecks. (Actually, Buster was on the verge of another collapse and ended up in a hospital soon after finishing the film.) In any event, the first Keaton-Sennett collaboration is hardly a momentous event. The two would do better in their next and final collaborative effort, *Hollywood Cavalcade,* made four years later for Twentieth Century-Fox.

THREE ON A LIMB

CREDITS:

An Educational Pictures Production Presented by E. W. Hammons; Distributed by Twentieth Century-Fox. *Director:* Charles Lamont; *Story:* Vernon Smith; *Photography:* Gus Peterson. *Release Date:* January 3, 1936. *Length:* two reels.

CAST:

Buster Keaton, Lona Andre, Harold Goodwin, Grant Withers, Barbara Bedford, John Ince, Fern Emmett, Phyllis Crane.

Three on a Limb comes close to being an above-average Educational short, maintaining a quirky charm until it loses its equilibrium during the climax.

Buster (called Elmer Brown), dressed amusingly in a scoutmaster outfit—short pants, Canadian Mountie–style hat—pulls into a drive-in restaurant and is immediately smitten by carhop Lona Andre. He can barely give her his order as he stares longingly into her eyes. When she delivers his food, he drops it on the ground and watches as another car pulls up and runs over it. Buster continues to moon over Lona even after her patrolman boyfriend (Harold Goodwin) appears and

Scoutmaster Buster checks policeman Harold Goodwin's list of traffic violations to make sure he didn't miss any, in *Three on a Limb.* Lona Andre waits for the final tally.

starts writing him up for as many violations as he can think of. When Harold runs out of inspiration, Buster helps out by mentioning that he recently ran a stoplight, and he gets written up for that, too.

Lona thinks Harold is a stinker for treating Buster so badly and accepts the latter's invitation to drive her home. On the way to her apartment, Buster learns that Lona is engaged to Harold, but her mother wants her to marry another suitor, Oscar (Grant Withers). In the film's frenetic finale, Oscar, Harold, and Buster all vie for Lona's hand. Her parents get into the act with Dad wanting Lona to marry Harold and Mom pulling for Oscar. Oscar's former girlfriend shows up and joins in the melee, too. After much pushing and shoving and several false starts at the altar, Buster and Lona end up married, and the attending preacher collapses from exhaustion while the others continue to tussle.

As a farce, *Three on a Limb* remains clever enough to survive most of its cartoonish shenanigans. However, Lona Andre's stiff acting damages key scenes, especially the finale when, standing placidly in front of the justice of the peace as her future husband is replaced again and again, she never objects in any overt way, her expression of outrage unconvincing. The scene itself, a variation of the finale to *His Wedding Night,* is interesting if predictable, the pace lively enough without its becoming a noisy brawl.

Buster looks more alert and in a much more playful mood, not as haggard as in some of the Educationals. He had recently gone through one of his worst alcoholic bouts, ending up in a veterans hospital in a straitjacket. During his hospitalization, he was informed that if he drank anymore, he would kill himself. After his release, he managed to stay dry for five years.

GRAND SLAM OPERA

CREDITS:

An Educational Pictures Production Presented by E. W. Hammons; Distributed by Twentieth Century-Fox. *Producer:* E. H. Allen; *Director:* Charles Lamont; *Story:* Buster Keaton and Charles Lamont; *Photography:* Gus Peterson. *Release Date:* February 21, 1936. *Length:* two reels.

CAST:

Buster Keaton, Diana Lewis, Harold Goodwin, John Ince, Melrose Coakley, Bud Jamison.

"It's awfully good of all you boys to see me to the train."

"So long, Elmer."

"I didn't think you cared if you should ne'er see me again."

"You're right, Elmer."

With his hilarious parody of George M. Cohan's "So Long Mary," Buster begins the only Educational two-reeler that he felt proud enough of to take scriptwriting credit for: *Grand Slam Opera*. This is a joy from beginning to end, full of playfully satirical routines from his days in vaudeville, all performed with vitality and assurance in classic Keaton style.

In his opening-song parody, sung in his strong and distinctive baritone from the back of a train, Buster is accompanied by his fellow townspeople who have gathered to serenade him as he leaves his hometown of Gopher City, Arizona, for New York to seek his fame. With a final farewell ("Good-bye, my Arizona, my mountains, my desert, my valley, my hat"), he disappears down the tracks. Then to the tune of "Sidewalks of New York," and to a visual collage of churning train wheels and rolling taxis, Buster arrives at a broadcasting studio to audition for the "Colonel Crow Amateur Night" radio show, an obvious parody of the popular "Major Bowes Amateur Hour."

After Buster watches pretty tap dancer Diana Lewis finish her number, Colonel Crow wraps up the show. Buster must wait until the next week for a chance to perform. Back in his hotel room, he prepares for his radio debut by attempting to perfect his talents. He tries juggling, but after flipping a lit cigar and then

accidentally sitting on it, he switches to balancing various objects on the tip of a billiard cue. When one of his objects, a bowling ball, nearly falls through the floor and into the room below, occupied by—who else?—Diana, Buster attempts dancing. Taking his inspiration from a dance-studio magazine advertisement featuring Fred Astaire, Buster sends up a couple of dance segments from *Top Hat*. Cranking up the record player, Buster begins tapping around the floor, then on top of a nightstand, a chair, along the fireplace mantel, and finally with a graceless leap, onto the bed, sending ceiling plaster raining down on Diana in the room below.

The subsequent week, Buster waits in the reception room of the broadcast studio while Colonel Crow introduces his next act, a corny-looking musical group called the Hoboken Canal Boat Boys. When the group launches into ethnic dance tunes, Buster rises from his seat, plucks a rose from a nearby flower arrangement, and performs along, changing his style of dance to

Orchestra conductor Harold Goodwin is not impressed with Buster's broom-balancing abilities in *Grand Slam Opera*, the only Educational two-reeler on which Keaton took scriptwriting credit.

Buster proudly poses with studio president Earl W. Hammons (left of Buster), director Charles Lamont (right of Buster), and Harold Goodwin (background in tux) on the set of *Grand Slam Opera*, one of his best post-silent films.

match the tunes played by the group: first several ballet leaps, then a Spanish tango (the rose clutched firmly in his teeth), followed by a Highland fling, an Irish jig, a modest tummy shake (to slinky Middle Eastern music), and finally a spectacular Russian deep-knee shuffle across the floor, ending with a half-twisting flip onto his back.

When Buster gets his turn to perform, he is to juggle—not exactly the best choice for a radio audience—an empty whiskey bottle and catch it on his finger. When asked by orchestra conductor Harold Goodwin if the bottle is empty, Buster replies, "Oh, yeah, I made sure of that," in a self-mocking reference to his problems with alcohol.

Buster ends up "gonged" after his first trick, and the orchestra quickly launches into a musical interlude. Ignoring these minor distractions, Buster attempts his next trick, balancing a broom on the end of his foot. When the broom ends up toppling Harold's music stand, the two men re-create Buster's old broom-bashing vaudeville routine done in time to the "Anvil Chorus." Buster smashes Harold in the rump with his broom, and Harold slaps Buster's head with a baton, and so on until Buster misses with one of his broom bashes and instead destroys an orchestra drum. Realizing his chances of winning the amateur contest are now fairly remote, Buster races out of the building, leaving a thoroughly flustered Colonel Crow and a decimated studio orchestra in his wake.

After another film montage featuring speeding trains, cars, bicycles, roller skates, and finally his two feet as he trudges painfully down a stretch of highway, Buster hears on a car radio that he has won the amateur radio contest after all. Again a flurry of images of travel fills the screen, ending with Buster bursting into the broadcast studio and crashing into the orchestra. He then runs over to Colonel Crow, who stuffs the contest check into his hand. Diana suddenly materializes, cooing, "My hero," and Buster utters his "How about a little dinner and a show?" line from *Doughboys,* to which she replies, "Swell!" and the two walk off together in the film's fade-out.

Grand Slam Opera is a mini-showcase of Buster's wildly varied talents: he sings, dances, performs acrobatic and juggling feats, stages pantomime routines, pokes fun at radio, movie musicals, and himself, and throws in several astounding sight gags for good measure. Throughout, Keaton remains his brilliantly understated self, the quiet eye surrounded by the film's hurricane-paced action.

Buster was sober during production and managed to stay away from alcohol throughout the rest of the decade. He had also recently been divorced from his second wife, Mae Scribbens. *Grand Slam Opera* could, therefore, be viewed as Buster's personal inventory of his talents, proving to himself and to the film community that he was still very much alive and kicking. Unfortunately, since Educational's reputation as the studio for has-beens was still firmly intact, Keaton's artistic gifts were once again ignored by the studio heads.

BLUE BLAZES

CREDITS:

An Educational Pictures Production Presented by E. W. Hammons; Distributed by Twentieth Century-Fox. *Producer:* E. H. Allen; *Director:* Raymond Kane; *Story:* David Freedman; *Photography:* George Webber. *Release Date:* August 21, 1936. *Length:* two reels.

CAST:

Buster Keaton, Arthur Jarrett, Rose Kessner, Patty Wilson, Marlyn Stuart.

Blue Blazes is a large step backward from Buster's previous Educational short, *Grand Slam Opera*. It is one of the talkiest of the Educationals, its shrill verbal jokes detracting from the visual horseplay. It is also ineptly made, with faked stunts, crude editing, and blatantly artificial outdoor night scenes filmed on a cavernous, echoing soundstage and then combined with shots staged out of doors in broad daylight.

Buster plays a fire-fighting Elmer in a large, noisy city. After being reprimanded by the chief (Arthur Jarrett) for falling off the back of the fire truck one too many times, Buster is transferred to a less desirable station located in a small suburb that also happens to be his old boss's hometown. Buster watches entranced as the firemen go about their daily chores: sewing, gardening, flower arranging, and doll repairing. When he asks a colleague how frequent fires are in the area, he is told there hasn't been one for weeks.

Naturally, the tranquillity is shattered the moment Buster attempts to relax in the station's bunkhouse. A proud Buster stands at the back of a truck preparing to race off to a fire, then watches as it pulls away, leaving him standing on a small bench (a gag originally used in *The Goat*). Catching up with the truck, he is thrown off—in a terrifically staged physical stunt—when it rounds a corner.

Buster ends up wandering the local streets in his uniform, a fire hose draped over one shoulder, finally making it back to the deserted station. As he attempts to rest once more, his efforts are again interrupted by the alarm, and he races off to battle a fire alone, riding on a bicycle laden with fire-fighting equipment. The burning house turns out to be the chief's, and after some inept stumbling and faked acrobatics, Buster saves the chief's wife and is pronounced a hero.

Buster is reinstated at his old, noisy fire station and

ends up falling out a window. He lands comfortably on a canvas awning, finally finding the right place for an undisturbed nap.

Blue Blazes is one of three Educationals Buster made in New York. The new environment, along with the new technical crew, obviously failed to provide any creative spark. Buster would do better in future Educationals after being reunited with his favorite low-budget director, Charles Lamont.

The Chemist: Buster seems unimpressed with his status as top dog of the least prestigious film studio in Hollywood.

THE CHEMIST

CREDITS:

An Educational Pictures Production Presented by E. W. Hammons; Distributed by Twentieth Century-Fox. *Producer/Director:* Al Christie; *Story:* David Freedman; *Photography:* George Webber. *Release Date:* October 9, 1936. *Length:* two reels.

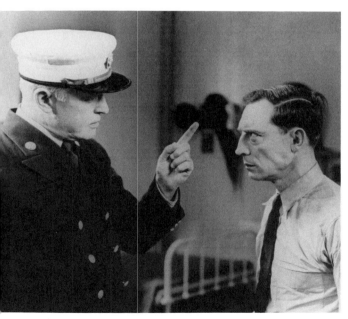

Fireman Buster is reprimanded by chief Arthur Jarrett for falling off the fire truck one too many times, in *Blue Blazes*.

CAST:

Buster Keaton, Marlyn Stuart, Earl Gilbert, Donald McBride, Herman Lieb.

The Chemist was produced and directed by early filmmaking veteran Al Christie, the founder of Nestor Studios, one of Hollywood's first film studios, established in 1911. Buster's old friend Roscoe Arbuckle had worked at Nestor for a brief period early in his career before moving on to Sennett's Keystone Studios. Like so many other talents—Keaton, Arbuckle, and Mack Sennett included—Christie ended up at Educational churning out two-reel cheapies.

The Chemist, unlike Buster's mediocre collaboration with Sennett, *The Timid Young Man*, is a fast-paced charmer with a solid story line slightly reminiscent of Laurel and Hardy's 1933 short *Dirty Work*. In that film, Stan and Ollie, working as chimney sweeps, become mixed up with a demented scientist whose rejuvenation formula has disastrously funny results. However, the lab shenanigans in that film take a backseat to the team's bumbling attempts to clean the professor's chimney. With *The Chemist,* the story emphasis is solidly on the wacky formulas Buster cooks up as an assistant to a chemistry professor at Duncemore College.

The first half of the short is dominated by Buster's experiments with a love potion that gets him into trouble with his girlfriend, Marlyn Stuart, when he inadvertently douses himself with the powder and pounces on her. The film's second half has him experimenting with a silent explosive, an invention that so excites the chemistry department's dean that he shouts, "Now we can have war in peace!" Unfortunately, the formula falls into the hands of safecrackers. Buster manages to douse the crooks with the explosive powder, then, because the powder is activated by water, he uses a seltzer bottle as a gun and marches the hoods to the police station. After turning over the crooks to the cops, he celebrates with a group of professors by offering them cups of water containing another formula of his, which triples a person's strength. Unfortunately, Buster has mixed up this powder with a shrinking formula, and *The Chemist* ends with Buster being chased down the street by his midget-sized colleagues.

Although one of Buster's better Educationals, *The Chemist* is not exactly a Keaton-type film, its pacing more fitting for a Three Stooges two-reeler, very broad and cartoonish, punctuated with snappy, wisecracking dialogue spoken by caricatural performers. Its most Keatonesque touch is the trademark porkpie, which he wears here for the first time since ripping it off his head in the hat-fitting scene from *Steamboat Bill, Jr.* The hat receives one of the film's biggest laughs when Buster, hiding from the crooks in a crowd, is finally spotted and the gang leader tells one of his cronies, "Look under that flat rock."

MIXED MAGIC

CREDITS:

An Educational Pictures Production Prestented by E. W. Hammons; Distributed by Twentieth Century-Fox. *Producer:* E. H. Allen; *Director:* Raymond Kane; *Story:* Arthur Jarrett and Marcy Klauber; *Photography:* George Webber. *Release Date:* November 20, 1936. *Length:* two reels.

CAST:

Buster Keaton, Marlyn Stuart, Eddie Lambert, Eddie Hall, Jimmie Fox, Walter Fenner, Pass Le Noir, Harry Myers.

A fairly predictable Educational two-reeler, *Mixed Magic* has mildly amusing variations of the show-wrecking shenanigans Buster performed previously in *Spite Marriage, Free and Easy*, and *Speak Easily.* The opening images quickly establish the film's colorful carnival setting. Buster is glimpsed before a billboard advertising The Great Spumoni, the show's featured magician, who is illustrated in the poster along with his pretty assistant.

Entering a cafeteria, Buster buys a plateful of spaghetti, then gasps at the sight of Spumoni (Eddie Lambert), and his assistant (Marlyn Stuart) at a nearby table. When Spumoni rises to fetch more food, Buster introduces himself to the girl, who informs him that her boss is looking for another assistant for his magic act. Spumoni returns and asks Buster if he has had any experience performing magic. Buster picks up a menu and places it with an inept flourish in front of his dinner plate, then pulls out a juicy steak and various other pilfered treats from underneath his spaghetti. An astonished Spumoni ends up hiring him on the spot.

When it comes time for Buster to help out with Spumoni's magic act, he thoroughly destroys it. During the "levitating woman" illusion, Buster stands backstage manipulating two ropes, lifting Marlyn off her couch, then tipping her at ridiculously extreme angles, first forward then backward, until she is nearly perpendicular instead of horizontal. Finally he manages to lower her back to the couch, but then pulls up on the ropes and catches Spumoni on the secret levitating

Buster is either in a hypnotic trance or suffering from boredom as he helps the Great Spumoni (Eddie Lambert) levitate pretty assistant Marlyn Stuart in *Mixed Magic*.

platform, hoisting him above the stage where the panicked magician calls for the curtain to be brought down. Instead, Buster lowers several backdrops, including an Egyptian desert scene complete with pyramids, before finally dropping the curtain, which collapses in a heap onstage.

Buster throws "magically appearing" ducks through the wrong trapdoor from underneath the stage, making Spumoni run from one end to the other trying to position his magic cape in front of the ducks to save the trick.

While Buster and Spumoni prepare for the show's finale, the magician's former assistant, seeking revenge against his ex-boss, lowers a hook from above the stage and yanks Marlyn into the rafters. Buster then springs into action in an ineptly staged bit of bravado ending with a faked rope-swinging rescue stunt.

In spite of its overly familiar material, *Mixed Magic* still includes a few unique Keaton touches. The film was the last he made for Educational in its New York–based studios.

JAIL BAIT

CREDITS:

An Educational Pictures Production Presented by E. W. Hammons; Distributed by Twentieth Century-Fox. *Producer:* E. H. Allen; *Director:* Charles Lamont; *Story:* Paul Gerard Smith; *Photography:* Dwight Warren. *Release Date:* January 8, 1937. *Length:* two reels.

Buster helps newspaper reporter Harold Goodwin catch a murderer by posing as the criminal himself in *Jail Bait*, another superior Educational two-reeler.

CAST:

Buster Keaton, Harold Goodwin, Matthew Betz, Bud Jamison, Betty Andre.

After having made three uninspired two-reelers for Educational in its East Coast studios, Buster celebrated his return to Los Angeles by filling his next three shorts with some of his best postsilent material. The first, *Jail Bait,* slightly reminiscent of *Convict 13,* has Buster working in a newspaper office as a lowly copyboy pining over pretty reporter Betty Andre. Then, with a newspaper headline screaming, "Kidnapped Victim's Body Found!" the scene shifts to the crime scene where police gather around the body and answer questions from probing reporters. As the police chief admits he hasn't a clue to the identity of the murderer, reporter Harold Goodwin spots an incriminating piece of evidence and runs off to the apartment he shares with Buster.

Harold announces to his roommate that he knows who the murderer is, then shocks Buster by suggesting that he (Buster) pose as the killer and confess to the crime so the cops will stop looking for the real one.

This will give Harold enough time to round up the criminal in his Arizona hideout and bring him to justice. Harold's offer to split the reward convinces the unenthusiastic Buster, who needs money to buy Betty an engagement ring.

Buster accompanies Harold back to the crime scene to plant incriminating evidence. While Harold boards a plane for Arizona, Buster goes off to get himself arrested by a not-too-observant policeman. After Buster's hat falls off and lands on a lawn with a "Keep off the Grass" sign, he ends up in the slammer and confesses to the murder—only to learn that Harold's plane has crashed. Buster is now stuck behind bars.

When a guard arrives to secure the bars on his cell window, Buster uses one of the bars as a club, subdues the guard, and switches uniforms. However, the moment Buster emerges from his cell, a prison break erupts. A stream of convicts dashes past him, one pausing long enough to conk the guard-uniformed Buster on the head. Realizing he would be better off in a convict's uniform, he switches again and steps out of his cell once more just in time to watch a parade of guards rush by, one of whom lands another blow on Buster's head. Staggering back inside his cell, Buster fixes the guard's uniform to the front of his body and the convict's to his back, then stands out in the hall once more, turning around and around, satisfying the

dress code for each group running past him. (Buster re-created this clever double-uniform gag for Red Skelton's later *A Southern Yankee,* a remake of *The General.*)

Buster finally escapes with a group of convicts, concealing himself with the others in a truckload of barrels. He ends up in a remote Arizona hideout where he runs into the real murderer. When cops arrive and surround the shack—saving Buster from a near-fatal encounter with the crooks—he escapes by following the murderer through a secret passageway and hitching a ride on the back of the criminal's escape vehicle. Buster ultimately hauls the killer back to the police station and is immediately pronounced a hero, receiving a pardon and a reward, which he uses to purchase the engagement ring for his girl in the fade-out.

Jail Bait is dominated not only by Buster's visual style but also by many of his favorite themes. Mistaken and switched identities, ironic plot twists, and the inability to control one's fate are all well represented in the film's lively, episodic story line. Although the influence of *Convict 13* and to a lesser degree *The Goat* are felt in several scenes, the film stands on its own as a prime example of Buster striving—and succeeding—to make something distinctively Keatonesque out of his scant production resources.

In *Ditto*, one of the finest examples of his post-silent film work, Buster tries to explain to Harold Goodwin and twins Barbara and Gloria Brewster how Lynton Brent received that nasty bump on his head.

DITTO

CREDITS:

An Educational Pictures Production Prestented by E. W. Hammons; Distributed by Twentieth Century-Fox. *Producer:* E. H. Allen; *Director:* Charles Lamont; *Story:* Paul Gerard Smith; *Photography:* Dwight Warren. *Release Date:* February 21, 1937. *Length:* two reels.

CAST:

Buster Keaton, Gloria and Barbara Brewster, Harold Goodwin, Lynton Brent, Al Thompson, Bob Ellsworth.

In *The Great Movie Shorts,* film historian and critic Leonard Maltin singles out *Ditto,* calling it "embarrassingly bad . . . , a film that starts out promisingly . . . but quickly deteriorates." Since this notice is one of the film's only existing reviews aside from Buster's general, disparaging comments about the work he produced at Educational, it is no wonder that *Ditto* was shrugged off as just another piece of cheap two-reeler trash from the trashiest of studios. In my own initial viewing, I also found the film lacking. However, after spending months watching and rewatching Buster's films—in sequential order for the most part—I was pleasantly surprised (make that stunned and shocked) to find *Ditto* to be, in fact, a minor masterpiece, one of Keaton's best since his silent films. It not only showcases his favorite themes of mistaken identities, multiple images, and misconstrued actions, but also contains autobiographical references, absurdist humor, outrageous satire, intricately timed mayhem, and superb pantomime routines as well as some of the finest examples of his sparse yet concise use of sound.

The film begins with a title card reading "The Forgotten Man," which fades to show Buster sitting in an ice truck reading a book. The title card supposedly refers to the anachronistic iceman, whose service was rapidly becoming obsolete with the growing popularity of electric refrigerators, but it's pretty obvious that Buster was referring to himself.

Buster spots an "Ice Wanted" sign hanging in a window and is invited in by an attractive young woman (Gloria Brewster), who is struggling with the door of her oven while balancing an unbaked pie in one hand. Handing the pie to Buster, she uses both hands to yank at the door, but finally gives up. Buster then gives the pie back to her and tries his luck. After three hat-jarring heaves, he backs off and steps aside just as the oven door falls open by itself, seemingly out of spite. Throwing the pie into the oven, Gloria inadvertently burns her wrist, and Buster slaps butter on her wound with a knife while gazing rapturously into her eyes. Gloria returns his swooning look, their expressions blissful, then, waking from her reverie, she looks at her arm and screams as she realizes that Buster has buttered her from shoulder to thumb.

Finally fetching Gloria a block of ice, Buster absentmindedly deposits it in the oven rather than the icebox. Later, when Gloria checks on her pie and finds it looking very unappetizing, she cuts into it and is squirted in the face with water.

Returning to Gloria's house, thinking he has a chance to woo her, Buster spots whom he believes is Gloria but who is actually her twin sister, Barbara, who lives next door. This sets up an extended bit of mixed identities as Buster ends up wooing both sisters while dodging their respective husbands. When Buster finally realizes twins are involved and both are married, he believes the women have been leading him on and walks off dejectedly, vowing to become a hermit.

After the title card "Fifteen Years Later . . . ," hermit Buster, adorned with a blatantly fake beard, sits forlornly by a campfire sheltered by a pitiful shack. As the camera moves back, the surrounding wilderness is revealed, choked with camping trailers and hundreds of noisy vacationers. Then to illustrate just how

crowded the world has become fifteen years into the future, Buster gazes skyward, and watches a fleet of airplanes fly overhead, each pulling a Winnebago trailer.

Buster next runs off to help a pretty woman untangle herself from her fishing line. Taken by her beauty, he asks if he can visit her later at her campsite. When she says yes, Buster rushes off and tries to shave off his fake beard, an inspired bit of comedy, faintly reminiscent of the beard gluing scene from *Spite Marriage*, but still solidly original. After several hysterical hair-pulling moments, Buster dons a fancy suit and approaches the girl's campsite, only to see five sets of identical-twin girls (seen from behind—a cheap effect but handled well enough to get the point across). A horrified Buster dashes off.

Watching *Ditto* is like watching a sloe-eyed hobo pull a string of shabby baubles out of a garbage can and fashion a dazzling object of unexpected, whimsical beauty. It is Buster at his subtly ironic best. Throughout, Buster's performance is assured, his motions swift and concise. With its "Forgotten Man" title card intro, the film plays like a visual résumé of his talents as the complete and total moviemaker.

LOVE NEST ON WHEELS

CREDITS:

An Educational Pictures Production Presented by E. W. Hammons; Distributed by Twentieth Century-Fox. *Producer:* E. H. Allen; *Director:* Charles Lamont; *Story:* William Hazlett Upson; *Adaptation:* Paul Gerard Smith; *Photography:* Dwight Warren. *Release Date:* March 26, 1937. *Length:* two reels.

CAST:

Buster Keaton, Myra Keaton, Louise Keaton, Harry Keaton, Al St. John, Lynton Brent, Diana Lewis, Bud Jamison.

Love Nest on Wheels, Keaton's final two-reeler for Educational, is a companion piece to his earlier *Palooka from Paducah.* Here, once again he stars with his mother and sister, with his younger brother, Harry, filling in for papa Joe. At this time, Buster was supporting his family, all of them—with the exception of Joe—living together in a modest home in the Cheviot Hills area of Los Angeles. Featuring his family in the Educationals, therefore, was not wholly an artistic decision but a way to earn some extra cash for the financially strapped Keatons.

Although nearly a remake of the Arbuckle-Keaton

Buster's younger brother, Harry, appears in *Love Nest on Wheels*, a companion film to the earlier Educational short, *Palooka From Paducah*. Like the previous two-reeler, this one also stars Keaton's mother, Myra, and sister, Louise.

short *The Bell Boy*, this is still an absolute delight. In the opening long shot, the Keatons are sprawled in front of their dilapidated hotel located in some remote backwoods area. Ma, sitting in her rocking chair and puffing on her corncob pipe, mumbles to her near-comatose family that the nefarious local banker (Bud Jamison) plans to foreclose on the mortgage the following day unless they come up with $350. No one seems all that concerned; in fact, Buster seems more interested in the fly on his nose, telling the others, "It'll fall off first cold spell."

When a car pulls up carrying newlyweds Diana Lewis and Lynton Brent, the family slumps into action. Buster and Harry help them to their room, using the horse-powered elevator straight out of *The Bell Boy*. When Diana bursts into tears at the sight of her suite, Buster recommends she and Lynton purchase a car trailer and spend their honeymoon traveling the countryside. Buster can sell the couple a trailer for, oh, let's say $350, and Lynton agrees. Running to Ma, who is chopping wood in the hotel lobby, Buster asks where he can find the trailer that was abandoned by a former

guest, then races off when she says that Uncle Jed has it stored in his barn.

Uncle Jed is played by Buster's old costar from the Arbuckle days, Al St. John, who looks marvelously cartoonish in his scraggly beard, floppy hat, and baggy pants. He tells Buster—in a whining voice—that he has the trailer but it is presently occupied by a stubborn cow that refuses to vacate. After a few tugs on the cow's collar, Buster agrees and dashes off to think of another way to solve the family dilemma.

Meanwhile, the banker Jamison shows up demanding payment on the mortgage. As he stalks around inspecting the property, Buster and family re-create two classic extended routines from *The Bell Boy*. In the first, originally staged by Buster and dad Joe, a tray of hot towels running on a conveyor belt from the hotel's barbershop to the kitchen knocks off Jamison's hat along its route, leading to a fight between Buster and the banker. In the second routine, an elevator full of guests gets stuck between floors when the horse powering the elevator refuses to budge. Both scenes are near-exact re-creations of the originals, but they play well here and are integrated into the story even more adeptly than in *The Bell Boy*.

In the end, the cow stuck in the trailer finally exits, followed by her newborn calf. Diana and Lynton pay cash for their new love nest, enabling the family to pay off its mortgage. The family assumes the same positions as in the opening scene and Ma mumbles, "Looks like we'll be keeping the hotel," which receives the same lackadaisical response as her first comment about losing it.

Love Nest on Wheels, smoothly logical with wonderfully deadpan acting by the Keatons, is nearly a parody of their personal life, the family living together and struggling to make financial ends meet.

Buster never spoke very highly of the short films he made for Educational, but considering their appallingly meager budgets, many have examples of his best post-silent-film work. As a whole, the Educationals put his MGM sound features to shame, vividly illustrating that, if given the proper resources and creative freedom, Keaton was still very capable of producing cinematic magic.

PEST FROM THE WEST

CREDITS:

A Columbia Pictures Production. *Producer:* Jules White; *Director:* Del Lord; *Script:* Clyde Bruckman. *Release Date:* June 16, 1939. *Length:* two reels.

After a two-year absence from the screen, Buster stars in *Pest From the West*, the first of a series of two-reelers for Columbia Pictures. The short was a remake of his British-produced feature, *The Invader*, and proved to be the best of the series.

CAST:

Buster Keaton, Lorna Gray [later Adrian Booth], Gino Corrado, Richard Fiske, Eddie Laughton, Forbes Murray, Bud Jamison.

After completing his final Educational two-reeler in the spring of 1937 shortly before the studio went bankrupt, Buster didn't appear on-screen for two years. With the assistance of several friends from his MGM days, Buster found work at his old studio as a gag writer. He was paid $200 per week, quite a comedown from the $3,000 in his days as the studio's featured comic.

It wasn't until early 1939 that Buster was offered a chance to appear once again in front of the camera, thanks to old friend and collaborator Clyde Bruckman, who was working as a scriptwriter for Columbia Pictures' short-film division, where the Three Stooges were then toiling. Buster was hired to star in a series of two-reelers. The Columbia shorts had more generous budgets than those at Educational, but despite the improved production values, the films suffer from a lack of originality. Both Buster and Bruckman (who receives writing credit for eight of the ten films) were satisfied with recycling jokes from the old days. The majority of these shorts were produced and directed by Jules White, Buster's least favorite director from his MGM days. White's forte was shrill, frenetic, roughhouse humor, which was much more suitable for Moe, Larry, and Curly than for Buster's more subtly elaborate approach. Most of Keaton's Columbia shorts suffer from this clash in comedic styles.

The best in the series is the first, *Pest From the West*, directed by one of Columbia's top short-film directors, Del Lord. A blatant remake of Buster's cheap British fiasco, *The Invader*, it manages to tell the feature's flimsy story in two reels as opposed to six without sacrificing any of the limp plot. However, the short does sacrifice some of Buster's more effectively subtle bits without adding anything substantially new.

Set in Mexico this time instead of Spain, *Pest From the West* finds Buster posing as a rich yachtsman who docks in the harbor of a small coastal town and ventures forth to find adventure and romance. He falls in love with Conchita, a beautiful Mexican dancer played by Lorna Gray, who in turn is in love with a caddish gigolo (Gino Corrado). She and her lover attempt to take over the local cantina by using a stooge, Buster, to make its owner murderously jealous. But Conchita falls in love with Buster, leading to a duel at dawn between Conchita's three suitors. Two of the suitors die, and Buster ends up running back to his yacht to escape the wrath of Conchita's husband, who suddenly turns up at the film's climax.

In the fade-out joke, when Conchita's husband suddenly appears, he turns out to be the man who dropped various objects on Buster's head as he serenaded Conchita with the song "In a Little Spanish Town," which, as in the feature, provides the film's best moment. The ending of *Pest From the West* differs from the original in that it is blessedly brief—two of Conchita's lovers appear, draw their pistols, and shoot each other dead in a matter of seconds—and in that Buster fails to get the girl in the end.

There is an interesting extraneous tidbit relating to the scene in which Conchita tries to seduce Buster to enrage the cantina owner. Conchita paws him, embraces him, and then calls him "my little Pamplinas," the nickname by which he was known in Spanish-speaking countries. Buster was called by several different names throughout the world, some of the more colorful and well-known being Malec (French), Zybsko (Polish), Prysmylenco (Czech), Wong Wong (Chinese), Glo Glo (Icelandic), and Kofreto (Siamese). In Rudi Blesh's biography, Keaton comments on the meaning of these international nicknames: "No one as yet has given me authentic translations, but I imagine that most of these terms of endearment signify null and void, and their combined meaning, if totaled up, would equal zero." According to Buster, the closest translation for Pampliñas is "a little bit of nothing." For the French name, the equivalent in English is "a blank piece of paper," or better yet, "the hole in the dough-nut," all marvelously appropriate monikers for the Great Stone Face.

MOOCHING THROUGH GEORGIA

CREDITS:

A Columbia Pictures Production. *Producer/Director:* Jules White; *Script:* Clyde Bruckman. *Release Date:* August 11, 1939. *Length:* two reels.

CAST:

Buster Keaton, Ned Glass, Bud Jamison, Monty Collins, Jill Martin (aka Harley Wood), Lynton Brent, Jack Hill, Stanley Mack.

Mooching Through Georgia is a typical Columbia two-reeler, full of broad, frenetic slapstick. Still, Buster manages to insert a trace of his more subtle style, and the film's plot and its central gag are very much in the Keaton tradition.

Buster first appears as a resident of a soldiers' retirement home. Sporting a bushy, artificial beard and dressed in Confederate gray, he runs into another old-timer, played by Ned Glass, dressed in Union blue, who asks Buster about the medal pinned on his lapel. Buster tells how he earned it in a flashback to a grand old Georgia plantation where Buster, his brother, Cyrus (Monty Collins), and his father, Titus (Bud Jamison), are lounging on the veranda. When a neighbor appears with news of war between the states, the two brothers decide to enlist. However, when they return home, Buster is dressed in Confederate gray, Cyrus in Union blue.

In the rest of *Mooching Through Georgia,* first Buster and then Cyrus change outfits according to which army happens to be on the premises at a given moment. In one segment, Buster is nearly executed by a Union firing squad. Cyrus tries to save him by sneaking blanks into the squad's rifles, but the guns end up in a larger pile of weapons so Buster's fate is left hanging. Buster does a comically hammy death scene for the benefit of the Union troops when he realizes he's been

Confederate veteran Buster relates to Union veteran Ned Glass how he won his Civil War medal, in *Mooching Through Georgia*.

In *Mooching Through Georgia*, Buster pitches some woo to his Southern Belle sweetheart, Jill Martin, while hiding from Union troops. The film is definitely not a sequel to *The General*.

HOLLYWOOD CAVALCADE

CREDITS:

A Twentieth Century-Fox Production. *Producer:* Darryl F. Zanuck; *Director:* Irving Cummings (Keystone Kops segment directed by Mal St. Clair); *Script:* Ernest Pascal; *Story:* Hilary Lynn and Brown Holmes, based on an idea by Lou Breslow; *Photography:* Allen M. Davey and Ernest Palmer; *Editor:* Walter Thompson; *Technical Adviser:* Mack Sennett and Buster Keaton (uncredited). Technicolor. *Release Date:* October 13, 1939. *Running Time:* 96 minutes.

CAST:

Buster Keaton, Alice Faye, Don Ameche, Stuart Erwin, Mary Forbes, Chester Conklin, Mack Sennett, Al Jolson, Ben Turpin, Harold Goodwin, Willie Fung.

shot with blanks. Later, when two soldiers try to bury him, Buster keeps scooting farther and farther away from the men when they're not looking, an effective variation of a gag from *The Paleface.* After finally managing to escape, Buster runs off to warn the Confederate army of a Yankee battle plan and saves the day. The film concludes with the two old Civil War veterans battling each other on the rest home grounds when Buster's acquaintance turns out to be one of the Union soldiers he fought on his front lawn many years ago.

Mooching Through Georgia is hardly the sequel to *The General* (or even the later *A Southern Yankee,* which it somewhat resembles with its extended uniform-switching segments). A typical noisy, chaotic Columbia two-reeler, the film was later the basis for the Three Stooges' short *Uncivil Warbirds,* made in 1946, also directed by Jules White. As Three Stooges material, it works fine. As a Keaton vehicle, well, not quite.

Buster was asked by friend and collaborator Mal St. Clair to assist as technical adviser for the film-within-a-film segments to this entertaining feature set during the pioneer days of Hollywood. He received no credit, although his assistance led to a juicy costarring part, his first work in a feature film for a major studio since his MGM days.

Ironically, what convinced Fox to take a chance on Buster, who still had a reputation as an unreliable drunk despite not having had a drink in nearly five years, was the success of his Columbia two-reelers. His first two Columbia shorts, benefiting from a much wider distribution than his Educationals, received a very positive public response not lost on the Hollywood moguls. Of course, it didn't hurt that Buster's old boss and former brother-in-law, Joseph Schenck, was now running Fox. Schenck had remained in contact with Buster during his lowest periods and had helped him out financially on several occasions.

A lavish, big-budget Technicolor production (Buster's first color picture), *Hollywood Cavalcade* chronicles the rise and fall and rise again of a pioneer filmmaker, played by Don Ameche and modeled after Mack Sennett, who also appears in the film. Ameche's featured star in most of his slapstick two-reel comedies is Alice Faye (as a Mabel Normand type). Buster appears with Alice in two early segments.

In the first, Ameche directs a scene with Buster proposing to Alice in front of a jewelry store. When Alice accepts his proposal, Buster runs inside to buy her a ring, only to return to find a rival suitor (George Givot) attempting to woo her. With Ameche screaming at Buster to hurry up and find something with which to

In his first appearance in a major studio-produced feature since being fired from MGM, Buster defends Alice Faye with a barrage of expertly tossed pies in *Hollywood Cavalcade*.

In this gag photo, Alice thanks Buster for defending her honor by splattering a pie in his face. Keaton's erroneous reputation as a pie-tossing silent film comedian ironically landed him the part here.

Buster retrieves Alice from a mud puddle after losing her off the back of his motorcycle in one of the best scenes from *Hollywood Cavalcade*.

hit George before the film runs out, Buster gazes off-camera and spots a man carrying a custard pie on a lunch tray. Picking up the pie, Buster flings it at George but ends up hitting Alice. When she screams in protest and Ameche screams at Buster for wrecking the scene, suddenly director Ameche becomes aware of the stagehands laughing uproariously at the sight of the pie-spattered Alice. And that, ladies and gentlemen, is how pie-slinging in the movies was born. The rest of the segment neatly segues into a black-and-white re-creation of a silent two-reel comedy, picking up on the action of the previous scene with Buster and George staging an elaborate pie fight. The irony is that, except for a very brief scene in *The Butcher Boy,* this is the first time Buster threw a pie in a film, showing how muddled his reputation, now that of a pie-throwing slapstick comic, had become in the collective Hollywood memory.

Buster's second segment is a re-creation of a Keystone Kops car chase. Playing a messenger boy, he drives Alice to her house on his teetering motorcycle. When he hits a bump in the road, Alice flies off into a mud puddle. Then, after picking her up and taking off again, Buster is thrown from the vehicle while Alice rides the bike off a cliff where she ends up dangling from a tree branch over the chasm. Buster uses gags from *Hard Luck* (the exploding bullets in the stove), *The Goat* (attempting to sit on the back of a vehicle but ending up stranded on a stationary plug), and *Sherlock Jr.* (riding on the handlebars of a driverless motorcycle). None of the re-created gags match the effectiveness of the originals because of the use of back projection and cartoonish sound effects. Again, Buster is perceived as a Sennett protégé, a former low-humor Keystone Kop, something he never was.

One of the joys of *Hollywood Cavalcade* is seeing Buster in glorious Technicolor. Dressed for the most part in his traditional outfit—flat hat, dark suit, vest, clip-on tie, and slap shoes—he plays his scenes with a quiet seriousness, looking beautifully and vibrantly sad. However, the film's most poignant moment occurs before Buster appears on-screen. A film lot is shown with a large fat man—his back to the camera—dressed in a bowler hat, checkered shirt, and ankle-length pants, walking down a western-style street. A nearby stagehand looks up, spots the figure, and says, "Hi, Rosoce." The fat man (played by Marshall Ruth) acknowledges the greeting with a tip of his hat and walks on. The scene is a touching tribute to another comedy pioneer whose accomplishments and career were distorted and smashed by the Hollywood studio machine.

NOTHING BUT PLEASURE

CREDITS:

A Columbia Pictures Production. *Producer/Director:* Jules White; *Script:* Clyde Bruckman; *Photography:* Henry Freulich; *Release Date:* January 19, 1940. *Length:* two reels.

CAST:

Buster Keaton, Dorothy Appleby, Johnny Tyrell, Richard Fiske, Bud Jamison, Jack Randall, Beatrice Blinn, Robert Sterling, Eddie Laughton, Victor Tramers, Lynton Brent.

Nothing But Pleasure is one of the better shorts Buster made at Columbia. According to Alan Hoffman in his book, *Buster*, the story is based on Keaton's

fondness for buying new cars direct from the factory in Detroit, driving them back to the West Coast to save shipping costs, and sight-seeing along the way. (Hoffman quotes Eleanor Keaton, who says she accompanied Buster on more than one of these journeys.)

In the short, Buster and Dorothy Appleby—his attractive costar for many of the Columbia shorts—sell their reliable old car, then hop a Detroit-bound bus to pick up their new one. The bus ride is complete with screaming babies, slovenly fellow passengers, and clouds of dust blowing through the windows.

When they arrive in Detroit and pick out their new dream car, Buster promptly drives it through the showcase window, resulting in additional expenses that whittle down the couple's cash. In a segment lifted straight from W. C. Fields's *The Man on the Flying Trapeze* (a sequence written by Clyde Bruckman, who also directed the Fields film), Buster tries pulling away from the curb in his new auto, but finds himself stuck between two cars. He yanks at the steering wheel trying to squeeze out, not realizing that the car behind him has been driven off. When a policeman finally

Taking time out from his cross-country driving duties, Buster assists an inebriated acquaintance, played by Beatrice Blinn, in *Nothing But Pleasure*, as his wife (Dorothy Appleby) studies his Good Samaritan techniques.

calls his attention to this fact, Buster guns the motor and slams his car into reverse just as another car pulls up behind him, resulting in crunched fenders and another chunk of money for repairs.

After the couple spends several days on the road, sleeping in the car to save dough, Dorothy insists they enjoy a night in a bed rather than the backseat. At a motel, after Buster encounters a drunk female, two gangsters end up stealing the new car and wrecking it after an extended chase. In one blessedly quiet scene occurring before the chase finale, Buster makes a stew in the motel room, with potatoes, zucchini, garlic, grapes, a mousetrap (sans mouse), a kitten (rescued from the boiling pot at the last minute), and a huge pumpkin.

Nothing But Pleasure reflects the overbearing presence of director/producer Jules White. His cinematic philosophy was "Make 'em move so fast, if they're not funny, no one will realize it or get bored." His approach is glaringly evident in nearly every Columbia short with which he was involved from the late 1930s to the early 1950s. His formulaic, assembly-line approach to filmmaking, favored by the major studios, was deplored by Keaton.

PARDON MY BERTH MARKS

CREDITS:

A Columbia Pictures Production. *Producer/Director:* Jules White; *Script:* Clyde Bruckman; *Photography:* Benjamin Kline. *Release Date:* March 22, 1940. *Length:* two reels.

CAST:

Buster Keaton, Dorothy Appleby, Vernon Dent, Dick Curtis, Eva McKenzie, Bud Jamison, Billy Gilbert, Richard Fiske, Clarice (the parrot).

Pardon My Berth Marks is the best of the Jules White–directed two-reelers Buster made for Columbia. For once, White permits Buster some more extended, silent-comedy segments before cranking up the slapstick machine to full throttle.

Buster plays a newsroom office boy who longs to be a reporter. The opening scene finds him destroying city editor Vernon Dent's office while delivering the mail. After Dent leaves, having told Buster to clean up the office, the latter takes a phone call from a mobster

Buster's impromptu visit to Dorothy Appleby's train berth is not appreciated by her racketeer husband, played by Richard Fiske, in *Pardon My Berth Marks*, one of Buster's better Columbia two-reelers. Bud Jamison is the train conductor.

who threatens to break Dent's neck if he prints a story implicating the hood in a bribery plot. Assuming Dent's aggressive demeanor, Buster tells off the caller, setting up a predictable confrontation between the crook and Dent. This ends with Buster wandering into Dent's office after the mobster has left to find Dent wearing various office articles and sporting a black eye. Before this, a desperate Dent has assigned Buster to follow high-society woman (Dorothy Appleby) as she travels by train to Reno for a quickie divorce after discovering her husband, (Richard Fiske), to be a racketeer.

After Buster boards the train—accompanied by his pet parrot, Clarice—he ends up amorously involved with Dorothy when the two are mistaken for newlyweds. When the passengers bed down for the evening, Buster spots Dorothy's arm dangling out of her compartment. Although he doesn't realize it, Dorothy is applying lotion to her arm, and he watches transfixed as she wiggles her limb in a "come hither" motion, followed by a "go away" gesture, leaving Buster thoroughly confused about her intentions. When Buster finally makes it into his bunk and tries undressing in the cramped quarters, he becomes entangled in his clothing and various suitcases while dodging the love pecks of Clarice. The other passengers delight in Clarice's cooing, which they mistake as spirited love-making between Buster and Dorothy.

Clarice's amorous squawks are also misinterpreted by Dorothy's husband, who boards the train in search of his wife. A chase erupts with Buster racing around, diving into various berths in his attempts to escape from the maniacal gangster. Finally subduing Fiske by tying him up with the train's emergency chord, Buster earns the respect of his editor boss with his report of the events and is promoted to full-fledged reporter.

Pardon My Berth Marks is a rare example of White's knockabout comedy approach complementing Keaton's more sedate style. The extended undressing routine, followed by a funny bit in which Buster imitates the squawkings of Clarice to escape from Dorothy's husband, not only provide the film's best moments but also offer a much-needed break in its frenetic tempo.

THE TAMING OF THE SNOOD
(aka Four-Thirds Off)

CREDITS:

A Columbia Pictures Production. *Producer/Director:* Jules White; *Script:* Ewart Adamson and Clyde Bruckman; *Photography:* Henry Freulich. *Release Date:* June 28, 1940. *Length:* two reels.

CAST:

Buster Keaton, Dorothy Appleby, Elsie Ames, Richard Fiske, Bruce Bennett.

The Taming of the Snood, an example of producer/director Jules White's "fast is funny" approach to comedy, starts promisingly with hat shop owner Buster modeling some of his creations for customer Dorothy Appleby. One of his originals is adorned with insect eyes (he calls it his Jiminy Cricket model); another is in the shape of a skyscraper-high pretzel; and the funniest is topped with a miniature clothesline complete with tiny clothes pinned to it. Dorothy, however, is more interested in stashing some hot jewelry in one of Buster's hats. After stuffing a gem in a familiar-looking porkpie model, then noticing two

police detectives lingering outside the store, she asks Buster to deliver the hat to her apartment later in the afternoon.

Buster shows up at Dorothy's place and is greeted by the maid, played by Elsie Ames, one of the loudest, most flailingly unsubtle comediennes in film history, and one who, unfortunately, was Buster's costar in several other Columbia shorts. Elsie gives a great example of her less-than-sedate style of comedy shortly after Buster arrives when she manages to knock herself out while dusting furniture. Buster foolishly comes to her aid and revives her by pouring a bottle of booze down her throat. This, unfortunately, gives Elsie an excuse to overact as she staggers around the apartment performing some of the most brutal physical stunts ever attempted by an inebriated maid. Ironically, most of them are taken from the roughhouse vaudeville act Buster performed with his father. At one point, Elsie executes Buster's "placing one leg on the tabletop, then the other leg" pratfall, then later climbs on his shoulders for a piggyback ride, causing him to swing her around and around and fling her headfirst into the wall. So much for the film's gentler moments.

When Dorothy shows up, she sneaks the hot rock

FBI agents Richard Fiske (left) and Bruce Bennett (right) think enough people have touched Buster's hat for one day, in *The Taming of the Snood.* The Columbia two-reeler is the first to team Buster with obstreperous comedienne Elsie Ames.

out of Buster's porkpie and attaches it to the leg of her pet parrot, which then flies out the window. Forced to retrieve the bird, Buster performs Harold Lloyd–type stunts on the side of the building, all of them obviously faked with the use of back projection. Elsie soon joins Buster and pulls his pants down while the two of them cling to a flagpole. When it breaks, the two are propelled back through Dorothy's window, and Buster hands her the rescued jewel, which she promptly turns over to the two detectives, who have caught up with her. Then Buster, Elsie, Dorothy, and one of the detectives collapse from exhaustion as the film reaches its wearisome fade-out.

If Buster's films were less than satisfactory during this period, his personal life was on a definite upswing. On May 29, 1940, between the filming of his previous Columbia short and this one, Buster married his third wife, Eleanor Norris, a nineteen-year-old dancer and MGM bit player. The two remained happily married for the rest of Buster's life.

THE SPOOK SPEAKS

CREDITS:

A Columbia Pictures Production. *Producer/Director:* Jules White; *Script:* Clyde Bruckman and Ewart Adamson; *Photography:* Henry Freulich. *Release Date:* September 20, 1940. *Length:* two reels.

CAST:

Buster Keaton, Elsie Ames, Dorothy Appleby, Lynton Brent, Bruce Bennett, Don Beddoe, Orson (the penguin).

The Spook Speaks is a fifth-rate remake of Buster's *The Haunted House* with a touch of *The Navigator* thrown in. When a movie's best moments are provided by an inebriated penguin on roller skates, something is definitely lacking in the film's human creativity.

Buster and wife Elsie Ames are caretakers in a house owned by Professor Mordini, a spiritualist/magician played by Lynton Brent. They arrive just as Mordini is commanding a woman to jump through a window that miraculously re-forms after she disappears (a weak variation of Buster's gag from *Sherlock Jr.* where he jumps through the stomach of his assistant and disappears through a seemingly solid wall). Noticing a dead body on the floor and a decapitated head sticking out of a trunk, Buster and Elsie decide on a hasty retreat. However, they are persuaded to stay after Mordini explains his sleight-of-hand tricks and points out the

house's trapdoors, secret compartments, and hidden passageways.

The magician's parting words to the couple are not to let anyone in the house while he is away on a six-week tour. He is especially concerned that his former assistant will break in and steal his secrets.

A series of tired spook-house gags follows. The worst is the insulting re-creation of the scene from *The Navigator* in which a spooky portrait—this time of Mordini instead of the ship's captain—dangles outside Buster's bedroom window, giving him a nasty fright (for some reason, Mordini's window is in the shape of a porthole; apparently when Buster decided to lift *The Navigator* gag, he took the porthole with him).

The film's best moments arrive on roller skates. Mordini's pet penguin, Orson, skitters through the house, a pair of tiny skates on his feet. Whenever the haunted-house hysterics begin to flag, Orson skates in and revives the film's sophisticated tone. In a weak running gag, Buster, Elsie, and Orson take turns chug-alugging from a liquor jug that chimes "How Dry I Am" whenever it is picked up. The imbibing is done off-camera and is signaled by the tinkling song and some bowling-ball sound effects.

The trio is joined by a newlywed couple and Mordini's nefarious former assistant (Bruce Bennett). The bride (Dorothy Appleby) is also a spiritualist and tries to demonstrate her powers to her husband (Don Beddoe), who remains dubious until the evil assistant stages some shenanigans of his own. Skeletons dance in the hallway, dummies talk, and musical instruments fly through the air playing a peppy tune, resulting in Buster, Elsie, and the newlyweds fleeing in the uninspired fade-out.

Except for Orson, none of the cast members are able to scare up a decent laugh.

THE VILLAIN STILL PURSUED HER

CREDITS:

A Franklin-Blank Production; Distributed by RKO Pictures. *Producer:* Harold B. Franklin; *Director:* Edward Cline; *Script:* Elbert Franklin, based on the play *The Fallen Saved,* also known as *The Drunkard; Additional Dialogue:* Ethel La Blanche; *Photography:* Lucien Ballard; *Editor:* Arthur Hilton. *Release Date:* October 11, 1940. *Running Time:* 66 minutes.

CAST:

Buster Keaton (*William Dalton*), Anita Louise (*Mary Wilson*), Richard Cromwell (*Edward Middleton*), Alan Mowbray (*Silas Cribbs*), Hugh Herbert (*Frederick Healy*), Margaret Hamilton (*Widow Wilson*), Joyce Compton (*Hazel Dalton*), Billy Gilbert (*Emcee*), Diane Fisher (*Julia Wilson*), Charles Judels (*Pie Vendor*), Jack Norton (*Pie Customer*), Vernon Dent (*Police Officer*), Carlotta Monti (*Streetwalker*).

Buster is reunited with his favorite codirector/collaborator from the silent two-reeler days, Eddie Cline, in *The Villain Still Pursued Her*, an entertaining spoof of florid melodramas. It was, most probably, Cline's influence that landed Buster his part in the film. Another factor might have been the success of Buster's previous feature film, *Hollywood Cavalcade*, which, like *The Villain Still Pursued Her*, is a period piece that derives its charm from its playful re-creation of silent screen comedy. Buster was hired for *Hollywood Cavalcade* primarily because of his erroneous reputation as a pie-slinging silent film comic, and in *The Villain Still Pursued Her*, he is given the chance to repeat his custard-tossing technique. Although a financial flop, the film is still thoroughly delightful, providing Buster with the meatiest subordinate role of his screen career.

Buster pauses to indulge in a pie-throwing interlude with policeman Vernon Dent and pie vendor Charles Judels before escorting inebriated friend Richard Cromwell back home to his loved ones, in *The Villain Still Pursued Her*.

Buster plays William Dalton, the real hero of *The Villain Still Pursued Her*, a hilarious send-up of florid melodramas. The feature reunites him with his old collaborator, Eddie Cline, resulting in the best supporting role performance of his career. Here, he helps his rattle-brained sister (Joyce Compton) locate the long-lost will of his alcoholic best friend.

The film is based on one of the most durable of melodramas, *The Fallen Saved* (also known as *The Drunkard*), first performed in 1844. The feature, also done earlier as *The Drunkard* (1935), is in a filmed-play format, introduced by a heavily accented Billy Gilbert, who addresses the "stage" audience, laying out the simple plot and encouraging the viewers to hiss the villain and cheer the hero. Set in the midnineteenth century, the film follows the rise and fall of a simple, charitable fellow, Edward Middleton (Richard Cromwell), as he is led to ruin by his villainous lawyer/adviser, Silas Cribbs (Alan Mowbray). After encouraging him to take his first sip of alcohol, Cribbs succeeds in corrupting Edward, who ultimately abandons his wife, Mary (Anita Louise), child, and friends as he falls under the spell of the devil's brew.

Buster plays William Dalton, Edward's best friend, who saves Edward after introducing him to an eccentric philanthropist, Frederick Healy (Hugh Herbert in a colorfully comical performance), head of a rehabilitation clinic for drunks. Buster is also on hand both to rescue his own half-crazy sister, Hazel (Joyce Compton), from Cribbs' lecherous clutches, and to thwart Cribbs' dastardly plan to sell Edward's beautiful, long-suffering Mary into prostitution.

The film's action is all deliciously overwrought, acted out by the spirited cast with exaggerated physical flourishes, heightened speech inflections, and flowery soliloquies. Verbal and visual jokes abound, all calling attention to the film's simplistic, black-and-white morality as well as the artificiality of the entire production. One of the running gags has Buster, every time he appears, punctuating his animated speeches with the phrase, "Or I'm not called William Dalton!" which he delivers while staring straight into the camera. In one scene he has to crawl over another actor blocking him from a clear view of the lens before he can utter his line. Other floridly dramatic lines are reacted to comically by the actors, as when Buster finds Edward passed out on a barroom floor. After being revived by his best friend, the eternally repentant Edward suddenly exclaims, "I've seen the light!" causing Buster to take a quick glance at the ceiling. Many of the visual jokes are in keeping with Buster's own satirical approach to florid melodrama, which he first parodied on-screen in the 1918 Arbuckle-Keaton short *Moonshine*. For instance, when Edward and Mary first meet, the scene switches back and forth between the two entranced characters in quick-cutting close-ups, each close-up more magnified until only their eyeballs are visible on-screen.

Buster's pie-flinging scene is the film's weakest segment, being totally irrelevant to the plot, inserted merely as a bit of crude slapstick. Overall, however, the film sustains its exaggerated style without becoming overly silly or resorting to low-brow antics, which would have destroyed its more sedate pacing.

With Eddie Cline behind the camera, Buster gives the most assured and accomplished supporting performance of his career. An ironic footnote to the film is that, shortly after its completion, Buster began drinking again, the first time in five years, resulting in a frightening series of blackouts that soon forced him back on the wagon.

LI'L ABNER

CREDITS:

A Vogue-RKO Pictures Production; Distributed by RKO. *Producers:* Lou Ostrow and Herman Schlom; *Director:* Albert S. Rogell; *Script:* Charles Kerr and Tyler Johnson, based on the comic strip by Al Capp; *Editors:* Otto Ludwig and Donn Hayes; *Photography:* Harry Jackson. *Release Date:* November 1, 1940. *Running Time:* 75 minutes.

CAST:

Buster Keaton (*Lonesome Polecat*), Granville Owen (*Li'l Abner*), Martha O'Driscoll (*Daisy Mae*), Mona Ray (*Mammy Yokum*), Johnnie Morris (*Pappy Yokum*), Billie Seward (*Cousin Delightful*), Kay Sutton (*Wendy Wilecat*), Maude Eburne (*Granny Scraggs*), Edgar Kennedy (*Cornelius Cornpone*), Charles A. Post (*Earthquake McGoon*), Bud Jamison (*Hairless Joe*), Dick Elliott (*Marryin' Sam*), Johnny Arthur (*Montague*), Walter Catlett (*Barber*), Chester Conklin (*Mayor Gurgle),* Doodles Weaver (*Hannibal Hoops*), Al St. John (*Joe Smithpan*), Hank Mann (*A Bachelor*), Blanche Payson (*Large Spinster*), Louise Keaton (*Small Spinster*), Lucien Littlefield (*Sheriff/Old Timer*), Mickey Daniels (*Cicero Grunts*).

Most movie fans have their personal best and worst film lists. *Li'l Abner* is a firm member of my "worst films of all time" list. It is stupefyingly unfunny, not a laugh to be found in its tedious seventy-five minutes. Based on Al Capp's popular cartoon strip featuring the colorful hillbilly inhabitants of Dogpatch, U.S.A., the film is an insult to Capp's wonderfully detailed, fully realized universe. Capp filled his comic strip world with bold, sexy, satirical humor, all presented from the perspective of supposedly dim-witted yokels. The film is merely dim-witted, an ineptly conceived, directed, and acted mess. Most of the cast members are so busy trying to speak in fake hillbilly accents that they never get around to acting.

The plot, such as it is, revolves around handsome hillbilly lug Li'l Abner Yokum (Granville Owen) and his attempts to remain blissfully single while tempted by Dogpatch's legion of man-hungry Amazons. Buster has a small role as Lonesome Polecat, Dogpatch's token Indian. He first appears early in the film, dressed in buckskins, braying at the heavens like a rabid coyote and thumping his chest, then performing an abbreviated ceremonial dance after successfully starting a campfire—with the assistance of a pocket lighter. He speaks a few lines in simplistic, Pidgin English before disappearing for a couple reels.

Buster shows up again for the climactic Sadie Hawkins race festivities, first standing proudly on display with Dogpatch's other eligible bachelors before racing, where he purposely tries to get caught by the pursuing females. In the film's only marginally funny scene, Buster and his giant, bushy sidekick, Hairless Joe (Bud Jamison, unrecognizable in a shoulder-length wig that conceals his face except for a bulbous, artificial nose) lag behind in the race, waiting for the women to catch up. When the women ignore the two, preferring to chase after more attractive men, Buster jumps into the arms of Blanche Payson, his prehistoric

Ugh! is the appropriate word to describe this very unfunny film adapted from Al Capp's very funny comic strip *Li'l Abner*, in which Buster appears along with a cavalcade of character actors. Pictured here are (from left to right): Dick Elliott as Marryin' Sam, Granville Owen as Li'l Abner, Buster as Lonesome Polecat, Bud Jamison as Hairless Joe, and Hank Mann and Doodles Weaver as a couple of eligible Dogpatch bachelors.

costar from *The Three Ages,* who dumps him in a nearby river in disgust.

The film's one attribute is its colorful supporting cast, a who's who of character actors (including Buster's pal from the Arbuckle days Al St. John), most of whom have virtually nothing to do except to look appropriately yokelesque. The film would have been a much more successful and accurate depiction of Capp's hillbilly universe if the footage had been replaced with the two Educational shorts Buster made with his family in which they played backwoods hicks. Speaking of family, Buster's sister, Louise, is part of the cast of backwoods bachelorette hopefuls, speaking a quick line of dialogue during the prerace dance festivities.

HIS EX MARKS THE SPOT

CREDITS:

A Columbia Pictures Production. *Producer/Director:* Jules White; *Script:* Felix Adler; *Photography:* Benjamin Kline. *Release Date:* December 13, 1940. *Length:* two reels.

CAST:

Buster Keaton, Dorothy Appleby, Elsie Ames, Matt McHugh.

His Ex Marks the Spot is easily the loudest, most abrasive short film Buster made at Columbia, totally devoid of his type of humor.

The highlight is its opening shot: Buster stands in the living room of his modest, two-bedroom apartment, smoking a pipe and wearing a woman's dress while his wife, played by Dorothy Appleby, finishes hemming it. When Dorothy complains that she never has enough money to buy her clothes, Buster reminds her that his alimony payments come first. After two burly moving men show up to repossess their furniture, Buster concocts a brilliant solution to their problem: "If I can get my ex-wife to move in with us, I won't have to pay her alimony and our troubles will be over!" Yes, absolutely brilliant.

Soon their apartment is invaded by Buster's ex (Elsie Ames) and her boyfriend (Matt McHugh). Both are loud, crass, and obnoxious, a match made in heaven. However, Buster and Dorothy are determined to remain polite and offer their guests a bedroom each. When Buster tries to lug Elsie's huge storage trunks into the bedroom, he staggers around the apartment

Buster and wife Dorothy Appleby have a hard time remaining civil to Buster's ex-wife and new boyfriend Matt McHugh after the couple moves in with them in *His Ex Marks the Spot*, the shrillest of all the high-velocity two-reelers he made at Columbia.

with the heavy trunk on his back, then returns hunched over for another, but grabs Elsie by the neck and throws her over his shoulder. The gag is ruined, though, by Matt's hyenalike laughter, which reverberates off the walls of the cheap apartment set.

For dinner, Dorothy prepares an elegant roast duck, and Buster repeats an uninspired duck-carving routine from *Sidewalks of New York*. Several obnoxious food jokes follow as Buster and Dorothy watch the other two gorge themselves. Turning in for the evening, the host couple set up their bedding in the living room on top of two of Elsie's trunks. When Dorothy lights a cigarette in bed, she throws the match into Buster's blankets and a fire breaks out. Predictably, the two couples scream, flail about, and throw buckets of water on one another.

In the morning, Dorothy and Elsie get into a plate-flinging, hair-pulling fight. Dorothy threatens to kill Elsie if she and Matt don't vacate the premises. Before they do, Buster persuades the couple to get hitched so he won't have to pay any more alimony. A quickie wedding ceremony is held in the living room with Dorothy holding a gun to the about-to-be-married couple as an incentive.

The only truly Keatonesque aspect about the film is that it accurately reflects Buster's personal situation at the time: he was supporting his mother, sister, and

brother, as well as a new wife, while still making monthly payments to Natalie. Fortunately, he dealt with his problem in a more logical and less odious manner than that depicted in the film.

SO YOU WON'T SQUAWK

CREDITS:

A Columbia Pictures Production. *Producers:* Del Lord and Hugh McCollum; *Director:* Del Lord; *Script:* Elwood Ullman; *Photography:* Benjamin Kline. *Release Date:* February 21, 1941. *Length:* two reels.

CAST:

Buster Keaton, Matt McHugh, Eddie Featherstone, Bud Jamison, Hank Mann, Vernon Dent, Edmund Cobb.

One of Buster's better Columbia shorts, *So You Won't Squawk* benefits from a more typically Keaton-type story line with identity mix-ups and falsely accused victims. He plays a handyman hired to help put the finishing touches on a new nightclub owned by a local gangster, Louie the Wolf (Eddie Featherstone). When he is mistaken for Louie by two thugs from a rival gang, the gangster takes advantage of the mix-up by having Buster impersonate him while collecting protection money from local establishments. Louie hopes Buster's impersonation will be convincing enough to get him bumped off by rival mobster Slugger McGraw (Matt McHugh).

As Buster visits various businesses, he is tailed by two of Slugger's thugs, who make a series of attempts to kill him. Walking out of one bar after collecting Louie's money, Buster slips on a banana peel just as one of Slugger's goons shoots at him. Thinking they have killed Louie, the mugs drive off to tell Slugger the good news. Buster, however, recovers from his fall and catches up with them on a bicycle, scaring them nearly to death with his undead presence. When the goons insist on taking Buster for a "friendly" ride, they jump out of the car as it approaches a cliff. Buster manages, though, to guide the car down the steep embankment. Then, with the action speeded up for a cheap, Keystone Kop effect, he careens through traffic and doubles back to pick up the disbelieving goons.

For the film's finale, Buster restages the climactic chase scene from *Le Roi des Champs-Élysées*, hurling objects at various policemen to get them to follow him back to Louie's hideout after he realizes that Louie has set him up. The scene is actually an improvement on the original with Buster scoring direct hits, splattering cops with tomatoes, breaking one patrol car's windshield with an expertly tossed tire iron, then swerving his car into a gully and covering an entire squadron of policemen with mud. Soon, he is leading a massive procession of officers on a chase through city streets and country lanes. (As in the French film, stock footage is used during the chase scene; this time, instead of an old Fritz Lang thriller, clips from *She Couldn't Take It*, a 1935 George Raft gangster movie, are used.)

So You Won't Squawk at least has the flavor of a Keaton-influenced film, as in the climactic chase scene lifted from Buster's French feature. The miserable attempts of the gangsters on Buster's life are reminiscent of the suicide gags in *Hard Luck*. The short, though, is so riddled with cheap effects—back projection, speeded-up action, cartoonish sounds, stock footage—that, in the end, it remains more in the traditional Columbia two-reeler style than Buster's own.

GENERAL NUISANCE (aka The Private General)

CREDITS:

A Columbia Pictures Production. *Producer/Director:* Jules White; *Script:* Felix Adler and Clyde Bruckman. *Release Date:* September 18, 1941. *Length:* two reels.

CAST:

Buster Keaton, Dorothy Appleby, Elsie Ames, Monty Collins, Nick Arno, Bud Jamison, Lynton Brent, Harry Semels.

Private Buster is on the brink of disaster in the hands of army nurse Elsie Ames in *General Nuisance*, a pseudo remake of *Doughboys*.

A full-fledged stylistic war rages throughout *General Nuisance,* with Buster's comic touches battling with producer/director Jules White's bombastic approach to the Keaton-inspired material. The film, based loosely on Keaton's MGM feature *Doughboys,* also tries to reprise the ethnic dance sequence from his favorite Educational short, *Grand Slam Opera,* and even contains an original song just as in that one. However, the dictatorial director once again wins the battle but loses the war.

Buster plays Peter Hedley Lamar, Jr., a well-known aristocratic millionaire, first seen dressed in formal attire standing by the side of a road examining the flat tire on his limousine. When he flags down a car for help, he is immediately smitten by its driver, Dorothy Appleby, who, with passenger Elsie Ames, play army nurses on their way to the nearby hospital. When Buster gives Dorothy the eye, she gives him the brush-off since she is only interested in enlisted men. Naturally, Buster decides to join up so he can be closer to his dream girl.

When Buster tries to enlist, he restages one of the best scenes from *Doughboys,* but here it's ruined by excessively broad slapstick. An identity mix-up follows when Buster, still dressed in formal attire, is mistaken for one of a group of diplomats touring the army base. Later, when it's discovered that he's only a lowly private, Buster is assigned to clean a mountain of spittoons. When Elsie shows up and attempts to woo millionaire Buster, she sings a comical song to him ("Your eyes are like taillights at night / They're red but they're not very bright. . . . Though you're low in the ranks / You've got dough in the banks / That is why I am falling for you"). The two then engage in a series of dance routines—a waltz, a jitterbug, Russian kicks, ballet twirls—all punctuated with Stooge-like falls, slaps, and slugs.

Buster remains more interested in wooing Dorothy, and after purposely wounding himself (with an unintentional assist from Elsie, who dumps him into a ditch), he is assigned to Dorothy's ward to recover from his multiple fractures. Predictably, Elsie once again attempts to help Buster, but nearly hangs him when she adjusts the pulleys attached to his splinted arms and legs. In the film's contrived finale, Buster wins Dorothy by rescuing her from a hatchet-wielding maniac.

No matter how much of Buster's material shows up in the Columbia shorts, the films still reflect White's unsubtle approach. Buster obviously realized this and seemed content to recycle old gags, most of them from his MGM period, which was fitting since the two studios shared a manipulative disregard for their artists.

SHE'S OIL MINE

CREDITS:

A Columbia Pictures Production. *Producer/Director:* Jules White; *Script:* Felix Adler. *Release Date:* November 20, 1941. *Length:* two reels.

CAST:

Buster Keaton, Monty Collins, Elsie Ames, Eddie Laughton, Jacqueline Dalya, Bud Jamison.

She's Oil Mine is Buster's final Columbia two-reeler. Like *General Nuisance,* it is a two-reel remake of one of his MGM features, this time *The Passionate Plumber.* Again, the result is a poor melding of antagonistic comedic styles with director Jules White manipulating Buster's material, turning it into a Stooge-like slapstick melee.

As in the MGM feature, Buster is a plumber, here getting mixed up with Oklahoma oil heiress Elsie Ames. Elsie has a problem: a persistent French suitor (Eddie Laughton). She fully realizes Eddie is more interested in her loot than in her; however, because he's a great kisser, Elsie can't resist him.

When the amorous Eddie shows up at her apart-

ment, Elsie escapes his passionate advances by falling out the window and running down the street, where she ends up in the shop run by Buster and his assistant Monty Collins. Unknown to them, Elsie hides in a water heater they are working on. Then, as they seal it, she begins squawking, "Oh, it's the end of the world!" which prompts Buster to utter the film's cleverest line: "It's Orson Welles broadcasting again." Turning to switch the channel on the radio, Buster realizes it is missing. The two plumbers think they have sealed it up in the water heater and promptly cut it open again with a blowtorch. Reaching into the heater, Buster pulls out Elsie's leg and nearly retires from the plumbing business on the spot. The newly rescued Elsie clears up the misunderstanding and hires the men to fix her broken shower. At her apartment to begin work in one of the tackiest-looking bathrooms ever owned by a million-airess, Buster restages both the shower-repair scene from *The Passionate Plumber* and the follow-up one, in which Eddie shows up, mistakes him for Elsie's new lover, and challenges him to a duel at dawn.

The dueling scene is a near-exact restaging of the original routine, with Monty Collins substituting for Jimmy Durante, even repeating some of Durante's joke-choked lines, several of which make no sense in this context. The funniest moments are supplied by character actor Bud Jamison, who, as part of Eddie's duel entourage, attempts a French accent, resulting in several unintended humorous asides. The routine concludes predictably with a hunter suddenly appear-

ing and scaring off the participants with a couple shotgun blasts. Elsie soon drives up and pronounces Buster the victor of the duel, then permits him to plant a passionate kiss on her lips. The smooch makes her forget all about boyfriend Eddie as she collapses in ecstasy to the ground.

In his autobiography, Keaton talked of the relief of finishing his last Columbia short: "I just got to the point where I couldn't stomach turning out even one more crummy two-reeler." That, unfortunately, is an accurate summation of the series.

FOREVER AND A DAY

CREDITS:

An Anglo-American/RKO Pictures Production; Distributed by RKO. *Production Supervisor:* Lloyd Richards; *Directors:* René Clair, Edmund Goulding, Cedric Hardwicke, Frank Lloyd, Victor Saville, Robert Stevenson, Herbert Wilcox; *Script:* Charles Bennett, C. S. Forrester, Lawrence Hazard, Michael Hogan, W. P. Lipscomb, Alice Duer Miller, John Van Druten, Alan Campbell, Peter Godfrey, S. M. Herzig, Christopher Isherwood, Gene Lockhart, R. C. Sherriff, Claudine West, Norman Corwin, Jack Hartfield, James Hilton, Emmett Lavery, Frederick Lonsdale, Donald Ogden Stewart, Keith Winter; *Photography:* Robert De Grasse, Lee Garmes, Russell Metty, Nicholas Musuraca; *Music Director:* Anthony Collins; *Editors:* Elmo J. Williams and George Crone. *Release Date:* March 26, 1943. *Running Time:* 104 minutes.

CAST:

Buster Keaton, Brian Aherne, Robert Cummings, Charles Laughton, Ida Lupino, Herbert Marshall, Ray Milland, Anna Neagle, Merle Oberon, C. Aubrey Smith, Claude Rains, Ian Hunter, Roland Young, Jessie Matthews, Gladys Cooper, Edward Everett Horton, Ruth Warrick, Donald Crisp, Anna Lee, Reginald Owen, Gene Lockhart, Victor McLaglen, Elsa Lanchester, Dame May Whitty, Edmund Gwenn, Arthur Treacher, Nigel Bruce, Una O'Connor, Eric Blore, Wendy Barrie, Cecil Kellaway, Cedric Hardwicke, George Kirby, June Lockhart, June Duprez, and a cast of hundreds.

Buster remained off the screen for over a year after completing his last "crummy two-reeler" for Columbia. When he finally showed up again, it was to offer his services for free as part of an international cast assembled to aid charities involved with the Allied war effort. *Forever and a Day,* with its huge, stellar cast, was the first war charity film ever offered to the public and proved to be a commercial success. The film is a series of vignettes chronicling the history of one English

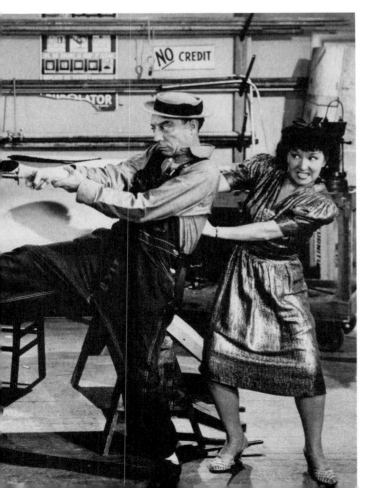

Eddie Laughton (left), Monty Collins, and Elsie Ames give Buster a few pointers on how to unclog a stopped-up drain in *She's Oil Mine*, the last "crummy two-reeler" Buster made for Columbia. The short is a remake of *The Passionate Plumber.*

Master plumber Cedric Hardwicke explains to house mistress Jessie Matthews the benefits of frequent bathing while Buster demonstrates a revolutionary new way to take a shower in *Forever and a Day*. The film was made to benefit the war relief effort and features nearly every major English actor working in World War II Hollywood.

mansion built in the early nineteenth century and destroyed during a World War II air raid.

Buster appears in an early segment set during the reign of Queen Victoria. Echoing his role from *The Passionate Plumber*, Buster is an assistant to master plumber Cedric Hardwicke, who also directed this particular segment. The two have been hired to install a bathtub in the mansion of Jessie Matthews, while she naps in the downstairs bedroom. Naturally, Keaton and Hardwicke raise a ruckus upstairs as they install the new tub. Buster drops a pile of tools, then stumbles over them, staggering backward and falling downstairs while Hardwicke patiently goes about his business, humming to himself as he works (finally, a costar who is in tune with Buster's more sedate approach to humor!). When the plumbers finally finish putting in the tub, Buster demonstrates for Matthews its unusual features. First, he shows how to take a shower by using

a series of buckets hooked up to a pulley, then shows the proper use of a metal shower cap that resembles a dunce cap. Finally, he points out the back-scratching scrub brush that folds out of the wall. The tub and its eccentric features could only have been conceived by Buster himself.

The segment is easily one of the film's highlights—of which there are many—and also features Ian Hunter as the gruff master of the house and Charles Laughton as an inebriated butler. To see all these talented actors on the same screen performing impeccably timed and executed movie magic is quite a refreshing change, because Keaton had for years been surrounded by inept and/or unappreciative collaborators.

SAN DIEGO, I LOVE YOU

CREDITS:

A Universal Pictures Production. *Producers/Script:* Michael Fessier and Ernest Pagano, based on a story by Ruth McKenney and Richard Branstein; *Director:* Reginald LeBorg; *Photography:* Hal Mohr; *Editor:* Charles Maynard. *Release Date:* September 29, 1944. *Running Time:* 83 minutes.

CAST:

Buster Keaton, Jon Hall, Louise Allbritton, Edward Everett Horton, Eric Blore, Irene Ryan, Rudy Wissler, Chester Clute, Hobart Cavanaugh.

Buster made character role appearances in three midforties features for Universal Pictures beginning with *San Diego, I Love You*. Ernest Pagano, Keaton's scriptwriting friend from his MGM and Educational Pictures days, was influential in getting Buster on-screen after an eighteen-month absence.

Appearing late in the film, Buster is a San Diego bus driver who has driven the same unglamorous route for ten years. The film's two principal characters, played by Jon Hall and Louise Allbritton, board Buster's bus, thinking it will take them on a scenic drive along the beach. When he informs them that the bus will not go anywhere near the beach nor will he alter his route to accommodate them, Louise, an inventor's daughter, begins to use a little inventive psychology on him.

She begins talking about how people can get so stuck in a boring routine that eventually they think the rut they are in is unalterable. While she talks, Buster's face is shown in a beautiful close-up, registering deep thought, which turns to fierce determination as he suddenly cranks the steering wheel and pulls the bus over. He then stuns his passengers, most of them regulars, by announcing that he is going to drive by the beach for a change of scenery and those who object can get off. At first outraged, they one by one confess that the change in their normal, dreary routines will do them good.

In the next scene, Louise and Jon snuggle, hum, and sing as a troupe of musicians/passengers sit at the back of the bus serenading the others. Buster, his official uniform loosened, a cigarette dangling from his bottom lip, guides his bus onto the beach right next to the pounding surf. The scene is absolutely delightful, just one of several extended subplot highlights that fill this quirky comedy. Also featured in the film are such great character actors as Edward Everett Horton as an eccentric high school teacher-turned-inventor, scrawny Irene Ryan as a hyper secretary in search of a room to rent, Eric Blore as a demented, accident-prone butler, and silent film veteran Chester Clute.

Buster, in a role with an autobiographical undercurrent, speaks his lines with strong conviction that quickly establishes his character as a person who, for years, has done his job without thinking about whether it has brought him any satisfaction or joy. It is obvious that Buster enjoyed playing this part because of the

Municipal bus driver Buster takes passengers Hobart Cavanaugh (left), Jon Hall, and Louise Allbritton for a joy ride along the beach in *San Diego, I Love You*. Although his part is brief, he gives one of his best supporting role performances in this modest screwball comedy.

Buster, his deadpan face registering newfound determination, makes the decision to turn his bus around and head for the beach.

One of the rarest and most startling sights of the cinema: Buster flashes a beatific smile in *San Diego, I Love You*, the only such time in a major studio-produced feature.

expressiveness he brings to his lines and the fact that, at the end of his segment, when he drops off Louise and Jon in front of Louise's house, he shakes their hands, thanks them for a wonderful evening, and leaves them with a beatific smile.

When I first saw the film, I had no idea that Buster smiled in it. So, when the Great Stone Face suddenly cracked a joyously sincere smile, I nearly fell out of my seat, the moment was so unexpected and his smile so obviously heartfelt, unlike the grin he flashes at the end of his 1934 French feature, *Le Roi de Champs-Él-*

ysées, which was obviously tacked on as a gimmick. In the earlier film, his pasty-faced grin is accompanied by a hollow, soulless glare, reflecting the dismal state of his personal life at the time. In contrast, Buster's *San Diego, I Love You* smile, although startling, still complements his character perfectly. It is also a reflection of his forties life, which was definitely on the upswing: his third marriage, to Eleanor, was solid and happy, he was still in demand at MGM, writing gags for various films as well as once again working for friends in front of the camera. After a long period of dread and disaster, he was once again a genuinely happy man—and smiling.

THAT'S THE SPIRIT

CREDITS:

A Universal Pictures Production. *Producers/Script:* Michael Fessier and Ernest Pagano; *Director:* Charles Lamont; *Photography:* Charles Van Enger; *Editor:* Fred R. Feitshans, Jr. *Release Date:* June 1, 1945. *Running Time:* 93 minutes.

CAST:

Buster Keaton, Peggy Ryan, Jack Oakie, June Vincent, Gene Lockhart, Andy Devine, Johnny Coy, Arthur Treacher, Irene Ryan.

Buster's friends at Universal, Ernest Pagano and Michael Fessier, fashioned another sterling supporting role for him in this delightful musical about a vaudeville performer, played by Jack Oakie, who marries the daughter of an ultraconservative banker. When Oakie's wife (June Vincent) nearly dies during childbirth in 1900, he makes a pact with the angel of death to take him instead. Oakie, however, is upset over the way he's snatched from earth and ends up at heaven's complaint department headed by Buster.

Buster, whose character is called L.M. (the significance of the initials is never explained), first appears sitting behind his glass desk sorting out stacks of complaint memos in his cloud-enshrouded office located on the outskirts of heaven. He is dressed in a wonderfully elegant white suit—even his trademark porkpie hat is white! Oakie then appears out of a backdrop of endless clouds and approaches Buster's desk to file his complaint, explaining that, because several people saw him walk off with the angel of death—a beautiful brunette—his acquaintances on earth now believe that he left his wife for another woman. Oakie wants to be sent back to earth to straighten things out, but Buster tells him that "green spirits" have to serve a probationary period first since most don't know how to behave on earth. A quick sixteen years pass—depicted by the standard scrolling-number effect, which stops at the year 1916—and Oakie returns to Buster's department. Buster looks up scowlingly at him and decides to prove to him that he isn't needed back on earth by showing him a television-type monitor that flashes images of Oakie's earthly family situation. However, after watching a scene where Oakie's daughter (Peggy Ryan), now a pretty teen, is ridiculed by her uptight grandpa (Gene Lockhart) for displaying too many of her two-timing father's low-class vaudeville talents, Buster agrees to send Oakie back to straighten things out. "But don't go around clankin' chains," Buster warns. "It's absolutely forbidden. Besides, it's corny."

Unfortunately, Buster disappears after dispatching Oakie back to earth. The Keaton influence is felt though, through the way his old Educational Studios director Charles Lamont handles the film's supernatural aspects, which are presented matter-of-factly, a rarity for a fantasy dealing with spirits and otherworldly

Buster heads Heaven's complaint department in *That's the Spirit*, another superb supporting role effort. Here he counsels newly-dead Jack Oakie in proper celestial procedures.

Buster and Jack Oakie pose with heavenly costars Gloria Marlen and young Teddy Infuhr in *That's the Spirit*.

With *That Night With You,* Keaton's third supporting appearance for Universal, the Ernest Pagano–Michael Fessier magic vanished. Buster nearly vanished as well: his part is severely restricted and undistinguished, lacking the spirited quirkiness of his roles in *San Diego, I Love You* and *That's the Spirit*.

Buster plays Sam (even his name is undistinguished), a short-order cook in an all-night diner where featured actress Susanna Foster works as a waitress. His best scene is his first. When a customer wanders in early one morning and orders a bowl of chili, Buster gets nauseous at the thought of eating such a dish at the crack of dawn and refuses to serve the man. Before a riot breaks out between the two, the diner's owner (David Bruce) steps in and solves the problem by cooking up the chili himself.

The only unusual aspect about the scene is that Buster, who usually plays a nonaggressive-type character, gets to display a little anger. Otherwise, it could have been played by just about any other character actor.

The rest of the film is a semifantasy, with Susanna dreaming about becoming a successful singer, com-

goings-on. Buster's presence is also reflected in the film's various vaudeville-style musical numbers staged during the era when he was a top vaudeville entertainer. Although his part is absolutely delightful, it's too bad Keaton wasn't offered the rather substantial part of the vaudeville theater manager, played quite well by Andy Devine, but seemingly more in keeping with Buster's personality.

THAT NIGHT WITH YOU

CREDITS:

A Universal Pictures Production. *Producers/Script:* Michael Fessier and Ernest Pagano, based on a story by Arnold Belgard; *Director:* William A. Seiter; *Photography:* Charles Van Enger; *Editor:* Fred R. Feitshans, Jr. *Release Date:* September 28, 1945. *Running Time:* 84 minutes.

CAST:

Buster Keaton, Franchot Tone, Susanna Foster, David Bruce, Louise Allbritton, Jacqueline de Wit, Irene Ryan.

Buster plays a chili-hating short-order cook in *That Night With You*, one of his non-outstanding supporting role performances.

Buster catches flies with friends Michael Fessier (left) and Ernest Pagano, the men responsible for providing him with two out of three superlative supporting roles for Universal Studios.

plete with elaborate musical numbers. She gets her break by claiming to be the long-lost daughter of theatrical producer Franchot Tone. However, when Tone's ex-wife (Jacqueline de Wit) shows up, and also tries to finagle her way into the show, it is finally revealed that Susanna is indeed—in her words—"the echo of a duet you sang twenty years ago." Pretty racy stuff for a musical comedy. Unfortunately, that's about as spicy as the film gets, discounting the chili.

Most of the film's best comical moments are supplied by Louise Allbritton, who plays Susanna's best friend. Otherwise, *That Night With You* is an assembly-line Universal musical, a disappointment, especially coming after Pagano and Fessier's two sparkling previous efforts, which provided Buster with two of his top supporting roles.

GOD'S COUNTRY

CREDITS:

An Action Pictures and Screen Guild Production. *Producer:* William B. David; *Director/Script:* Robert E. Tansey; *Photography:* Carl Webster. Cinecolor. *Release Date:* April 1946. *Running Time:* 62 minutes.

Dan'l Buster makes friends with mountain girl Helen Gilbert's dog while Gabby Hayes-clone Si Jenks prepares for a confrontation with heaven knows what in *God's Country*. This obscure and cheaply made outdoors picture offered Buster little to do but frolic with an assortment of wild animals and stay out of the way of falling trees.

CAST:

Buster Keaton, Robert Lowery, Helen Gilbert, William Farnum, Stanley Andrews, Trevor Bardette, Si Jenks, Estelle Zarco, Juan Reyes, Al Ferguson.

God's Country is a shoestring-budget outdoor film about a fugitive from the law, played by Robert Lowery. Lowery takes refuge in a remote mountain community and becomes involved with several local residents whose way of life is threatened by the unscrupulous owner of a neighboring lumber firm. Buster plays a character called Mr. Boone (although listed as Old Tarp in the credits). He is the sidekick to a grizzled Gabby Hayes–type character, played by Si Jenks, both of whom are companions of Lowery's.

Dressed in buckskins and sporting a coonskin cap, Buster has only one substantial comedy scene, and even here, Buster's role is subordinate, this time to some animals. As he labors over a kettle, studying a chili recipe from a cookbook, a crow suddenly flies into the modest wilderness campground and lands on Buster's shoulder. Borrowing a cigarette, the crow then adds extra ingredients to the kettle while Buster studies the cookbook. The crow later flips the pages of the book to a recipe for nutcake, and Buster methodically adds the ingredients for this dish as well.

Later, a squirrel appears and eats from a cup of

walnuts, followed by a raccoon that helps knead a bowlful of dough. When an exasperated Buster finally shouts, "Is there anybody else that wants to get in on this?" a mountain lion saunters out of the brush and Buster races from the campsite, ending up in a nearby lake.

As usual, Buster performs well with his animal costars, accepting their appearances matter-of-factly until the final interruption by the mountain lion. The scene, like the rest of the film, suffers from amateurish staging and an unsubtle music score that accentuates the segment's already obvious, lighthearted tone.

Buster has little else to do for the rest of the film except stumble around in the background. The film's only other attribute is a brief nude swimming scene by the female lead, Helen Gilbert. The rest contains lots of stock footage of lumberjacks cutting down trees, wooden actors speaking unmemorable dialogue, and animals frolicking in the wilds.

Obviously, Buster was most interested here in collecting his paycheck. The film's setting probably appealed to him, since he was an avid outdoorsman and the movie was filmed on location in southern California's picturesque Big Bear area. Perhaps he felt that he was getting paid for camping out. In any event, *God's Country* remains appropriately obscure.

EL MODERNO BARBA AZUL
(aka Boom in the Moon)

CREDITS:

An Alsa Films Production (Mexico). *Producer:* Alexander Salkind; *Director:* Jaime Salvador; *Scenario:* Victor Trivas; *Photography:* Agustin Jiminez. *Release Date:* August 2, 1946. *Running Time:* 90 minutes.

CAST:

Buster Keaton, Angel Garasa, Virginia Seret, Luis Barreiro, Fernando Soto, Jorge Mondragon, Luis Mondragon.

Buster's last starring role in a feature was in the low-budget, Mexican-produced opus *El Moderno Barba Azul* (or *The Modern Bluebeard*), movie historian Kevin Brownlow's choice as the worst film ever made. At this point in Keaton's life, he was still experiencing severe financial hardships and was willing to accept just about any screen role offered to him.

After Buster is accused of killing eight women, he is offered a chance to become a moon astronaut in *El Moderno Barba Azul* (*The Modern Bluebeard*). This Mexican-produced fantasy/comedy is his last starring role in a feature film.

Buster plays a World War II survivor who doesn't realize the war is over. Getting out of a plane crash alive, he drifts for days in a tiny lifeboat until spotting land, which he believes to be Japan but turns out to be Mexico! Buster, a scraggly, long-bearded mess, wades ashore and wanders into a small village, where he is mistaken for a murderer of six women when he fits the modern bluebeard's description ("The man has a long beard, never laughs, and never eats any sugar—a real sourpuss"). The police chief, believing he has captured the notorious criminal, is ecstatic and begins to treat Buster like a celebrity.

Buster's celebrity status comes to a sudden end, however, with the arrival of a group of authorities with special instructions to transfer the modern bluebeard and his cellmate (Angel Garasa). What the two prisoners don't realize is that these men represent a rocket scientist who has made a deal with the police to use the condemned duo as guinea pigs in an experimental flight to the moon.

After the group rides off on horseback, Buster restages several gags from *Hard Luck,* the best occurring when he attempts to remount his horse by positioning the animal on the opposite side of a low wall, then jumping to the top of the wall and onto the horse. However, in a great, unexpected gag (marred by the use of a double), Buster ends up riding a wild bull—unseen on the other side of the wall—and bounds off into the foliage until he is thrown, flipping onto his back. The routine, which originated in *Hard Luck* and was later used in *Go West,* is more startlingly humorous here than before.

Buster and Angel are finally delivered to the professor's estate where they prepare for their reluctant journey into space. Their bargain-basement spacecraft resembles one of the models used in the old Flash Gordon serials starring that other Buster—Crabbe. During the countdown, a malfunction occurs and the professor's pretty assistant (Virginia Seret) enters the craft to investigate, at which point the rocket lifts off and blasts into space. After the use of cheap, stock aerial footage, the rocket finally lands in a remote part of Mexico, which the three astronauts naturally mistake for the moon. In one of the best moments, Buster dons a space suit and steps outside the craft, then panics when his face mask falls apart. He spends several inspired minutes trying to put it back together to avoid suffocating until he finally realizes he can breathe without it.

When the three explorers decide to venture out into this strange new landscape, they all slip into ridiculous-looking sorcerer-type gowns adorned with stars and comets, topped by pointy magician's hats (except for Buster, who prefers to wear his familiar porkpie). Soon, they encounter a beekeeper, whom they mistake for a moon man, and the poor, confused soul finally runs off in fright to warn village authorities. The trio is soon arrested and thrown into a cell, then subjected to some extremely bad overacting by the local psychiatrist, who ends up acting crazier than his patients. Meanwhile, the real bluebeard suspect has been captured and Buster and Angel are pronounced innocent and reasonably sane enough to be released from jail.

Overall, the film has the look and spirit of one of Buster's cheap Educational shorts. However, the pacing is lively and the restagings of old gags work well within the kooky plot. Costar Angel Garasa turns out to be a perfect match for Buster's more sedate approach to comedy. Garasa, with his thoroughly deadpan expression and underacting, complements Buster much better than the majority of Keaton's previous costars.

The version I saw of *El Moderno Barba Azul* was a badly dubbed print with Buster's low-croaking voice replaced by someone else's gruff baritone. According to Alan Hoffman, who saw the original Spanish-language version, Buster starts off talking in broken English and finishes up in broken Spanish. In any language, *El Moderno Barba Azul* is nothing to croak about; however, it is hardly Buster's least sterling feature film effort, the majority of his MGM features being worse.

THE LOVABLE CHEAT

CREDITS:

A Skyline Pictures Production; Distributed by Film Classics, Inc. *Producers/Script:* Richard Oswald and Edward Lewis, based on the play *Mercadet le Falseur* by Honoré de Balzac; *Director:* Richard Oswald; *Photography:* Paul Wang; *Editor:* Douglas Bagier. *Release Date:* May 11, 1949. *Running Time:* 74 minutes.

CAST:

Buster Keaton, Charles Ruggles, Peggy Ann Garner, Richard Ney, Alan Mowbray, Iris Adrian, Ludwig Donath, Fritz Feld, John Wengraf, Edna Holland, Minerva Urecal, Helen Servis, Jody Gilbert, Judith Trafford.

Buster was unofficially rediscovered after James Agee's excellent article "Comedy's Greatest Era" appeared in the *Life* magazine issue of September 3, 1949. Of the four silent comedy masters lauded in the piece—Chaplin, Keaton, Lloyd, and Langdon—Buster was the one who benefited most from Agee's praise, and his increased work in film, theater, and television reflect this. Strangely, all three of the films Buster made

Buster and his rather tall wife (Helen Servis) provide the silver for a dinner party given by French con man Charlie Ruggles (right) in *The Lovable Cheat*. Except for some funny stuff involving loose false teeth, Keaton's role remains undistinguished.

in 1949 were released before Agee's article was published. Stranger still is the star billing Buster receives in *The Lovable Cheat*—his title credit is more prominent than the film's nominal lead, Charles Ruggles. Unfortunately, this is the most interesting aspect about the film, based on a Balzac play, a parlor room farce set almost exclusively in a nineteenth-century French mansion.

Ruggles plays Claude Mercadet, a con artist who tries to pass off his family and himself as members of a long line of rich French aristocrats. To maintain his cover, Ruggles borrows money from a legion of creditors, always promising to pay them back but inevitably borrowing more and more. Buster plays Goulard, one of the creditors. Although he is featured throughout the film, his best scene is his first, when he arrives at Ruggles's home demanding to be paid back. Buster has just bought a new pair of false teeth, which, when they are not slipping out of his mouth, cause him to speak in a mushy, whistling manner. He gets a lot of gag mileage with his prop dentures, continually adjusting them, stumbling over words, and avoiding phrases that might cause the teeth to eject from his mouth.

Predictably, Ruggles ends up convincing Buster to lend him even more money so that he can impress a visiting count (Richard Ney) who has shown interest in marrying Ruggles's pert daughter (Peggy Ann Garner). Buster even lends Ruggles his silverware so the count will be impressed. To show his gratitude, Ruggles invites Buster and his wife (Helen Servis) to the soiree,

causing Buster to remark, "Good, that way I'll be able to watch my silver very carefully." He then spits out his teeth again and leaves.

Buster shows up later for the dinner party, accompanied by his lean giant of a wife. In the film's weakest segment, the guests indulge in some anemic dinner-table slapstick involving spilled food, broken glassware, and seating mix-ups. All ends well when Ruggles's long-lost business partner suddenly returns from America with a fortune.

Buster's part, although substantial, is essentially one that almost any good character actor could have played. The film is far too tame, too polite, to give Buster the chance to inject more of his irreverent comedy style. His only real comedic bits, his teeth-fumbling antics, are good, but they are overused by the film's end.

IN THE GOOD OLD SUMMERTIME

CREDITS:

A Metro-Goldwyn-Mayer Production. *Producer:* Joe Pasternak; *Director:* Robert Z. Leonard; *Script:* Samson Raphaelson; *Adaptation:* Albert Hackett, Frances Goodrich, and Ivan Tors, based on the play *Parfumerie* by Miklos Laszlo; *Pho-*

Buster is back on the screen for MGM, the first time since the studio fired him in 1933. Here, he dances with Judy Garland while sweethearts S. Z. Sakall and Spring Byington cuddle in *In the Good Old Summertime*.

tography: Harry Stradling: *Editor:* Adrienne Fazan. *Release Date:* July 29, 1949. Technicolor. *Running Time:* 102 minutes.

CAST:

Buster Keaton, Judy Garland, Van Johnson, S. Z. Sakall, Spring Byington, Clinton Sundberg, Marcia Van Dyke, Lillian Bronson, Liza Minnelli.

In the Good Old Summertime marks Keaton's first credited screen appearance for MGM since his days as one of the studio's featured performers. Buster had made uncredited cameos in some of the films for which he had supplied gags (see the "Miscellaneous and Uncredited Film Appearances" section). Ironically, his appearance here was a result of his gag-writing expertise. Eleanor Keaton, in Alan Hoffman's book, *Buster,* describes how Buster landed his part in the film:

> [Director Robert Leonard] had to break this violin as a plot point at the end of the picture. And he didn't know how to break it. It had to be an accident, it couldn't be deliberate or vicious. So he came down to Buster's office and said, "Take this damn [script] home and read it and tell me how to break this violin." Buster mulled it around over the weekend and came back and said, "You do this and do this. [But] be careful because if you get a stuntman who looks like he's doing a stunt, it's gonna be a phony pratfall." Four days later, Bob called Buster again and says, "I got the whole thing figured out. It's all solved. You're gonna be in the picture . . . so you can break it and I'll know it'll be done right."

Buster was assigned the role of Hickey, a clerk in his uncle Oberkugen's (S. Z. "Cuddles" Sakall) music shop in turn-of-the-century New York, along with Van Johnson and Judy Garland. He spends most of the time fumbling around in the background, a yes-man for Uncle Otto, the only person who can stand to listen to his uncle's inept violin playing, which sets up the scene that earned Buster his part. Buster is supposed to hand Uncle Otto his violin, a rare Stradivarius, so that he can show off his nebulous musical talents to a group of friends gathered to honor him and his fiancée (Spring Byington). When Buster rises from the dinner table and approaches Uncle Otto with the violin, he trips, staggers back, then does a tremendously effective bellyflop, landing squarely on top of the violin and smashing it to pieces—one of his best pratfalls.

Buster wrote and directed another segment, although he doesn't appear in the scene, where Van and Judy meet for the first time, literally bumping into one another on a street corner. Van knocks Judy down and messes up her hat, hairdo, and parasol, then spends the next several minutes attempting to put her back together but musses her up even further. Finally, in a panic, he pedals off on his bicycle with her dress caught in the bike's spokes. In his autobiography, Keaton comments on the staging of this marvelous scene, how he worked very closely with Johnson in order to ensure that the intricately timed mayhem would look unrehearsed. It strongly reflects Buster's careful but seemingly off-the-cuff filmmaking approach and contrasts dramatically with director Leonard's more conservative style.

SUNSET BOULEVARD

CREDITS:

A Paramount Pictures Production. *Producer:* Charles Brackett; *Director:* Billy Wilder; *Script:* Charles Brackett, Billy Wilder, and D. M. Marshman, Jr., from the short story "A Can of Beans." *Photography:* John R. Seitz; *Editors:* Doane Harrison and Arthur Schmidt; *Music:* Franz Waxman. *Release Date:* August 1950. *Running Time:* 110 minutes.

CAST:

Buster Keaton, Gloria Swanson, William Holden, Erich Von Stroheim, Nancy Olson, Fred Clark, Jack Webb, Cecil B. DeMille, H. B. Warner, Anna Q. Nilsson, Hedda Hopper.

Sunset Boulevard, one of the film greats, provides Buster Keaton with one of his most famous—and briefest—supporting roles. The film's story could easily apply to his own experiences with the Hollywood studio system: a young, aspiring performer becomes one of the giants of the silent screen, only to fall into obscurity during the advent of sound pictures, ending up a forgotten, reclusive nobody. What gives the film its power is that its forgotten nobodys are indeed some of Hollywood's legendary figures: Swanson, Von Stroheim, Keaton, even the still-very-much-in-the-public-eye DeMille,—they just don't get any more legendary than that.

Buster was friends with nearly all of *Sunset Boulevard*'s illustrious figures. He was especially close with Anna Q. Nilsson, a friend from his Arbuckle days, and Erich Von Stroheim, an old bridge-playing pal. Buster's appearance, one of his one-day working assignments, occurs nearly halfway through the film. Gloria Swanson, playing Norma Desmond, the once-legendary

Buster does one of the best "poker-faced and befuddled" looks of his career in his very brief but effective cameo in the magnificent *Sunset Boulevard*.

Buster called his brief cameo assignment for *Sunset Boulevard*, "like old home week." Here, he compares his veteran status with such fellow Hollywood legends as (from left) Anna Q. Nilsson, William Holden (in background), Cecil B. DeMille, Gloria Swanson, and H. B. Warner.

queen of the silent screen, a character essentially modeled after herself, has invited some of her old movie acquaintances over for a friendly bridge game. According to William Holden's character, Joe Gillis, who is dead in the opening scene but acts as the film's narrator, "the others around the table would be actor friends, dim figures you may still remember from the silent days. I used to think of them as her waxworks."

A series of close-ups follows, first of Swanson, then Anna Q. Nilsson, then H. B. Warner (best known for his portrayal of Jesus in DeMille's *King of Kings*), then Buster. The camera holds on Buster the longest as he utters his only line of dialogue, "Pass . . . Pass." His wistful expression, conveying a hint of bewilderment,

contrasts with the faces of the others, who seem much more hardened, their eyes reflecting a cynical acceptance of their low-profile existence.

Many have commented on the film's almost exploitive use of its faded, legendary greats. However, it is more of a comment on Hollywood than on its stars, how some of the greatest cinematic talents were drained of their creative energies and then cast aside. Buster himself felt no qualms about playing a Hollywood has-been. To him it was a day's work for a day's pay. He enjoyed working with his old friends and called the experience "like old home week." When the now-legendary film was released, he never even bothered to see it since he preferred comedies to dramas.

PARADISE FOR BUSTER

CREDITS:

A Wilding Pictures Production Presented by John Deere and Company, Inc. *Production Supervisors:* H. M. Railsback and G. M. Rohrbach; *Director:* Del Lord; *Story:* J. P. Prindle, John Grey, and Harold Goodwin; *Photography:* J. J. La Fleur and Robert Sable; *Editor:* William Minnerly; *Music:* Albert Glasser. *Release Date:* October 15, 1952. *Running Time:* 39 minutes.

CAST:

Buster Keaton, Harold Goodwin.

In addition to his supporting roles in features and his theater and television work at home and abroad, Buster made several films for private firms. For the most part, these industrial films are pretty much glorified commercials made to promote a company's products or to inform the public about the functions of a particular organization. Since they were made for private businesses, none received any wide distribution and they remain relatively obscure.

Buster's first industrial film, *Paradise for Buster,* made for John Deere and Company, is the best, namely because it promotes nothing, explains no organization's functions, and doesn't clarify any public service. It is essentially a four-reel comedy short directed by Del Lord, who worked with Buster on two of his best Columbia two-reelers.

In this grab bag of recycled and revamped routines from his old movies, Buster plays a bored, inept bookkeeper of a Midwestern mining company. Learning that he has inherited the farm of his recently deceased uncle, Burr McKeaton, Buster storms into the offices of the various vice presidents, slamming their doors and breaking the glass in each until he arrives at the president's suite, where he speaks his only line of dialogue, "I quit!" before vacating the premises.

Arriving at his new "estate," Buster learns that his uncle has left him a run-down farm on the brink of foreclosure. After gaining access to the farmhouse, he finds a piggy bank hidden behind the portrait of his beloved uncle Burr (the portrait is of Buster adorned with a bushy beard and a tam-o'-shanter). He then restages a scene from *The Cameraman* as he attempts to crack open the tiny bank. In the original, Buster nearly destroyed his small apartment trying to break open the stubborn bank. Here, he actually destroys the entire farmhouse. Along the way, he restages the "spilled molasses" routine from *The Butcher Boy* before finally burning the house down. Although the segment is a tad too long, the sight of Buster in one bit of chaotic comedy business after another while the

Made for John Deere and Company, *Paradise for Buster* is his first and best "industrial film," basically a four-reel comedy made up of some of the best gags from several of his previous movies.

Buster recreates the "gun fishing" gag from *The Love Nest* in this scene from *Paradise for Buster*.

effectively restages the "fish shooting" gag from *The Love Nest*. Afterward, a passing fisherman, played by old Keaton friend Harold Goodwin, spies Buster's catch and pays him for the privilege of fishing in the lake. Buster gazes at the money, then gets a twinkle in his eye as he hits on a plan to save his farm from foreclosure. In the follow-up scene, a long line of cars drives onto Buster's property, each passing under a huge banner: "Fisherman's Paradise—Buster Keaton, Prop." Hundreds of fishermen line the banks of the lake while Buster stuffs wads of money into various piggy banks.

Although hardly original, *Paradise for Buster* is filled with charm and clever variations on memorable routines. It also benefits from its unhurried pacing—a luxury for Buster—and its beautiful outdoor settings, to which Buster always seems perfectly suited.

LIMELIGHT

CREDITS:

A Celebrated Films Corporation Production; Distributed by United Artists. *Producer/Director/Script/Music:* Charles Chaplin; *Photography:* Karl Struss (*Photographic Consultant:* Roland Totheroh); *Editor:* Joe Inge. *Release Date:* February 6, 1953. *Running Time:* 145 minutes.

CAST:

Buster Keaton, Charles Chaplin, Claire Bloom, Nigel Bruce, Sydney Chaplin, Norman Lloyd, Marjorie Bennett, Wheeler Dryden, Barry Bernard, Stapleton Kent, Mollie Blessing, Leonard Mudie, Julian Ludwig, Snub Pollard, Loyal Underwood, Charley Rogers, Geraldine Chaplin, Michael Chaplin, Josephine Chaplin, Charles Chaplin, Jr., Edna Purviance.

house burns to the ground is truly a joy to watch.

Having destroyed the farmhouse, Buster explores the rest of his new estate. As an antagonistic neighboring farmer secretly watches from below, Buster fools around with the blades of a windmill, then gets stuck on them and is tossed off down to a truckload of hay, the impact of his fall throwing the other farmer out of his hiding place and into a pigsty. Buster's angry neighbor then chases him across the rest of the farm to a nearby lake, which is also part of his estate. Feeling despondent over the recent disastrous events, Buster decides to end it all and marches off to the lake to drown himself. As he is about to jump in, he notices a swarm of hyperactive fish jumping friskily out of the water. Forgetting about suicide, Buster breaks out his fishing gear. When the trout ignore his line, Buster

Buster's most famous supporting role is in *Limelight*, where he appears for the only time with the man he referred to in his autobiography as the greatest screen comedian of all time (and the man who makes no mention of Buster in his own autobiography). Chaplin decided to employ Buster for the simple fact that he badly needed someone familiar with pantomime and Buster was readily available. Buster jumped at the opportunity to appear with the master, later saying that he would have done the part for free. As it was, he was paid $1,000 for three weeks' work. Most of his time was spent watching Chaplin rehearse and rerehearse their scenes.

The film, set in turn-of-the-century England, tells of a fading music-hall performer and his struggles to sur-

197

The two greatest film comedians of all time finally play together on screen in Charlie Chaplin's *Limelight*.

vive in a world that has forgotten his former triumphs, a timely subject for both Chaplin and Keaton. Chaplin's character, Calvero, has suffered through a series of humiliating setbacks before finally getting the chance to headline a gala variety show. Before his performance, he dons his costume and makeup in the star dressing room, chatting with an old performer friend (Buster) who will assist him in the act.

The first sight of the two comic giants dressed in clownlike-costumes is a classic cinematic moment that leaves an indelible impression. Their act consists of Buster, sporting a walrus mustache and thick glasses, accompanying Charlie on the piano while the latter stages a comical violin recital. Buster does an extended bit, struggling to keep his sheet music from falling on the floor. Finally, after he indicates that he has his music in order, the two men try tuning their instruments and end up disemboweling the piano. As Charlie finally begins sawing away on his instrument,

flashing an intense, impish grin, Buster bangs away at the piano, falling off his stool as the tempo picks up. When it becomes even more frenzied, Charlie himself loses his balance and falls into the orchestra pit, landing in a bass drum, still fiddling away. In the bittersweet follow-up scene, Charlie suffers a heart attack and ends up on a couch backstage while Buster watches his old friend die, finally shuffling backward as the theater doctor pulls a sheet over Charlie's face.

Although their comical musical number is quite good, Buster really has little to do except drop his sheet music and look intensely befuddled as he pounds away at the piano. Chaplin's death scene has much more punch. Buster's hunched shoulders, shuffling gait, and forlorn stare as his friend slips away are extremely poignant, another timeless cinematic moment that transcends its context.

In his autobiography, Buster mentions his encounter with Chaplin on the set of *Limelight* after not having seen the master for twenty years: "Apparently, he had expected to see a physical and mental wreck. But I was in fine fettle. I'd just been in New York for four months doing an average of two TV guest shots a week. So I was prosperous and looked it." According to Buster, Chaplin was shocked to find out that he was so involved with television. Unlike Chaplin, who hated television, Buster loved watching and performing on TV and, in fact, starred in two Los Angeles–based series in the early 1950s, one filmed live in front of a studio audience, the other done without an audience.

Much has been written about Chaplin's efforts to sabotage Buster's performance in *Limelight* by editing out some of the latter's best moments. Although Chaplin had an ego the size of Jupiter, it seems unlikely that he would have gone to the trouble of hiring Buster just so he could edit him out of the picture. In his book, *Remembering Charlie*, Jerry Epstein (Chaplin's assistant on *Limelight*) states that the star shot enough footage for his one scene with Buster to make five feature films. "Of course Charlie cut some of Keaton's gags," he writes. "If he hadn't, the picture would have run forever. But he cut just as many of his own best laughs." Considering Chaplin's reputation as an egomaniac, he must be praised for having had the guts to use Buster at all.

AROUND THE WORLD IN EIGHTY DAYS

CREDITS:

A United Artists Release. *Producer:* Michael Todd; *Director:* Michael Anderson; *Script:* James Poe, John Farrow, and S. J. Perelman, based on the novel by Jules Verne; *Photography:* Lionel Lindon; *Editors:* Gene Ruggiero and Howard Epstein; *Music:* Victor Young. Todd-AO and Eastman Color. *Release Date:* March 1956. *Running Time:* 168 minutes.

CAST:

Buster Keaton, David Niven, Cantinflas, Shirley MacLaine, Robert Newton, Joe E. Brown, John Carradine, Charles Coburn, Ronald Colman, Noel Coward, Reginald Denny, Andy Devine, Marlene Dietrich, John Gielgud, Cedric Hardwicke, Trevor Howard, Glynis Johns, Evelyn Keyes, Beatrice Lillie, Peter Lorre, Victor McLaglen, Col. Tim McCoy, Alan Mowbray, Robert Morley, Jack Oakie, George Raft, Gilbert Roland, Frank Sinatra, Red Skelton, and a cast of billions.

For his appearance in the Academy Award–winning extravaganza *Around the World in Eighty Days*, Buster is typecast as a nineteenth-century railroad conductor who commandeers his train across the Indian-infested Western frontier. On board are the principal characters, David Niven as the globe-hopping Phileas Fogg, and Mexican clown Cantinflas as his manservant Passepartout, along with a bevy of other star players.

Train conductor Buster gives a lift to world travelers Shirley MacLaine, David Niven, and Cantinflas in the Academy Award-winning *Around the World in Eighty Days*.

Although Buster had absolutely no creative control over his scenes, his segment conjures up memories from three of his films. First, in a scene strongly reminiscent of the climactic bridge-crossing from *The General,* Buster stops the train at the end of a long, wobbly bridge spanning a chasm and pronounces the structure unsafe to cross. With a little urging from crusty gambler John Carradine, along with a quick swig from his whiskey bottle, Buster decides, however, to risk the crossing, then holds his breath along with the engineer as the bridge begins to disintegrate behind them.

The second film recalled is *The Passionate Plumber,* when Carradine, who has been antagonizing Niven throughout the train trip, throws out one insult too many and is challenged to a duel. Buster arranges the duel between the two while the train is still moving. After herding the rest of the passengers out of the "dueling car," he warns the two men, "Now don't miss, boys, and damage the woodwork. The company's liable to take it out of my salary." As in *The Passionate Plumber,* the duel never occurs, interrupted this time by a horde of attacking savages. Buster is wounded in the battle, receiving an arrow in the side, which he pulls out and hands to Niven, growling, "I'm all right, but look what they've done to my coat."

The third memory-jogger occurs when Cantinflas tries to walk atop the train to the engine room to aid the wounded engineer. However, along the way he falls off and is captured by the Indians, who attempt to burn him at the stake in a comical bit slightly reminiscent of *The Paleface.* Unlike Buster in the original short, Cantinflas has forgotten his asbestos underwear and has to rely on the cavalry to get him out of his predicament.

Buster's character was originally supposed to die during the Indian attack. However, even with such a small role, he proved too sympathetic and was spared at the last minute. It is too bad that he wasn't offered the key role of Passepartout. Although Cantinflas is a marvelous comic actor and pantomimist, Buster would have been able to give the role much more expressive shading.

THE ADVENTURES OF HUCKLEBERRY FINN

CREDITS:

A Metro-Goldwyn-Mayer Production. *Producer:* Samuel Goldwyn, Jr.; *Director:* Michael Curtiz; *Script:* James Lee, from the novel by Mark Twain; *Photography:* Ted McCord; *Editor:* Frederic Steinkamp. CinemaScope and MetroColor. *Release Date:* June 17, 1960. *Running Time:* 107 minutes.

CAST:

Buster Keaton, Eddie Hodges, Archie Moore, Tony Randall, Neville Brand, Mickey Shaughnessy, Patty McCormack, Judy Canova, Andy Devine, Sherry Jackson, John Carradine, Josephine Hutchinson, Sterling Holloway, (Harry) Dean Stanton.

Like every other filmed version of Mark Twain's novel (there are at least seven so far), this one fails to do justice to its source. This was MGM's second attempt, the previous version filmed in 1939 and starring Mickey Rooney in the title role. This time, Eddie Hodges, a Rooney look-alike two decades removed, plays the immortal lost boy and river rat, with former heavyweight boxing champ Archie Moore as Jim, the runaway slave.

Buster's part is superfluous; his scene isn't even in the novel. Attempting to make it to free territory where Jim will be safe from slave hunters, Huck and Jim join up with a decrepit traveling circus troupe. Buster plays an old lion tamer, with an even older lion, Orville. Buster pulls the old lion's tail to get it to move, and it just yelps feebly. When the circus owner (Andy Devine) appears with food for the ancient beast—a bag of turnips—Buster remarks, "If Orville doesn't get meat soon, I'm gonna be afraid to get in the cage with him."

For the evening's performance, Huck dresses up Jim as a native monarch, then acts as his interpreter while Buster plays a drum. Huck and Jim's act nearly works until their old con artist acquaintances, the Duke and the Dauphin (Tony Randall and Mickey Shaughnessy), turn up and accuse Jim of being a runaway slave. Covering for Huck and Jim, the circus owner tells the con men that Jim was brought from Patagonia by his young interpreter, who is also the World's Youngest Lion Tamer. The two scoundrels then demand that Huck prove he is a lion tamer by getting into the cage with Orville.

Buster tries to give Huck a crash taming course, handing him a chair and telling him not to show any fear. When Orville lets out a roar (he sounds as if he were dubbed by the MGM lion), Buster tells Huck, "That's those darn turnips."

When Jim tries to prevent Huck from entering the cage, a fight breaks out and Huck ends up locking the Duke and the Dauphin in with Orville. Buster, however, repeating his line about Orville's not having eaten meat for weeks, yanks the two rapscallions out of the cage.

Buster's scene was seemingly inserted as a bit of comic relief. Devine dominates the segment with Keaton acting almost as his sidekick, throwing out an occasional comment about the sad shape of his beloved Orville. The lion used was truly ancient, and the scene's best moments are the shots of Buster and Orville together, two ancient kings struggling to inject some much-needed color to yet another sanitized version of America's greatest literary achievement.

TEN GIRLS AGO

CREDITS:

An Am-Can Production. *Producer:* Edward A. Gollin; *Director:* Harold Daniels; *Script:* Peter Farrow and Diane Lampert; *Photography:* Lee Garmes and Jackson Samuels; *Music/ Lyrics:* Diane Lampert and Sammy Fain; *Musical Director:* Joseph Harnell; *Choreography:* Bill Foster. *Release Date:* never released (filming completed in April 1962). *Running Time:* 92 minutes (approximate).

CAST:

Buster Keaton, Bert Lahr, Eddie Foy, Jr., Dion DiMucci, Austin Willis, Jan Miner, Jennifer Billingsley, Risella Bain.

Throughout his career, Buster was involved in a number of films that, for various reasons, were never completed, such as MGM's *The March of Time* (also known as *Hollywood Revue of 1930*), *The Fisherman* and *The Little King* (both abandoned in 1933 after Buster's producer friend Marshall Neilan went bankrupt), and much later in his career, something called *Pajama Party in a Haunted House*, a sequel to one of the "beach party" movies he made for American-International in the 1960s. He also abandoned a project in the midtwenties, conceived by film critic/

Buster plays a lion tamer worried that Huck Finn (Eddie Hodges) is going to upset Orville, the ancient but still meat-obsessed lion, in *The Adventures of Huckleberry Finn*. Archie Moore (left) as Jim and Andy Devine as the circus owner look on.

Buster with Eddie Foy, Jr., and Bert Lahr on the set of *Ten Girls Ago*, a Canadian-produced youth-oriented film that remains unreleased.

Bert Lahr, Austin Willis (in checkered jacket), and Eddie Foy, Jr. (on bench) rehearse a scene with Buster for *Ten Girls Ago*.

Buster takes a break during the filming of *Ten Girls Ago*.

playwright Robert E. Sherwood, where Buster gets stuck with his girlfriend atop a partially completed skyscraper in the middle of the night. (Many years later, Buster ran into Sherwood in the lobby of a hotel, and the famed playwright acknowledged Buster's presence by shouting, "Don't worry, Buster, I'll get you down from that skyscraper yet!")

Of all the abandoned projects on which Buster worked, the one that came the closest to completion was *Ten Girls Ago*. Planned as a sort of Canadian beach-party movie without the beach, the film also starred such veteran actors as Bert Lahr and Eddie Foy, Jr., along with pop idol Dion DiMucci and a bevy of dancing go-go girls (at least ten of them, anyway). In the film, an aging comic, played by Lahr, has a long-running television variety show that is being trounced in the ratings by a sitcom starring a collie named Nellie. With the help of some of his old pals—Keaton and Foy—along with a basset hound of his own, Lahr stages a comeback and ultimately triumphs. The film features several song-and-dance numbers, an extended scene in a delicatessen, and much comical interplay among the three veteran actors.

According to John Sebert, who covered the project as a newspaper still photographer, the film was in financial trouble from the very beginning, and producer Edward Gollin called it quits after failing to raise additional funds to finance postproduction work. Alan Hoffman, in his book, *Buster*, talked to celebrated cinematographer Lee Garmes, who told him that the film was 98 percent complete, requiring only a few scene inserts and opticals. Shooting was held up when Bert Lahr came down with pneumonia, then later when the film's musical director, Joe Harnell, was in a car crash and broke several bones. Buster himself was injured on the set, nearly biting off a large chunk of his tongue while trying to execute a routine pratfall. A crude, thirty-minute version of the film is said to be preserved in the vaults of the National Archives of Canada. Perhaps somebody will some day provide the funds to bring this film, in its entirety, to the silver screen.

Buster back on the set with Bert Lahr, Eddie Foy, Jr., and Austin Willis.

Ten Girls Ago: Jennifer Billingsley and Buster rehearse dance steps before wriggling in front of the cameras.

Buster is eye to nose with Jennifer Billingsley, one of at least ten female cast members from *Ten Girls Ago*.

Buster asks a turn-of-the-century policeman for directions to the nearest Fotomat in *The Triumph of Lester Snapwell*, an industrial film made for the Eastman Kodak Company.

THE TRIUMPH OF LESTER SNAPWELL

CREDITS:

An Eastman Kodak Company Production. *Director:* James Calhoun. *Release Date:* 1963. *Running Time:* 22 minutes.

CAST:

Buster Keaton, Sigrid Nelsson, Nina Varela.

Buster appeared in dozens of television commercials beginning in the 1950s and continuing right up to the time of his death. He enjoyed doing them very much, saying it was good pay for a minimal amount of work. He pitched a wide variety of products—toothpaste, power tools, airlines, beer, gasoline, and antacids to name a few. *The Triumph of Lester Snapwell,* one of Keaton's industrial-film efforts, is essentially a lengthy commercial for the Eastman Kodak Company and its then-revolutionary advance in amateur home photography, the Instamatic camera.

A low-budget effort, shot in mock-silent-movie style—no dialogue, speeded-up action, and title cards supplemented with voice-over narration—the film gives a thumbnail history of amateur photography. Buster plays Lester Snapwell, a photography enthusiast who, according to the opening title card, "had two loves . . . his camera and his girl (in that order)." This

card's resemblance to one of the opening titles to Buster's *The General* is purely intentional. The film then opens on the Dawn of Photography, back in the 1860s and, through a series of vignettes, ends in the trendy 1960s with that most revolutionary breakthrough in modern photographic technology. Until that momentous occasion, Buster, in each vignette, struggles with his cumbersome camera equipment as he tries to photograph his sweetie, Clementine (Sigrid Nelsson), and her matronly mother (Nina Varela). Naturally, he fails miserably in every epoch until-. . . well, you know.

Several of the segments contain cute Keatonesque gags. In one, Buster battles his Mathew Brady–model camera, adjusting the tripod, juggling chemicals, mistaking the back of Mama's dress for the camera's drape, then finally setting the dress on fire with the photo chemicals and escaping from the matronly dervish by jumping headfirst through the top portion of a Dutch door. In another segment, a turn-of-the-century Buster tells his subjects to "Hold that pose!" as he dashes off to the post office to send for another roll of film. Two months later, the film arrives and he races back to Clementine's to find his sweetheart and her mom still frozen in position, although looking somewhat saggy after the delay. In the end, Buster triumphs when the knucklehead-proof Instamatic is finally invented.

Hardly a cinematic triumph, the film is amateurish, even more stilted and cheap-looking than Buster's Educational shorts. It isn't his best industrial film and is hardly comparable to some of his television commercials, most of which are quite entertaining. Still, it has an innocent charm and some startlingly effective stunt work for a then-sixty-seven-year-old funnyman. Since there are hints of gags from some of Buster's earlier films sprinkled throughout, I kept on waiting for Buster to restage the "collapsing tripod" gag from *My Wife's Relations*. According to Alan Hoffman, the gag does appear in a French version.

IT'S A MAD, MAD, MAD, MAD WORLD

CREDITS:

A United Artists Production. *Producer/Director:* Stanley Kramer; *Script:* William and Tania Rose; *Photography:* Ernest Laszlo; *Music:* Ernest Gold; *Editor:* Fred Knudtson. Ultra Panavision and Technicolor. *Release Date:* November 7, 1963. *Running Time:* 192 minutes (cut to 154 minutes; later rereleased with some restored footage).

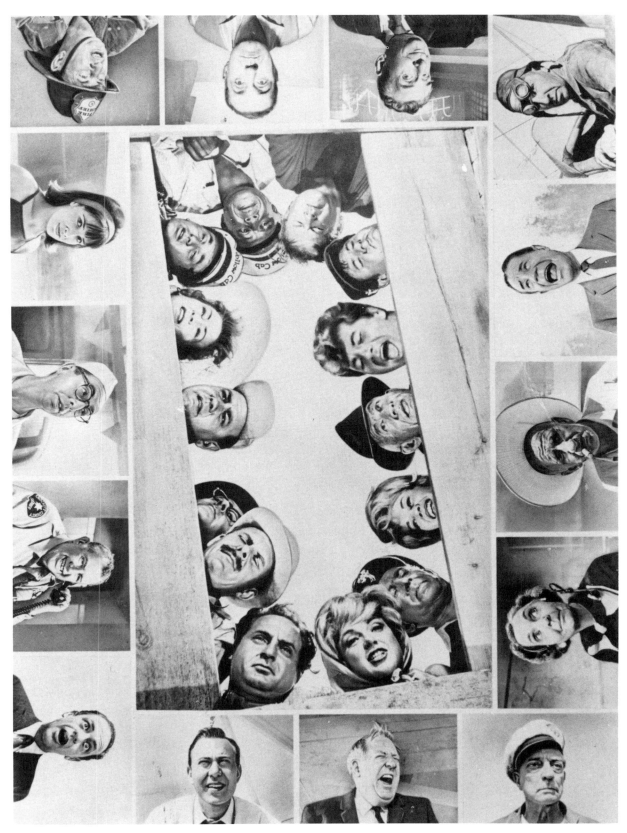

You name 'em, they're in *It's a Mad, Mad, Mad, Mad World*. However, when theater owners insisted the film be cut to a more reasonable showing time, Buster's part was almost totally eliminated from all existing prints.

CAST:

Buster Keaton, Spencer Tracy, Milton Berle, Sid Caesar, Buddy Hackett, Ethel Merman, Mickey Rooney, Dick Shawn, Phil Silvers, Terry-Thomas, Jonathan Winters, Edie Adams, Dorothy Provine, Jimmy Durante, Eddie "Rochester" Anderson, Jim Backus, Barrie Chase, Peter Falk, Paul Ford, Leo Gorcey, Don Knotts, Carl Reiner, The Three Stooges, Joe E. Brown, Andy Devine, Sterling Holloway, Charles McGraw, ZaSu Pitts, Arnold Stang, Jesse White, Stan Freberg, Norman Fell, Doodles Weaver, Jack Benny, Jerry Lewis, and a cast of zillions.

The ultimate example of the "more is better" approach to comedy is Stanley Kramer's loud, long, elephantine extravanganza, *It's a Mad, Mad, Mad, Mad World* (even the title is a joke that goes on for too long). Apparently, the film's original distributors also felt that Kramer's "kitchen sink" approach to comedy was excessive and demanded that it be cut from its gargantuan 192-minute length to a running time that would permit them to fit in an additional evening screening. Nearly forty minutes were trimmed, which further sabotages the already wildly chaotic pacing. It also resulted in the near-total elimination of Buster from the film.

In the original version, Buster played a character called Jimmy the Crook, a friend of Spencer Tracy's police chief who, along with everyone else in the film, is obsessed with finding the whereabouts of a suitcase full of money stolen by Jimmy Durante. Tracy wants the cash so he can retire far away from his loudmouth wife and incorrigible teenage daughter. He phones Buster, who owns a boat, and in a lengthy telephone conversation arranges an escape plan. After following the frenzied mob of comedians to the money's hiding place, Tracy steals the loot from them and drives to the harbor where Buster has his boat docked. When Tracy arrives and pulls into Buster's nearby garage, the money-mad mob comes on the scene. "What's goin' on?" croaks Buster. "Sorry, Jimmy," replies Tracy, then pulls out of Buster's garage and drives away, leaving his partner in crime to dodge the swarm of vehicles piloted by the manic money-grubbers.

In the film's existing version, all of Buster's conversations with Tracy are missing. His one remaining scene, the brief encounter with Tracy outside the garage, now stands as the most blatant example of the hackneyed editing job forced on the film after its initial release. This scene, with Buster running hesitantly in all directions, now makes no sense since the viewer doesn't know for sure why Tracy is driving to the harbor, or why he would address this new character by his first name, only to drive off and never refer to him again.

Although loud, chaotic, and almost primitive in its approach to comedy, the film nevertheless is distinguished by its amazing cast of comedians and character actors. However, since it remains the premier example of comedy overkill, it seems illogical to edit anything out. Give us more, not less—especially more of Buster. (According to film historian Bruce Lawton, there *was* more of Buster that Kramer edited out of the original 192-minute version: a scene where Buster struggles to put a donkey in his boat garage.)

PAJAMA PARTY

CREDITS:

An American-International Pictures Production. *Producers:* James H. Nicholson and Samuel Z. Arkoff. *Director:* Don Weis; *Script:* Louis M. Heyward; *Photography:* Floyd Crosby; *Editors:* Fred Feitshans and Eve Newman. Panavision and Pathécolor. *Release Date:* November 11, 1964. *Running Time:* 85 minutes.

CAST:

Buster Keaton, Tommy Kirk, Annette Funicello, Elsa Lanchester, Harvey Lembeck, Jesse White, Jody McCrea, Susan Hart, Bobbi Shaw, Don Rickles, Frankie Avalon, Dorothy Lamour.

Buster received the widest public exposure of his post-MGM film career with his appearances in the series of "beach movies" he made for American-International. Ironically, while he was appearing on-screen with a bevy of bikini-clad babes in some of the most ineptly made—and financially successful—teen exploitation movies, the international film community was officially rediscovering his earlier, classic silents and hailing him as a cinematic genius. As usual, Buster himself treated his beach-movie work and the international acclaim equally—he didn't take any of it seriously. Basically, he just loved working, always feeling at his best when he was performing. As he said in his autobiography, "I never knew a real actor who was happy when he wasn't working. And working is something I manage to do a lot of these days."

The beach movies are essentially all alike, made primarily to show scantily clad youths gyrating together in various party locales, usually on a stretch of California beach. They feature some of the worst acting, writing, directing, camera work, choreography,

"Kowabunga!" exclaims Buster as Chief Rotten Eagle, "Me already get to hold Annette and this only my first beach party movie!" Also pictured is Tommy Kirk as a Martian with a strong Earthly craving for a wild *Pajama Party*.

and music ever recorded on film. However, as a long-standing member of the Cult of the Annette Idolaters, I must admit that I find them highly inspiring.

As a whole, the films have the same basic premise: a horde of parentless (on-screen at least) beach kids who just want to have fun keep on having their fun interrupted by petty jealousies, by boy-girl misunderstandings, and by various doltish outsiders. The outsiders include numerous, eccentric adults, and a rival group of lunkheaded bikers headed by the past president of the Al St. John School of Subtle Acting, Harvey Lembeck. Among the interloping do-gooders (and do-badders) are Vincent Price, Robert Cummings, Boris Karloff, Elsa Lanchester, Dorothy Lamour, and Basil Rathbone, as well as such comics as Don Rickles, Buddy Hackett, Mickey Rooney, and Jesse White.

Buster's character in *Pajama Party* is similar to the one he played in *Li'l Abner*, an imbecilic Indian caricature, here called Chief Rotten Eagle. Dressed in standard buckskins (except for his trademark flat hat, which sports one tall feather), and speaking in stilted Pidgin English, Buster is a crony of con man Jesse White, who is plotting to steal the fortune of eccentric millionairess Elsa Lanchester. Elsa has her fortune

hidden somewhere in her huge Victorian-style mansion, and Buster, Jesse, and another character (Ben Lessy) spend most of the film trying to figure out how to gain access to her house and search for the loot without arousing her suspicions.

This is all a distraction from the main story, which centers on a Martian, played by Tommy Kirk, who infiltrates the group of beach kids to master their behavior so he can more successfully lead an invasion of the planet. As in all of the beach films, plot, characters, and motivation are secondary to showing lots of jiggling babes and bouncing breasts and bulges.

Buster has a sidekick of his own, Helga, a dim-witted, buxom blonde with a fake Swedish accent. Bobbi Shaw plays Helga and she is beautiful to look at, which is obviously why she was hired for the part. Since Buster has no cleavage to show off, he has little to do in the film. He does have a mildly amusing running gag with one of the beach girls—the two continually douse each other with a variety of liquids. And he does provide one of the film's key phrases—"Kowabunga!" (and this is long before the Teenage Mutant Ninja Turtles).

Buster's best moments occur when he dances with Lanchester and some of the beach girls as the end credits roll. He gets in some cute variations of his powwow dance steps from *The Paleface* and *Li'l Abner*, as well as a couple of contemporary moves. The film, however, belongs to Don Rickles as a sarcastic Martian who belittles Tommy Kirk's activities to his boss, played by surprise guest Frankie Avalon.

By the way, this is one of the rare beach movies where Annette actually gets her hair wet.

BEACH BLANKET BINGO

CREDITS:

An American-International Pictures Production. *Producers:* James H. Nicholson and Samuel Z. Arkoff. *Director:* William Asher; *Script:* William Asher and Leo Townsend; *Photography:* Floyd Crosby; *Editors:* Fred Feitshans and Eve Newman. Panavision and Pathécolor. *Release Date:* April 15, 1965. *Running Time:* 98 minutes.

CAST:

Buster Keaton, Frankie Avalon, Annette Funicello, Deborah Walley, Harvey Lembeck, John Ashley, Jody McCrea, Donna Loren, Marta Kristen, Linda Evans, Bobbi Shaw, Timothy Carey, Don Rickles, Paul Lynde, Earl Wilson.

Buster perfects his surfboarding skills in *Beach Blanket Bingo*, arguably the best of the beach party movies of the 1960s.

Buster's second beach movie was the most popular of the series and contains one of his worst supporting roles. Dressed in his traditional Keaton outfit, he plays an assistant to Don Rickles, who runs a skydiving outfit and a nightclub catering to the beach crowd. Buster has really nothing to do in the film except chase around Bobbi Shaw, the buxom blond assistant from his previous beach opus, *Pajama Party*.

In his first scene, just after the credits and the title song crooned by Frankie and Annette, Buster is seen fishing along the beach and reeling in a bikini top belonging to a gyrating blond. He absentmindedly tosses the top back into the ocean, then, realizing what he has done, frantically gazes out to sea trying to catch a glimpse of its owner.

Buster shows up a little later standing on the shoreline painting a seascape. When a beach girl passes by and rips off her robe revealing her bikini-clad body, Buster falls over his easel and then chases the girl down the beach, only to return moments later running in the opposite direction, the two now pursued by a dog.

Next, he shows up at the airport where Rickles is extolling the joys of skydiving to the beach kids. In the middle of his sales pitch, Buster runs across the airport in pursuit of curvy Bobbi Shaw. When Frankie remarks that it looks as though Bobbi is in need of some assistance, Rickles replies, "That's just Buster . . . It's just clean fun. Keeps them out of pool halls." Later, in a reprise of the pursuer-pursued joke from his previous scene, Buster and bouncing Bobbi are glimpsed dashing across the airport chased by a Piper Cub.

In his best scene, which occurs in Rickles's nightclub, Buster first commands Bobbi to dance, then gets up to join her and executes some funny "surfer stomp" movements before accidentally hitting himself in the face and tumbling backward over a chair. At age sixty-nine he is still able to make the fall look brutally unrehearsed. A while later, he and Bobbi do a mock minuet to a slow dance number.

Buster and Bobbi are on hand for the climactic fight scene, joining the surfers to trounce the rival biker gang led by Harvey Lembeck. Buster is also part of the ineptly filmed Keystone Kop–style car chase where a low-hanging branch yanks him from his vehicle just before it careens over a cliff. And finally, while trying to save a girl from the clutches of a demented pool-hall creep, Buster scales a pile of kids and is the first person upstairs to confront the no-goodnik in his secret hiding place, then is the first to fall through his trapdoor.

Buster repeats his over-the-credits dance routine from *Pajama Party,* comically gyrating with various beach bunnies and supplying some last-minute laughs to this painfully inept, yet hugely successful, sand and surf spectacular.

HOW TO STUFF A WILD BIKINI

CREDITS:

An American-International Pictures Production. *Producers:* James H. Nicholson and Samuel Z. Arkoff. *Director:* William Asher; *Script:* William Asher and Leo Townsend; *Photography:* Floyd Crosby; *Editors:* Fred Feitshans and Eve Newman. Panavision and Pathécolor. *Release Date:* July 14, 1965. *Running Time:* 98 minutes.

CAST:

Buster Keaton, Annette Funicello, Dwayne Hickman, Mickey Rooney, Brian Donlevy, Frankie Avalon, Harvey Lembeck, Beverly Adams, Jody McCrea, John Ashley, Marianne Gaba, Irene Tsu, Bobbi Shaw, Alberta Nelson, Elizabeth Montgomery (uncredited cameo).

As the profits from the beach movies increased, their production values decreased. *How to Stuff a Wild Bikini* is arguably the worst of the series with the songs, dance numbers, and acting all more hopelessly inept than ever. (To be fair, the film does contain more jiggling scenes with gyrating bodies than any of the others, so in that sense, it is the series masterpiece.) Two dance numbers, one featuring veteran dramatic

Buster demonstrates *How to Stuff a Wild Bikini* with help from his sexy assistant, Bobbi Shaw.

actor on the skids, Brian Donlevy, as a frisky advertising executive, and the second with regular cast member/bad guy Harvey Lembeck, are so achingly bad that they come close to qualifying the film for the Ed Wood, Jr., Memorial "Bad-Is-Good" Cinema Hall of Fame.

Buster plays Bwana, a tropical-island witch doctor specializing in love potions. Dressed in a grass skirt and traditional porkpie hat, he again speaks in Pidgin English while endlessly stirring a smoldering caldron in his little grass shack. He is once again assisted by faithful, bouncy Bobbi Shaw, as well as another island beauty, played by Irene Tsu.

Coast Guard recruit Frankie Avalon, who is stationed on Buster's island and dallying with sexy Tsu, wants to find out whether sweetheart Annette is remaining faithful to him back home. Buster agrees to help him out by dispatching a pelican back to California to spy on Annette. He also fashions a shapely girl and stuffs her in the famed wild bikini, then sends her to join the beach crowd to keep the guys busy ogling her instead of lusting after Annette.

When he isn't stirring his caldron or conjuring up large-breasted women, Buster indulges in a series of painfully unfunny alcohol jokes, swigging from a jug of "torpedo juice" that produces puffs of smoke from his ears. He has one funny line—a comment on the convoluted plot—and also sets up the film's final big joke, one that makes little sense to the modern viewer not familiar with a 1960s television sitcom featuring a bewitching nose-twitching housewife.

Unlike in his two previous beach films, Buster doesn't get the chance to dance over the end credits. The film's strongest attribute is the song segment by the legendary 1960s garage band The Kingsmen, whose version of "Louie Louie" spawned a plethora of

Buster helps cool off *Sergeant Deadhead*, played by Frankie Avalon, after the accident-prone sergeant overheats by standing too close to recruit Deborah Walley (pictured with bucket).

pseudosubliminal dirty-message songs. Unfortunately, the group performs a less notorious number here, then acts as the backup band for a lively number featuring the Holy Virgin of the Beach, Annette.

SERGEANT DEADHEAD

CREDITS:

An American-International Production. *Producers:* James H. Nicholson and Samuel Z. Arkoff. *Director:* Norman Taurog; *Script:* Louis M. Heyward; *Photography:* Floyd Crosby; *Editors:* Ronald Sinclair, Fred Feitshans, and Eve Newman. Panavision and Pathécolor. *Release Date:* August 18, 1965. *Running Time:* 89 minutes.

CAST:

Buster Keaton, Frankie Avalon, Deborah Walley, Cesar Romero, Fred Clark, Eve Arden, Gale Gordon, Harvey Lembeck, Reginald Gardiner, John Ashley, Donna Loren, Norman Grabowski, Pat Buttram, Patti Chandler, Luree Holmes, Bobbi Shaw.

With the exception of Buster, most of the beach movies' worst moments were provided by the adult character actors engaged to provide various plot complications for the beach regulars. In *Sergeant Deadhead,* the character-actor quotient increases, resulting in a near-unwatchable disaster that doesn't even take place near a large body of water. Worse than that, Annette isn't in it.

Almost nonexistent is Buster's role as Airman Blinken, an ancient handyman who works on a military base populated, for the most part, by nubile female cadets. When one of the few male soldiers, the accident-prone Sergeant Deadhead, played by Frankie Avalon, injures himself while trying to launch a toy rocket, Buster and a bevy of comely recruits come to his aid, with Buster helping out by throwing a bucket of water in Frankie's face. Afterward, Buster is ordered by Officer Eve Arden to lead a troop of female recruits in a

drilling exercise and ends up trampled when the girls fail to successfully execute an about-face maneuver.

Then called upon to rewire base commander Fred Clark's office, Buster installs a "panic button," which naturally goes off and causes a base-wide panic. Before the riot occurs, he takes turns nearly electrocuting himself, Clark, and Arden during his rewiring efforts. Then, in the panic scene, he restages a weak gag from *Three on a Limb,* racing around with a faulty fire hose and poking at the nozzle until it explodes with a gush of water, knocking him flat on his rear. He then quietly disappears from the scene, letting Frankie provide the bulk of the film's loud, banal humor.

THE RAILRODDER

CREDITS:

A National Film Board of Canada Production. *Producer:* Julian Biggs; *Director/Script:* Gerald Potterton; *Photography:* Robert Humble; *Music:* Eldon Rathburn; *Editor:* J. Kilpatrick. *Release Date:* 1965. *Running Time:* 21 minutes.

CAST:

Buster Keaton.

Keaton spent his final few years as a living legend, his reputation as a cinematic genius finally recognized. He continued to accept offers to appear in a variety of productions—at home and abroad—none of which were especially outstanding but which kept him busy right up to the end. *The Railrodder,* filmed in the autumn of 1964, gave Buster the chance to tour the gorgeous Canadian wilderness while traveling pell-mell across the country aboard a small, motorized rail car. Fast paced, beautifully filmed, expertly edited, and featuring an effectively quirky original music score, the two-reeler nevertheless is a disappointment, more of a travelogue than a comedy in which the real star is Canada rather than the man in the porkpie hat.

Inspired by a newspaper ad—"See Canada Now!"—Buster imagines wild, untamed excitement awaits him if he dares to explore that country's wilderness. He decides to take the dare and jumps from a bridge, disappearing into the sea below, then later reemerging and wading ashore to begin his journey. After pausing to read a sign, "Pacific Ocean, West $3,982\frac{1}{2}$ Miles," he starts trudging westward, following a set of deserted tracks, and soon encounters what appears to be an abandoned railroad car, which resembles a sit-down lawn mower on rails. Getting into the vehicle's single seat, Buster then inadvertently starts up the machine and zooms off down the tracks, much to the shock of

It's a tea time break for Buster before resuming his journey across the Canadian wilderness in a motorized train car built-for-one in the Canadian-produced *The Railrodder.*

the car's owner, who pops up from behind a nearby mound of dirt just in time to witness Buster's departure.

The rest of the film is made up of a series of random gags as Buster travels the Canadian countryside. In the car's small storage trunk, Buster finds an endless stream of items—food, clothing, toiletries, reading material, maps, even his trademark coat and flat hat—all of which he puts to good use. When he passes a hotel and spots some guests enjoying their midafternoon tea, he joins them by producing a complete formal tea set and sipping away as he continues to speed down the tracks. Later, he hangs his laundry out to dry over a makeshift clothesline attached to the rail car. He re-creates a variation of the "giant newspaper" gag from *The High Sign* when he pulls out a map and becomes enveloped in its folds. Struggling to free himself from the unwieldy map, he remains unaware of crossing a massive bridge, and of chasing a convoy of train enthusiasts—also riding on motorized handcars—back to their point of departure. In another effective gag, Buster spots a flock of geese overhead and covers his car with tree branches, then pulls out a rifle from his storage trunk and begins shooting at the birds just as the car enters a tunnel.

Finally reaching the Pacific and his journey's end, Buster gets out of his car to take a look around, only to catch sight of another man dressed just like him emerging from the ocean, spotting a similar direction sign ("Atlantic Ocean, East 3,982$\frac{1}{2}$ Miles"), hopping on the car, and speeding off in the opposite direction.

The film is basically a one-joke affair with Buster's pulling various items out of the storage trunk and playing with them while passing through the lush landscape. Buster contributed many gags for *The Railrodder,* but he was limited by the premise. Director Gerald Potterton, an accomplished Canadian filmmaker and great Keaton enthusiast, nevertheless spends too much time on shots of the scenery. He also sabotages many of the gags by filming them in panoramic long shots that show off the landscape but reduce Buster's activities to such minuscule proportions that it's frequently difficult to see just what the hell is going on. Potterton obviously wanted to take advantage of Buster's long association with—and love for—trains, and his shots of Keaton racing his tiny car down the tracks at a dizzying speed are all excellent, reminiscent of Buster's own in *The General.* A much more exciting film, however, is the documentary *Buster Keaton Rides Again,* done during the shooting of *The Railrodder.* In it, the focus is on Buster rather than the Canadian wilderness, as it should have been with *The Railrodder.*

FILM

CREDITS:

An Evergreen Theatre Production. *Producer:* Barney Rosset; *Director:* Alan Schneider; *Script:* Samuel Beckett; *Photography:* Boris Kaufman; *Editor:* Sydney Myers. *Release Date:* September 1965. *Running Time:* 22 minutes.

CAST:

Buster Keaton.

> To be is to be perceived.
> —*Samuel Beckett, on the meaning of* Film

> A man may keep away from everybody but he can't get away from himself.
> —*Buster Keaton, on the meaning of* Film

Buster meets Beckett, or the Pratfall King meets the Emperor of Ennui. Buster himself would have been the first to admit that his and Beckett's artistic styles are slightly different. Make that totally different. Make that not even in the same galaxy.

In an essay written to accompany Beckett's published script, the author's longtime friend Alan Schneider, the director of *Film,* spoke on his experiences with Buster during the making of the short. His comments, for the most part, are quite condescending toward the star, who comes across as a burnt-out old Hollywood dolt. While belittling Buster for his unfamiliarity with Beckett, Schneider reveals his own general unfamiliarity with Buster's artistic achievements. He also admits that, after his first conversation with Buster, he was quite worried about working with him. He felt that Buster's confessed bafflement over the material would harm the production. Schneider and Beckett had originally wanted to get either Chaplin, Zero Mostel, or Jack MacGowran for the essentially one-character film. Only after their first choices proved to be unavailable did Beckett himself suggest Buster. However, despite their differences in attitudes, opinions, hobbies, hats, and generally everything else, Buster proved to be the perfect choice for Beckett's study in despair and isolation.

The film is silent—except for one character's "Shhhh"—and shot in beautifully stark black and white, being pure Beckett, his only cinematic effort. It opens with an extreme close-up of a jaundiced eyeball, Buster's, as it stares directly into the camera

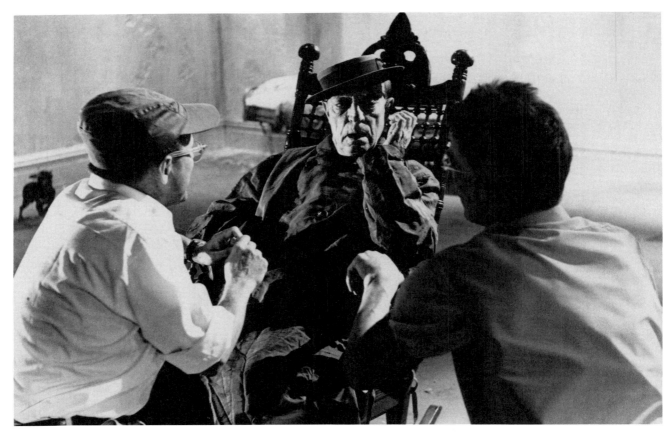

Buster confers with director Bert Schneider (left) and author Samuel
Beckett during the shooting of *Film*, the only work written specifically for
the screen by the Nobel Prize-winning author.

before closing. The camera then pans across an ancient cityscape before settling on a crumbling brick
wall. Buster then appears, his back to the camera, and
is photographed that way virtually throughout the rest
of the film. He is dressed in a thick, heavy overcoat; his
flat hat is his only recognizable feature until he begins
to move in his familiar shuffling, childlike manner
across the desolate landscape. Suddenly, he bumps
into a man and a woman dressed in Victorian-style
clothing who give him a condescending stare along
with a "Shhhh!" Then, from the point of view of Buster,
the two appear distorted and hazy, their haughty
expressions suddenly transforming into looks of
shocked horror.

Buster shuffles into an old apartment building and,
after scaring an old woman with his stare, enters a
shabby, sparsely decorated apartment. A picture of a
saucer-eyed, Babylonian-style figure hangs on one
wall and a mirror on another. Sneaking up on the
mirror, Buster puts a blanket over it and later tears up
the picture after its wide-eyed stare becomes too
unsettling for him. Then, from Buster's bleary point of

view, we see his menagerie of pets—a dog, a cat, a
caged bird, and a goldfish—each animal returning his
steady glare. In the only scene with a hint of comedy,
Buster methodically removes the dog and cat from the
room, both sneaking back in several times before
being locked out. He then covers the bird and the bowl
of the fish with a towel. Later, he tears up a pile of
photographs after looking at them and becoming
disturbed by the people in the shots. After he sits down
in a rocking chair, the camera slowly pans around the
room, taking in all the various objects before returning
to Buster, this time revealing his face for the first time.
Buster wears a patch over one eye, his other eye
reflecting horror as he stares at an object in front of
him. The camera shifts to his point of view to reveal
another Buster wickedly leering back at his double in
the chair. The original Buster gasps, then covers his
face with his hands, finally collapsing in a heap of
despair. The film's final image is the same as its first, a
close-up of Buster's ancient, unblinking eyeball.

The most fascinating aspect about *Film* is how
Buster manages to adapt to Beckett's bleak view while

maintaining his own strongly identifiable persona. Although he is filmed almost exclusively from behind, his performance is amazingly expressive, his distinct physical mannerisms communicating an animated aliveness while surrounded by dread and despair. The contrast between *Film*'s deliberately slow pacing and Buster's movements results in a perfect blending of two disparate styles that ultimately complement one another and give the constricted action a sense of urgency while the film maintains its unhurried pace.

Buster's interpretation of the film—you can't escape from yourself—although not as highfalutin as Beckett's, seems to be accurate, very much in line with the author's favorite themes of isolation, alienation, and despair. Although hardly reflective of Buster's stylistic approach to filmmaking, the film reflects many of his favorite themes of multiple images and false first impressions. However, in the end, the film is too single-minded, its theme too minuscule, for Buster's more irreverent tastes. If *Film* had been a more truly collaborative effort between the two men, Buster would have picked up where Beckett left off, having his cringing character recovering from the shocking sight of his leering double, then standing up to examine this curious specter, possibly even staging a reprise of the scene from *The Playhouse* where the two minstrel-show Busters dance together onstage. As for the film's final image of the wrinkled, unblinking eyeball, a much more Keatonesque ending would have been for the ancient peeper to be splattered with a custard pie.

In September 1965, *Film* premiered at the Venice Film Festival with Keaton in attendance. Schneider had been worried that the audience would come expecting to see a Keaton film rather than a Beckett film. Schneider's worst fears were realized when Buster received a tumultuous standing ovation, which left the veteran actor visibly moved. Obviously, the applause was for Buster's brilliant, lifetime contributions to the screen and had little to do with the merits of *Film,* which remains Beckett's and Schneider's only filmmaking effort.

WAR ITALIAN STYLE

CREDITS:

An American-International Pictures Production. *Producer:* Fulvio Lucisano; *Director:* Luigi Scattini; *Script:* Franco Castellano and Pipolo; *Photography:* Fausto Zuccoli; *Music:* Piero Umiliani. Techniscope and Technicolor. *Release Date:* January 18, 1967 (filming completed in September 1965). *Running Time:* 84 minutes. (Italian Title: *Due Marines e un Generale.*)

Those sultans of subtlety, Italian comics Franco (left) and Ciccio, try to revive Nazi general Buster after torturing him with a barrage of facial contortions in *War Italian Style.*

CAST:

Buster Keaton, Franco Franchi, Ciccio Ingrassia, Martha Hyer, Fred Clark.

Buster's connections with American-International and its beach movies landed him his substantial supporting role in this Italian-American World War II coproduction. The film's stars are Franco and Ciccio, an inexplicably popular Italian comedy team in the Abbott and Costello mold possessing all the subtlety and finesse of a roomful of screaming two-year-olds. The contrast between Buster's expressive quietness and Franco and Ciccio's excessive shrillness gives the film a schizophrenic quality, as if two stylistically varied movies were edited together. Thankfully, Buster and the comedy duo spend most of the film avoiding one another. Buster supplied most of his gags for the film, a few of which are quite good.

Buster plays, of all things, General von Kessler, a Nazi general and former concert pianist. In one of the film's few good scenes, Franco and Ciccio, as Ameri- can Marines (more inspired casting), invade Buster's palatial Italian headquarters posing as plumbers assigned to fix his bathroom. Buster then tests the plumbers' handiwork, turning on various faucets and watching the water spew forth with terrific force until his entire bathroom is a series of geyserlike waterfalls.

When Buster prepares to review his troops, with some assistance from his buxom blond assistant, played by Martha Hyer (still more inspired casting), Buster removes his general's coat and dons another customized model. This one contains a built-in fake arm that sticks straight out in a "Heil, Hitler" salute, allowing him to review his troops without effort. The sight of Buster driving around with his artificial limb in a perpetual Nazi salute is the film's comedy highlight.

The film's most effective moment is its last. After Franco and Ciccio almost single-handedly succeed in destroying a huge cannon, thus allowing the Allies to stage the Anzio invasion, the two then capture Buster and hunt down their battalion to turn him in. However, after finally catching sight of their battalion, they turn to Buster and confess, "General, you're the nicest

The powerfully effective final scene from the otherwise ineffective *War Italian Style*: Buster steps out of his Nazi general's uniform and into his trademark outfit, then disappears into the Italian countryside. Since the picture wasn't released until 1967, this is Keaton's final screen image.

214

enemy we've ever known," then hand him civilian clothing and set him free. Buster removes his general's uniform and puts on the civilian clothing, which turns out to be his trademark outfit—porkpie hat, string tie, baggy black suit, and slap shoes. With a final look at his former captors, Buster turns and walks off into the Italian countryside. Since the film was released nearly a year and a half after being completed in September 1965—and eleven months after Buster's death—the final wistful shot of him wandering away from the camera is the last Keaton image the public saw on film. No more fitting final image could have been planned for the funny, unsmiling little man in the flat hat.

A FUNNY THING HAPPENED ON THE WAY TO THE FORUM

CREDITS:

A United Artists/Quadrangle Production. *Producer:* Melvin Frank; *Director:* Richard Lester; *Script:* Michael Pertwee, based on the play by Burt Shevelove and Larry Gelbart; *Photography:* Nicolas Roeg; *Music and Lyrics:* Stephen Sondheim; *Editor:* John Victor Smith. DeLuxe Color. *Release Date:* October 16, 1966 (filming completed in October 1965). *Running Time:* 99 minutes.

CAST:

Buster Keaton, Zero Mostel, Phil Silvers, Jack Gilford, Michael Crawford, Annette Andre, Patricia Jessel, Michael Hordern, Inga Neilsen, Leon Greene, Myrna White, Pamela Brown, Roy Kinnear.

> He was just the first person that enchanted me totally in terms of sitting in the cinema and watching films. . . . I didn't really know anything about what the cinema had to offer until I started seeing Keaton's films. And I was just overwhelmed by what he did. So when the opportunity came up to have the chance of working with him, I leapt at it because to me, he was the master.
>
> —*Richard Lester, quoted from the documentary*
> Buster Keaton: A Hard Act to Follow
> *by Kevin Brownlow and David Gill*

Shortly after completing *War Italian Style,* in September 1965, Buster flew to Madrid to begin shooting what was to be the last feature film in which he appeared, *A Funny Thing Happened on the Way to the*

Forum. Buster's part in the film is minimal, but he received third billing, just after the film's principals, Zero Mostel and Phil Silvers. He was in bad health at the time and had to be doubled—by English stuntman Mick Dillon—in several scenes that showed him running across the Roman—actually Spanish—countryside. Although his performance suffers from his weakened condition, *Forum* itself is the perfect showcase for his final feature film appearance.

Buster plays Erronius, described by the film's star, Zero Mostel, as "a befuddled old man, abroad now in search of his children stolen in infancy by pirates," and the owner of one of the three principal houses that figure prominently in the story. The second one, owned by Phil Silvers's character, Lycus, is actually a brothel; and the third, owned by Michael Hordern's character, Senex, is also occupied by his wife and randy, teenage son, Hero, played by Michael Crawford (later to find a new career as the Phantom of the Opera). The third is also the home of Mostel's character, the Roman slave Pseudolus. The film's helter-skelter plot revolves around Mostel's attempts to buy his freedom from Hordern by helping Crawford woo one of Silvers's beautiful maidens, who is in turn betrothed to a Roman officer. To fulfill his desire to become free, supremely confident Mostel and edgy cohort Jack Gilford take over Buster's house while Buster is busy looking for his long-lost children. However, when Buster makes an unexpected return home, Mostel tries to keep him occupied by convincing him that the best way to find his children—and simultaneously rid his house of evil spirits—is to run around the Seven Hills of Rome seven times. Buster obliges and takes off running, occasionally showing up throughout the rest of the film as he jogs through town and the Roman countryside.

At one point, he is glimpsed clomping through the Roman environs as a swarm of chariots zoom by, some in front of him, some behind him, all barely missing him as he continues to trot along. Finally, after the chariots have all rushed past him, he pauses to comment on the refreshing Roman climate, then takes a few more steps and runs headfirst into a tree, the impact knocking him on his rear. In the Kevin Brownlow–David Gill television documentary, *Buster Keaton: A Hard Act to Follow,* stuntman Mick Dillon comments on watching Buster perform his pratfall: "He ran straight into the tree and took everybody's breath away. We thought he hadn't seen it. But that was the way he did it, he just ran straight into it—bang! It was marvelous!"

Buster is on hand for the film's denouement, supplying some much-needed sense to the convoluted plot. He is last seen running on a treadmill during the end credits, then being transformed into an animated figure that runs off the screen, a suitable image for Buster's final feature film appearance (though not as touching as the last scene in his previous *War Italian Style*).

Director Richard Lester, a Keaton worshiper, is one of the few contemporary directors to have consistently exhibited Keatonesque flourishes in his films, from *A Hard Day's Night* onward. His ability to orchestrate some of the most brutally realistic pratfalls, all of them solidly in Buster's dynamically sloppy style, is the most prominent example of his Keaton-influenced approaches to comedy. Lester is also a master of the throwaway gag, extraneous bits of comedy staged in an offhanded style that at first seem almost accidental yet are all expertly planned "background" routines. He manages, too, to endow his films with a low-key calmness even while the action is sliding into madness. His love of absurd cartoon jokes and wickedly biting satire, as well as his innovative, quick-cutting visual style, also reflect his understanding and appreciation of the man whom he calls "the master."

THE SCRIBE

CREDITS:

A Film-Tele Production for the Construction Safety Association of Ontario. *Executive Producers:* Raymond Walters and James Collier; *Producers:* Ann and Kenneth Heely-Ray; *Director:* John Sebert; *Script:* Paul Sutherland and Clifford Braggins; *Photography:* Mike Lente; *Editor:* Kenneth Heely-Ray. *Music:* Quartet Productions, Ltd. *Release Date:* May 1966 (filmed in October 1965). *Running Time:* 30 minutes.

CAST:

Buster Keaton, Larry Reynolds (stuntman/double).

The Scribe, an obscure, amateurish three-reel industrial film made for Ontario's Construction Safety Association, might at first seem to be a rather odd vehicle for Buster's last screen appearance. However, since Buster was able to find humor in every situation and every subject matter, what better way to end his career than in a film about construction-site safety tips.

Buster was quite sick when he made *The Scribe* in October 1965, shortly after completing his part in *A Funny Thing Happened on the Way to the Forum*. He was suffering from severe bronchitis, a symptom of the disease that finally led to his death, lung cancer. However, according to the film's director, John Sebert,

who had first met Buster in 1962 during the shooting of the never-released *Ten Girls Ago,* he worked with great enthusiasm once shooting began, performing endless takes where he was required to run around an actual construction site. He also had much to say about the script, his comments punctuated by one of his most often-repeated phrases, "This isn't funny," followed by suggestions on how to add to the humor. The film itself contains dozens of small bits of comedy, many of the gags variations on routines from *The Bell Boy, Cops, Daydreams, Seven Chances,* and *Pardon My Berth Marks*.

Buster plays a janitor for a Canadian newspaper. While in a reporter's office cleaning up, he intercepts a telephone call from the paper's editor, who, thinking he is talking to the reporter, assigns him a story on construction safety. Buster decides to impersonate the reporter and leaves to research the story himself. Spotting a construction site, he boldly walks into the

Buster is comforted by the vivacious Phil Silvers while Zero Mostel snuggles with the voluptuous Jack Gilford in the hilarious "toga party" comedy, *A Funny Thing Happened on the Way to the Forum*.

area and finds a poster listing various safety rules. After tucking the poster in his coat, he begins a series of confrontations with various construction workers. He approaches one worker and attempts to correct his unsafe behavior, pulling out his poster of safety rules and pointing to the one appropriate to the situation while an omniscient narrator speaks each rule over the sound track.

In one of the more clever segments, a man is pushing a wheelbarrow overloaded with bricks. Buster stops him to point out the importance of properly loading and balancing equipment, then begins to unload some of the bricks, dropping a few on the man's foot. When the man begins to hobble around in pain, Buster points out the importance of wearing safety boots. While the man is nursing his foot, another man hobbles up, his boot stuck in a bucket, a result of a previous encounter with Buster. Looking at the man's feet, Buster then grabs another brick and drops it on

Buster's appearance in *A Funny Thing Happened on the Way to the Forum* was his last in a feature film. Here, he paces with the love-struck Michael Crawford.

the worker's bucket-free foot to check if *he* is wearing safety boots. He isn't, and the two men end up hobbling after Buster as he dashes through the site.

A while later, still trying to escape from his two hobbling pursuers, Buster stops and whips off his coat, then grabs a shovel and pretends to be a worker filling in a hole. When his pursuers pass him by, Buster stops shoveling and congratulates himself on this latest maneuver, then jumps back when two other men pop up out of the hole he has been filling. The men end up as part of a long progression of pursuers in a sight gag reminiscent of the horde of policemen who chased Buster through *Cops*.

Keaton is doubled—very poorly—in a couple scenes by Larry Reynolds, a tall, lean Canadian actor

217

who looks nothing like him and whose wildly flailing mannerisms more closely resemble those of Buster's old Arbuckle costar Al St. John. Although Reynolds doubles for Buster when he's to be lifted to the top of a building by a huge crane (reminiscent of a similar scene from *Seven Chances*), Buster himself falls through a poorly constructed catwalk, topples backward off various stools, rides around in the shovel of a tractor, and runs, runs, runs across the rough, muddy construction site. Although he appears breathless at times, Buster performs all of his stunts with a youthful flair, a startling achievement for a seventy-year-old man dying of lung cancer.

The film's ending provides a most suitable coda to Keaton's seven-decade career. After eluding his construction-site pursuers, Buster returns to the newspaper to type up his story and turn it in to the editor, then goes back to the reporter's office to finish mopping the floor. Sitting down on the floor, his mop, scrub brush, and bucket by his side, he washes one small area at a time before scooting to another, covering himself with water as he works. When the film's credits begin to roll, he stops and plays with the words "The End" before resuming his mopping. This final image of Buster sitting on the floor mopping away repeats one from *The Bell Boy*. In the earlier film, the joke was performed by Roscoe Arbuckle. Nearly fifty years later in the last moments of his last film, Buster remembered his best friend, the man who introduced him to a new medium that he would eventually master to perfection, using it to create a unique body of work that ranks as one of the most innovative and inspiring artistic achievements ever.

Buster died three months after completing *The Scribe*. At the end of his autobiography, he talked of his desire to live to be one hundred: "I intend to do it. For who would not wish to live a hundred years in a world where there are so many people who remember with gratitude and affection a little man with a frozen face who made them laugh a bit long years ago when they and I were both young?"

They are still laughing, Buster, and they will continue to do so for long, long years to come.

Buster makes his last screen appearance in *The Scribe*, an industrial film made for the Construction Safety Association of Ontario, Canada. Here, John Sebert (with megaphone) directs Buster as he rides off into the sunset on the back of a tractor, a fitting final image for the civil engineer of screen comedy.

Buster acts as Lew Cody's stunt double and executes a tricky fall down a flight of stairs in *The Baby Cyclone*. The stunt earned him $7.50 and the wrath of both Louis B. Mayer and Irving Thalberg.

MISCELLANEOUS AND UNCREDITED FILM APPEARANCES

THE ROUND UP
(1920; Paramount)

Director: George Melford.
Cast: Roscoe Arbuckle.

This Arbuckle feature has Buster in an uncredited cameo as an Indian savage. After attacking a cowboy, Buster runs down a hilly incline, then does a spectacular head-over-heels fall when Roscoe, playing a sheriff, shoots him.

SCREEN SNAPSHOTS #3
(1922; Pathé Exchange)

Producers: Jack Cohn and Louis Lewyn.

Buster appears in this newsreel featuring popular celebrities of the day.

THE BABY CYCLONE
(1928; MGM)

Director: Edward Sutherland.
Cast: Lew Cody, Aileen Pringle, Robert Armstrong, Gwen Lee.

Buster doubles for Lew Cody, falling down a flight of stairs. Apparently, the stunt (done during a break in the filming of *The Cameraman*) looked so real that when Irving Thalberg saw *The Baby Cyclone* and found out Buster had performed it, both he and Louis B. Mayer

forbade him to attempt any more hazardous falls. For his stunt work here, Buster was given a check for $7.50, the standard stuntman's rate for such a fall. Instead of cashing the check, Buster framed it and hung it on his wall, where it remained as one of his prized possessions.

TIDE OF EMPIRE
(1929; MGM)

Director: Allan Dwan.
Cast: Renée Adorée, George Duryea (Tom Keene), George Fawcett, William Collier Jr., Fred Kohler.

Buster does a cameo as a mustached drunk tossed out of a saloon in this early California melodrama. Unfortunately, he was cut from the release print.

THE VOICE OF HOLLYWOOD
(1929; Tiffany Productions)

Director: Louis Lewyn.
Cast: Robert Woolsey (*Emcee*), with guests Buster Keaton, Al St. John, Nancy Welford, Johnny Walker, Mary Carr, the Meglin Kiddies, Lew Cody, Gwen Lee, Cliff Edwards, Raquel Torres.

Buster is featured along with other MGM stars in this rare one-reel promotional short. Keaton authority Alan Hoffman reports that Buster has a small scene with actress Raquel Torres and MGM's Leo the lion. How-

Admiral Buster poses with his land yacht in a scene from *Hollywood on Parade*. He lived in it part-time after he and first wife Natalie divorced in 1932.

ever, a conflicting report comes from Keaton devotee Chuck Harter, who claims that Buster appears in a Hollywood nightclub setting where he flips a spoon into a water glass, then picks up a saltshaker and sniffs it, as if it were filled with cocaine. Since it is believed that Buster appeared in two of the *Voice of Hollywood* shorts, this could explain the conflicting comments.

THE STOLEN JOOLS
(1931; Paramount/National Variety Artists)

Producer: Pat Casey; *Director:* William McGann; *Supervisor:* E. K. Nadel. (U.K. Title: *The Slippery Pearls*).

Cast: Buster Keaton, Wallace Beery, Edward G. Robinson, Stan Laurel, Oliver Hardy, Norma Shearer, the Our Gang Kids, Polly Moran, Joan Crawford, Victor McLaglen, Warner Baxter, Irene Dunne, Bert Wheeler, Robert Woolsey, Richard Dix, Lowell Sherman, Stu Erwin, Gary Cooper, Maurice Chevalier, Douglas Fairbanks, Jr., Loretta Young, Richard Barthelmess, Bebe Daniels, Ben Lyon, Barbara Stanwyck, Jack Oakie, Fay Wray, Joe E. Brown, George "Gabby" Hayes, Mitzi Green, and a cast of quadrillions.

Buster has a small role as a Keystone-type cop in the first few minutes of this two-reel, all-star extravaganza, a fund-raising effort to benefit the National Variety Artists. He appears with Wallace Beery, who plays a gruff desk sergeant, then disappears as the other stars parade through the rest of the film looking for Norma Shearer's stolen necklace.

HOLLYWOOD ON PARADE
(1933; Paramount)

Producer/Director: Louis Lewyn.

Cast: Buster Keaton, Lew Cody, Richard Arlen, Frances Dee, Clark Gable, Tallulah Bankhead.

Buster appears in his land yacht, the one he purchased shortly after his breakup with Natalie. He and Lew Cody pose in navy uniforms before reboarding and driving off.

LA FIESTA DE SANTA BARBARA
(1935; MGM)

Producer/Director: Louis Lewyn; *Script:* Alexander Van Dorn. Technicolor.

Cast: Buster Keaton, Andy Devine, Robert Taylor, Edmund Lowe, Maria Gamberelli, Gary Cooper, Harpo Marx, Leo Carrillo, Ida Lupino, Ted Healy, the Gumm Sisters (including Judy Garland).

Although not associated with MGM at the time, Buster was invited to participate in this Pete Smith Specialty short by its producer-director, Louis Lewyn, who was the husband of Marion Mack, Buster's leading lady in *The General*. Dressed in Spanish regalia and sounding horribly hung over, Buster referees a comical bullfight with Andy Devine as the matador and two guys in a bull costume as the ferocious El Toro.

SUNKIST STARS AT PALM SPRINGS
(1936; MGM)

Producer/Director: Louis Lewyn. Technicolor.

Cast: Buster Keaton, Johnny Weissmuller, Jackie Coogan, Betty Grable, Claire Trevor, Betty Furness, Walter Huston, Robert Benchley, Frances Langford.

In another Pete Smith Specialty short featuring a bevy of MGM stars, Buster, looking relaxed and dapper, snoozes on an inflatable mattress while a group of poolside beauties launch him into a swimming pool and, with an assist from Johnny Weissmuller, manage to rouse him from his slumber, at which point he falls off his raft and sinks to the bottom of the pool.

NEW MOON
(1940; MGM)

Producer/Director: Robert Z. Leonard.

Cast: Jeanette MacDonald, Nelson Eddy, Mary Boland, George Zucco, H. B. Warner, Grant Mitchell, Stanley Fields, Nat Pendleton.

According to Alan Hoffman, Buster had a substantial role in this lavish MacDonald-Eddy musical with a score by Sigmund Romberg and Oscar Hammerstein II. He was paired with character actor Nat Pendleton in a comic-relief subplot that was ultimately cut from the film. However, Buster can still be glimpsed briefly in the background in several scenes with Nelson Eddy as the latter leads his "stouthearted men" through various musical numbers. The sight of Buster as just another faceless extra in the crowd scenes is truly disturbing; yet, it serves as a fitting comment on the worth of his talents as perceived by MGM.

TWO GIRLS AND A SAILOR
(1944; MGM)

Producer: Joe Pasternak; Director: Richard Thorpe.
Cast: Van Johnson, June Allyson, Gloria DeHaven, Jimmy Durante, Tom Drake.

Buster makes a gag appearance as Durante's son in this big musical.

SHE WENT TO THE RACES
(1945; MGM)

Producer: Frederick Stephani; Director: Willis Goldbeck.
Cast: James Craig, Frances Gifford, Ava Gardner, Edmund Gwenn, Sig Ruman, Reginald Owen.

Buster has an uncredited bit as a hotel bellboy who carries suitcases and golf clubs into the room of gambler James Craig, then does a double take at the presence there of pajama-adorned Frances Gifford. As he stares at her, he turns and does a terrific face-forward fall over the suitcases and clubs. Buster also contributed gags to the film.

YOU'RE MY EVERYTHING
(1949; Twentieth Century-Fox)

Producer: Lamar Trotti; Director: Walter Lang. Technicolor.
Cast: Dan Dailey, Anne Baxter, Anne Revere, Stanley Ridges, Alan Mowbray, Selena Royle.

Buster does a walk-on as a butler in a silent-film-within-a-film segment with Anne Baxter, who accidentally throws a drink on him while he is serving the other guests. He reacts as if he were totally outraged, then pulls out his trademark flat hat, slaps it on his head, and storms off.

UN DUEL À MORT
(1950; Films Azur)

Director: Pierre Blondy; Script: Buster Keaton and Pierre Blondy.
Cast: Buster Keaton, Antonin Berval.

Buster recreates the dueling scene from *The Passionate Plumber* in this three-reel film made in Paris when he was on tour with the Cirque Medrano. It was never released in the U.S.

Buster imbibes with Jeanette MacDonald in a scene that was cut from *New Moon*, one of many eliminated from the film, reducing his part to an uncredited extra.

Buster discusses his uncredited walk-on part in *You're My Everything* with the film's director, Walter Lang.

SCREEN SNAPSHOTS: HOLLYWOOD PIE THROWERS
(1951; Columbia)

Compiler/Director: Ralph Staub.

Cast: Buster Keaton, Ken Murray, Joan Davis, Milton Berle, The Andrews Sisters, Ella Logan.

At a Hollywood Gay Nineties party hosted by Berle, star Murray is splattered in a pie-throwing demonstration by Buster and Joan. (Made several years earlier.)

L'INCANTEVOLE NEMICA
(1953; Orso Films–Italy)

Executive Producer: Ferruccio Biancini; *Director:* Claudio Gora.

Cast: Buster Keaton, Silvana Pampanini, Robert Lamoureux, Carlo Campinini, Ugo Tognazzi, Pina Renzi, Nyta Dover.

This Italian feature, also unreleased in the U.S., has Buster in an extraneous bit of comedy filmed onstage in a Milan theater where he was touring with Eleanor. Although the bit has nothing to do with the rest of the story, it also features the film's lead character, played by Robert Lamoureux.

MERTON OF THE MOVIES
(1957; Buckeye/Keaton)

Producer/Director/Script: Buster and Eleanor Keaton.
Cast: Buster Keaton.

Buster and Eleanor made this one-reel short as a filmed introduction to the revival of the play of the same name in which Buster was appearing as the title character. It is basically a re-creation of the duck-hunting scene from *Battling Butler*. While Buster is picking off ducks from a rowboat, the boat sinks, and the final image is of his porkpie hat floating across the lake.

THE DEVIL TO PAY
(1960; Educational Research Films/Rodel Productions)

Director: Herb Skobie; *Script/Editor:* Cummins-Betts.
Cast: Buster Keaton, Ralph Dunn, Ruth Gillette, Marion Morris, John Rodney.

Buster plays a devillike figure in this industrial film made for the National Association of Wholesalers. Dressed in a comical devil's costume, he visits earth and rids the world of wholesalers, then watches as the American economy crumbles. After an omniscient narrator explains the economic importance of wholesalers, Buster brings 'em all back from the bowels of hell and world order is restored.

THERE'S NO BUSINESS LIKE NO BUSINESS
(1963; Maremont Exhaust and Gabriel Shocks Division/Arvin Corporation)

In this one-reel short, actually more of a commercial than anything else, Buster plays a gas station attendant who inspects a car desperately in need of the company's products while a voice-over narrator explains their advantages.

THE FALL GUY
(1965; U.S. Steel)

Director: Darrel Bateman; *Production Assistant:* Jim Dearden.
Cast: Buster Keaton.

Buster has a dual role, playing Mr. Goodfarmer and Mr. Badfarmer, in this unpreviewed industrial film made for U.S. Steel about increasing agricultural efficiency.

Buster takes a break during filming of *The General,* his most often-anthologized feature.

COMPILATION FILMS, DOCUMENTARIES, AND FILMS ABOUT BUSTER KEATON

APRIL SHOWERS
(1948; Warner Bros.)

Producer: William Jacobs; *Director:* James V. Kern.
Cast: Jack Carson, Ann Sothern, Robert Alda, S. Z. Sakall, Robert Ellis.

Although Buster was not associated in any way with this film, the story is obviously based on his vaudeville experiences when he performed with his mother and father as The Three Keatons. It chronicles the ups and downs of a mother-father-son vaudeville act, The Three Tymes, as they tour the circuit in turn-of-the-century America. According to Alan Hoffman, Joe Laurie, Jr., a former vaudevillian who wrote the film, informed Buster about the script's obvious references to The Three Keatons and encouraged him to sue Warners. Buster was paid $5,000 in a quick, out-of-court settlement.

SCREEN SNAPSHOTS: MEMORIES OF FAMOUS HOLLYWOOD COMEDIANS
(1951; Columbia)

Compiler/Director: Ralph Staub.
Cast: Buster Keaton, Roscoe "Fatty" Arbuckle, ZaSu Pitts, Laurel and Hardy, W. C. Fields, Charley Chase, Ben

Turpin, the Marx Brothers, Joe E. Brown, Andy Clyde, Olsen and Johnson. Joe E. Brown narrates.

In this unpreviewed, one-reel short, Buster appears in some behind-the-scenes footage shot during the production of some of his independently produced films.

CA C'EST DE CINÉMA
(1951; France)

This unpreviewed French documentary on the hstory of the cinema includes scenes from Buster's silent shorts and features.

THE BUSTER KEATON STORY
(1957; Paramount)

Producer/Script: Robert Smith and Sidney Sheldon; *Director:* Sidney Sheldon.
Cast: Donald O'Connor, Ann Blyth, Rhonda Fleming, Peter Lorre, Larry Keating, Richard Anderson, Dave Willock, Claire Carleton, Larry White, Jackie Coogan, Richard Aherne, Cecil B. DeMille, Benny Rubin, Snub Pollard.

Buster was paid $50,000 as a technical consultant and for the use of his name, which, amazingly enough, is spelled correctly in the credits, a miracle considering the gross inaccuracies that permeate nearly every

Donald O'Connor and Ann Blyth look grim in the even grimmer *Buster Keaton Story*. Buster received a technical adviser credit for the film but most of his advice was ignored along with the facts of his life.

frame of the film. However, not even a total ignorance of the facts of Buster's life would increase the viewer's enjoyment of this ineptly written and poorly directed fiasco.

To be fair, Donald O'Connor gives a credible performance in the title role, especially during the re-created scenes from Buster's films, which Buster directed himself. When the film premiered, Buster and Eleanor were asked to attend and nearly walked out after the first five minutes. O'Connor was so infuriated over the bastardized interpretation of Buster's life (by Sidney Sheldon, of all people, before becoming the mega-author) that he refused to attend the premiere and to this day has reportedly never seen the film.

Fortunately, with the money Buster was paid for the use of his name and his technical advice (most of which was ignored), he was able to buy a ranch in California's San Fernando Valley where he lived comfortably for the rest of his life. Buster's mansion in the film is Norma Desmond's home from *Sunset Boulevard* (1950), in which he had a cameo.

WHEN COMEDY WAS KING
(1960; Ro-Co Productions and Twentieth Century-Fox)

Producer/Compiler/Script: Robert Youngson.
Cast: Buster Keaton, Charles Chaplin, Stan Laurel and Oliver Hardy, Ben Turpin, Roscoe "Fatty" Arbuckle, Charley Chase, Wallace Beery, Gloria Swanson.

Excerpts from some of Buster's classic shorts and features appear in this compilation film along with clips from the other famous comedians of the silent era.

SAD CLOWNS (Silents Please)
(1961; Sterling Educational Films)

Producers: Saul J. Turell and Paul Killiam.
Cast: Buster Keaton, Charles Chaplin, Harry Langdon.

This segment of *The History of Motion Pictures* film series discusses the similarities and differences of three of the silent era's four premier comedians.

THE GREAT CHASE
(1962; Janus Films)

Producer: Harvey Cort; *Script:* Harvey Cort, Saul Turell, and Paul Killiam.
Cast: Buster Keaton, Douglas Fairbanks, Pearl White, Richard Barthelmess, Lillian Gish.

This compilation film, featuring chase scenes from such silent classics as *The Mark of Zorro* and *Way Down East*, is primarily devoted to segments from Buster's *The General*.

THIRTY YEARS OF FUN
(1963; Twentieth Century-Fox)

Producer/Compiler/Script: Robert Youngson.
Cast: Buster Keaton, Charles Chaplin, Stan Laurel and Oliver Hardy, Harry Langdon, Charley Chase.

Buster is represented in this compilation film with excerpts from *Cops, Daydreams*, and *The Balloonatic*.

THE SOUND OF LAUGHTER
(1963; Union Films)

Producers: Barry B. Yellin and Irvin S. Dorfman; *Director:* John O'Shaughnessy.
Cast: Buster Keaton, Danny Kaye, Bing Crosby, Bob Hope.

Buster appears in clips from two of his Educational shorts: *One-Run Elmer* (the baseball game scene) and *Grand Slam Opera* (the juggling scene in the radio studio).

BUSTER KEATON RIDES AGAIN
(1965; National Film Board of Canada)

Producer: Julian Biggs; *Director/Photography:* John Spotton.
Cast: Buster Keaton, Eleanor Keaton, Gerald Potterton.

This fascinating documentary was shot during the filming of *The Railrodder* and catches Buster at his unguarded best. He appears relaxed and smiles freely while meeting with Gerald Potterton (director of *The Railrodder*), working out gags, advising on camera angles, choreographing extras, etc. Buster also reminisces about his days in vaudeville and at MGM, and his love for silent comedy (he acts out a scene from one of the Laurel and Hardy shorts). One harrowing scene catches Buster in a coughing spell—revealing how fragile his health was at the time—and later at a press conference he paces nervously about like a caged lion, his eyes darting around the crowded room looking for the nearest exit. In the film's poignant ending Buster relaxes with Eleanor as he strums on a ukulele and sings "Casey Jones."

THE GREAT STONE FACE
(1968; Funnyman Productions, Inc.)

Director/Script: Vernon P. Becker
Cast: Buster Keaton.

A poor documentary on Buster's life, mostly footage from his classic shorts and features—*Coney Island, Cops, The General*, and others. It also includes clips from *The Railrodder*.

THE COMIC
(1969; Columbia)

Producers/Script: Carl Reiner and Aaron Rubin; *Director:* Carl Reiner.
Cast: Dick Van Dyke, Michele Lee, Mickey Rooney, Cornel Wilde.

This excellent feature chronicles the life of fictional silent-film comedian Billy Bright, whose character is a composite of the era's four giants—Chaplin, Keaton, Langdon, and Lloyd—with some Stan Laurel sprinkled in for good measure. Dick Van Dyke plays the temperamental comic who successfully makes the transition from vaudeville to the screen and reaches the pinnacle of success only to be done in by alcohol and his boundless ego. Although the film is probably closer to Langdon and Laurel, there are definite touches of Buster's life as well, especially in the later scenes where Van Dyke is shown making television guest apperances and commercials. All in all, it more accurately captures Buster's life than does the dismal *Buster Keaton Story*.

FOUR CLOWNS
(1970; Twentieth Century-Fox)

Buster rehearses in front of some of the crew members of *Buster Keaton Rides Again*, an excellent documentary filmed during the making of *The Railrodder*.

Producer/Compiler/Script: Robert Youngson; *Associate Producer:* Raymond Rohauer.
Cast: Buster Keaton, Stan Laurel and Oliver Hardy, Charley Chase.

In this compilation film, Buster appears in a long excerpt from *Seven Chances*, practically the entire feature.

THE THREE STOOGES FOLLIES
(1974; Columbia)

Cast: Buster Keaton, The Three Stooges, Vera Vague, Krazy Kat.

Buster appears in one of his better Columbia shorts, *Nothing but Pleasure*, in this compilation film devoted primarily to the "nyuk nyuk" kings of roughhouse comedy.

HOLLYWOOD (EPISODE #8: COMEDY—A SERIOUS BUSINESS)
(1980; Thames Television)

Producers/Script: Kevin Brownlow and David Gill
Cast: Buster Keaton, Charles Chaplin, Harold Lloyd, Harry Langdon, Mack Sennett, Hal Roach, Frank Capra, Jackie Coogan.

This episode from the excellent thirteen-part BBC television documentary produced by film historians Kevin Browlow and David Gill features Buster in several of his classic films, including *The Goat, One*

Week, Sherlock Jr., Seven Chances, The General, and *Steamboat Bill, Jr.*, as well as commentary by Marion Mack, stuntman Harvey Parry, and Buster himself.

THE GOLDEN AGE OF BUSTER KEATON (aka Buster)

(1982; Jay Ward productions)

Producer: Raymond Rohauer; *Executive Producers:* Jay Ward and Bill Scott.
Cast: Buster Keaton, Roscoe "Fatty" Arbuckle, Al St. John.

Buster's film career is represented with excerpts from a number of the films he made with Roscoe Arbuckle as well as clips from his silent classics.

BUSTER KEATON: THE GREAT STONE FACE

(1982; S-L Film Productions)

Cast: Buster Keaton.

A short introduction touching on some of the highlights of Buster's life and film career is followed by excerpts from such films as *Coney Island, One Week, The Boat, The Playhouse, Cops*, and *The General*.

BUSTER KEATON: A HARD ACT TO FOLLOW

(In three parts: "From Vaudeville to Movies," "Star Without a Studio," and "A Genius Recognized")

(1987; Thames Television in association with Raymond Rohauer)

Producers/Script: Kevin Brownlow and David Gill.

I have watched this magnificent three-part documentary on Buster's life roughly 3 million times and still can't get enough of it. Packed with fascinating tidbits about every facet of his life, it includes lengthy interviews with Buster, Eleanor Keaton, Raymond Rohauer, Marion Mack, Charles Lamont, stuntman Harvey Parry, personal friends, and fellow filmmakers. It naturally has generous samplings from Buster's entire film career and explanations regarding how he achieved certain technical effects and staged various gags and stunts. The only problem is that, even at 165 minutes, it is still too short. A true achievement by film historians Kevin Brownlow and David Gill and a major inspiration for this book.

Buster is elected to the board of the country club featured in *Hard Luck,* his favorite short film. Long thought lost, the two-reeler was finally pieced together from foreign prints by film historians Kevin Brownlow and David Gill. An excerpt appears in their masterful three-part documentary, *Buster Keaton: A Hard Act to Follow.*

BUSTER'S BEDROOM

(1990; Metropolis Filmproduktion, Berlin; Les Productions du Versau, Canada; and Prole Film, Lisbon)

Producer: Luciano Gloor; *Director:* Rebecca Horn; *Script:* Rebecca Horn and Martin Mosebach.

Cast: Donald Sutherland, Geraldine Chaplin, Valentina Cortese, Amanda Ooms, David Warrilow, Taylor Mead, Ari Snyder, Martin Wuttke, Mary Woronov.

In this film by German artist-filmmaker Rebecca Horn, a young woman obsessed with every aspect of Buster's life decides to visit one of the sanatoriums where he was treated for his alcoholism. That's about as interesting as this movie gets, with the rest of the film chronicling the woman's encounters with the current residents of the sanatorium, all of them loonies. As Buster would have put it, "This isn't funny." Although one of the most boring, pretentious movies ever made, it does contain one brief excerpt from *Steamboat Bill, Jr.*, its only redeeming aspect.

Buster arrives on the MGM lot with his bag o' gags, ready to assume his new duties for the studio where he once reigned as premier comedian. Buster worked behind the scenes for MGM from 1937 to 1951.

WRITING/DIRECTING CREDITS, UNCREDITED GAGS, AND TECHNICAL ADVICE

SPLASH!
(1931; MGM)

Directors: Jules White and Zion Myers.

Buster worked briefly on this short about swimming.

A NIGHT AT THE OPERA
(1935; MGM)

Director: Sam Wood.
Cast: The Marx Brothers.

The famous scene in which the Marx Brothers and dozens of others crowd into Groucho's stateroom was inspired by the bathhouse changing-room scene from *The Cameraman*.

LIFE IN SOMETOWN, U.S.A.
(1938; MGM)

Producer: Louis Lewyn; *Director*: Buster Keaton.

One of three MGM one-reelers Buster directed in between his gag-writing assignments. In this one, the most Keatonesque of the three, a young boy is hauled into a police station by a rich society dame who demands that the youngster be locked up for breaking one of the windows of her mansion with his baseball.

The desk sergeant, sympathizing with the boy, decides to teach the woman and her friends a lesson by having them arrested for breaking antiquated laws, still on the books, all of which are highly nonsensical. Each quirky law is visually depicted, making for some interesting sight gags.

HOLLYWOOD HANDICAP
(1938; MGM)

Producer: Louis Lewyn; *Director*: Buster Keaton.

In this one-reel musical short, directed by Buster and set at the Santa Anita racetrack with a stadium full of celebrities (including Al Jolson, Ruby Keeler, Mickey Rooney, Stuart Erwin, June Collyer, Charles Butterworth), a black singing group, the Original Sing Band, has hocked its instruments and bet all its money on the slowest nag on the track. The members try to inspire the horse by singing and mimicking the sounds of the musical instruments they have hocked. This, however, only slows down the horse even more.

STREAMLINED SWING
(1938; MGM)

Producer: Louis Lewyn; *Director*: Buster Keaton.

Buster once again directs the Original Sing Band in this one-reel musical short. This time the members are train porters on a private car owned by the president of the railroad. When an eccentric millionaire makes a present of the car to the singers, they turn it into a nightclub, serving up hot food and hot music.

FAST COMPANY (aka The Rare Book Murder)
(1938; MGM).

Director: Edward Buzzell.

Cast: Melvyn Douglas, Florence Rice, Nat Pendleton, Louis Calhern.

Buster created a routine for Melvyn Douglas, as a rare-book buff turned amateur sleuth.

TOO HOT TO HANDLE
(1938; MGM)

Director: Jack Conway.

Cast: Clark Gable, Myrna Loy, Walter Pidgeon.

Buster directs some of the cast members of *Life in Sometown, U.S.A.* This one-reel MGM short was his first directorial effort for the studio. He later directed two others, *Hollywood Handicap* and *Streamlined Swing*.

Buster created gags, the most overtly Keatonesque one involving hotshot photographer Clark Gable faking a plane bombing to spice up his newsreel footage. Film historian William K. Everson has pointed out that Buster might have a cameo appearance in the film, disguised as a witch doctor in a ceremonial chicken costume. Although Buster would probably have jumped at the chance to play a giant chicken, the person in the costume displays no overtly Keaton-like physical mannerisms, leading one to conclude that, in this instance, the gags came first, not the chicken.

LOVE FINDS ANDY HARDY
(1938; MGM)

Director: George B. Seitz.

Cast: Mickey Rooney, Judy Garland, Lana Turner, Lewis Stone.

Buster was a technical consultant on this comedy, the third in MGM's Andy Hardy series.

THE JONES FAMILY IN HOLLYWOOD
(1939; Twentieth Century-Fox)

Director: Mal St. Clair; *Original Story:* Joseph Hoffman and Buster Keaton, based on characters created by Katharine Kavanaugh.

Cast: Jed Prouty, Spring Byington, Ken Howell, June Carlson, Florence Roberts.

With help from his old boss Joseph Schenck, and his former collaborator Mal St. Clair, Buster landed two writing assignments at Twentieth Century-Fox, supplying gags and the story line for two B-movie genre pictures featuring a "typical American family" headed by Mr. and Mrs. Jones, played by Jed Prouty and Spring Byington.

THE JONES FAMILY IN QUICK MILLIONS
(1939; Twentieth Century-Fox)

Director: Mal St. Clair; *Original Story:* Buster Keaton and Joseph Hoffman, based on characters created by Katharine Kavanaugh.

Cast: Jed Prouty, Spring Byington, Ken Howell, June Carlson, Florence Roberts.

This is Buster's second story effort for the Jones family series, genre pictures similar in style and content to modern-day television sitcoms.

AT THE CIRCUS
(1939; MGM)

Director: Edward Buzzell.
Cast: The Marx Brothers.

Buster created gags for Groucho, Chico, and Harpo. He didn't enjoy working with the zany brothers; they never took their comedy seriously, a cardinal sin in Buster's eyes.

COMRADE X
(1940; MGM)

Director: King Vidor.
Cast: Clark Gable, Hedy Lamarr.

Buster created gags.

GO WEST
(1940; MGM)

Director: Edward Buzzell.
Cast: The Marx Brothers.

Buster created more gags for those ungrateful brothers.

TALES OF MANHATTAN
(1942; Twentieth Century-Fox)

Director: Julien Duvivier.
Cast: Charles Boyer, Rita Hayworth, Henry Fonda, Ginger Rogers, Charles Laughton, Edward G. Robinson, Paul Robeson.

Buster worked on a twenty-minute segment featuring W. C. Fields in this (initially) five-episode film that chronicles the life of a dress tailcoat. The Fields segment, however, was ultimately cut from the film, but exists as a separate entity infrequently shown.

I DOOD IT
(1943; MGM)

Producer: Jack Cummings; *Director:* Vincente Minnelli.
Cast: Red Skelton, Eleanor Powell.

Buster created gags for this remake of his *Spite Marriage*. Although their comic styles are quite dissimilar, Keaton loved working with Skelton and they became very good friends, with Buster supplying much gag material for several of Red's films.

BATHING BEAUTY
(1944; MGM)

Director: George Sidney.
Cast: Red Skelton, Esther Williams.

Buster created Skelton gags for this musical comedy featuring swimming star Esther Williams and also suggested an alternate title for the film: *The Fatal Breast Stroke*. Louis B. Mayer was not amused.

NOTHING BUT TROUBLE
(1945; MGM)

Producer: Benny Zeidman; *Director:* Sam Taylor.
Cast: Stan Laurel and Oliver Hardy.

Buster was a big fan of Laurel and Hardy and supplied gags for this feature of theirs.

ABBOTT AND COSTELLO IN HOLLYWOOD
(1945; MGM)

Director: S. Sylvan Simon.
Cast: Bud Abbott and Lou Costello.

As with the Marx Brothers, Buster didn't care for Abbott and Costello's indifferent attitude toward their work. However, he did respect Lou Costello's comedic sensibilities. This film contains several scenes comparable to ones in Buster's first MGM talkie, *Free and Easy*, indicating that he had a hand in creating the gags.

THE EQUESTRIAN QUIZ
(1946; MGM)

A Pete Smith Short (Number 11)

For this Pete Smith Specialty one-reeler, Buster created gags and directed a segment involving horse racing.

EASY TO WED
(1946; MGM)

Director: Edward Buzzell.

Cast: Van Johnson, Esther Williams, Lucille Ball, Keenan Wynn.

Buster created gags for this musical remake of *Libeled Lady* and codirected a segment, along with friend Edward Sedgwick, involving Van Johnson duck hunting in a lake. He also suggested another alterna-

A bleary-eyed Buster, here serenaded by Stan Laurel and Oliver Hardy, supplies gags for their film *Nothing But Trouble.*

tive title for this Esther Williams vehicle: *The Bride Wore Spurs.* Louis B. Mayer was still not amused.

CYNTHIA
(1947; MGM)

Director: Robert Z. Leonard.
Cast: Elizabeth Taylor, George Murphy, Mary Astor.

Buster submitted five pages of script for this teen comedy.

IT HAPPENED IN BROOKLYN
(1947; MGM)

Director: Richard Whorf.
Cast: Frank Sinatra, Kathryn Grayson, Jimmy Durante, Peter Lawford, Gloria Grahame.

Buster created gags for this musical comedy featuring his old costar Jimmy Durante.

MERTON OF THE MOVIES
(1947; MGM)

Director: Robert Alton.
Cast: Red Skelton, Virginia O'Brien, Gloria Grahame.

Buster acted as script doctor and technical adviser for this film based on the George S. Kaufman–Marc Connelly play. He later toured in a 1957 production.

A SOUTHERN YANKEE
(1948; MGM)

Director: Edward Sedgwick.
Cast: Red Skelton, Arlene Dahl, Brian Donlevy.

Buster created gags for this unofficial remake of *The General.* However, two of his most distinctive touches are from other films of his: the "woman's dress on the back of the horse gag" from *Our Hospitality*, and the double-uniform gag from *Jail Bait*, are both effectively re-created.

NEPTUNE'S DAUGHTER
(1949; MGM)

Director: Edward Buzzell.
Cast: Esther Williams, Red Skelton, Ricardo Montalban, Betty Garrett, Keenan Wynn.

Buster contributed dialogue suggestions for this Esther Williams vehicle. Taking into consideration

Buster is arrested by an MGM guard for being funnier than featured actor Lou Costello during the making of *Abbott and Costello in Hollywood,* a film that restages some of the routines from Buster's own MGM feature, *Free and Easy.*

Esther's role as a bathing suit designer, Buster again suggested an alternative title: *Thar She Sews*. Mayer wept.

TAKE ME OUT TO THE BALL GAME
(1949; MGM)

Director: Busby Berkeley.
Cast: Gene Kelly, Frank Sinatra, Esther Williams, Betty Garrett, Jules Munshin.

Buster supplied baseball gags for this turn-of-the-century musical comedy.

WATCH THE BIRDIE
(1950; MGM)

Director: Jack Donohoe.
Cast: Red Skelton, Arlene Dahl, Ann Miller.

Buster created gags for this remake of his first MGM film, *The Cameraman*.

THE YELLOW CAB MAN
(1950; MGM)

Director: Jack Donohoe.
Cast: Red Skelton, Gloria DeHaven.

Combining material from *One Week* and *The Electric House*, Buster created gags involving a spinning, gadget-filled house belonging to neophyte inventor Red Skelton.

EXCUSE MY DUST (aka Mr. Belden's Amazing Gasmobile)
(1951; MGM)

Director: Roy Rowland.
Cast: Red Skelton, Sally Forrest, Macdonald Carey.

For his final gagman assignment for MGM, Buster created routines and codirected a racehorse segment with Edward Sedgwick.

Buster coaches Red Skelton for his featured role in *A Southern Yankee*, a remake of *The General*. Keaton worked on several films starring Skelton and the two men became good offscreen friends.

TELEVISION APPEARANCES

Buster made hundreds of television appearances as a guest on the variety shows of Ed Sullivan, Ed Wynn, Ken Murray, Steve Allen, Garry Moore, among others; and on Allen Funt's *Candid Camera*; game shows (*What's My Line, I've Got a Secret*); series episodes; network specials; and commercials. He also starred in *The Buster Keaton Comedy Show* (1949), filmed in front of a studio audience, and *The Buster Keaton Show* (1950–51), a taped series produced by Los Angeles' KTTV. (Various episodes from the taped series were edited together and shown in British theaters in 1951 and 1952 as *The Misadventures of Buster Keaton* and *Life With Buster Keaton*.) Since many of his appearances haven't survived, the following is a partial list of his television work.

DOUGLAS FAIRBANKS, JR., PRESENTS: THE RHEINGOLD THEATRE
Episode: "The Awakening." Aired July 1954, NBC. (30 minutes)

BEST OF BROADWAY
Episode: "The Man Who Came to Dinner." Aired October 1954. CBS (60 minutes).

EDDIE CANTOR COMEDY THEATRE
Episode: "The Square World of Alonzo Pennyworth." Aired October 1955, ABC (30 minutes).

SCREEN DIRECTORS PLAYHOUSE
Episode: "The Silent Partner." Aired December 1955, NBC (25 minutes).

THE MARTHA RAYE SHOW
Aired March 1956, NBC (60 minutes).

PRODUCERS' SHOWCASE
Episode: "The Lord Don't Play Favorites." Aired September 1956, NBC (90 minutes).

THIS IS YOUR LIFE
Episode: "Buster Keaton" (*Host:* Ralph Edwards). Aired 1957, NBC (30 minutes).

PLAYHOUSE 90
Episode: "The Innocent Sleep." Aired June 1958, CBS (90 minutes).

THE DONNA REED SHOW
Episode: "A Very Merry Christmas." Aired December 1958, ABC (30 minutes).

THE ADVENTURES OF MR. PASTRY
Aired 1958, British Television (26 minutes).

SUNDAY SHOWCASE
Episode: "After Hours." Aired February 1960, NBC (60 minutes).

THE TWILIGHT ZONE
Episode: "Once Upon a Time." Aired December 1961, CBS (30 minutes).

THE MEDICINE MAN
(Pilot for Ernie Kovacs series, produced in 1961)

THE SCENE STEALERS
(Benefit show for the March of Dimes) Aired April 1962, CBS (30 minutes).

ROUTE 66
Episode: "Journey to Nineveh." Aired September 1962, CBS (60 minutes).

MR. SMITH
Episode: "Think Mink." Aired January 1963, ABC (30 minutes).

TODAY SHOW
Episode: "Buster Keaton Tribute" (*Host:* Hugh Downs). Aired April 1963, NBC (120 minutes).

THE GREATEST SHOW ON EARTH
Episode: "You're All Right, Ivy." Aired April 1964, ABC (60 minutes).

BURKE'S LAW
Episode: "Who Killed 1/2 of Glory Lee?" Aired May 1964, ABC (60 minutes).

HOLLYWOOD PALACE
(*Host:* Gene Barry.) Aired June 1964, ABC (60 minutes).

THE MAN WHO BOUGHT PARADISE
(aka Hotel Paradise) Aired January 1965, CBS (60 minutes).

THE DONNA REED SHOW
Episode: "Now You See It, Now You Don't." Aired February 1965, ABC (30 minutes).

TELEVISION COMMERCIALS

Colgate Toothpaste (1956); Simon Pure Beer (1958); Alka-Seltzer (1958); North West Orient Airlines (1958); Shamrock Oil (1959); U.S. Steel (1959); 7-Up (1959); Wen Power Tools (1960); Marlboro Cigarettes (1961); Phillip's 66 Oil (1961); Milky Way Chocolate Bar (1961); Ford Motor Company (1962); Minute Cold Rub (1963); Seneca Apple Juice (1964); Budweiser Beer (1964); Pure Oil (1964).

SELECTED BIBLIOGRAPHY

Agee, James. *Agee on Film: Essays and Reviews*. New York: St. Martin's Press, 1958.

Benayoun, Robert. *The Look of Buster Keaton*. New York: St. Martin's Press, 1983.

Brownlow, Kevin. *The Parade's Gone By*. New York: Knopf, 1969.

Dardis, Tom. *Keaton: The Man Who Wouldn't Lie Down*. New York: Charles Scribner's Sons, 1979.

Edmonds, Andy. *Frame-Up! The Untold Story of Roscoe "Fatty" Arbuckle*. New York: William Morrow, 1991.

Keaton, Buster (with Charles Samuels). *My Wonderful World of Slapstick*. New York: Doubleday, 1960.

Kerr, Walter. *The Silent Clowns*. New York: Knopf, 1975.

Maltin, Leonard. *The Great Movie Shorts*. New York: Crown, 1972.

Meade, Marion. *Quiet! The Tumultuous Life of Buster Keaton*. New York: Villard Books/Random House, in press.

Moews, Daniel. *Keaton: The Silent Features Close Up*. Berkeley: University of California Press, 1977.

Rapf, Joanna, and Gary Green. *Buster Keaton: A Bio-Bibliography*. Westport, Conn.: Greenwood Press, 1992.

Robinson, David. *Buster Keaton*. Bloomington: University of Indiana Press, 1969.

Yallop, David. *The Day the Laughter Stopped*. New York: St. Martin's Press, 1976.

THE COMPLETE BUSTER KEATON FILM TITLE LISTING

Abbott and Costello in Hollywood
Adventures of Huckleberry Finn, The
Allez Oop
April Showers
Around the World in Eighty Days
At the Circus
Baby Cyclone, The
Back Stage
Balloonatic, The
Bathing Beauty
Battling Butler
Beach Blanket Bingo
Bell Boy, The
Blacksmith, The
Blue Blazes
Boat, The
Buster Keaton: A Hard Act to Follow
Buster Keaton Rides Again
Buster Keaton Story, The
Buster Keaton: The Great Stone Face
Buster's Bedroom
Butcher Boy, The
Ça C'Est de Cinéma
Cameraman, The
Chemist, The

College
Comic, The
Comrade X
Convict 13
Cook, The
Cops
Country Hero, A
Cynthia
Daydreams
Devil to Pay, The
Ditto
Doughboys
Easy to Wed
E-Flat Man, The
El Moderno Barba Azul
Electric House
Equestrian Quiz, The
Excuse My Dust

Fall Guy, The
Fast Company
Fatty at Coney Island
Film
Forever and a Day
Four Clowns
Free and Easy
Frozen North, The
Funny Thing Happened on the Way to the Forum, A

Garage, The
General, The
General Nuisance
Go West (1925)
Go West (1940)
Goat, The
God's Country
Gold Ghost, The
Golden Age of Buster Keaton, The

Good Night, Nurse!
Grand Slam Opera
Great Chase, The
Great Stone Face, The
Hard Luck
Haunted House, The
Hayseed, The
Hayseed Romance
High Sign, The
His Ex Marks the Spot
His Wedding Night
Hollywood Cavalcade
Hollywood (Episode 8: Comedy—A Serious Business)

Hollywood Handicap
Hollywood on Parade
Hollywood Revue of 1929
How to Stuff a Wild Bikini

ORDER NOW!
More Citadel Film Books

If you like this book, you'll love the other titles in the award-winning Citadel Film Series. From James Stewart to Moe Howard and The Three Stooges, Woody Allen to John Wayne, The Citadel Film Series is America's largest and oldest film book library.

With more than 150 titles--and more on the way!--Citadel Film Books make perfect gifts for a loved one, a friend, or best of all, yourself!

A complete listing of the Citadel Film Series appears below.
If you know what books you want, why not order now!
It's easy! Just call 1-800-447-BOOK and have your MasterCard or Visa ready.

STARS
Alan Ladd
Barbra Streisand: First Decade
Barbra Streisand: Second Decade
Bela Lugosi
Bette Davis
Boris Karloff
The Bowery Boys
Buster Keaton
Carole Lombard
Cary Grant
Charles Bronson
Charlie Chaplin
Clark Gable
Clint Eastwood
Curly
Dustin Hoffman
Edward G. Robinson
Elizabeth Taylor
Elvis Presley
Errol Flynn
Frank Sinatra
Gary Cooper
Gene Kelly
Gina Lollobrigida
Gloria Swanson
Gregory Peck
Greta Garbo
Henry Fonda
Humphrey Bogart
Ingrid Bergman
Jack Lemmon
Jack Nicholson
James Cagney
James Dean: Behind the Scene
Jane Fonda
Jeanette MacDonald & Nelson Eddy
Joan Crawford
John Wayne Films

John Wayne Reference Book
John Wayne Scrapbook
Judy Garland
Katharine Hepburn
Kirk Douglas
Laurel & Hardy
Lauren Bacall
Laurence Olivier
Mae West
Marilyn Monroe
Marlene Dietrich
Marlon Brando
Marx Brothers
Moe Howard & the Three Stooges
Norma Shearer
Olivia de Havilland
Orson Welles
Paul Newman
Peter Lorre
Rita Hayworth
Robert De Niro
Robert Redford
Sean Connery
Sexbomb: Jayne Mansfield
Shirley MacLaine
Shirley Temple
The Sinatra Scrapbook
Spencer Tracy
Steve McQueen
Three Stooges Scrapbook
Warren Beatty
W.C. Fields
William Holden
William Powell
A Wonderful Life: James Stewart
DIRECTORS
Alfred Hitchcock
Cecil B. DeMille
Federico Fellini

Frank Capra
John Ford
John Huston
Woody Allen
GENRE
Bad Guys
Black Hollywood
Black Hollywood: From 1970 to Today
Classics of the Gangster Film
Classics of the Horror Film
Divine Images: Jesus on Screen
Early Classics of Foreign Film
Great French Films
Great German Films
Great Romantic Films
Great Science Fiction Films
Harry Warren & the Hollywood Musical
Hispanic Hollywood: The Latins in Motion Pictures
The Hollywood Western
The Incredible World of 007
The Jewish Image in American Film
The Lavender Screen: The Gay and Lesbian Films
Martial Arts Movies
The Modern Horror Film
More Classics of the Horror Film
Movie Psychos & Madmen
Our Huckleberry Friend: Johnny Mercer
Second Feature: "B" Films
They Sang! They Danced! They Romanced!: Hollywood Musicals
Thrillers
The West That Never Was

Words and Shadows: Literature on the Screen
DECADE
Classics of the Silent Screen
Films of the Twenties
Films of the Thirties
More Films of the 30's
Films of the Forties
Films of the Fifties
Lost Films of the 50's
Films of the Sixties
Films of the Seventies
Films of the Eighties
SPECIAL INTEREST
America on the Rerun
Bugsy (Illustrated screenplay)
Comic Support
Dick Tracy
Favorite Families of TV
Film Flubs
Film Flubs: The Sequel
First Films
Forgotten Films to Remember
Hollywood Cheesecake
Hollywood's Hollywood
Howard Hughes in Hollywood
More Character People
The Nightmare Never Ends: Freddy Krueger & "A Night mare on Elm Street"
The "Northern Exposure" Book
The "Quantum Leap" Book
Sex In the Movies
Sherlock Holmes
Son of Film Flubs
Those Glorious Glamour Years
Who Is That?: Familiar Faces and Forgotten Names
"You Ain't Heard Nothin' Yet!"

For a free full-color brochure describing the Citadel Film Series in depth, call 1-800-447-BOOK; or send your name and address to Citadel Film Books, Distribution Center B, 120 Enterprise Ave., Secaucus, NJ 07094.